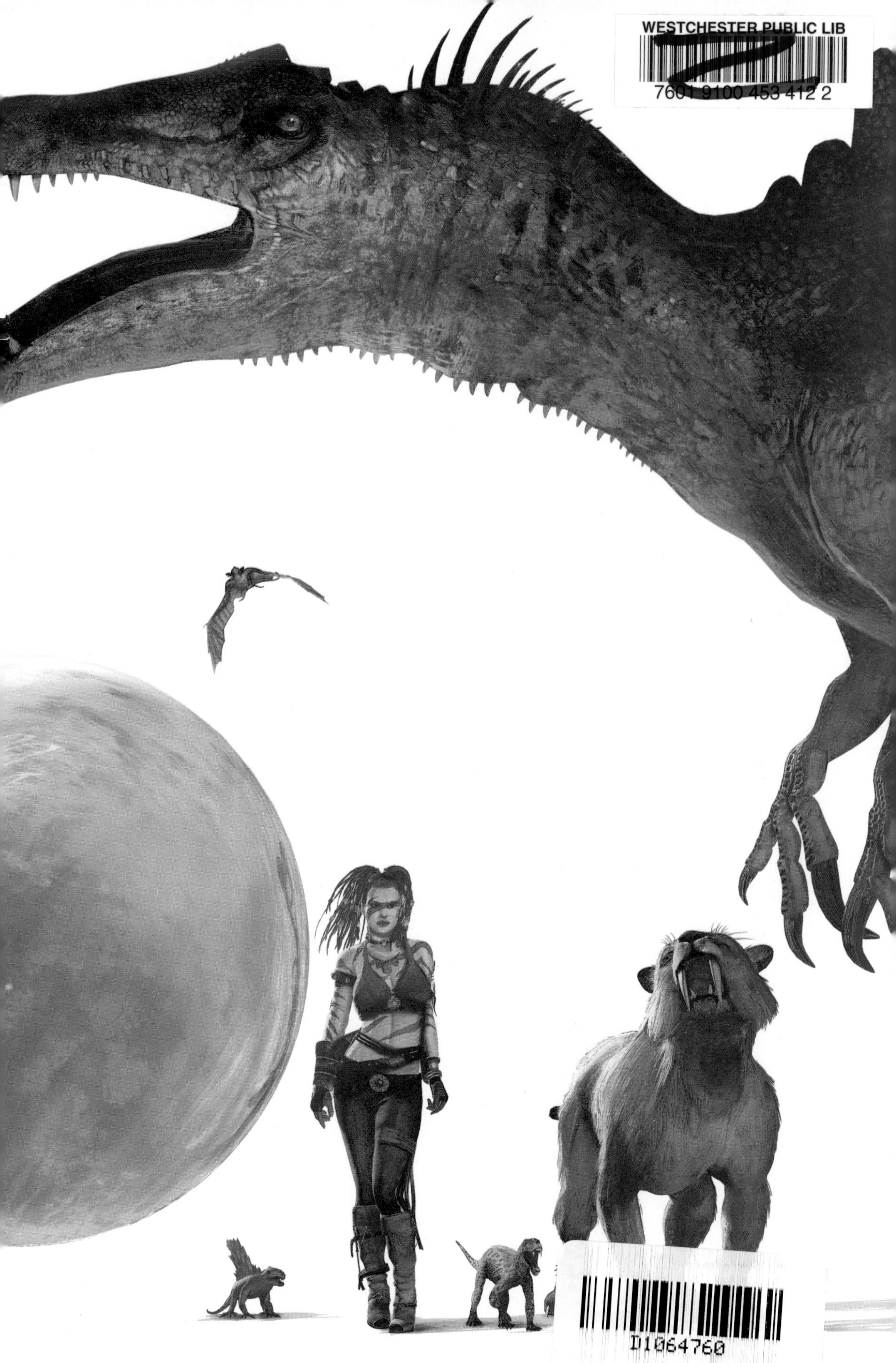

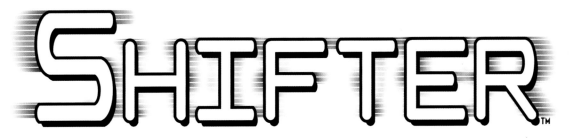

SHIFTER, Vol. 1. October 2013. Published by ANOMALY PUBLISHING, a division of ANOMALY PRODUCTIONS, INC. SHIFTER, its logo and characters are ™ and © 2013 Anomaly Productions, Inc. All rights reserved. The characters, events and stories in this publication are entirely fictional. With the exception of artwork used for review purposes, none of the contents may be reprinted without the permission of Anomaly Productions, Inc. Requests for permission should be addressed to: ANOMALY PRODUCTIONS, INC., 1801 Century Park West, Los Angeles, CA 90067.

For more information, please visit: experienceshifter.com

FIRST EDITION
Library of Congress Cataloging-In-Publication has been applied for.
ISBN-13: 978-0-9853342-1-5
Printed in the United States of America

ULTIMATE AUGMENTED REALITY™ (UAR
Quick Start Guide

1. Visit **experienceshifter.com/UAR** using your device browser.

2. Select the appropriate store (iOS or Android) and install the app . **The UAR app is FREE.**

3. Run the application and point at "live" pages to activate UAR.

UAR content pages will be listed within the app so you don't miss a thing.

New, **FREE** content will be added periodically.

Follow us on Facebook, Twitter and join our email list at **experienceshifter.com** to find out when the next UAR update is released.

How do I use it?

1) **Launch** the app.

2) **Point** your device camera at "live" pages (listed in-app).

3) **Let the magic begin!** Remember, most 3D items are **interactive**. Tap/swipe these objects to see how they react.

SHIFTER™

CREATED BY:

SKIP BRITTENHAM
AND
BRIAN HABERLIN

STORY:
BRIAN HABERLIN
AND BRIAN HOLGUIN

ILLUSTRATIONS:
BRIAN HABERLIN
GEIRROD VANDYKE
KUNRONG YAP
AND CHAN HYUK LEE

LETTERS:
FRANCIS TAKENAGA

TECHNOLOGY:
DAVID PENTZ

DIGITAL ASSISTS:
DIANA SANSON

EDITED BY:
SALLY HABERLIN
AND
SKIP BRITTENHAM

Genesis 1: 20-22
And God said, "Let the water teem with living creatures, and let birds fly above the earth across the expanse of the sky." So God created the great creatures of the sea and every living and moving thing with which the water teems, according to their kinds, and every winged bird according to its kind. And God saw that it was good. God blessed them and said, "Be fruitful and increase in number and fill the water in the seas, and let the birds increase on the earth."

Remember, democracy never lasts long. It soon wastes, exhausts, and murders itself. There never was a democracy yet that did not commit suicide.
- *John Adams*

We know better.
-*Mark Redding*
CEO, Morning Star Industries

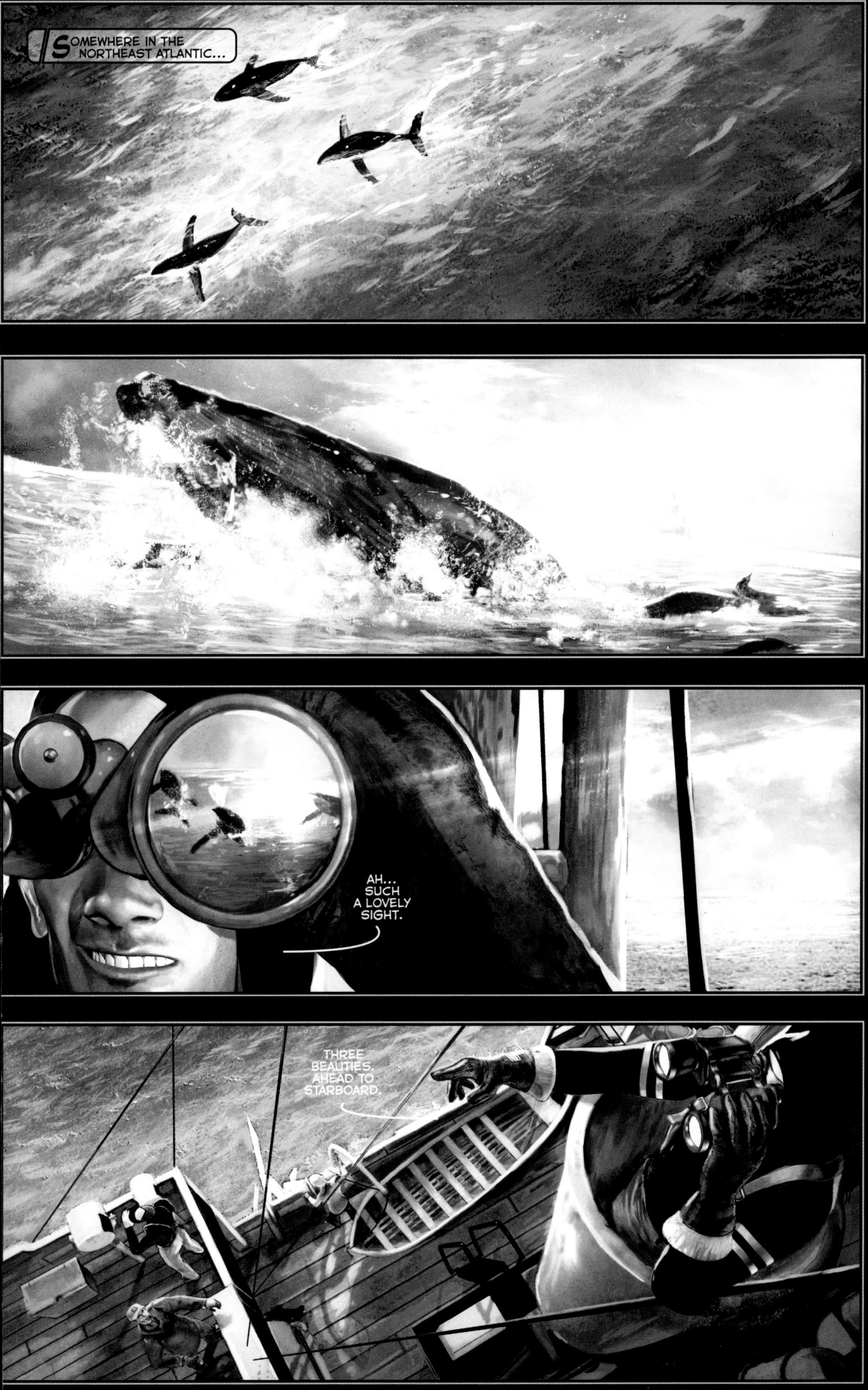
SOMEWHERE IN THE NORTHEAST ATLANTIC...
AH... SUCH A LOVELY SIGHT.
THREE BEAUTIES. AHEAD TO STARBOARD.

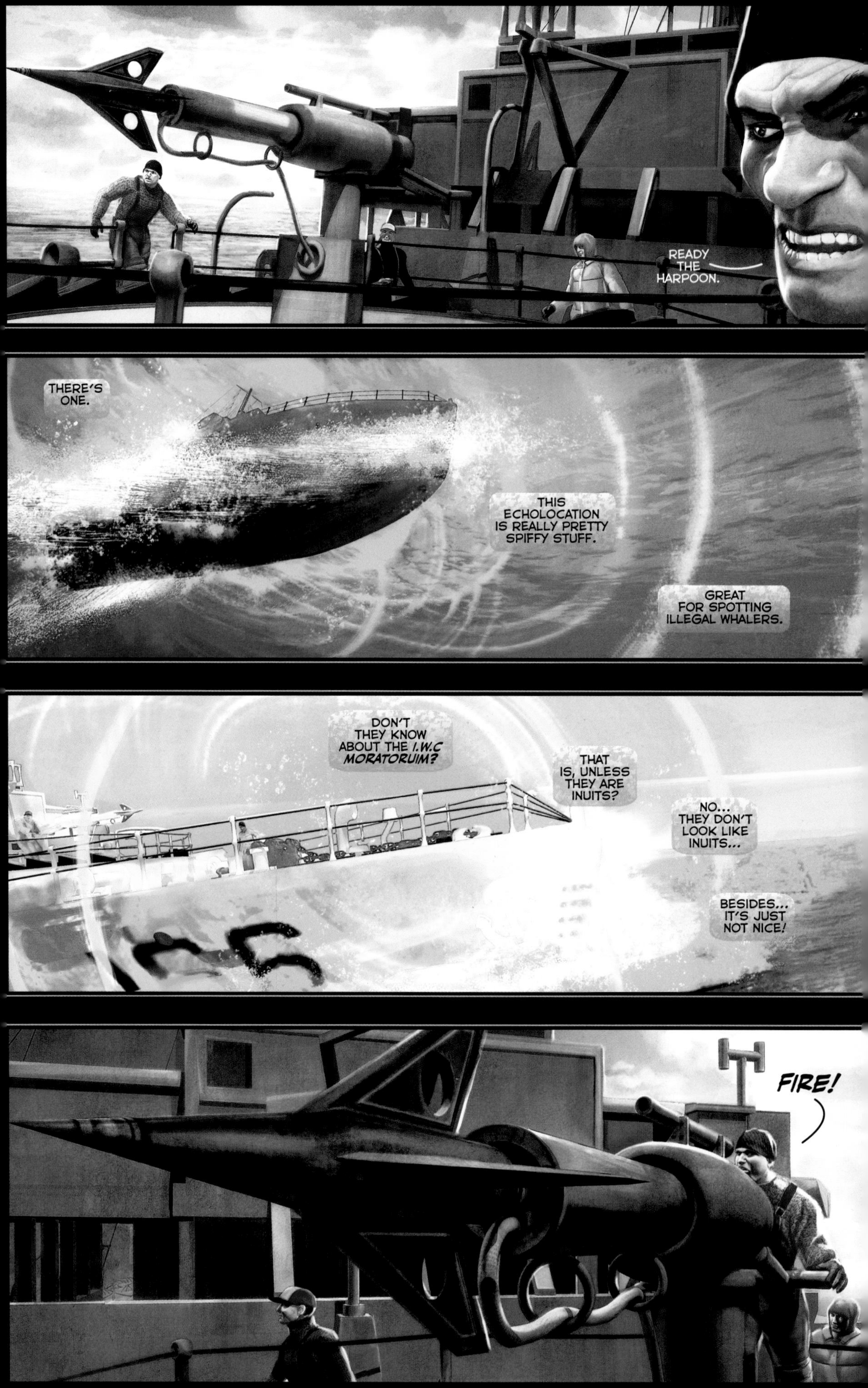
READY THE HARPOON.
THERE'S ONE.
THIS ECHOLOCATION IS REALLY PRETTY SPIFFY STUFF.
GREAT FOR SPOTTING ILLEGAL WHALERS.
DON'T THEY KNOW ABOUT THE *I.W.C MORATORUIM?*
THAT IS, UNLESS THEY ARE INUITS?
NO... THEY DON'T LOOK LIKE INUITS...
BESIDES... IT'S JUST NOT NICE!
FIRE!

WHOOSH

SPLASH

SNAP!

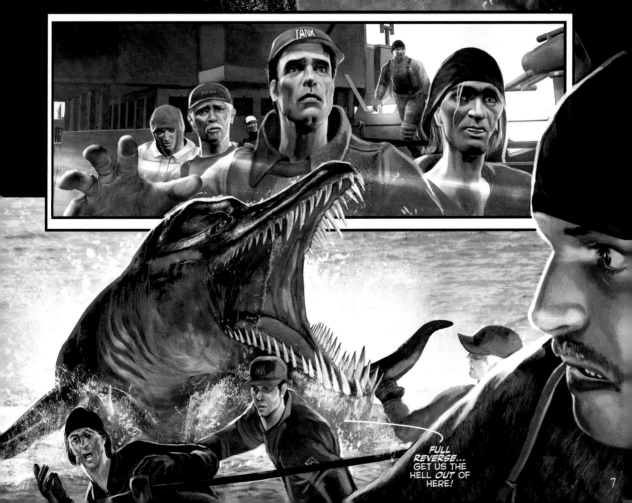

TANK

REDS

FULL REVERSE... GET US THE HELL *OUT* OF HERE!

7

RRROAR!

I THINK THAT PUT A GOOD SCARE IN THEM.

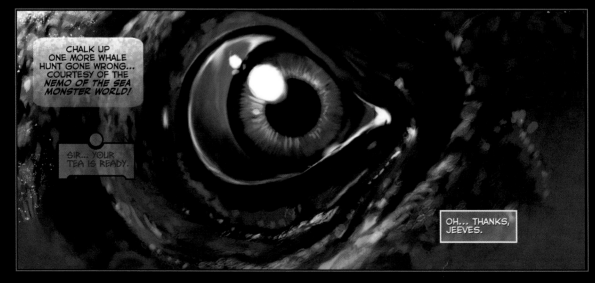

CHALK UP ONE MORE WHALE HUNT GONE WRONG... COURTESY OF THE *NEMO OF THE SEA MONSTER WORLD!*

SIR... YOUR TEA IS READY.

OH... THANKS, JEEVES.

SIX MONTHS EARLIER...

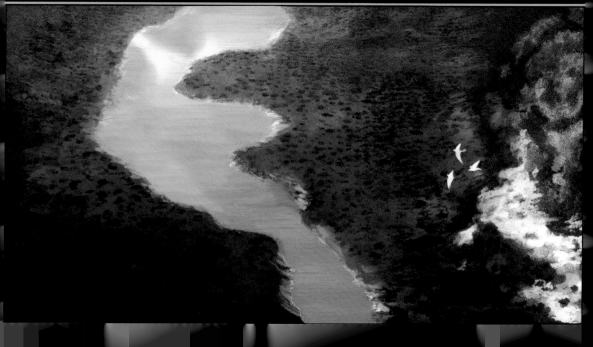

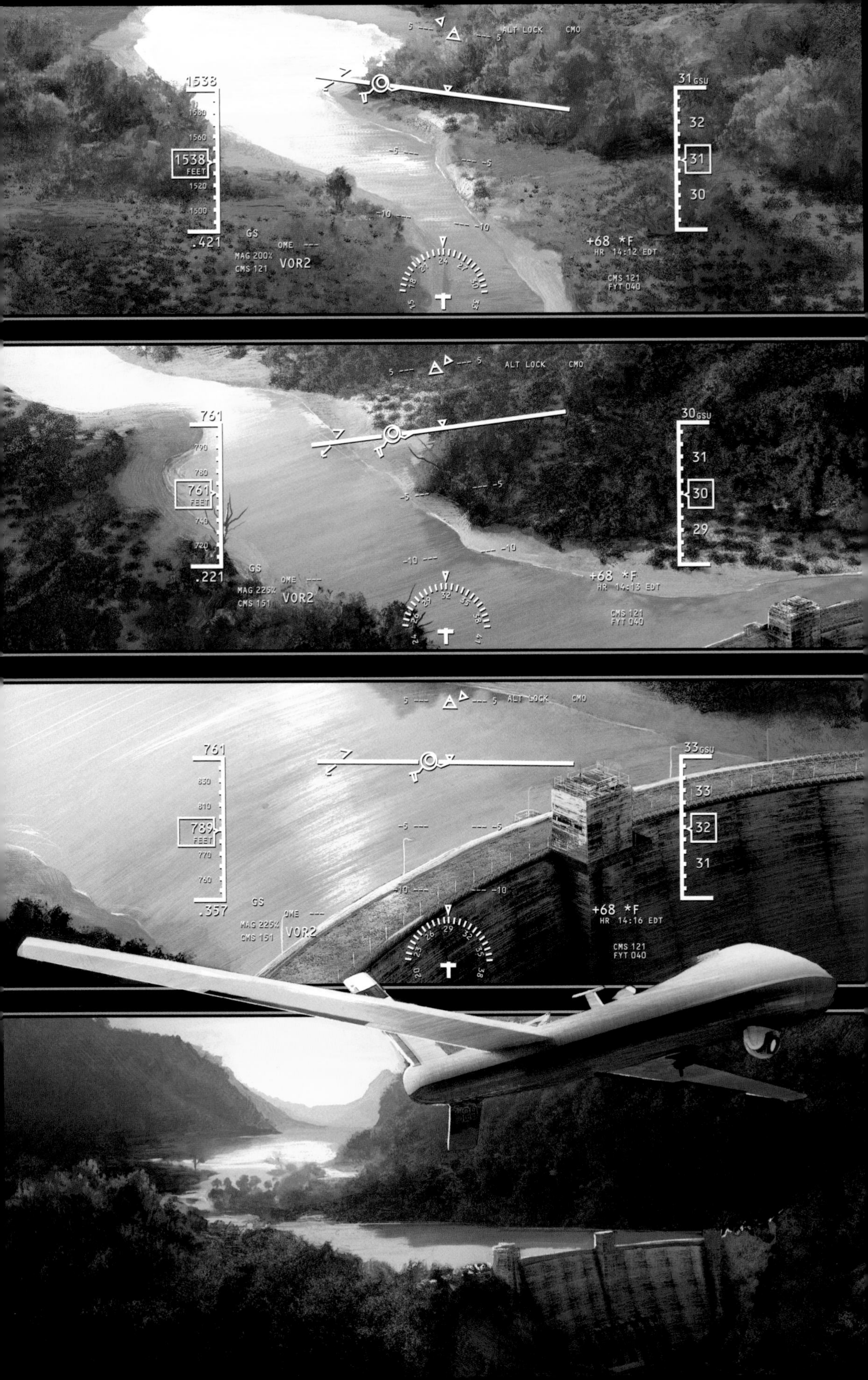
ALT LOCK
CMO
1538
1538 FEET
.421
GS
OME ---
MAG 200%
CMS 121
VOR2
31 GSU
32
31
30
+68 *F
HR 14:12 EDT
CMS 121
FYT 040
ALT LOCK
CMO
761
761 FEET
.221
GS
OME ---
MAG 225%
CMS 151
VOR2
30 GSU
31
30
29
+68 *F
HR 14:13 EDT
CMS 121
FYT 040
ALT LOCK
CMO
761
789 FEET
.357
GS
OME ---
MAG 225%
CMS 151
VOR2
33 GSU
33
32
31
+68 *F
HR 14:16 EDT
CMS 121
FYT 040

"I Became Insane
with Long Intervals
of Horrible
Sanity."
— E. A. Poe

brrrp
brrrp

NOAH
FREEMAN.

YOUR
DAYS ARE
NUMBERED,
NOAH FREEMAN...

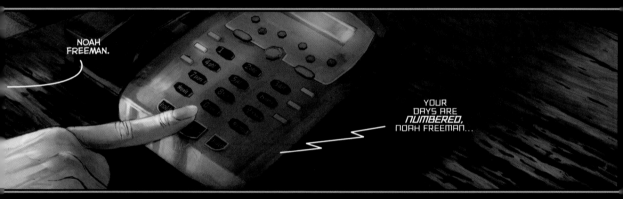

STILL
TIME TO
RUN.

STILL
TIME TO
*SAVE
YOURSELF!*

HEY,
TERRY...

HOW
LONG TILL
THE FUNERAL?

THREE
WEEKS.

I'M
GETTING
MARRIED,
TERRY.

NOT
DYING.

YOU
SAY
"TOMATO..."

IS THERE A POINT TO THIS CALL, TERRY? I'M TRYING REALLY HARD NOT TO CRASH A MILLION-DOLLAR PIECE OF GOVERNMENT HARDWARE HERE.
MILLION DOLLARS? ARE YOU KIDDING? THAT THING COSTS TEN TIMES THAT, AT LEAST.
WOW... REALLY? SHOULDN'T BE TRYING THOSE LOOP-DE-LOOPS THEN...
RIGHT.
ANYWAY, I THOUGHT YOU'D WANT TO GO OUT FOR A BEER AFTER WORK. WE STILL NEED TO PLAN YOUR WAKE... I MEAN BACHELOR PARTY.
I TOLD YOU I DON'T WANT...
HANG ON...
THAT'S WEIRD...
WHAT'S WEIRD?
NOTHING.
I THOUGHT I TOLD YOU I DIDN'T WANT A WAKE...
HA! SO IT IS A FUNERAL!
OKAY, BACHELOR PARTY. WHATEVER. I DON'T NEED ONE.
YEAH, BUT YOUR FRIENDS DO. EITHER WAY, LET'S GRAB A BEER. HELEN'S STILL IN ENGLAND, RIGHT?
SHE IS.

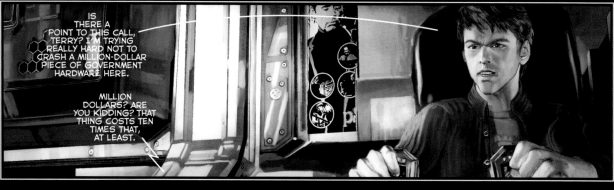

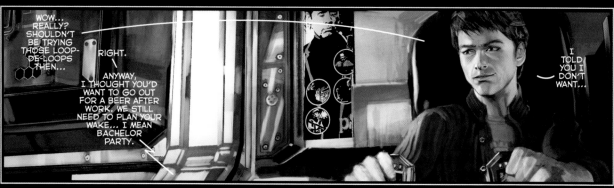

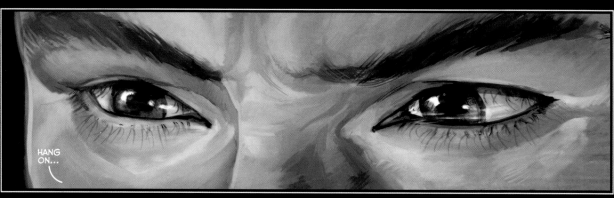

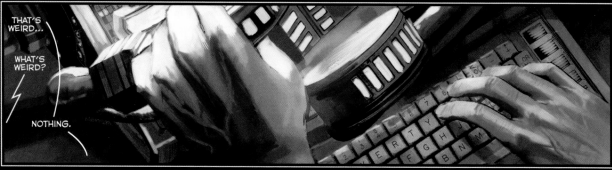

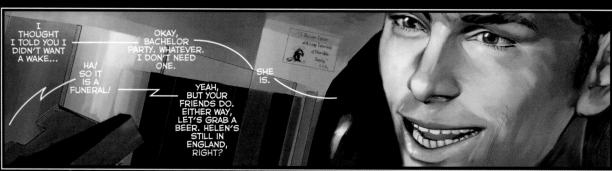

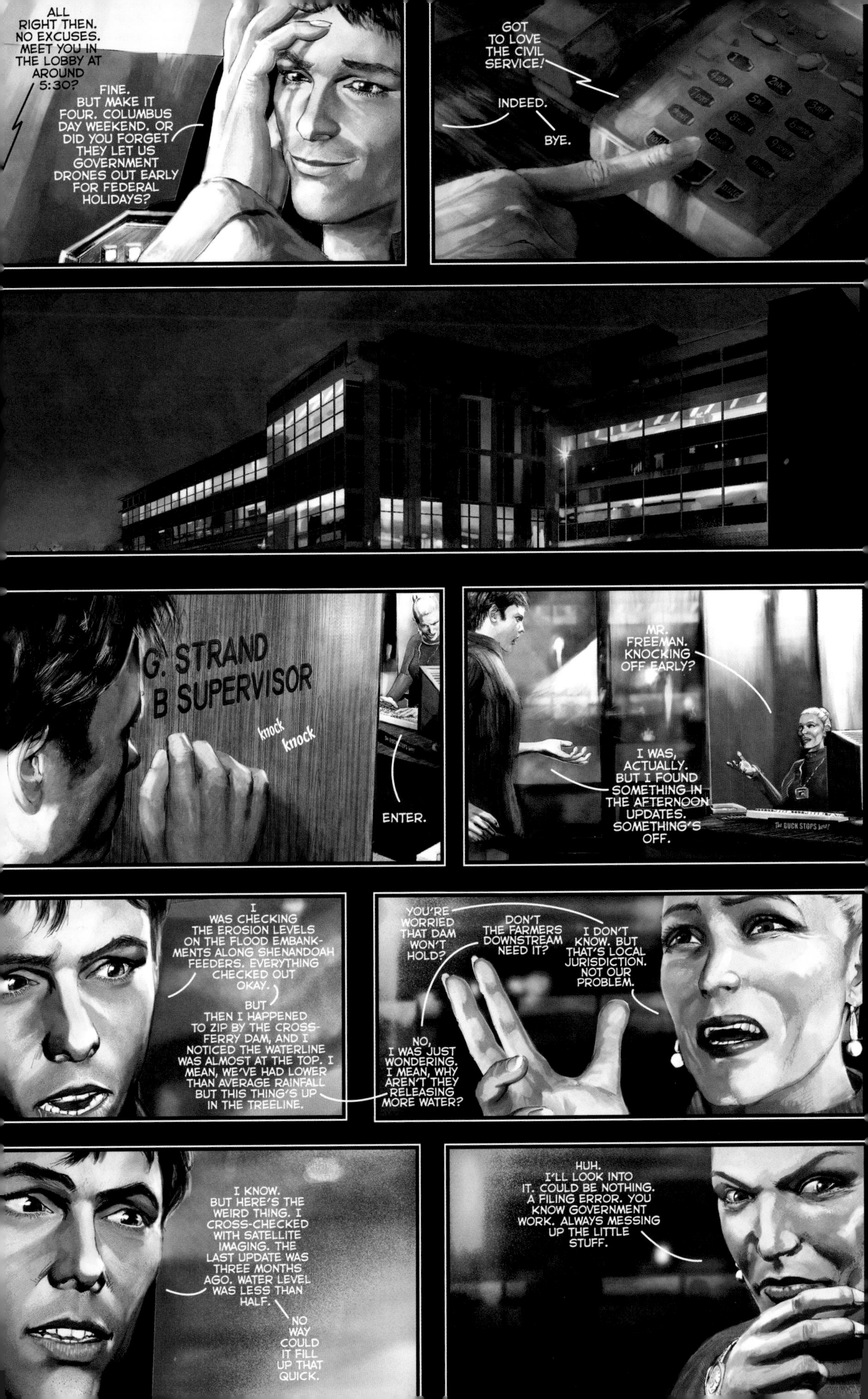
ALL RIGHT THEN. NO EXCUSES. MEET YOU IN THE LOBBY AT AROUND 5:30?
FINE. BUT MAKE IT FOUR. COLUMBUS DAY WEEKEND. OR DID YOU FORGET THEY LET US GOVERNMENT DRONES OUT EARLY FOR FEDERAL HOLIDAYS?
GOT TO LOVE THE CIVIL SERVICE!
INDEED.
BYE.
G. STRAND
B SUPERVISOR
knock knock
ENTER.
MR. FREEMAN. KNOCKING OFF EARLY?
I WAS, ACTUALLY. BUT I FOUND SOMETHING IN THE AFTERNOON UPDATES. SOMETHING'S OFF.
The BUCK STOPS here!
I WAS CHECKING THE EROSION LEVELS ON THE FLOOD EMBANK-MENTS ALONG SHENANDOAH FEEDERS. EVERYTHING CHECKED OUT OKAY.
BUT THEN I HAPPENED TO ZIP BY THE CROSS-FERRY DAM, AND I NOTICED THE WATERLINE WAS ALMOST AT THE TOP. I MEAN, WE'VE HAD LOWER THAN AVERAGE RAINFALL BUT THIS THING'S UP IN THE TREELINE.
YOU'RE WORRIED THAT DAM WON'T HOLD?
NO, I WAS JUST WONDERING. I MEAN, WHY AREN'T THEY RELEASING MORE WATER?
DON'T THE FARMERS DOWNSTREAM NEED IT?
I DON'T KNOW. BUT THAT'S LOCAL JURISDICTION. NOT OUR PROBLEM.
I KNOW. BUT HERE'S THE WEIRD THING. I CROSS-CHECKED WITH SATELLITE IMAGING. THE LAST UPDATE WAS THREE MONTHS AGO. WATER LEVEL WAS LESS THAN HALF.
NO WAY COULD IT FILL UP THAT QUICK.
HUH. I'LL LOOK INTO IT. COULD BE NOTHING. A FILING ERROR. YOU KNOW GOVERNMENT WORK. ALWAYS MESSING UP THE LITTLE STUFF.

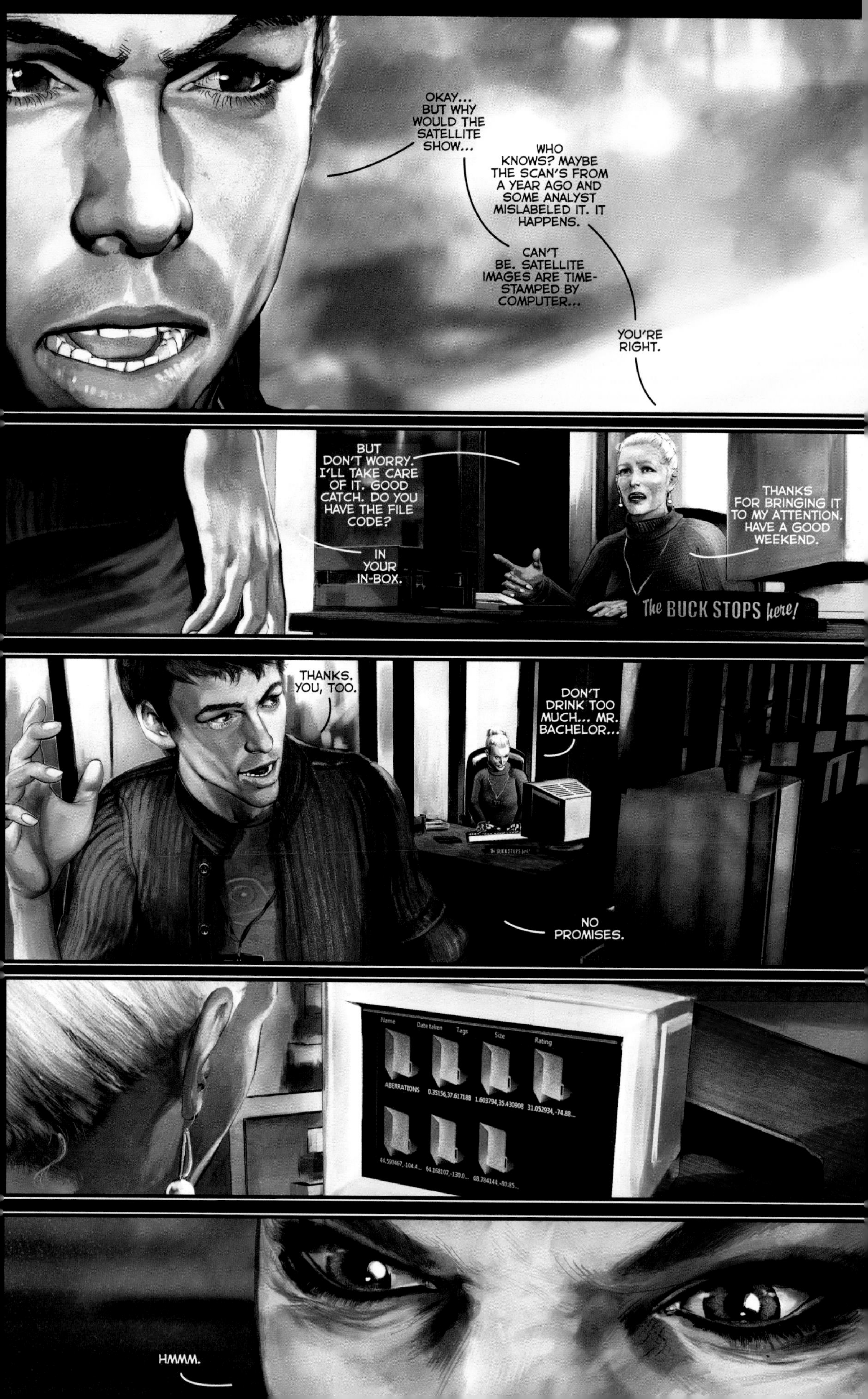
OKAY... BUT WHY WOULD THE SATELLITE SHOW...
WHO KNOWS? MAYBE THE SCAN'S FROM A YEAR AGO AND SOME ANALYST MISLABELED IT. IT HAPPENS.
CAN'T BE. SATELLITE IMAGES ARE TIME-STAMPED BY COMPUTER...
YOU'RE RIGHT.
BUT DON'T WORRY. I'LL TAKE CARE OF IT. GOOD CATCH. DO YOU HAVE THE FILE CODE?
IN YOUR IN-BOX.
THANKS FOR BRINGING IT TO MY ATTENTION. HAVE A GOOD WEEKEND.
The BUCK STOPS here!
THANKS. YOU, TOO.
DON'T DRINK TOO MUCH... MR. BACHELOR...
NO PROMISES.
Name
Date taken
Tags
Size
Rating
ABERRATIONS
0.35156,37.617188
1.603794,35.430908
31.052934,-74.88...
44.590467,-104.4...
64.168107,-130.0...
68.784144,-80.85...
HMMM.

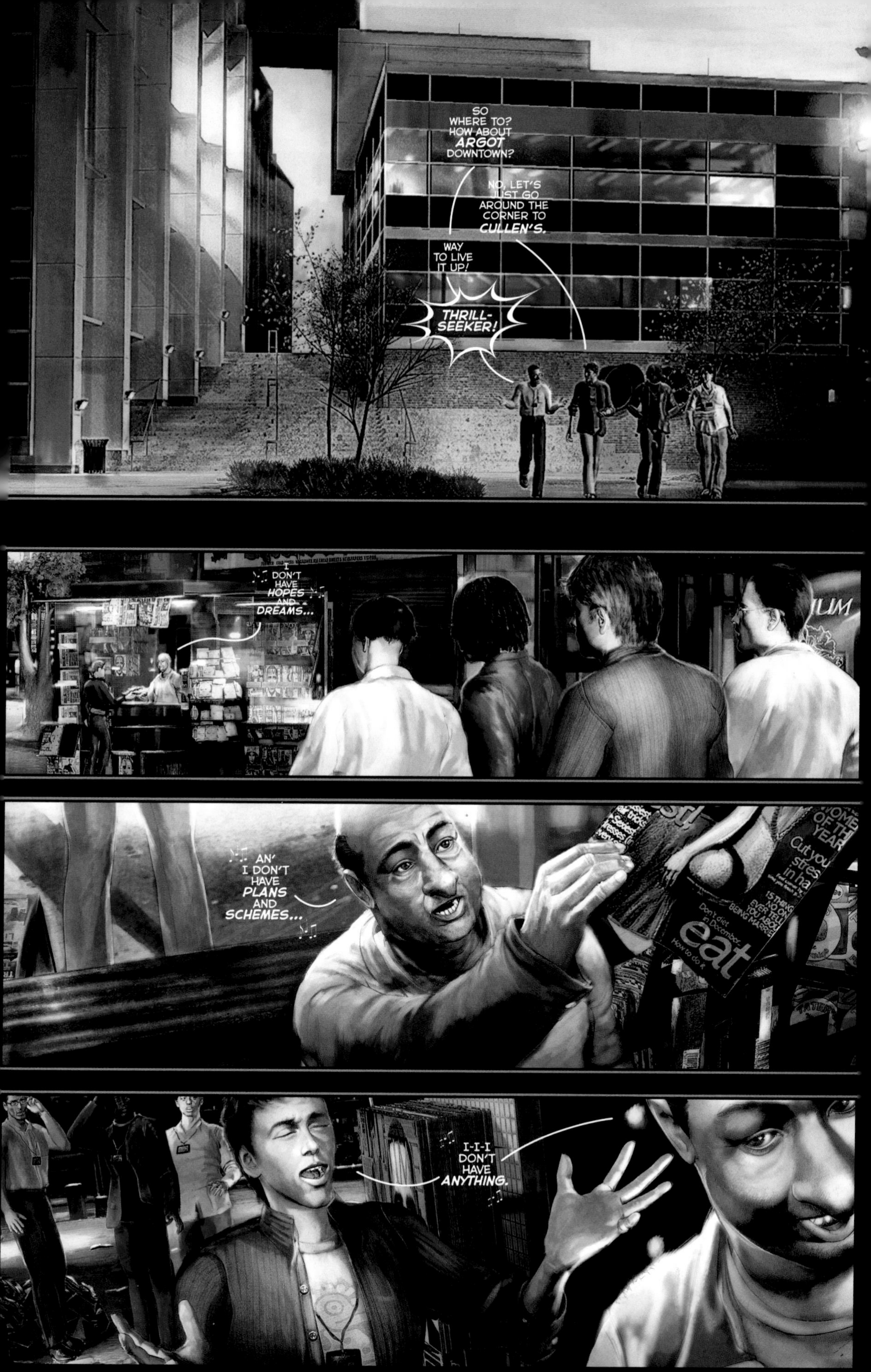
SO WHERE TO? HOW ABOUT ARGOT DOWNTOWN?
NO, LET'S JUST GO AROUND THE CORNER TO CULLEN'S.
WAY TO LIVE IT UP!
THRILL-SEEKER!
I DON'T HAVE HOPES AND DREAMS...
AN' I DON'T HAVE PLANS AND SCHEMES...
I-I-I DON'T HAVE ANYTHING.

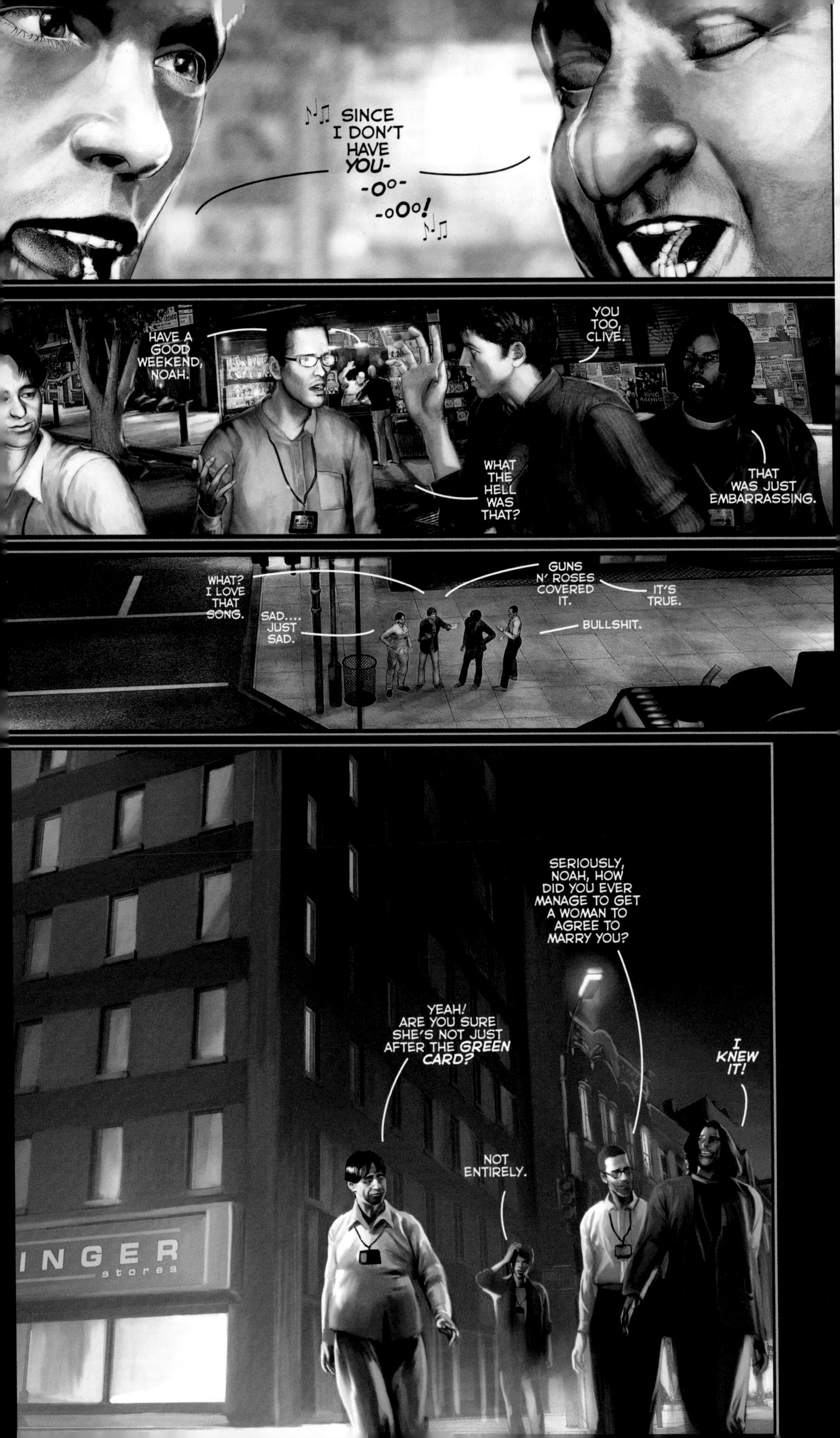
SINCE I DON'T HAVE *YOU*- -Oº- -oOo!
HAVE A GOOD WEEKEND, NOAH.
YOU TOO, CLIVE.
WHAT THE HELL WAS THAT?
THAT WAS JUST EMBARRASSING.
WHAT? I LOVE THAT SONG.
GUNS N' ROSES COVERED IT.
IT'S TRUE.
SAD.... JUST SAD.
BULLSHIT.
SERIOUSLY, NOAH, HOW DID YOU EVER MANAGE TO GET A WOMAN TO AGREE TO *MARRY* YOU?
YEAH! ARE YOU SURE SHE'S NOT JUST AFTER THE *GREEN CARD?*
I KNEW IT!
NOT ENTIRELY.
INGER stores

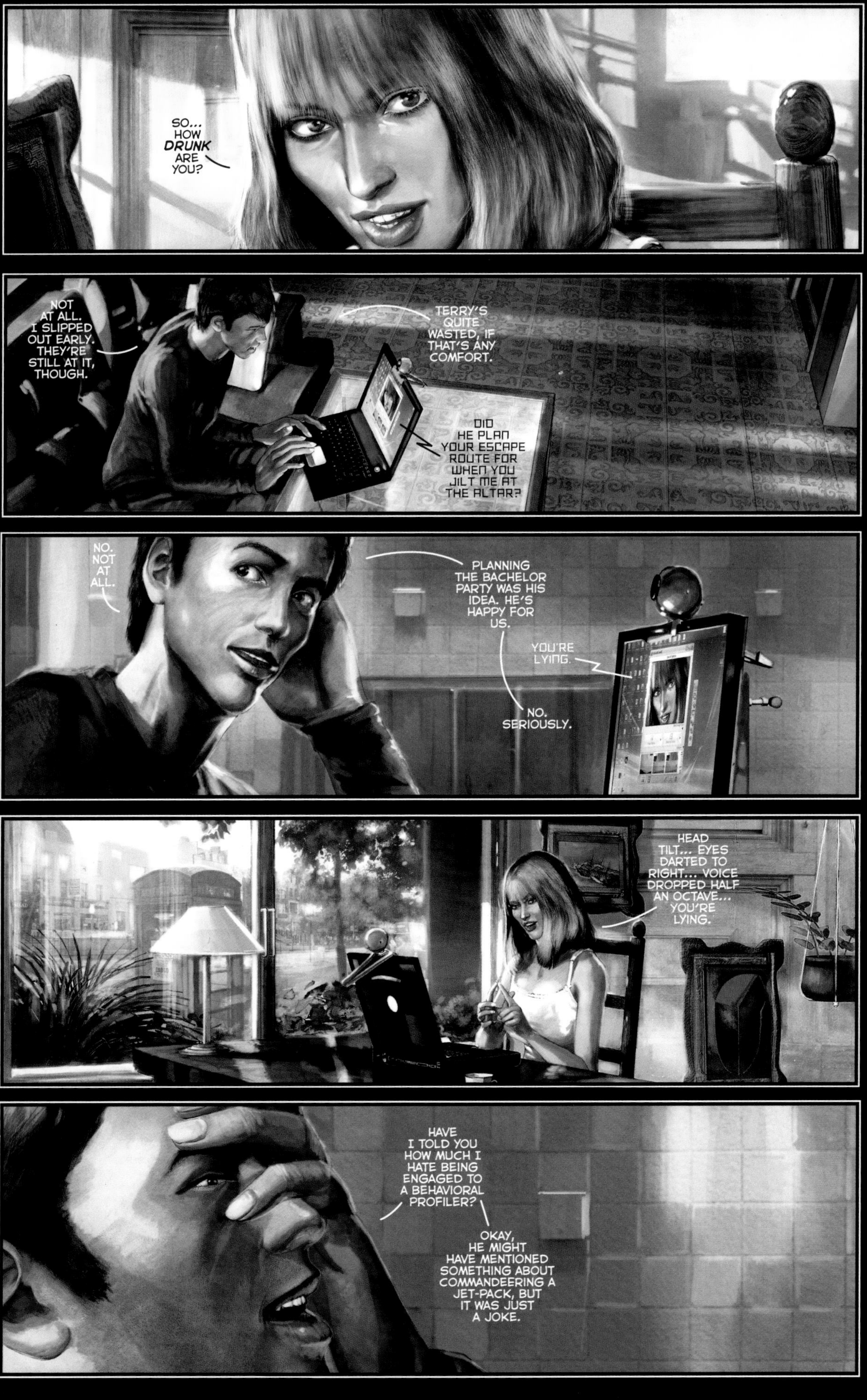
SO... HOW **DRUNK** ARE YOU?
NOT AT ALL. I SLIPPED OUT EARLY. THEY'RE STILL AT IT, THOUGH.
TERRY'S QUITE WASTED, IF THAT'S ANY COMFORT.
DID HE PLAN YOUR ESCAPE ROUTE FOR WHEN YOU JILT ME AT THE ALTAR?
NO. NOT AT ALL.
PLANNING THE BACHELOR PARTY WAS HIS IDEA. HE'S HAPPY FOR US.
YOU'RE LYING.
NO. SERIOUSLY.
HEAD TILT... EYES DARTED TO RIGHT... VOICE DROPPED HALF AN OCTAVE... YOU'RE LYING.
HAVE I TOLD YOU HOW MUCH I HATE BEING ENGAGED TO A BEHAVIORAL PROFILER?
OKAY, HE MIGHT HAVE MENTIONED SOMETHING ABOUT COMMANDEERING A JET-PACK, BUT IT WAS JUST A JOKE.

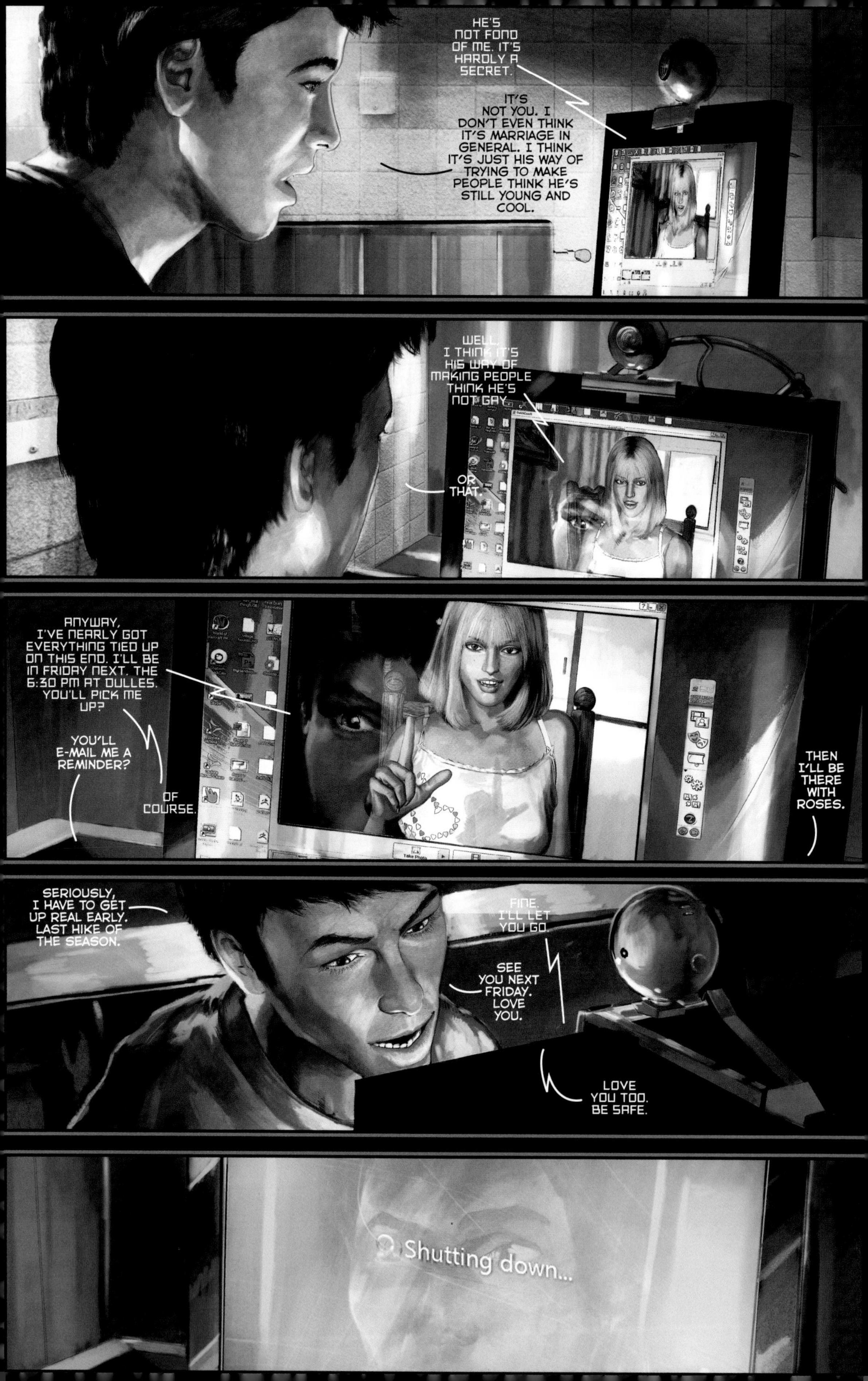
HE'S NOT FOND OF ME. IT'S HARDLY A SECRET.
IT'S NOT YOU. I DON'T EVEN THINK IT'S MARRIAGE IN GENERAL. I THINK IT'S JUST HIS WAY OF TRYING TO MAKE PEOPLE THINK HE'S STILL YOUNG AND COOL.
WELL, I THINK IT'S HIS WAY OF MAKING PEOPLE THINK HE'S NOT GAY.
OR THAT.
ANYWAY, I'VE NEARLY GOT EVERYTHING TIED UP ON THIS END. I'LL BE IN FRIDAY NEXT. THE 6:30 PM AT DULLES. YOU'LL PICK ME UP?
OF COURSE.
YOU'LL E-MAIL ME A REMINDER?
THEN I'LL BE THERE WITH ROSES.
SERIOUSLY, I HAVE TO GET UP REAL EARLY. LAST HIKE OF THE SEASON.
FINE. I'LL LET YOU GO.
SEE YOU NEXT FRIDAY. LOVE YOU.
LOVE YOU TOO. BE SAFE.
Shutting down...

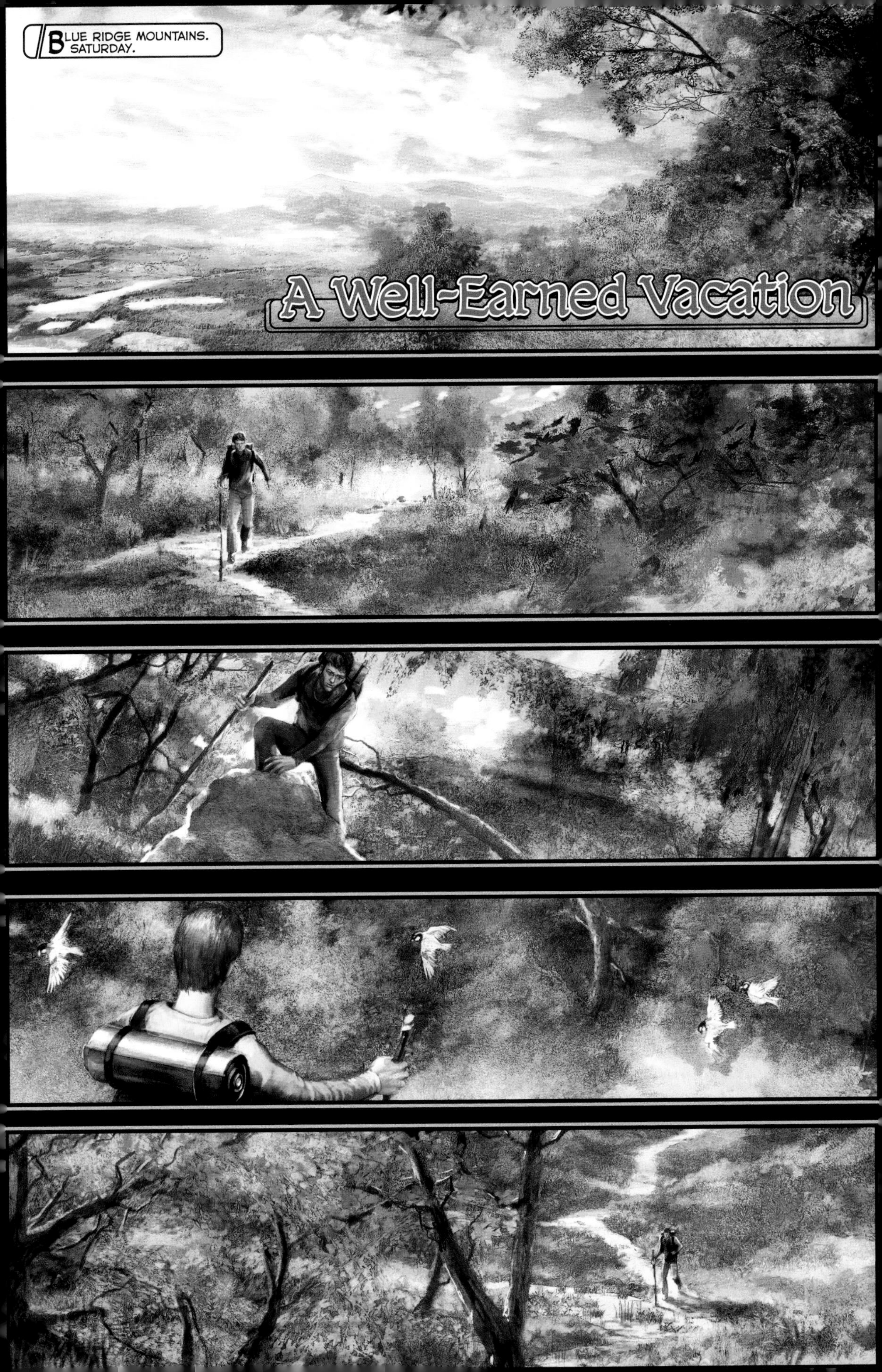
BLUE RIDGE MOUNTAINS. SATURDAY.
A Well-Earned Vacation

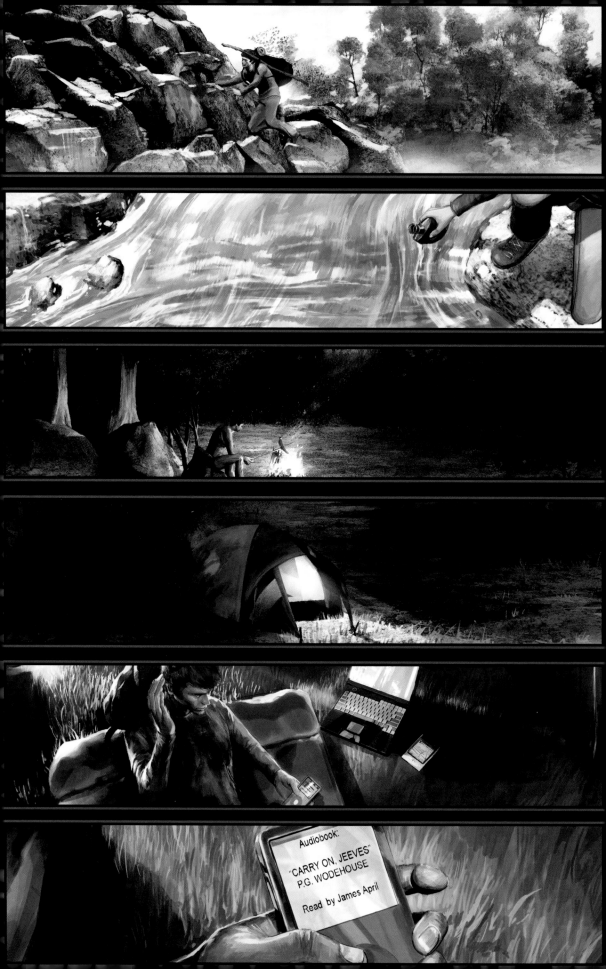

Audiobook:

"CARRY ON, JEEVES"
P.G. WODEHOUSE

Read by James April

...LOST. I'M TELLING YOU.

WE'RE NOT LOST. WE'RE JUST... DETOURED.

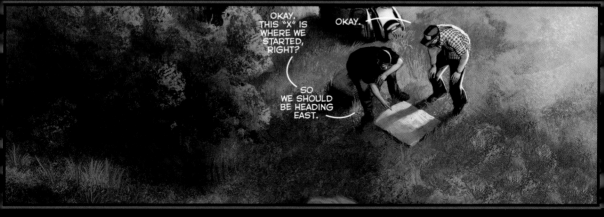

OKAY, THIS "X" IS WHERE WE STARTED, RIGHT?

OKAY.

SO WE SHOULD BE HEADING EAST.

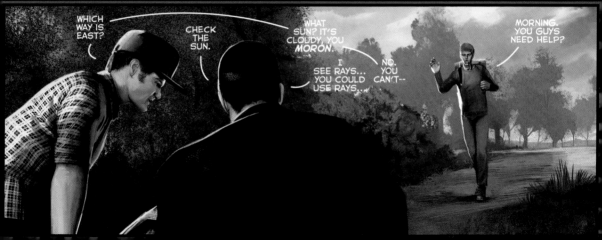

WHICH WAY IS EAST?

CHECK THE SUN.

WHAT SUN? IT'S CLOUDY, YOU MORON.

I SEE RAYS... YOU COULD USE RAYS...

NO. YOU CAN'T--

MORNING. YOU GUYS NEED HELP?

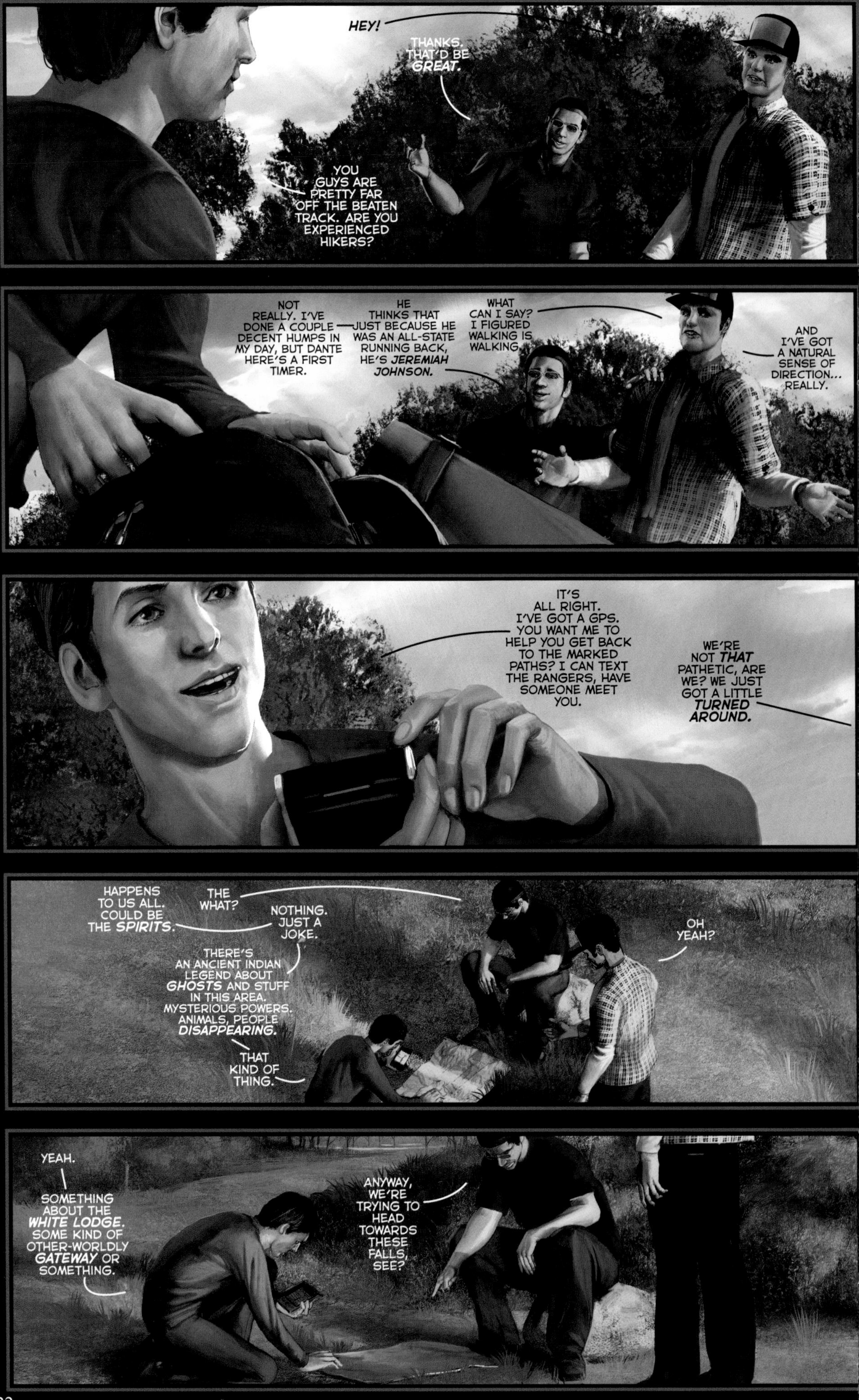
HEY!
THANKS. THAT'D BE GREAT.
YOU GUYS ARE PRETTY FAR OFF THE BEATEN TRACK. ARE YOU EXPERIENCED HIKERS?
NOT REALLY. I'VE DONE A COUPLE DECENT HUMPS IN MY DAY, BUT DANTE HERE'S A FIRST TIMER.
HE THINKS THAT JUST BECAUSE HE WAS AN ALL-STATE RUNNING BACK, HE'S JEREMIAH JOHNSON.
WHAT CAN I SAY? I FIGURED WALKING IS WALKING.
AND I'VE GOT A NATURAL SENSE OF DIRECTION... REALLY.
IT'S ALL RIGHT. I'VE GOT A GPS. YOU WANT ME TO HELP YOU GET BACK TO THE MARKED PATHS? I CAN TEXT THE RANGERS, HAVE SOMEONE MEET YOU.
WE'RE NOT THAT PATHETIC, ARE WE? WE JUST GOT A LITTLE TURNED AROUND.
HAPPENS TO US ALL. COULD BE THE SPIRITS.
THE WHAT?
NOTHING. JUST A JOKE.
THERE'S AN ANCIENT INDIAN LEGEND ABOUT GHOSTS AND STUFF IN THIS AREA. MYSTERIOUS POWERS. ANIMALS, PEOPLE DISAPPEARING.
THAT KIND OF THING.
OH YEAH?
YEAH.
SOMETHING ABOUT THE WHITE LODGE. SOME KIND OF OTHER-WORLDLY GATEWAY OR SOMETHING.
ANYWAY, WE'RE TRYING TO HEAD TOWARDS THESE FALLS, SEE?

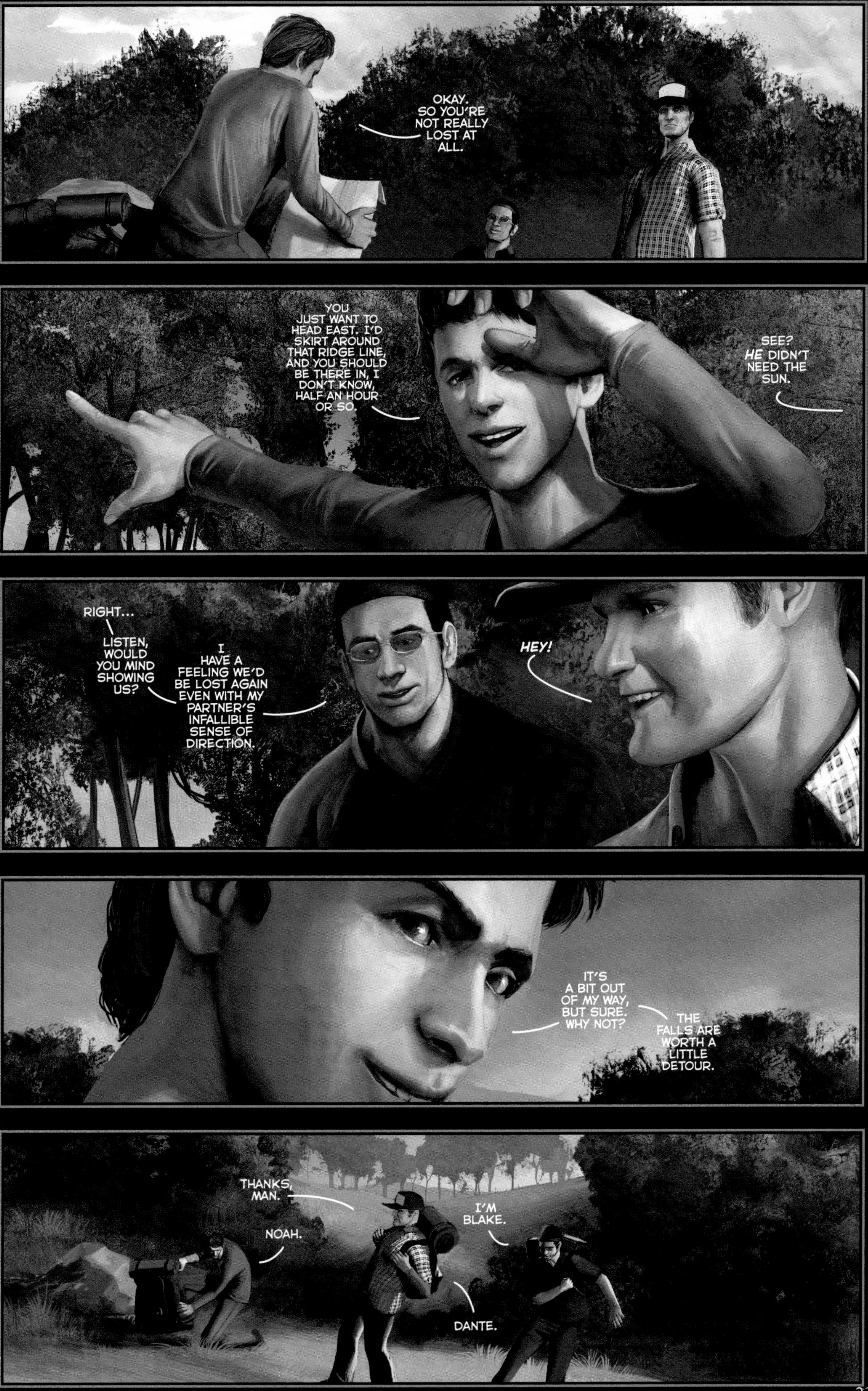
OKAY. SO YOU'RE NOT REALLY LOST AT ALL.
YOU JUST WANT TO HEAD EAST. I'D SKIRT AROUND THAT RIDGE LINE, AND YOU SHOULD BE THERE IN, I DON'T KNOW, HALF AN HOUR OR SO.
SEE? HE DIDN'T NEED THE SUN.
RIGHT...
LISTEN, WOULD YOU MIND SHOWING US?
I HAVE A FEELING WE'D BE LOST AGAIN EVEN WITH MY PARTNER'S INFALLIBLE SENSE OF DIRECTION.
HEY!
IT'S A BIT OUT OF MY WAY, BUT SURE. WHY NOT?
THE FALLS ARE WORTH A LITTLE DETOUR.
THANKS, MAN.
NOAH.
I'M BLAKE.
DANTE.

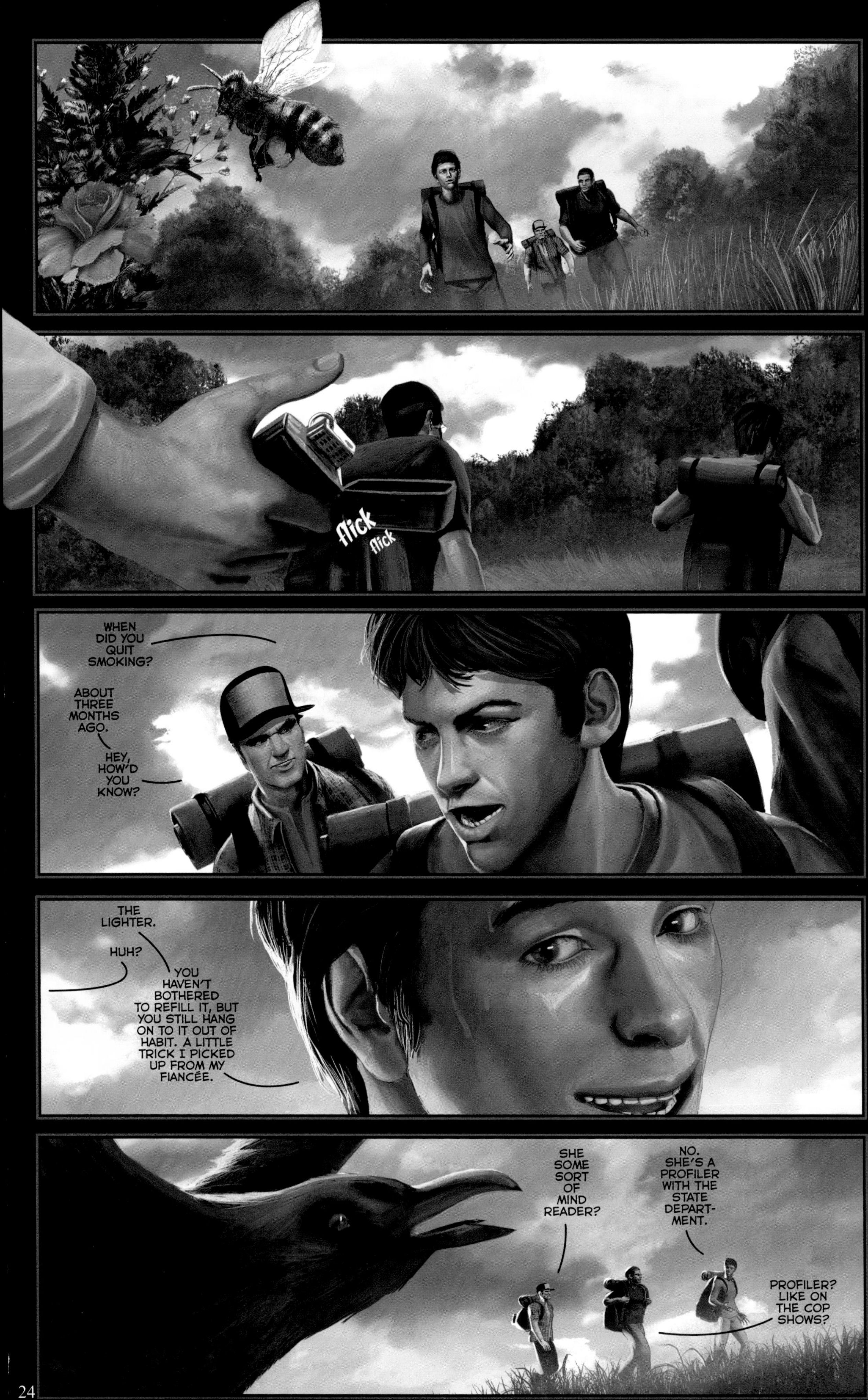
flick
flick
WHEN DID YOU QUIT SMOKING?
ABOUT THREE MONTHS AGO.
HEY, HOW'D YOU KNOW?
THE LIGHTER.
HUH?
YOU HAVEN'T BOTHERED TO REFILL IT, BUT YOU STILL HANG ON TO IT OUT OF HABIT. A LITTLE TRICK I PICKED UP FROM MY FIANCÉE.
SHE SOME SORT OF MIND READER?
NO. SHE'S A PROFILER WITH THE STATE DEPART-MENT.
PROFILER? LIKE ON THE COP SHOWS?

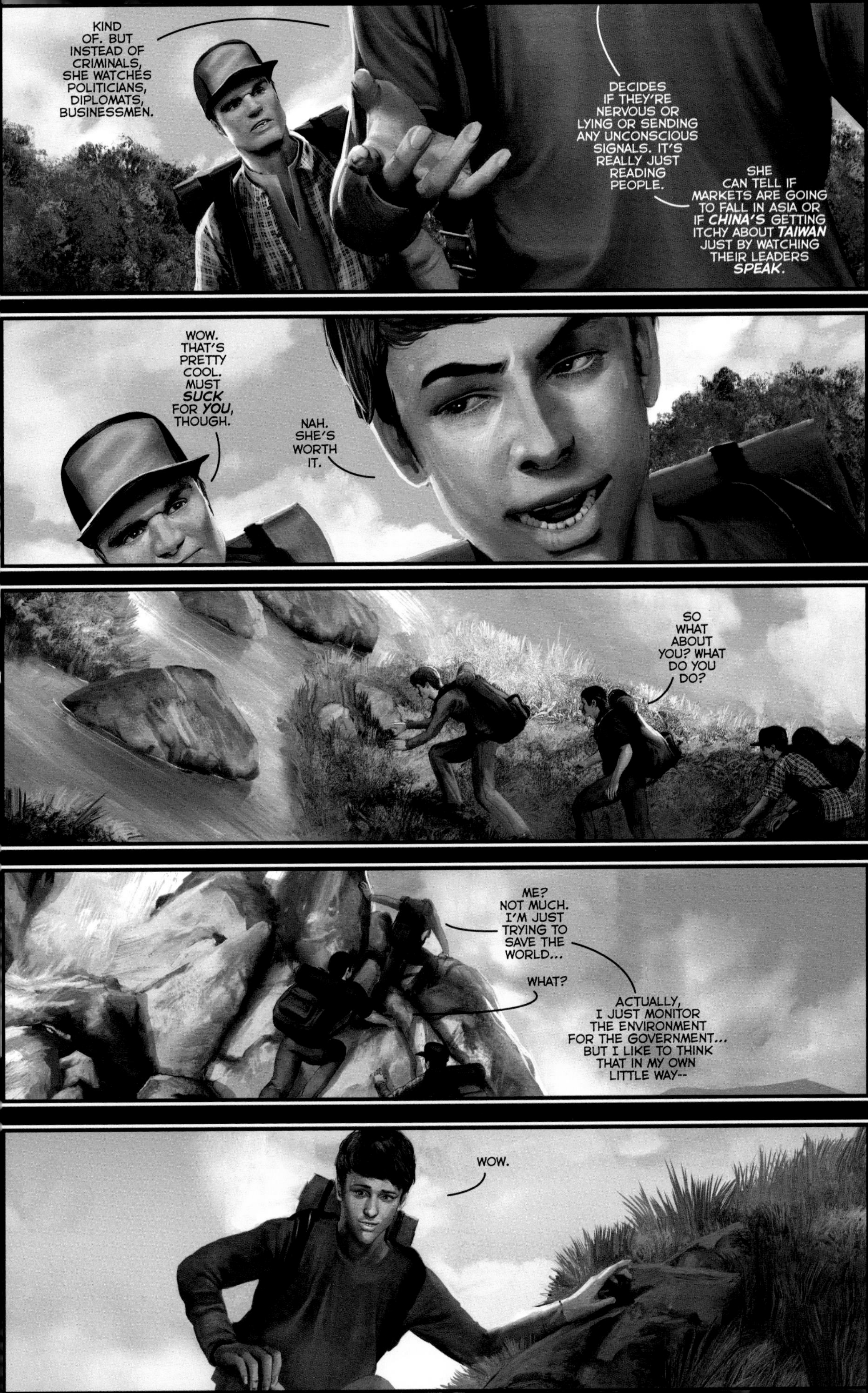
KIND OF. BUT INSTEAD OF CRIMINALS, SHE WATCHES POLITICIANS, DIPLOMATS, BUSINESSMEN.
DECIDES IF THEY'RE NERVOUS OR LYING OR SENDING ANY UNCONSCIOUS SIGNALS. IT'S REALLY JUST READING PEOPLE.
SHE CAN TELL IF MARKETS ARE GOING TO FALL IN ASIA OR IF CHINA'S GETTING ITCHY ABOUT TAIWAN JUST BY WATCHING THEIR LEADERS SPEAK.
WOW. THAT'S PRETTY COOL. MUST SUCK FOR YOU, THOUGH.
NAH. SHE'S WORTH IT.
SO WHAT ABOUT YOU? WHAT DO YOU DO?
ME? NOT MUCH. I'M JUST TRYING TO SAVE THE WORLD...
WHAT?
ACTUALLY, I JUST MONITOR THE ENVIRONMENT FOR THE GOVERNMENT... BUT I LIKE TO THINK THAT IN MY OWN LITTLE WAY--
WOW.

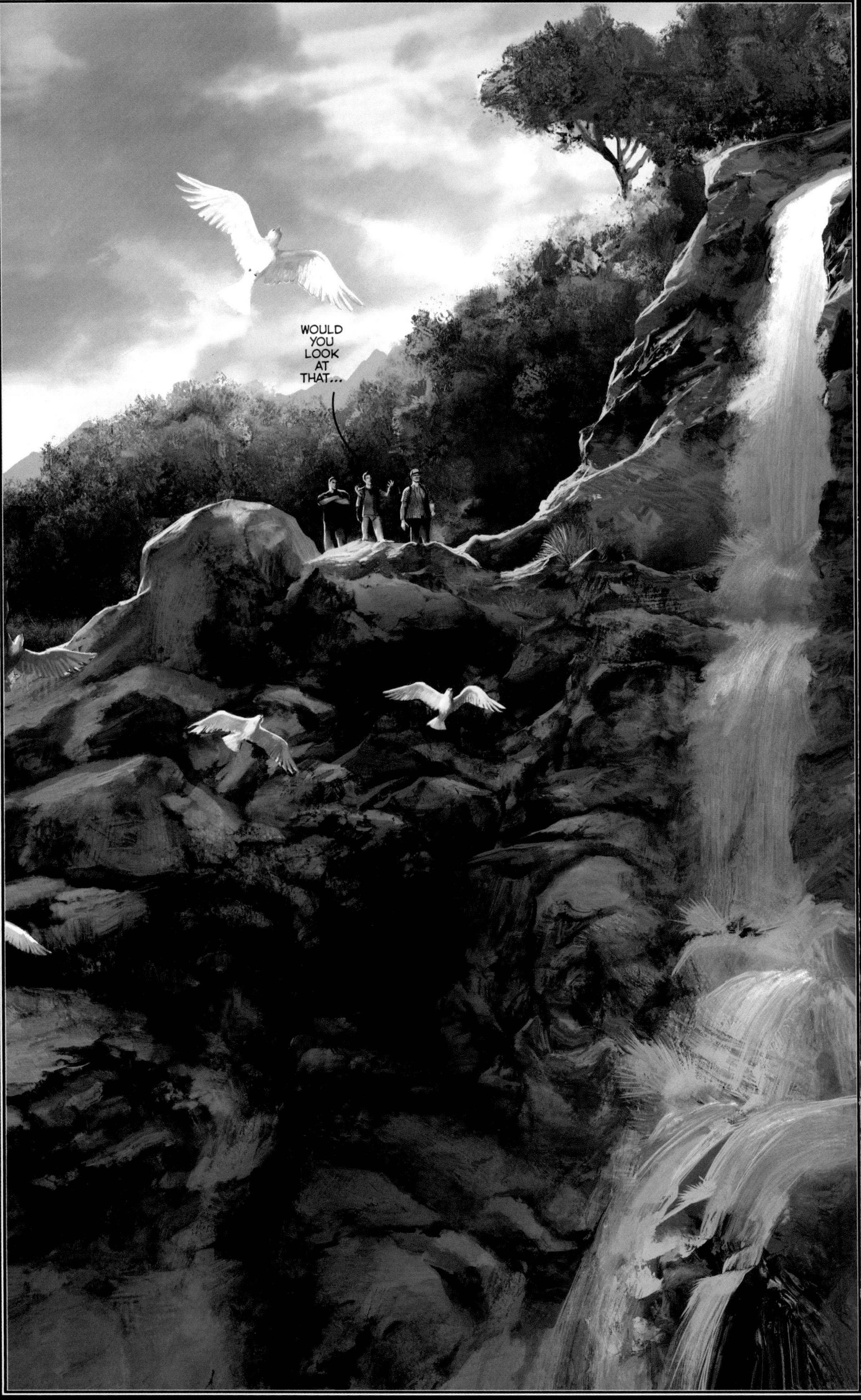
WOULD YOU LOOK AT THAT...

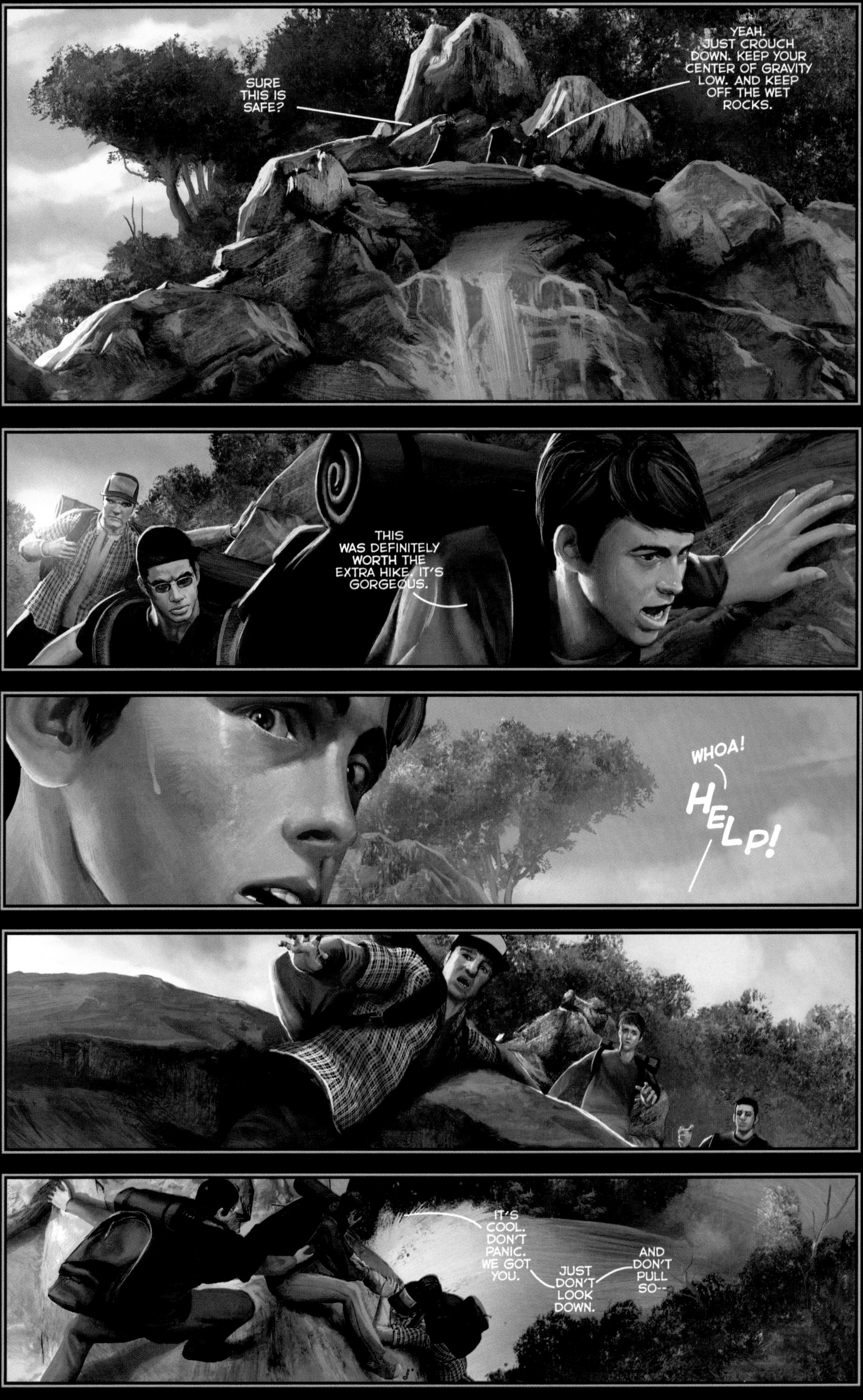

SURE THIS IS SAFE?
YEAH. JUST CROUCH DOWN. KEEP YOUR CENTER OF GRAVITY LOW. AND KEEP OFF THE WET ROCKS.
THIS WAS DEFINITELY WORTH THE EXTRA HIKE. IT'S GORGEOUS.
WHOA!
HELP!
IT'S COOL. DON'T PANIC. WE GOT YOU.
JUST DON'T LOOK DOWN.
AND DON'T PULL SO--

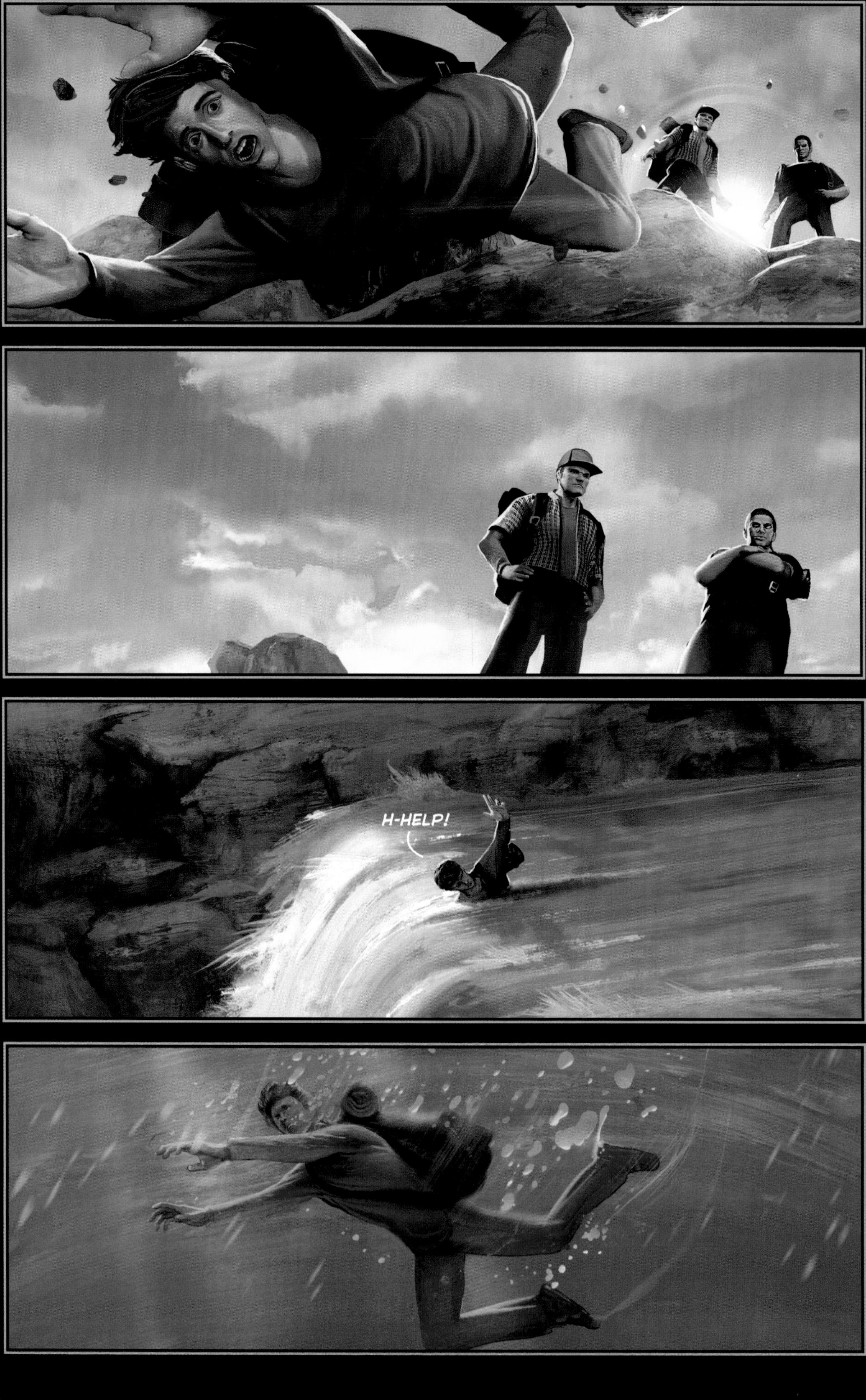
H-HELP!

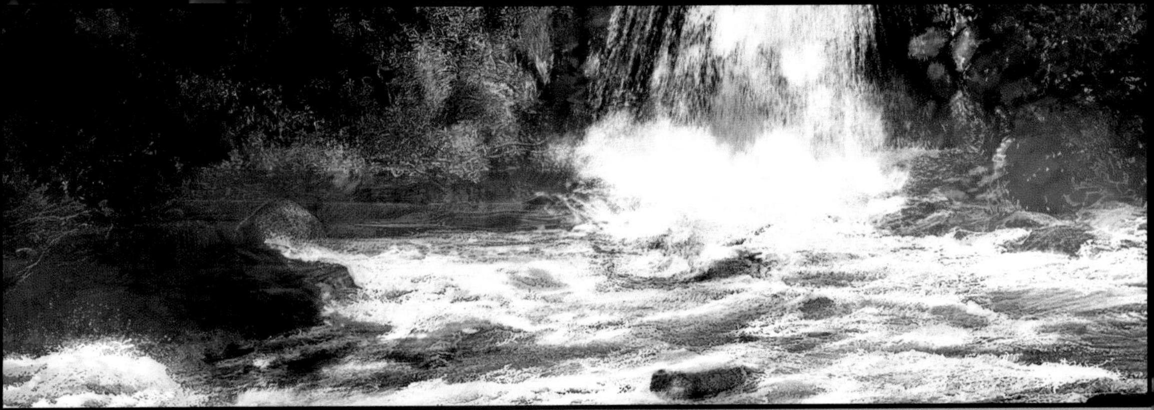

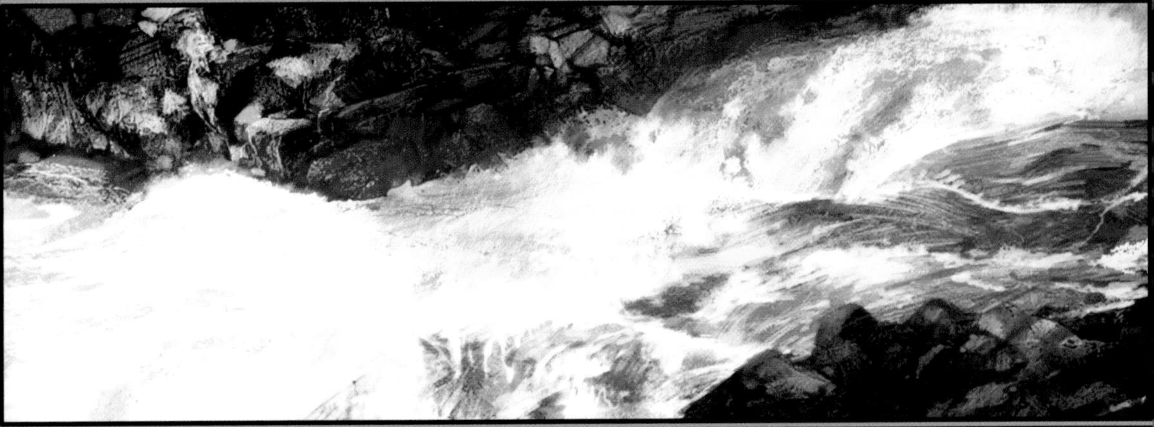

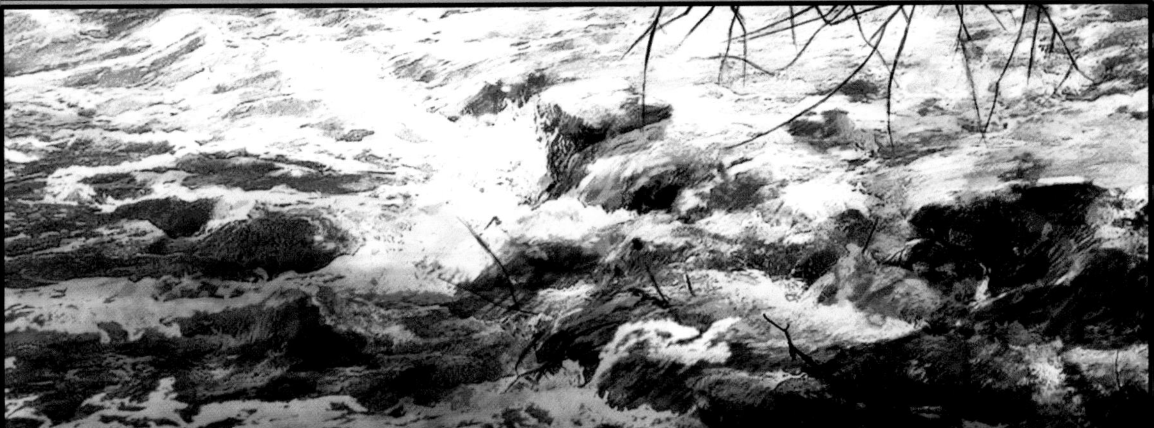

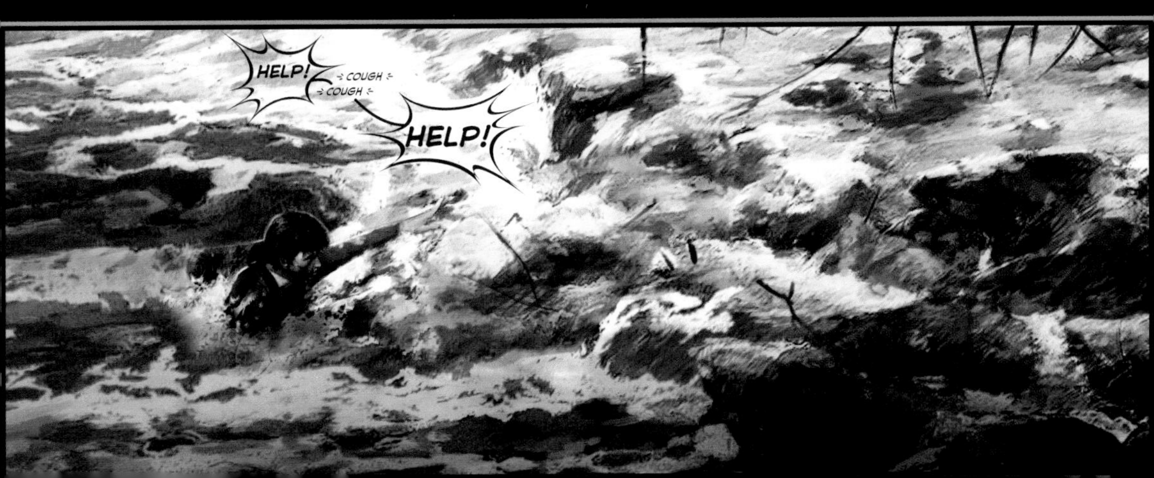
HELP!
COUGH
COUGH
HELP!

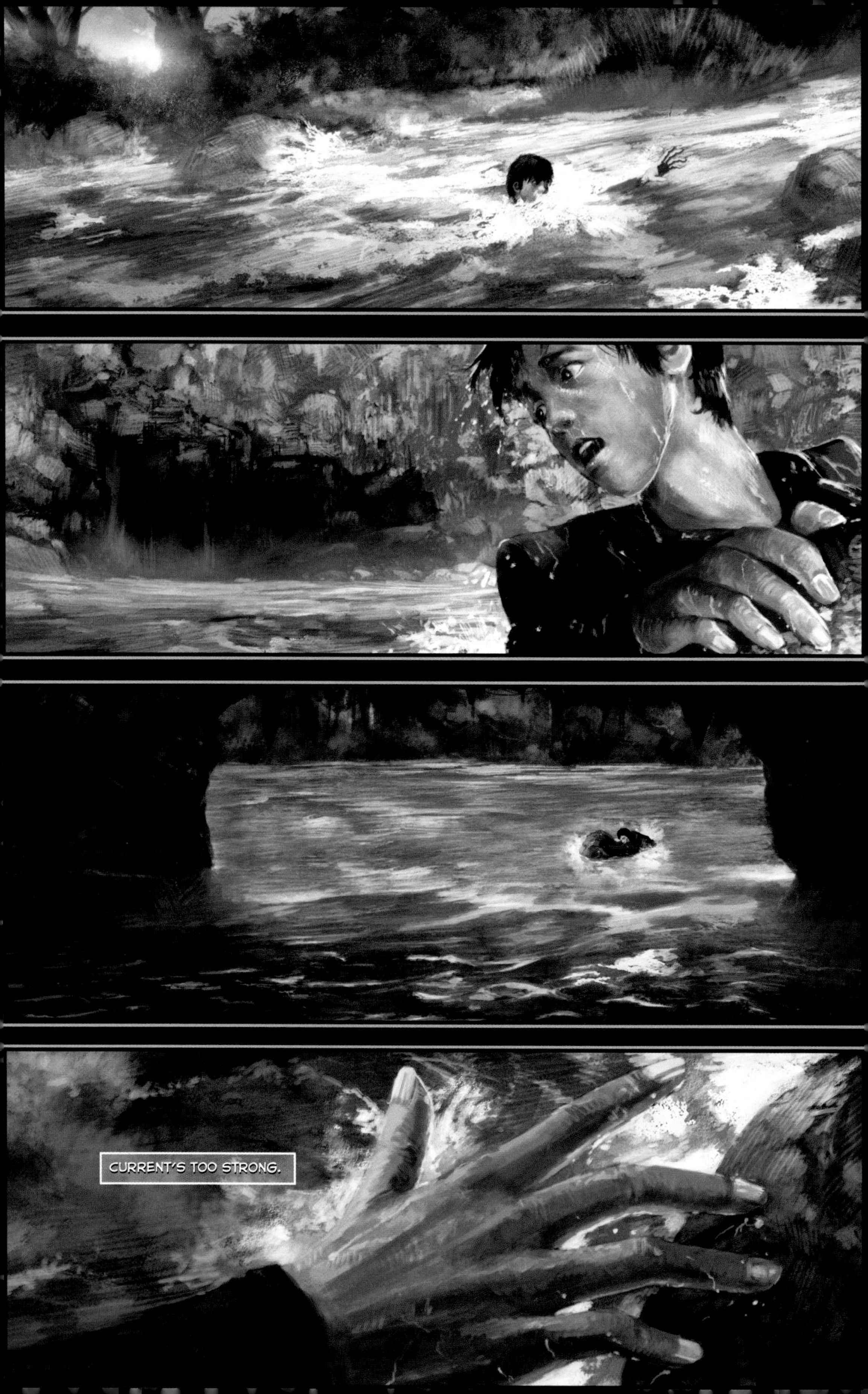
CURRENT'S TOO STRONG.

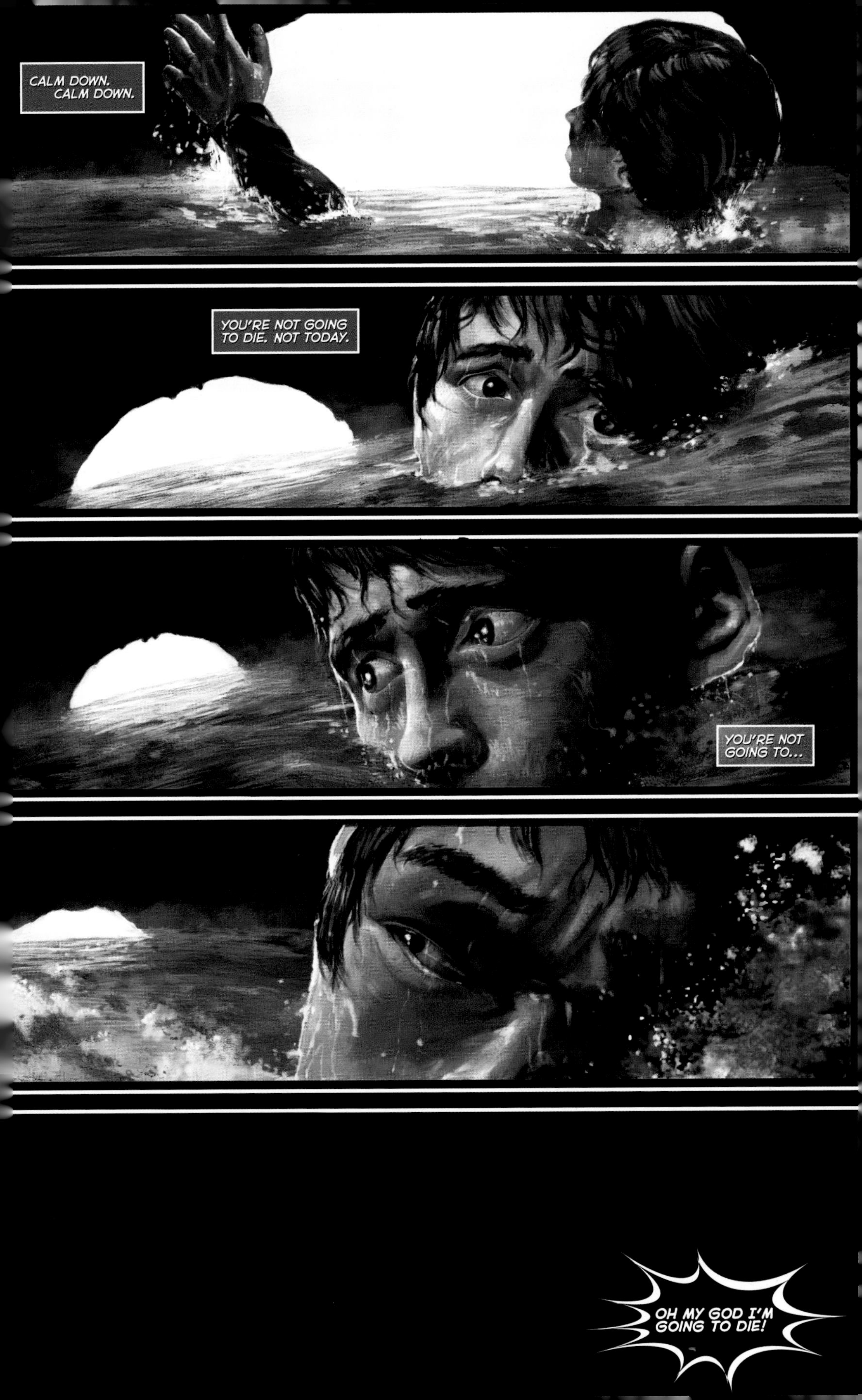
CALM DOWN. CALM DOWN.
YOU'RE NOT GOING TO DIE. NOT TODAY.
YOU'RE NOT GOING TO...
OH MY GOD I'M GOING TO DIE!

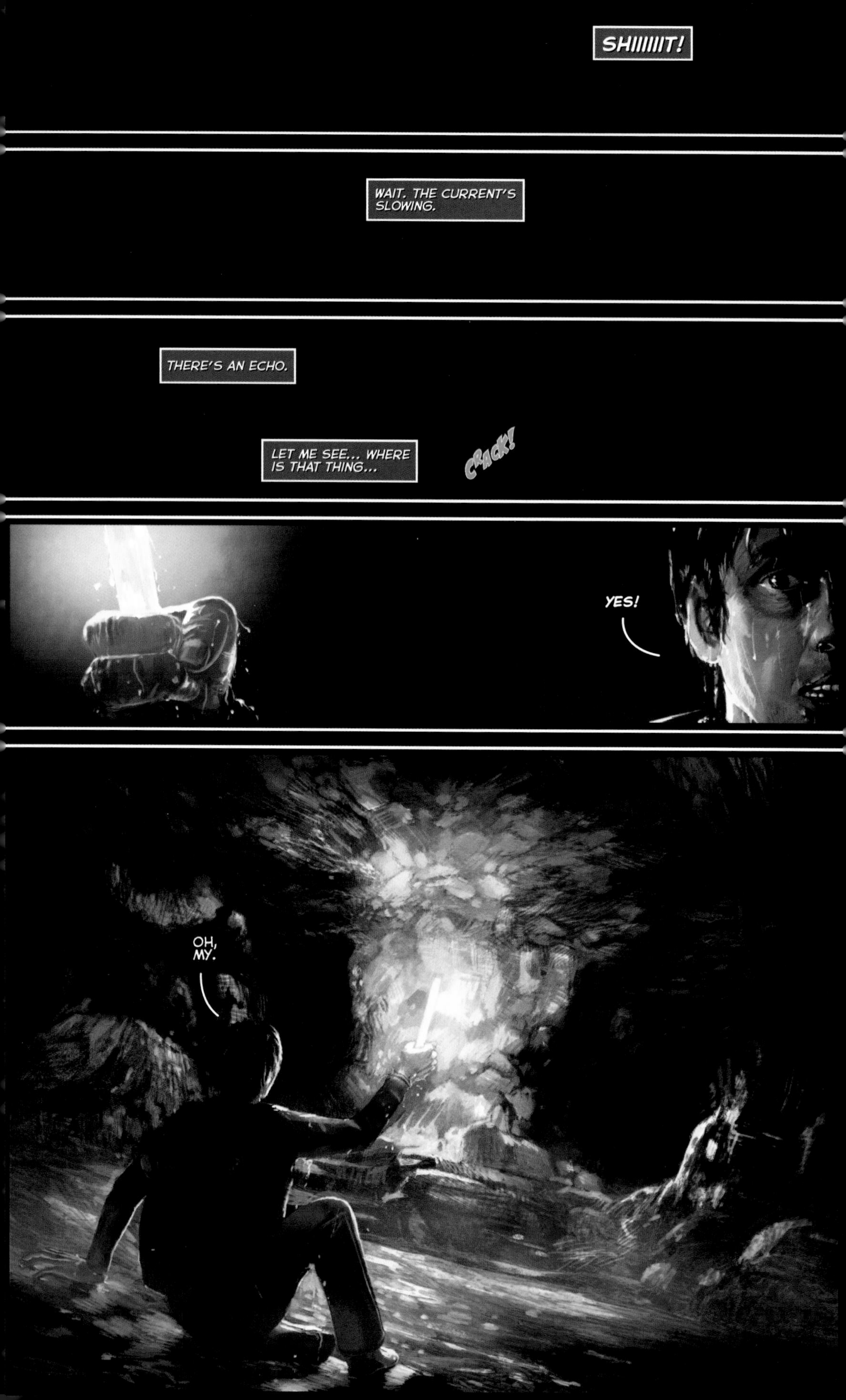
SHIIIIIIT!
WAIT. THE CURRENT'S SLOWING.
THERE'S AN ECHO.
LET ME SEE... WHERE IS THAT THING...
CRACK!
YES!
OH, MY.

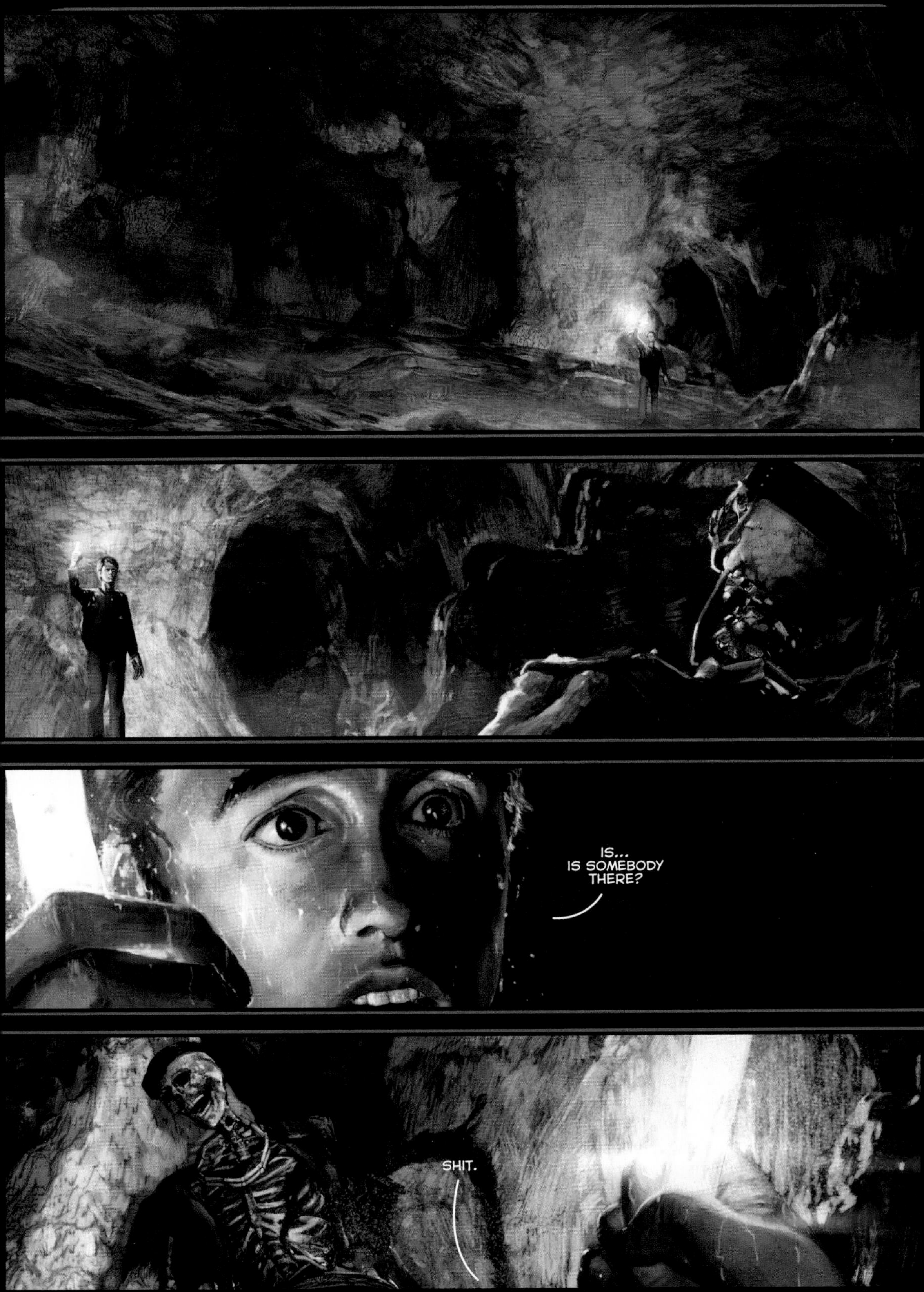
IS... IS SOMEBODY THERE?
SHIT.

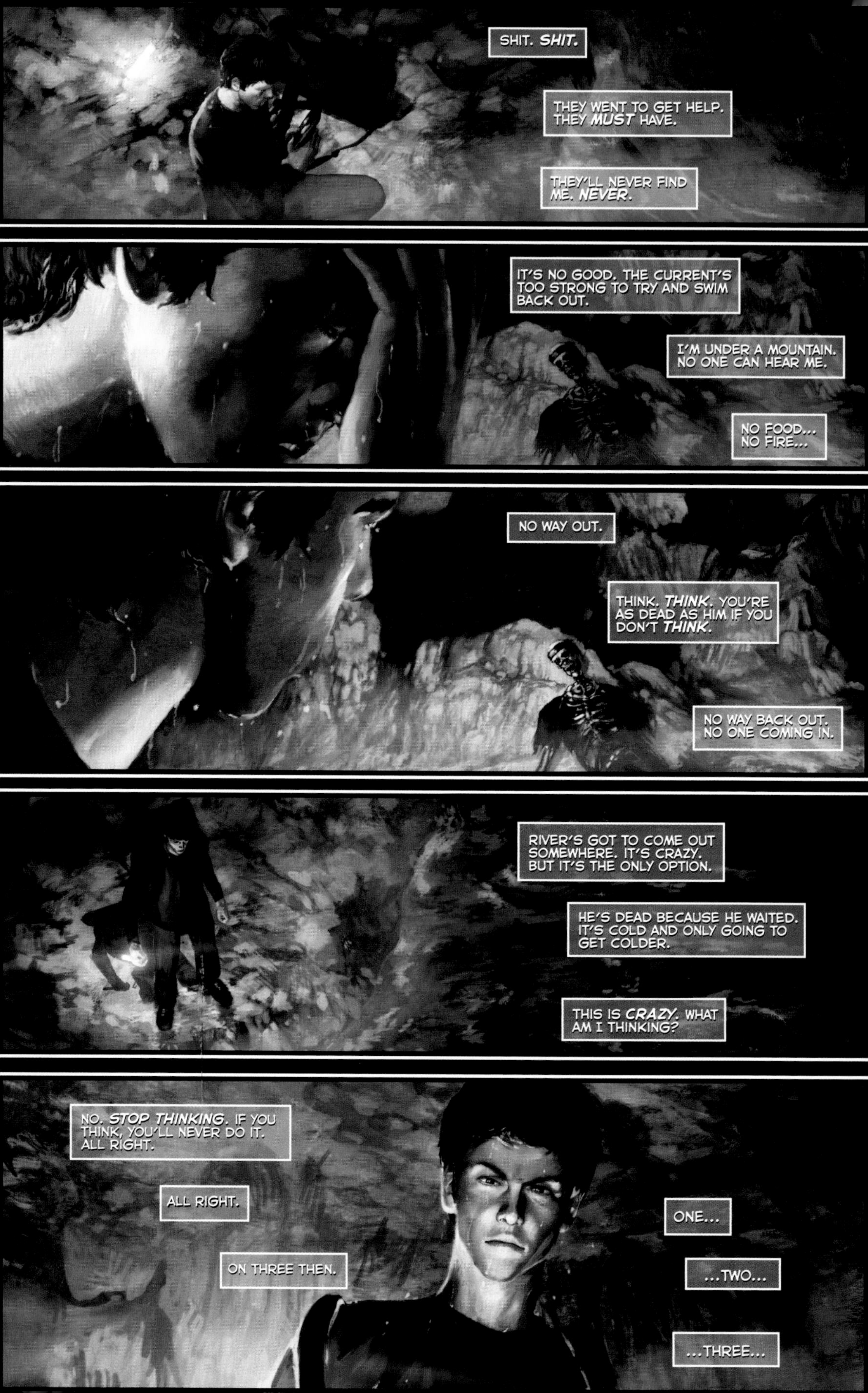
SHIT. SHIT.
THEY WENT TO GET HELP. THEY MUST HAVE.
THEY'LL NEVER FIND ME. NEVER.
IT'S NO GOOD. THE CURRENT'S TOO STRONG TO TRY AND SWIM BACK OUT.
I'M UNDER A MOUNTAIN. NO ONE CAN HEAR ME.
NO FOOD... NO FIRE...
NO WAY OUT.
THINK. THINK. YOU'RE AS DEAD AS HIM IF YOU DON'T THINK.
NO WAY BACK OUT. NO ONE COMING IN.
RIVER'S GOT TO COME OUT SOMEWHERE. IT'S CRAZY. BUT IT'S THE ONLY OPTION.
HE'S DEAD BECAUSE HE WAITED. IT'S COLD AND ONLY GOING TO GET COLDER.
THIS IS CRAZY. WHAT AM I THINKING?
NO. STOP THINKING. IF YOU THINK, YOU'LL NEVER DO IT. ALL RIGHT.
ALL RIGHT.
ON THREE THEN.
ONE...
...TWO...
...THREE...

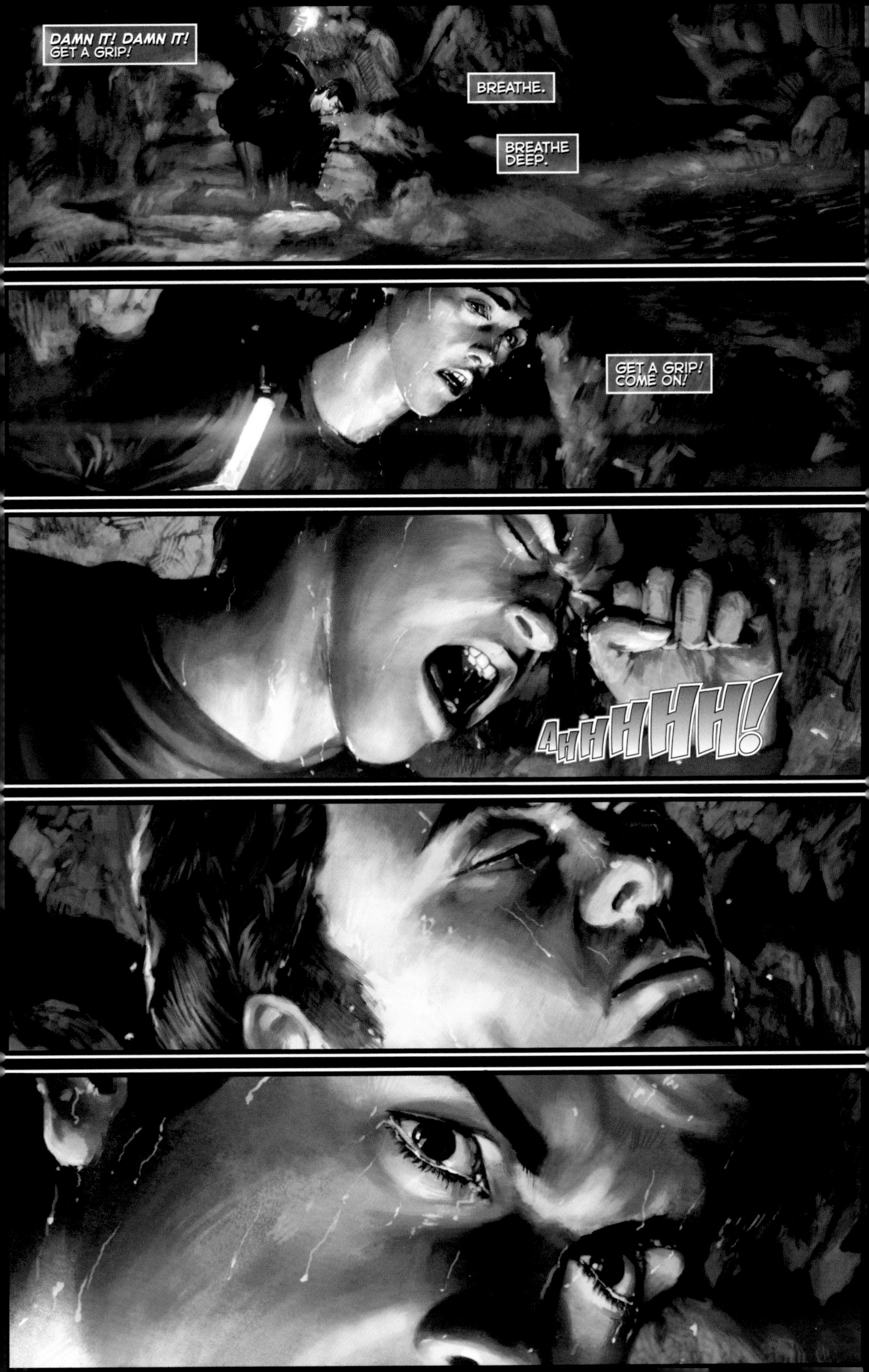
DAMN IT! DAMN IT! GET A GRIP!
BREATHE.
BREATHE DEEP.
GET A GRIP! COME ON!
AHHHHHH!

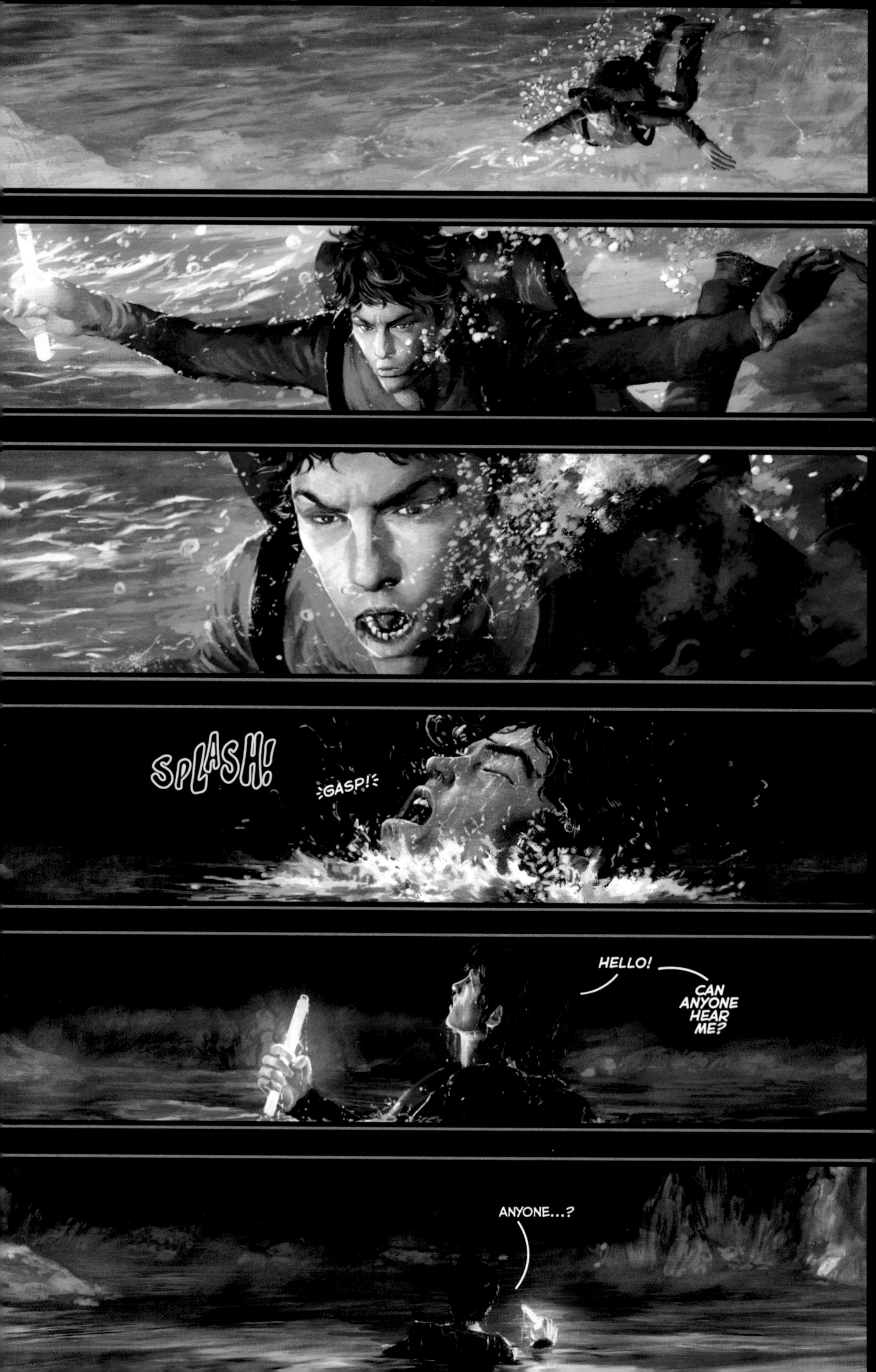
SPLASH!
GASP!
HELLO!
CAN ANYONE HEAR ME?
ANYONE...?

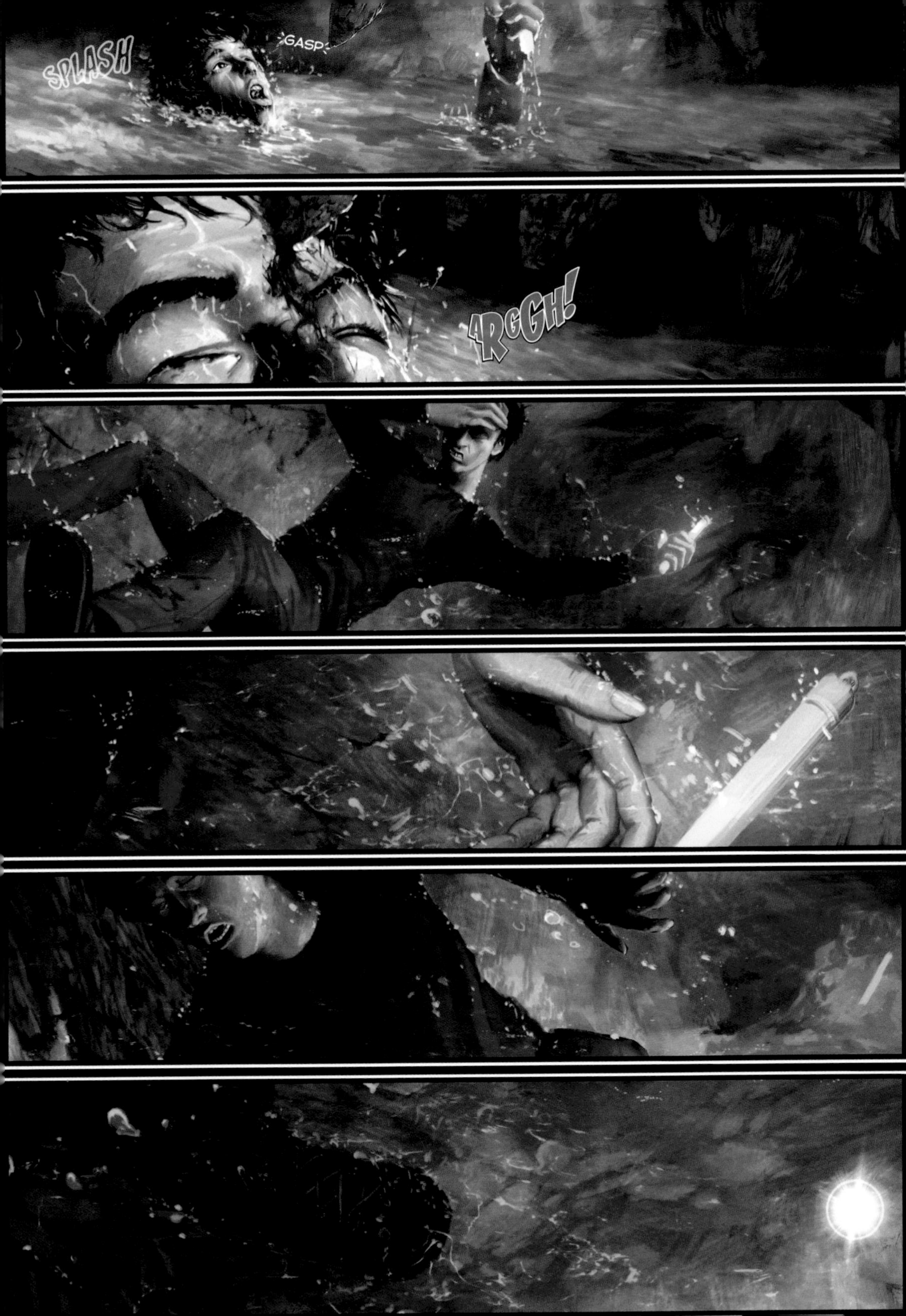
SPLASH
GASP
ARGGH!

IS THIS **HEAVEN**?

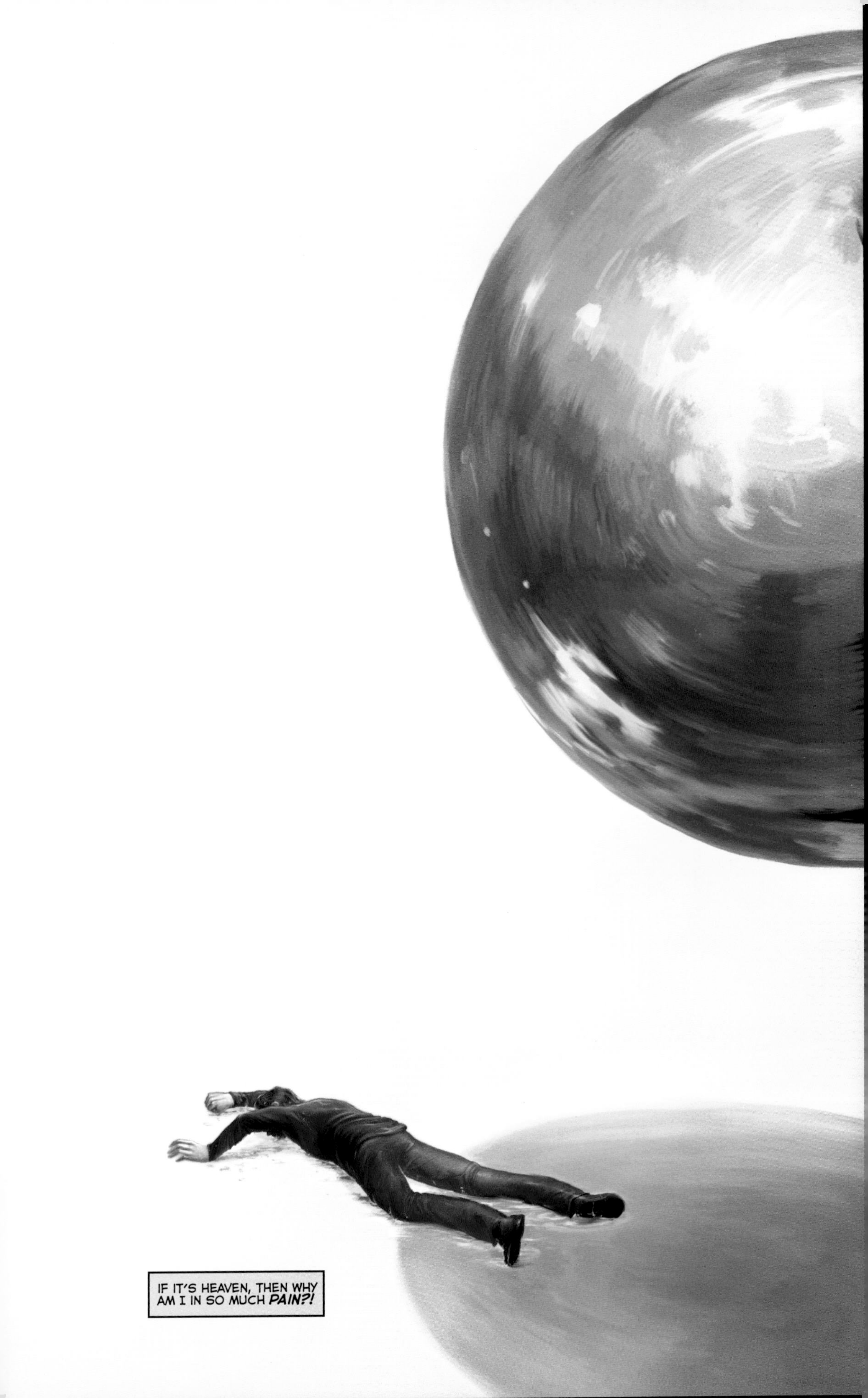
IF IT'S HEAVEN, THEN WHY AM I IN SO MUCH *PAIN?!*

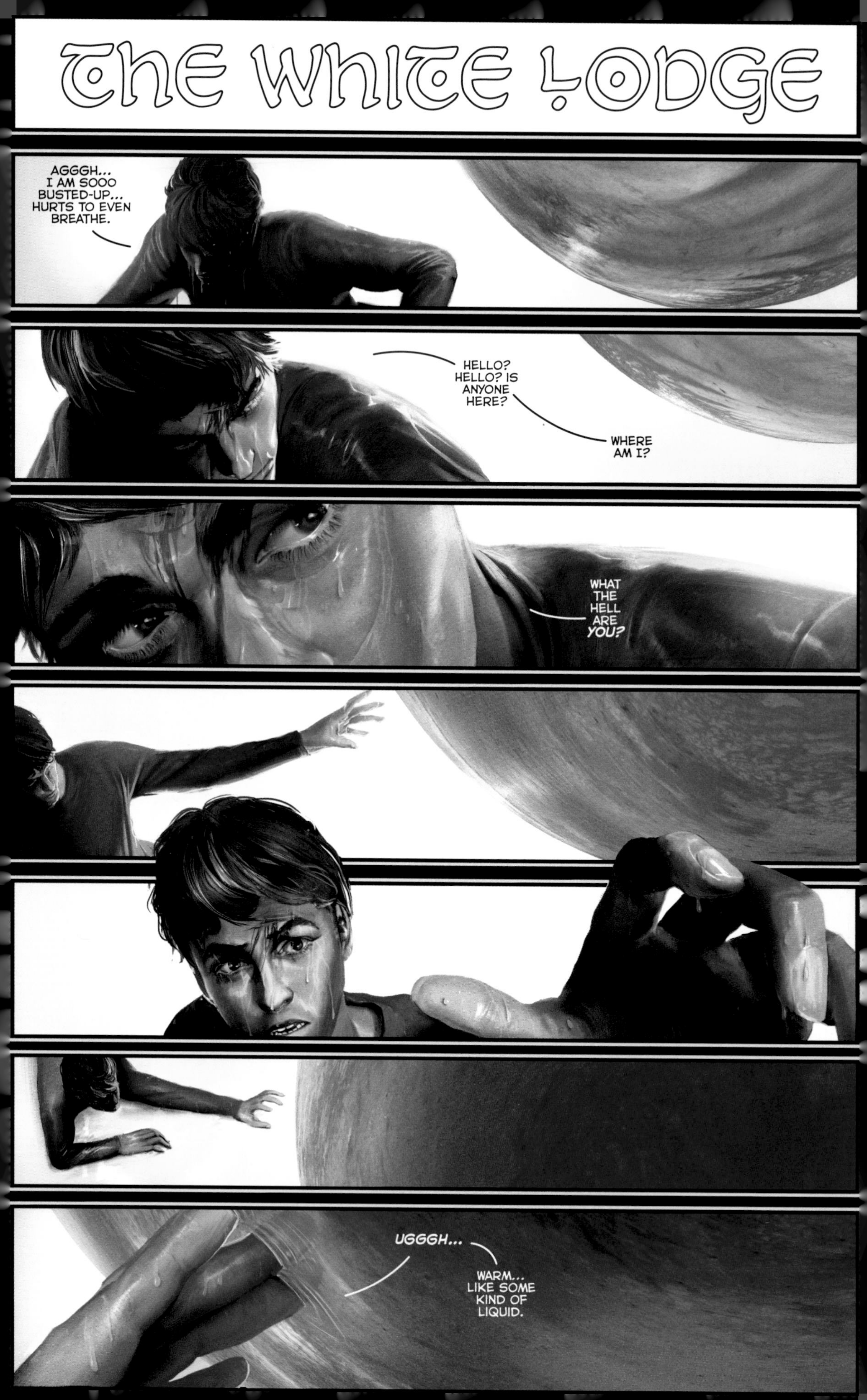
THE WHITE LODGE
AGGGH... I AM SOOO BUSTED-UP... HURTS TO EVEN BREATHE.
HELLO? HELLO? IS ANYONE HERE?
WHERE AM I?
WHAT THE HELL ARE YOU?
UGGGH...
WARM... LIKE SOME KIND OF LIQUID.

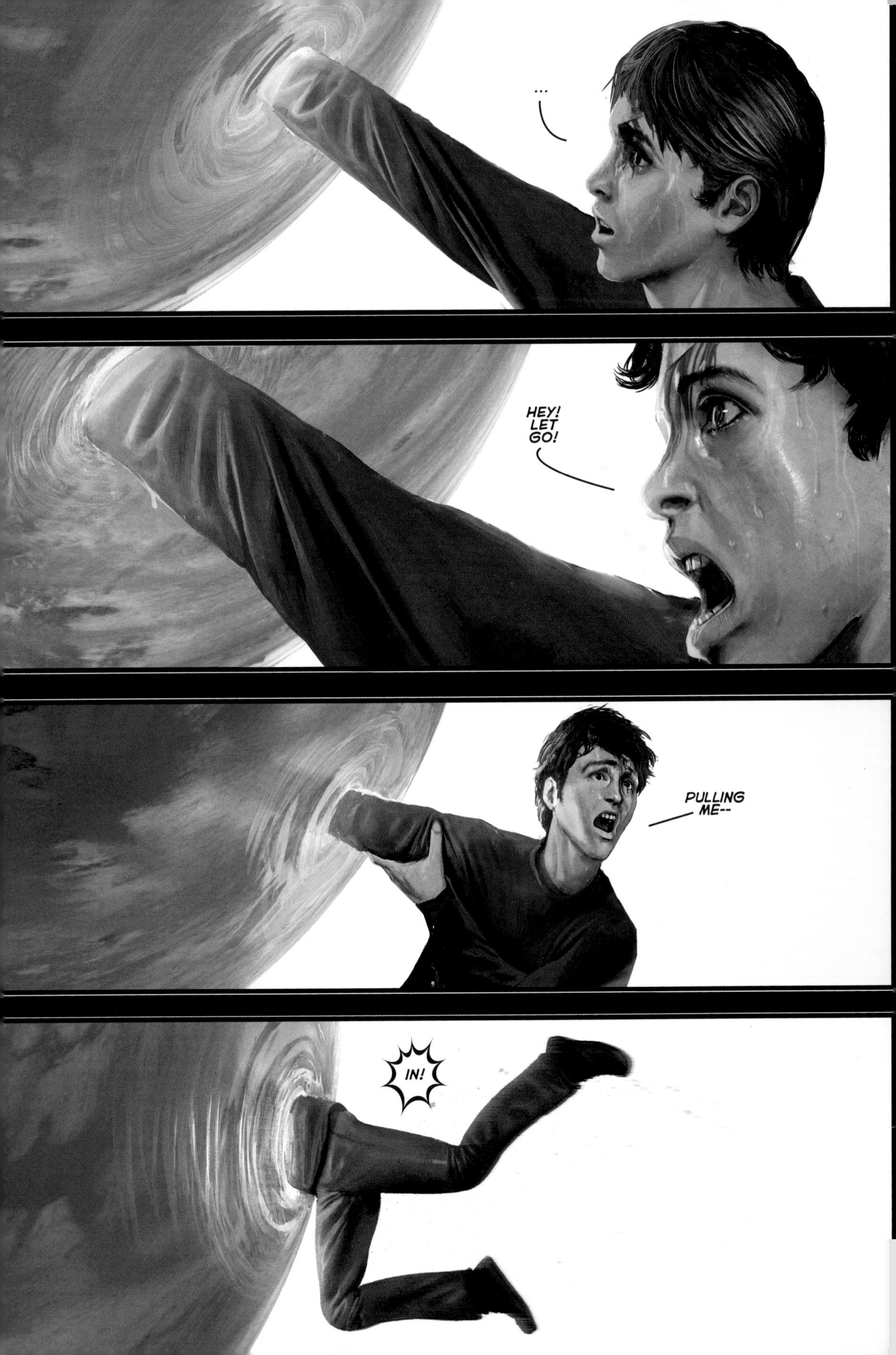
...
HEY! LET GO!
PULLING ME--
IN!

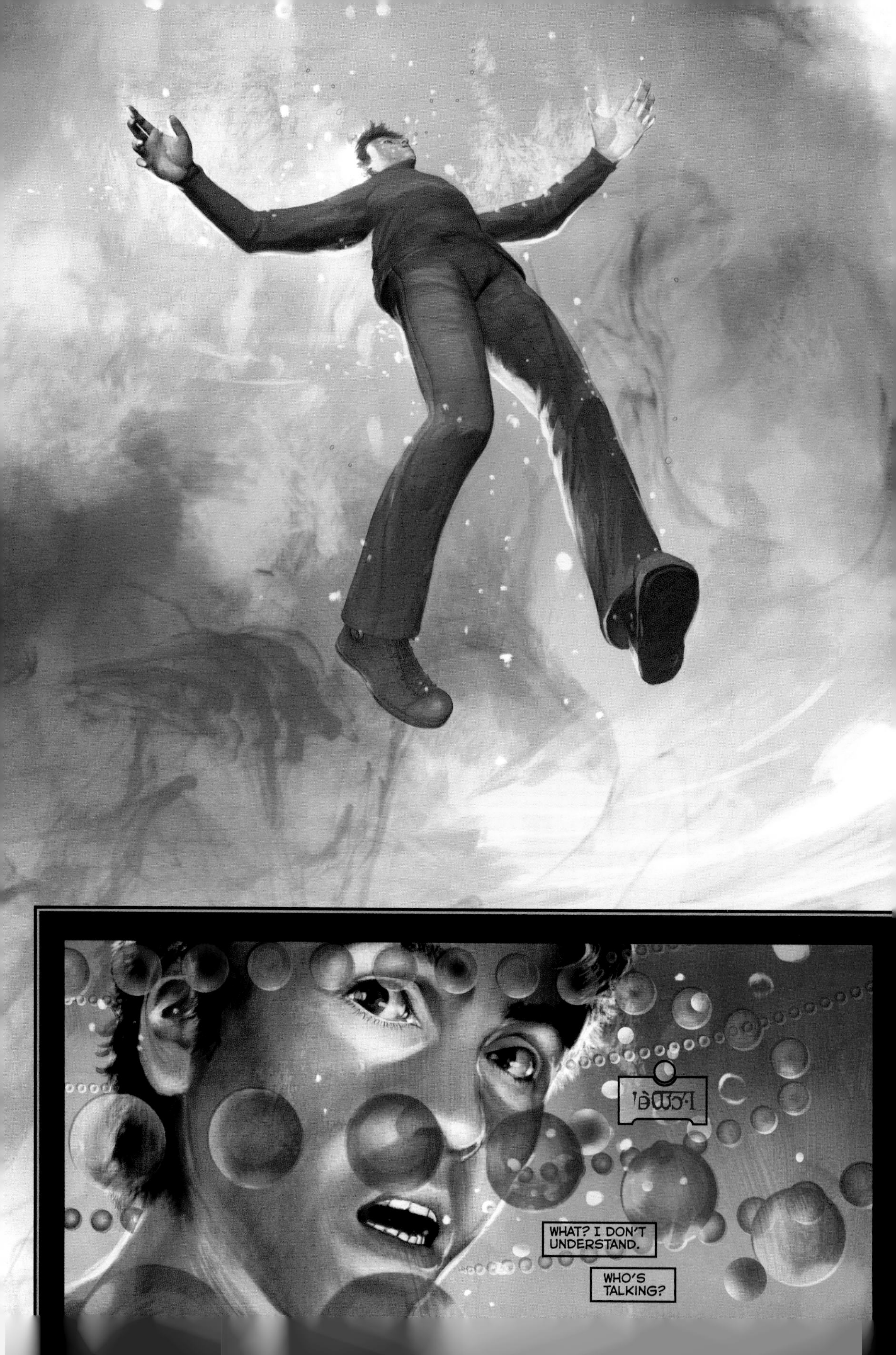
WHAT? I DON'T UNDERSTAND.
WHO'S TALKING?

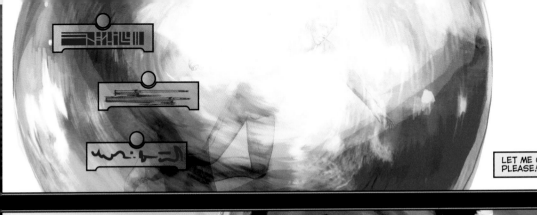

LET ME OUT! PLEASE!

WELCOME BACK, OPERATOR.

WHERE AM I? LET ME OUT... PLEASE... I'M DROWNING...

RESPIRATION FACILITATED. YOU ARE *NOT* IN WATER. NO RISK OF DROWNING.

OPERATOR SCAN COMMENCING.

OPERATOR IS SERIOUSLY INJURED.

SHALL I EFFECT REPAIR?

WHAT?

SHALL I REPAIR OPERATOR?

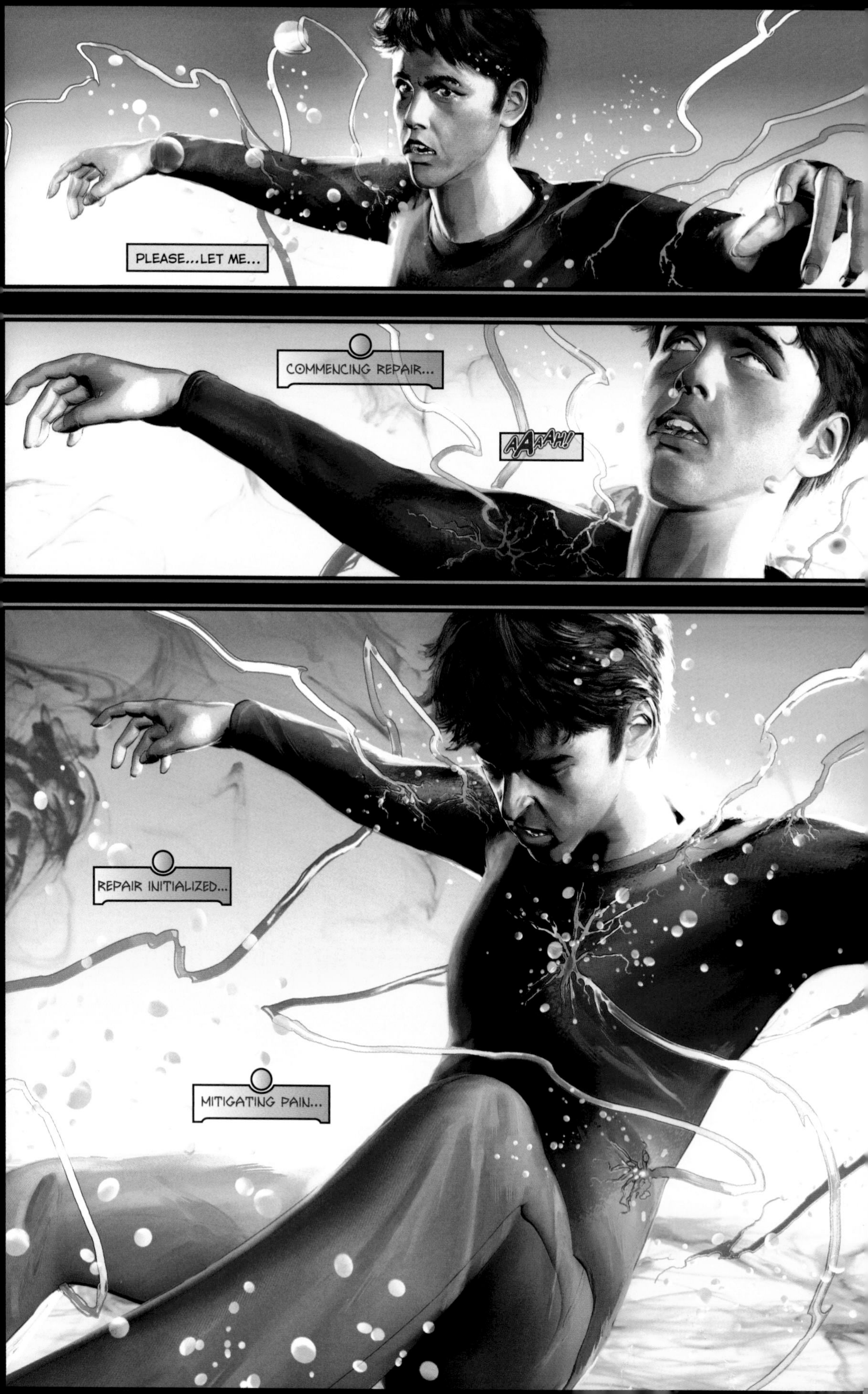
PLEASE...LET ME...
COMMENCING REPAIR...
AAAAH!
REPAIR INITIALIZED...
MITIGATING PAIN...

WHO ARE YOU? WHERE AM I?

THIS IS THE OUTPOST. I AM THE INTERFACE.

THE INTERFACE? FOR WHAT?

FOR THE OPERATOR.

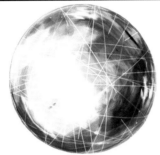

OPERATOR? WHO IS THE OPERATOR?

YOU ARE THE OPERATOR.

CAN YOU LET ME OUT? I NEED TO GET HOME.

IINJURIES ARE STILL CRITICAL. YOU HAVE SEVERAL BROKEN BONES AND INTERNAL INJURIES. REPAIR INCOMPLETE.

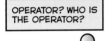

LET'S SLOW DOWN. YOU'RE THE INTERFACE?

CORRECT.

I AM THE OPERATOR?

CORRECT.

OKAY. WHO WAS THE *ORIGINAL* OPERATOR?

I DON'T UNDERSTAND?

NEVER MIND. LET'S SEE. UH, OPERATOR REQUESTS... A REMEDIAL.

EXPLAIN.

A MANUAL? A *TUTORIAL*.

OF COURSE. WHAT SUBJECT?

UM... THE *OUTPOST*. ITS HISTORY, PURPOSES AND USES.

THE OPERATOR *SHOULD* KNOW THESE THINGS.

...I WAS INJURED, REMEMBER? LET'S SAY MY UNDERSTANDING ISN'T CLEAR. PLEASE. A TUTORIAL.

OF COURSE.

OH WOW...

THIS IS WHAT? YOUR PLANET? YOUR GALAXY?
AND THAT'S HOW YOU TRAVEL? WARPING SPACE?
YOU'RE EXPLORERS... NO?
MISSIONARIES? IS THAT CLOSER?

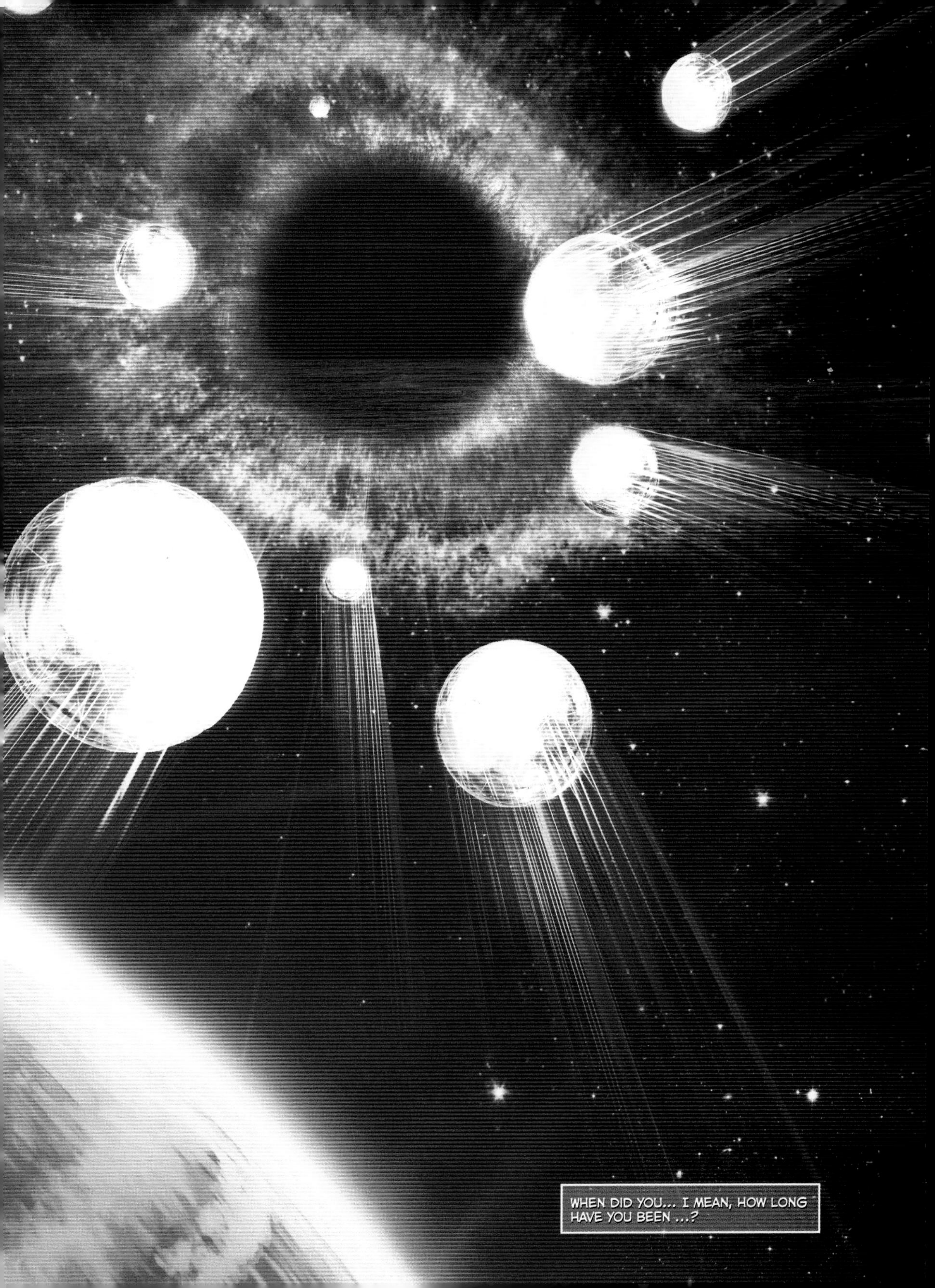
WHEN DID YOU... I MEAN, HOW LONG HAVE YOU BEEN ...?

THAT'S US. I MEAN EARTH...
YOU'VE BEEN HIDDEN AWAY ALL THESE MILLENNIA? TO DO WHAT?
TO WATCH?
OBSERVE?
I DON'T UNDERSTAND WHAT I'M SEEING.

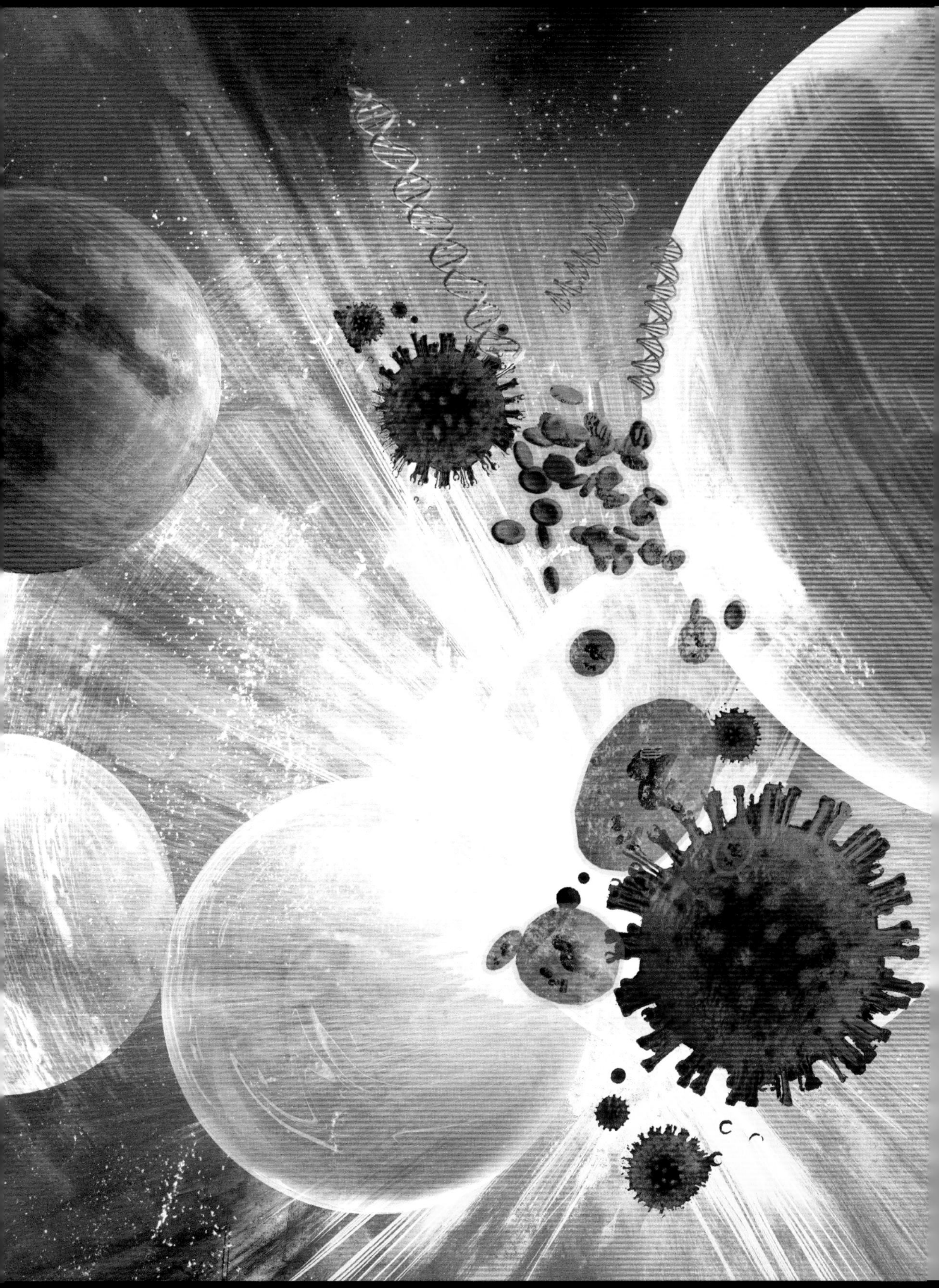

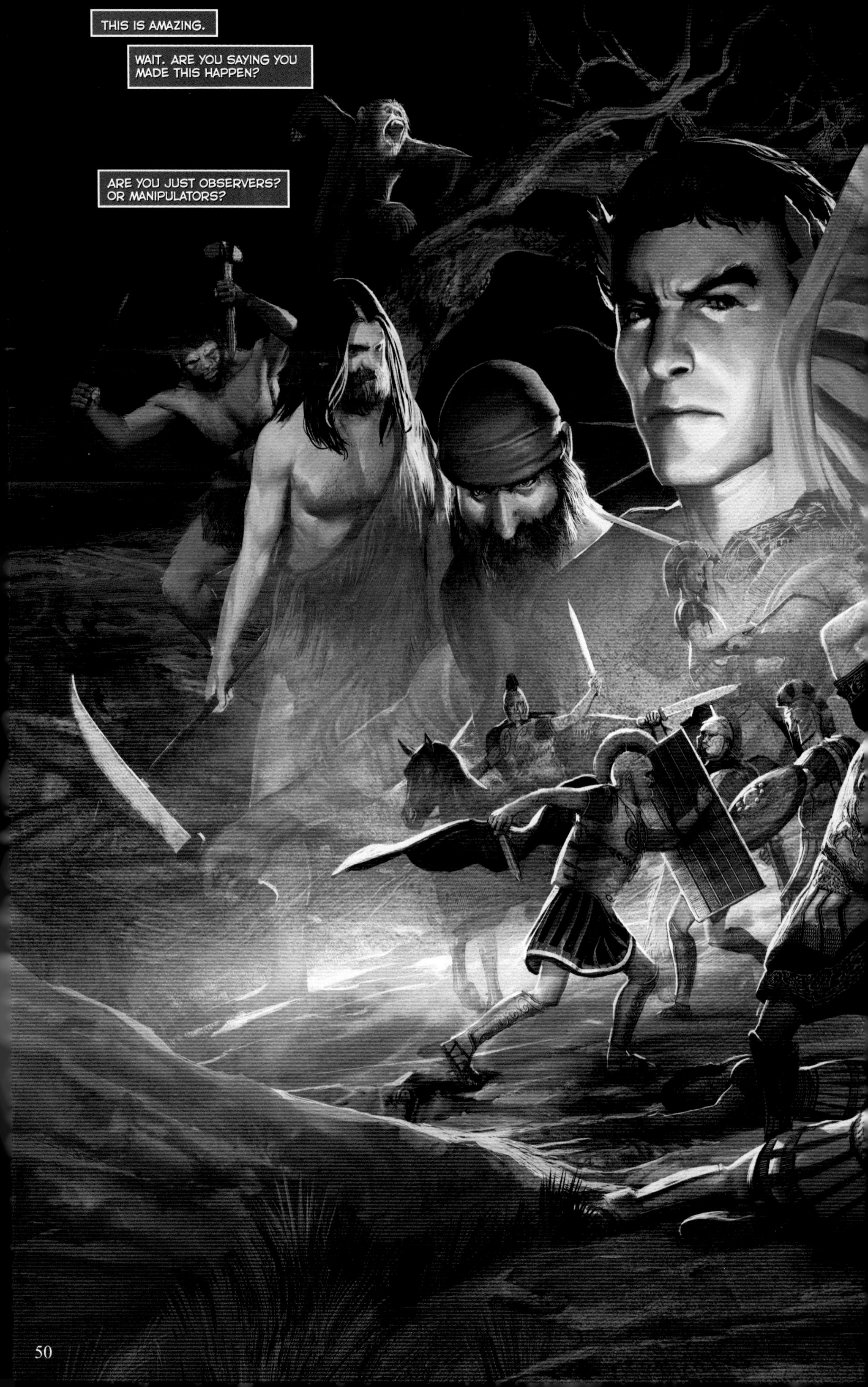
THIS IS AMAZING.
WAIT. ARE YOU SAYING YOU MADE THIS HAPPEN?
ARE YOU JUST OBSERVERS? OR MANIPULATORS?

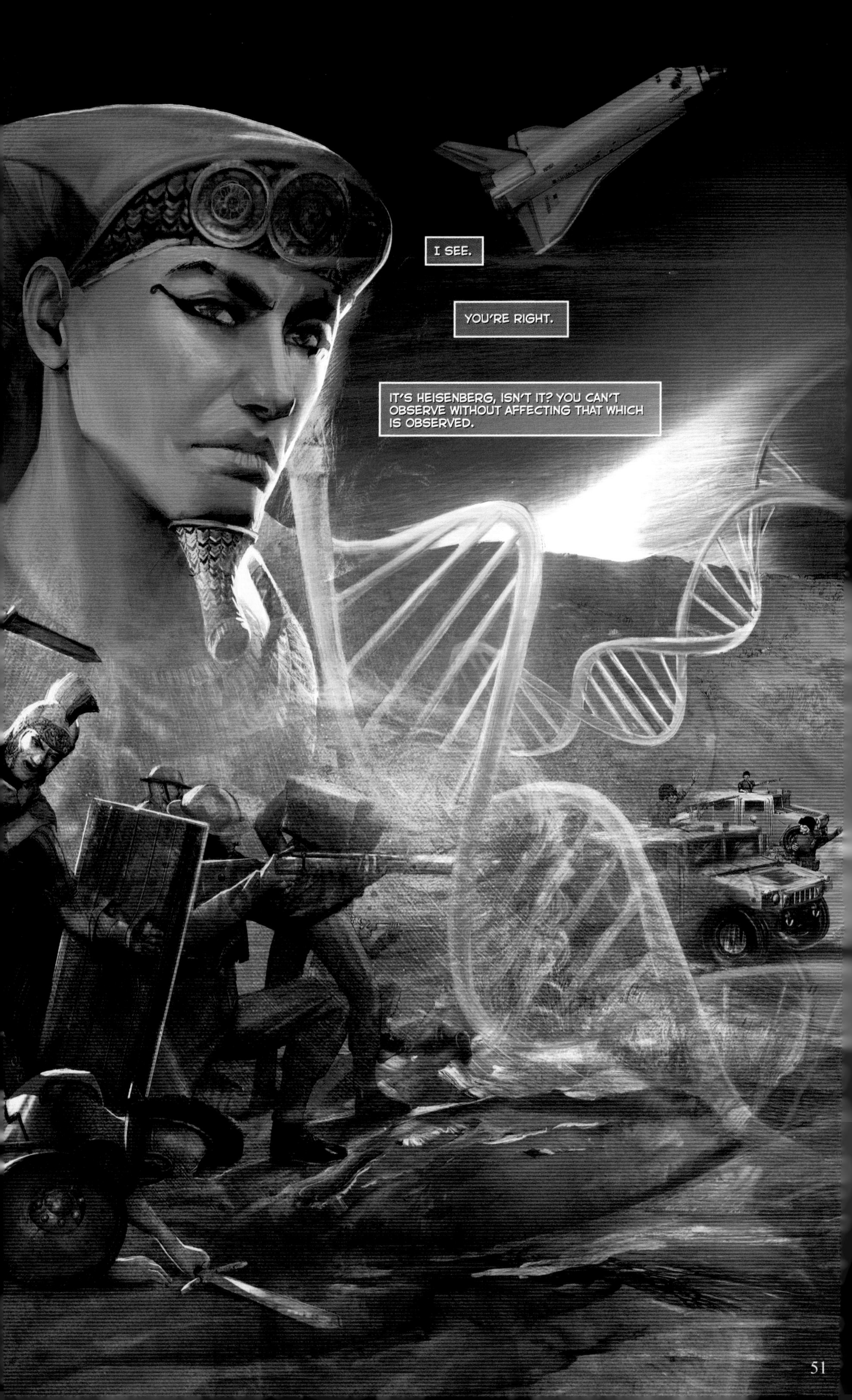
I SEE.
YOU'RE RIGHT.
IT'S HEISENBERG, ISN'T IT? YOU CAN'T OBSERVE WITHOUT AFFECTING THAT WHICH IS OBSERVED.

THAT WAS...BREATHTAKING!

YOUR RESPIRATORY RATE IS CURRENTLY IN THE NORMAL RANGE FOR YOUR SPECIES. SHALL I INCREASE THE OXYGEN IN THE SPHERE?

NO, THAT'S NOT WHAT I MEANT-- IT'S FINE.

WHAT IS THE MISSION? ULTIMATELY, WHAT IS THE GOAL FOR THIS UNDERTAKING?

TO ACHIEVE ᐃ𝖌𝖌ᐁ.

THAT HAS *ALWAYS* BEEN OUR PRIMARY GOAL.

I DON'T *UNDERSTAND*.

TO PROMOTE AND ENCOURAGE ᐃ𝖌𝖌ᐁ.

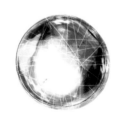

OKAY...

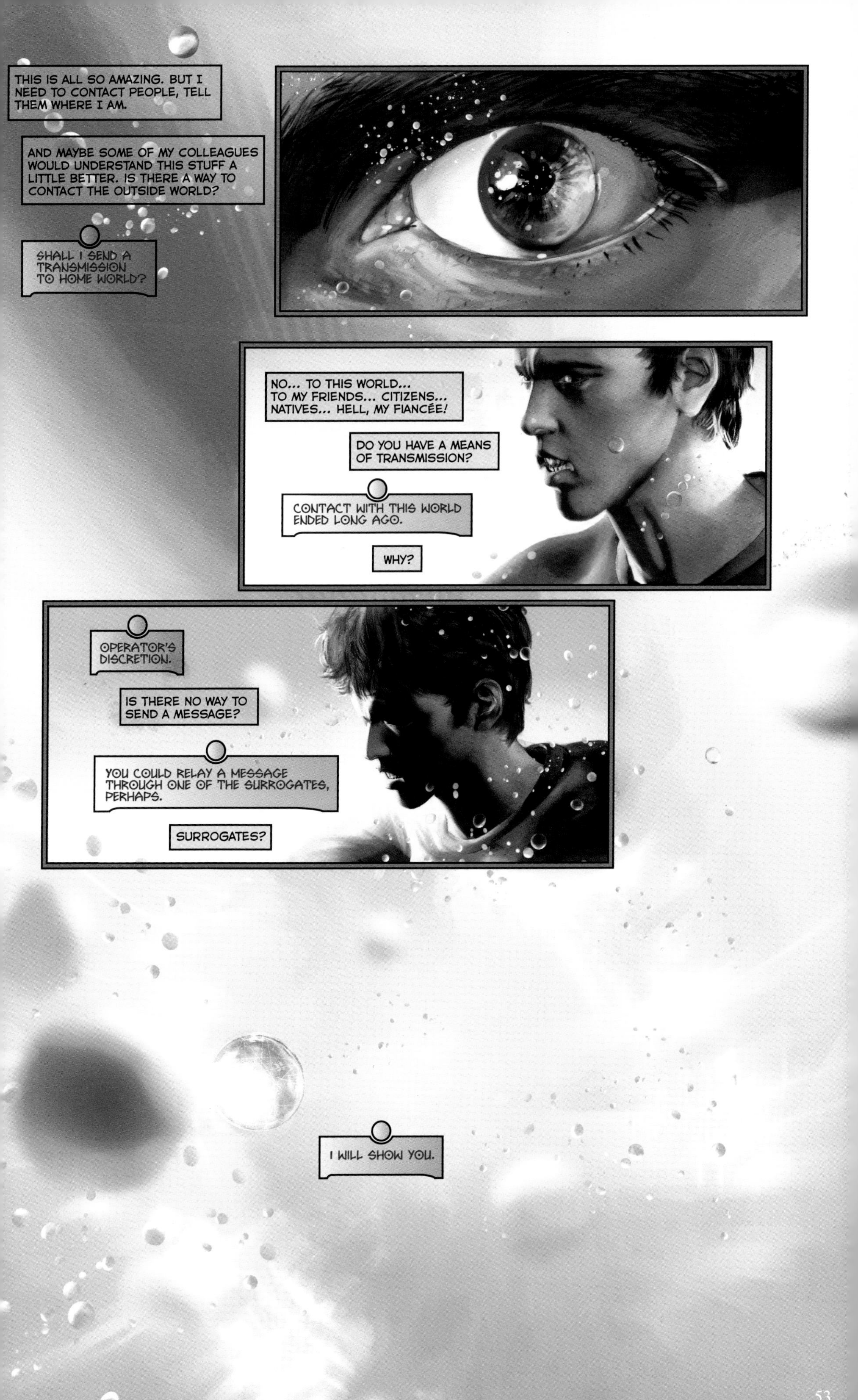

THIS IS ALL SO AMAZING. BUT I NEED TO CONTACT PEOPLE, TELL THEM WHERE I AM.
AND MAYBE SOME OF MY COLLEAGUES WOULD UNDERSTAND THIS STUFF A LITTLE BETTER. IS THERE A WAY TO CONTACT THE OUTSIDE WORLD?
SHALL I SEND A TRANSMISSION TO HOME WORLD?
NO... TO THIS WORLD... TO MY FRIENDS... CITIZENS... NATIVES... HELL, MY FIANCÉE!
DO YOU HAVE A MEANS OF TRANSMISSION?
CONTACT WITH THIS WORLD ENDED LONG AGO.
WHY?
OPERATOR'S DISCRETION.
IS THERE NO WAY TO SEND A MESSAGE?
YOU COULD RELAY A MESSAGE THROUGH ONE OF THE SURROGATES, PERHAPS.
SURROGATES?
I WILL SHOW YOU.

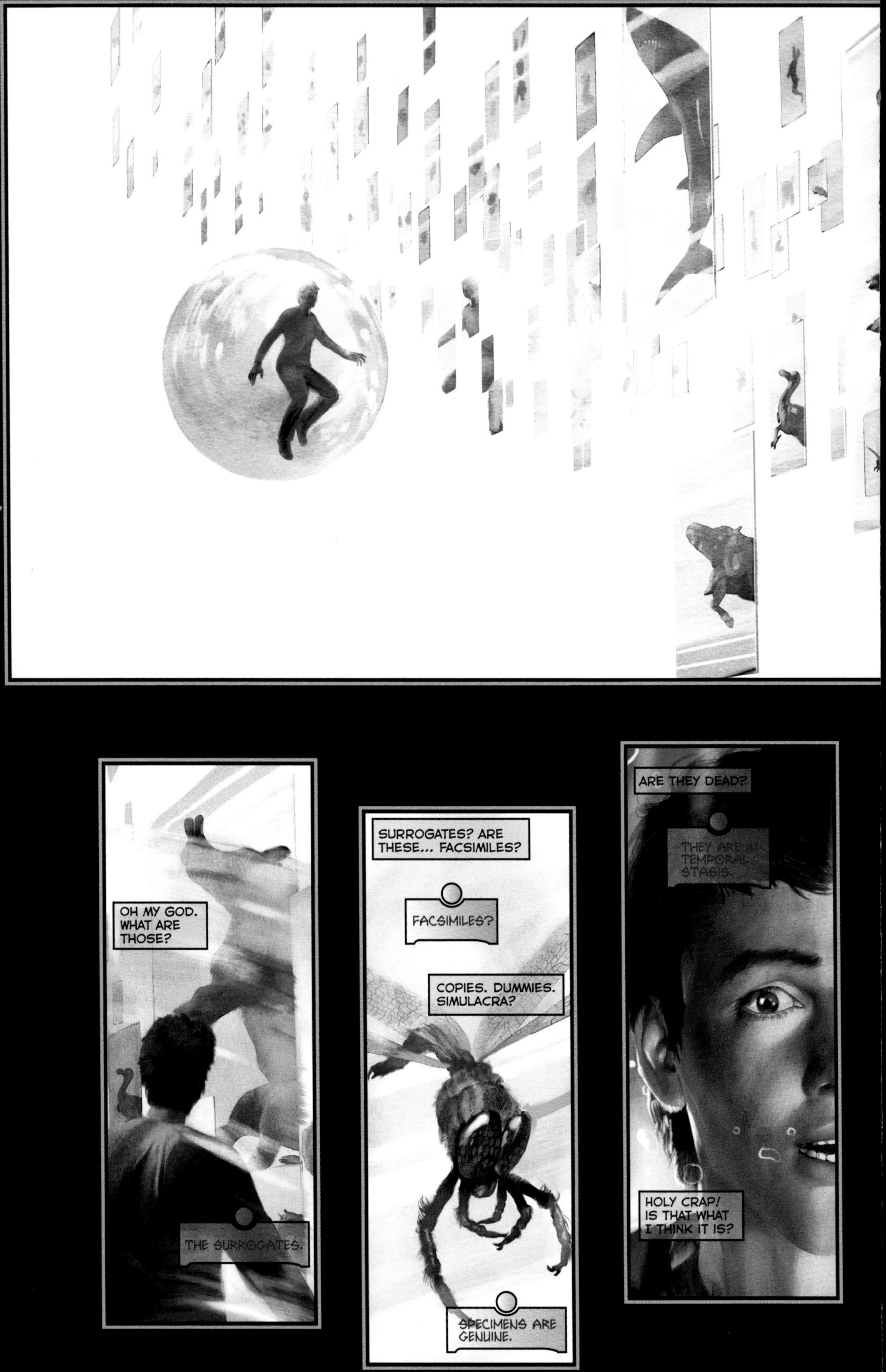
OH MY GOD. WHAT ARE THOSE?
THE SURROGATES.
SURROGATES? ARE THESE... FACSIMILES?
FACSIMILES?
COPIES. DUMMIES. SIMULACRA?
SPECIMENS ARE GENUINE.
ARE THEY DEAD?
THEY ARE IN TEMPORAL STASIS.
HOLY CRAP! IS THAT WHAT I THINK IT IS?

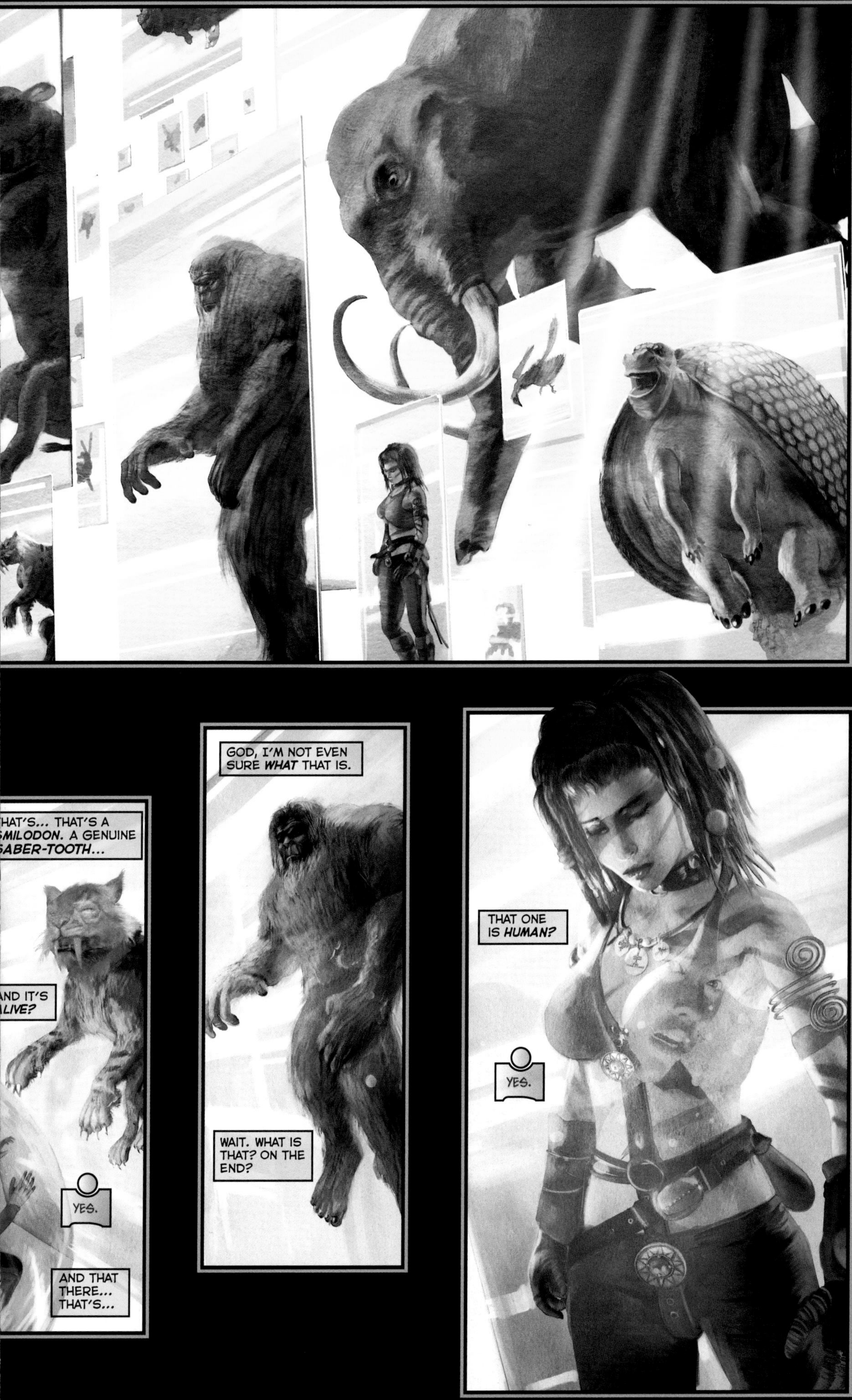
HAT'S... THAT'S A SMILODON. A GENUINE SABER-TOOTH...
AND IT'S ALIVE?
YES.
AND THAT THERE... THAT'S...
GOD, I'M NOT EVEN SURE *WHAT* THAT IS.
WAIT. WHAT IS THAT? ON THE END?
THAT ONE IS *HUMAN?*
YES.

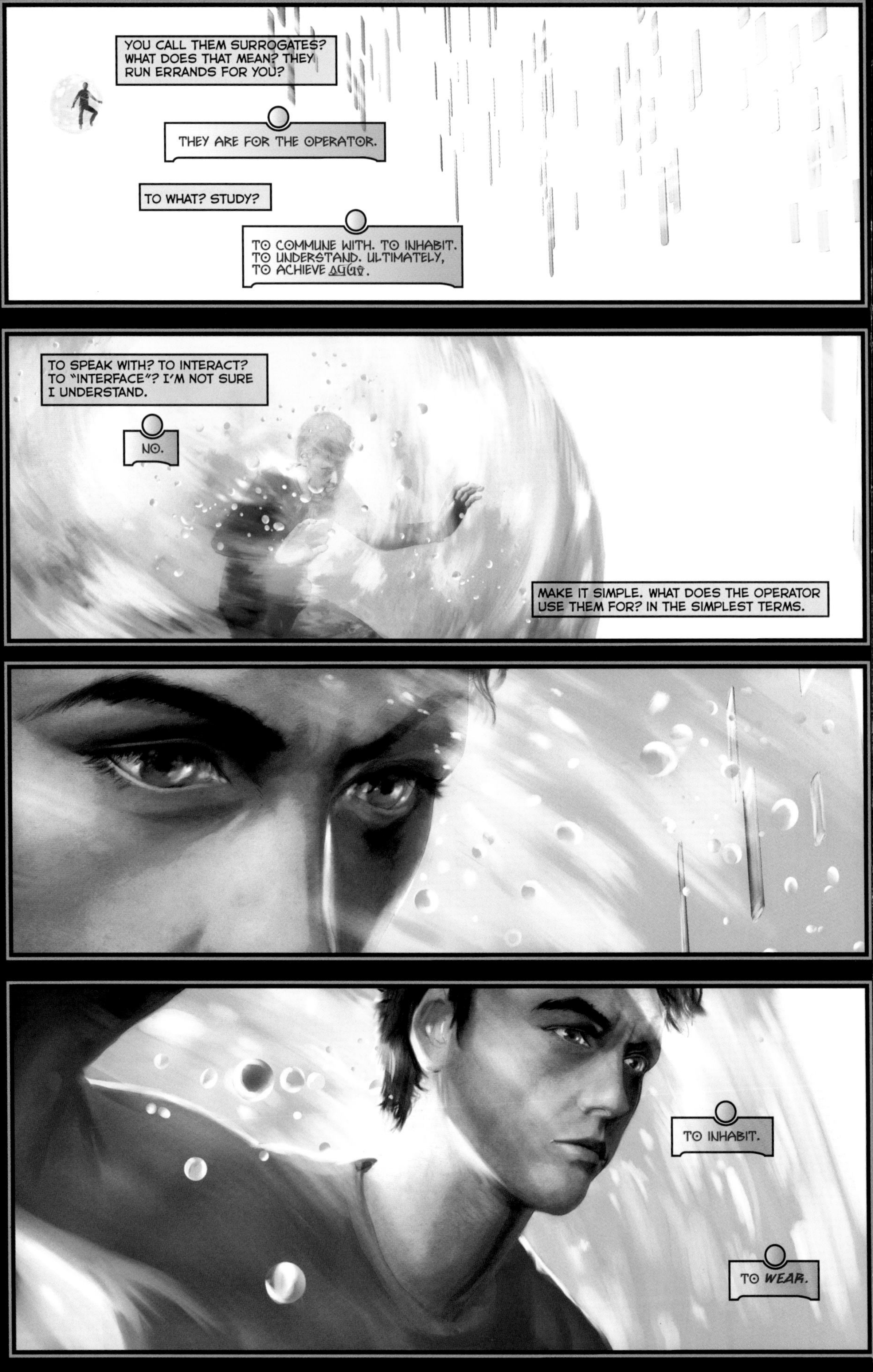
YOU CALL THEM SURROGATES? WHAT DOES THAT MEAN? THEY RUN ERRANDS FOR YOU?
THEY ARE FOR THE OPERATOR.
TO WHAT? STUDY?
TO COMMUNE WITH. TO INHABIT. TO UNDERSTAND. ULTIMATELY, TO ACHIEVE .
TO SPEAK WITH? TO INTERACT? TO "INTERFACE"? I'M NOT SURE I UNDERSTAND.
NO.
MAKE IT SIMPLE. WHAT DOES THE OPERATOR USE THEM FOR? IN THE SIMPLEST TERMS.
TO INHABIT.
TO WEAR.

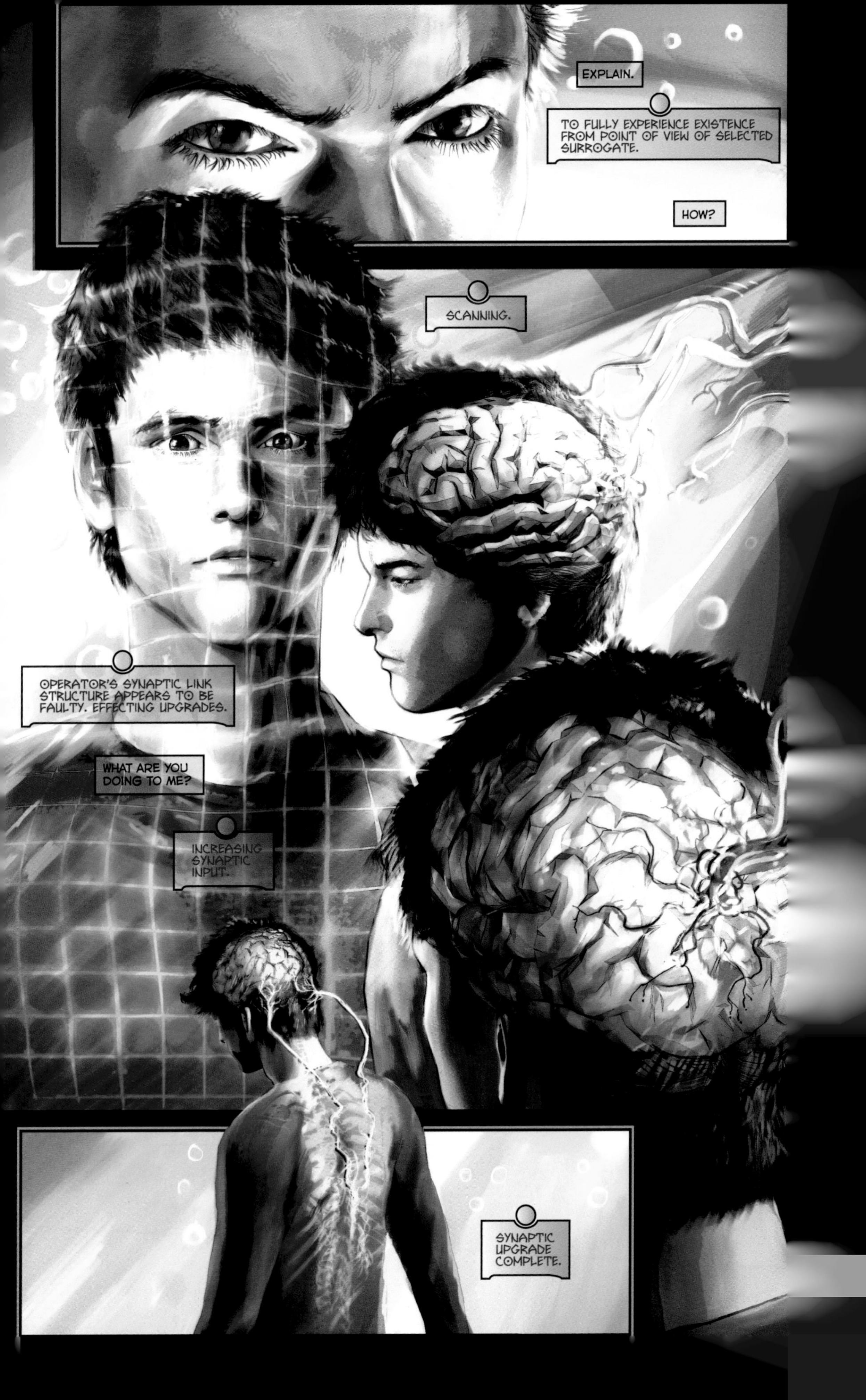
EXPLAIN.
TO FULLY EXPERIENCE EXISTENCE FROM POINT OF VIEW OF SELECTED SURROGATE.
HOW?
SCANNING.
OPERATOR'S SYNAPTIC LINK STRUCTURE APPEARS TO BE FAULTY. EFFECTING UPGRADES.
WHAT ARE YOU DOING TO ME?
INCREASING SYNAPTIC INPUT.
SYNAPTIC UPGRADE COMPLETE.

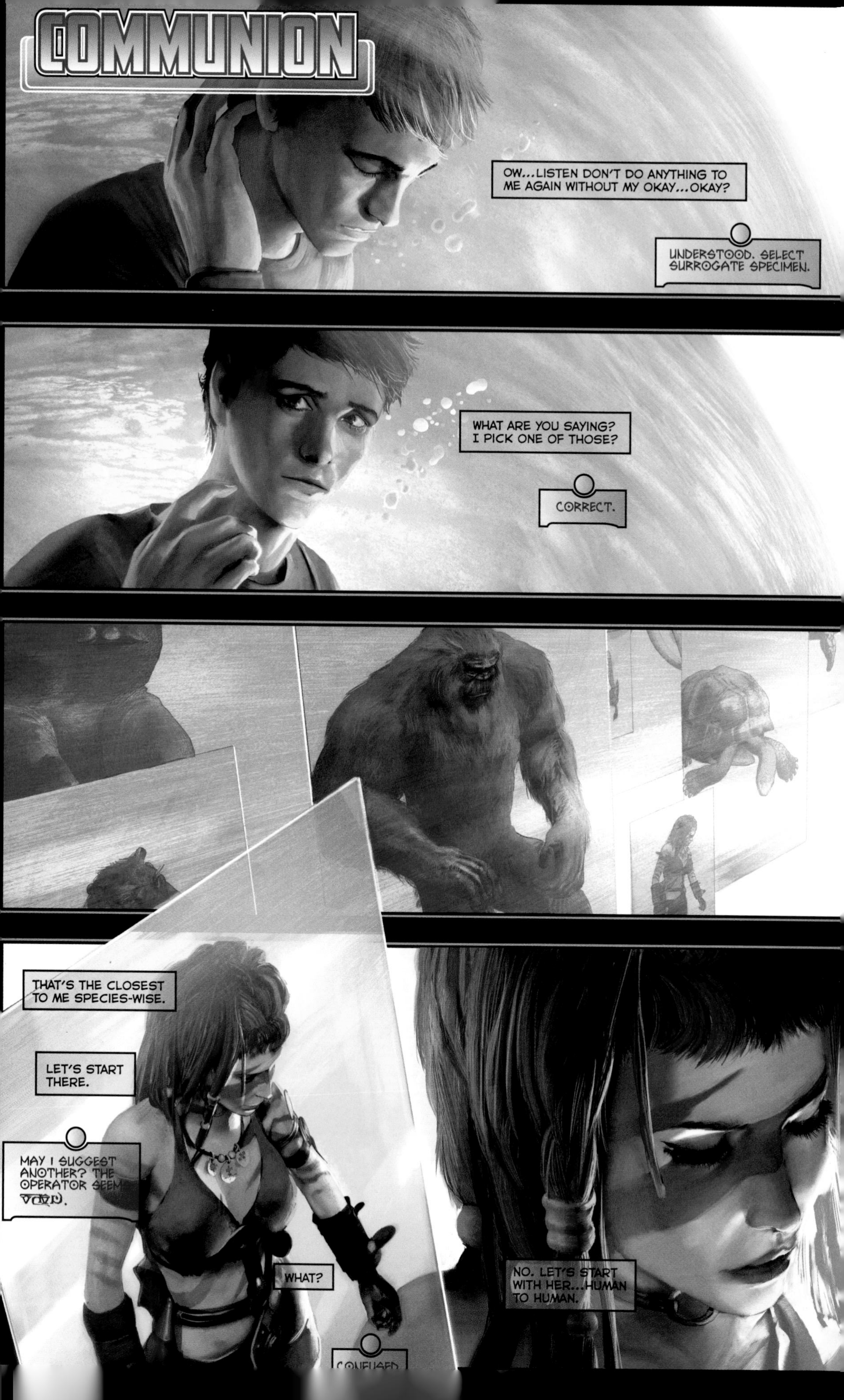
COMMUNION
OW...LISTEN DON'T DO ANYTHING TO ME AGAIN WITHOUT MY OKAY...OKAY?
UNDERSTOOD. SELECT SURROGATE SPECIMEN.
WHAT ARE YOU SAYING? I PICK ONE OF THOSE?
CORRECT.
THAT'S THE CLOSEST TO ME SPECIES-WISE.
LET'S START THERE.
MAY I SUGGEST ANOTHER? THE OPERATOR SEEM
WHAT?
NO. LET'S START WITH HER...HUMAN TO HUMAN.

THAT'S ME!
I'M OUTSIDE
NOW! I'M--

WHAT'S HAPPENING?
I DON'T UNDERSTAND--

I CAN'T CONTROL HER!

YEAAAAAA!

I'M SUPPOSED TO
CONTROL HER,
RIGHT?

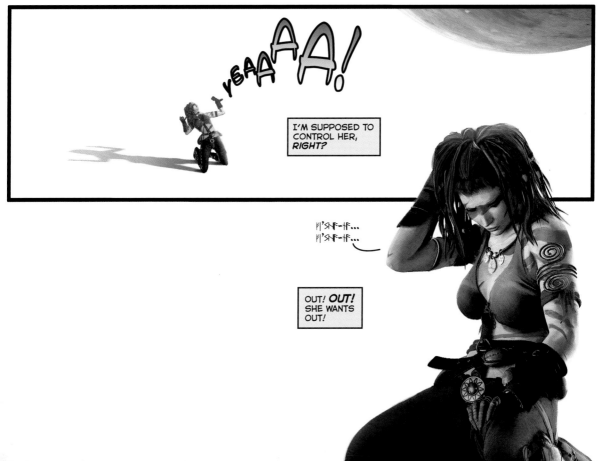

OUT! *OUT!*
SHE WANTS
OUT!

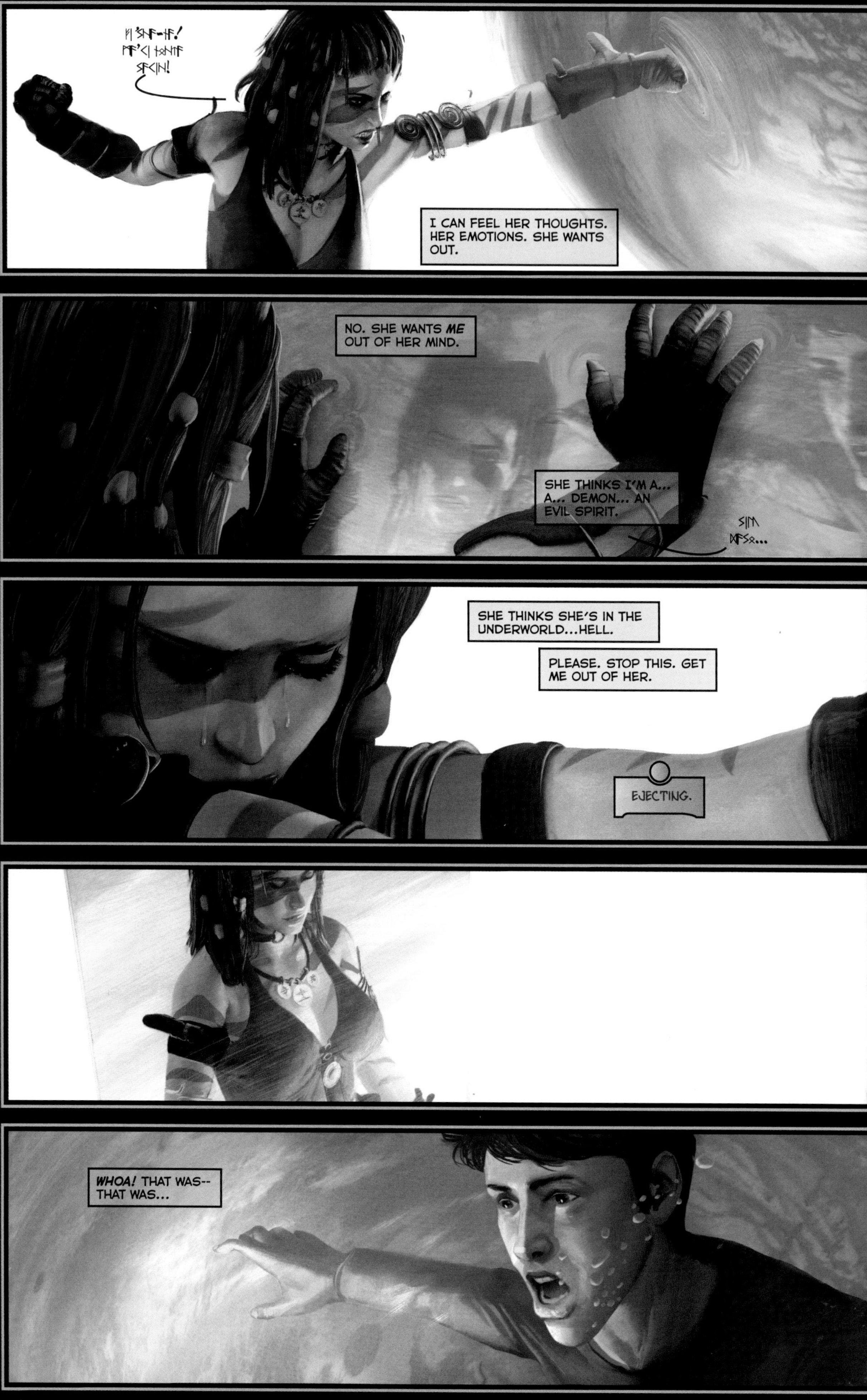
I CAN FEEL HER THOUGHTS. HER EMOTIONS. SHE WANTS OUT.
NO. SHE WANTS *ME* OUT OF HER MIND.
SHE THINKS I'M A... A... DEMON... AN EVIL SPIRIT.
SHE THINKS SHE'S IN THE UNDERWORLD...HELL.
PLEASE. STOP THIS. GET ME OUT OF HER.
EJECTING.
WHOA! THAT WAS-- THAT WAS...

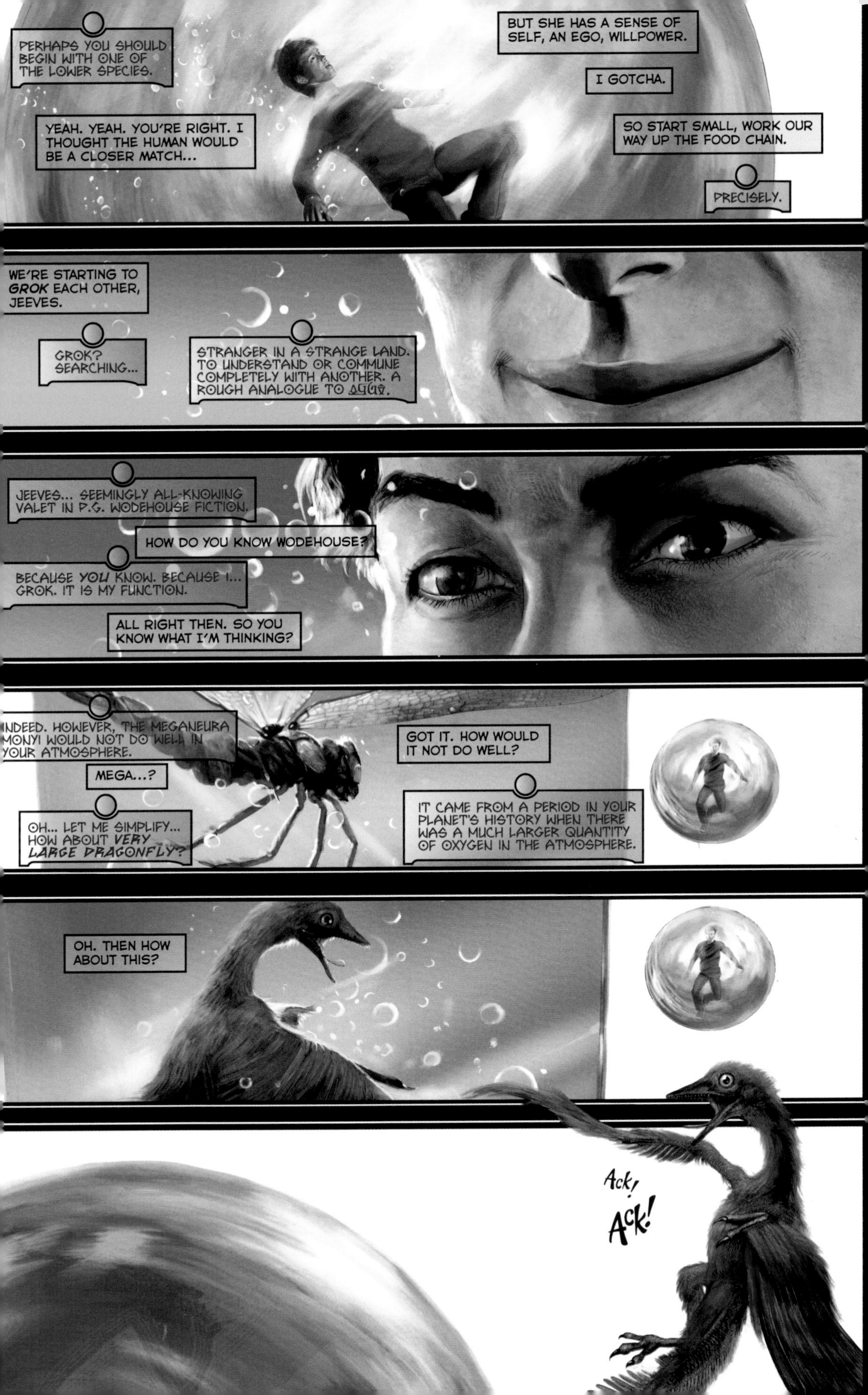
PERHAPS YOU SHOULD BEGIN WITH ONE OF THE LOWER SPECIES.
YEAH. YEAH. YOU'RE RIGHT. I THOUGHT THE HUMAN WOULD BE A CLOSER MATCH...
BUT SHE HAS A SENSE OF SELF, AN EGO, WILLPOWER.
I GOTCHA.
SO START SMALL, WORK OUR WAY UP THE FOOD CHAIN.
PRECISELY.
WE'RE STARTING TO GROK EACH OTHER, JEEVES.
GROK? SEARCHING...
STRANGER IN A STRANGE LAND. TO UNDERSTAND OR COMMUNE COMPLETELY WITH ANOTHER. A ROUGH ANALOGUE TO
JEEVES... SEEMINGLY ALL-KNOWING VALET IN P.G. WODEHOUSE FICTION.
HOW DO YOU KNOW WODEHOUSE?
BECAUSE YOU KNOW. BECAUSE I... GROK. IT IS MY FUNCTION.
ALL RIGHT THEN. SO YOU KNOW WHAT I'M THINKING?
INDEED. HOWEVER, THE MEGANEURA MONYI WOULD NOT DO WELL IN YOUR ATMOSPHERE.
MEGA...?
OH... LET ME SIMPLIFY... HOW ABOUT VERY LARGE DRAGONFLY?
GOT IT. HOW WOULD IT NOT DO WELL?
IT CAME FROM A PERIOD IN YOUR PLANET'S HISTORY WHEN THERE WAS A MUCH LARGER QUANTITY OF OXYGEN IN THE ATMOSPHERE.
OH. THEN HOW ABOUT THIS?
Ack!
Ack!

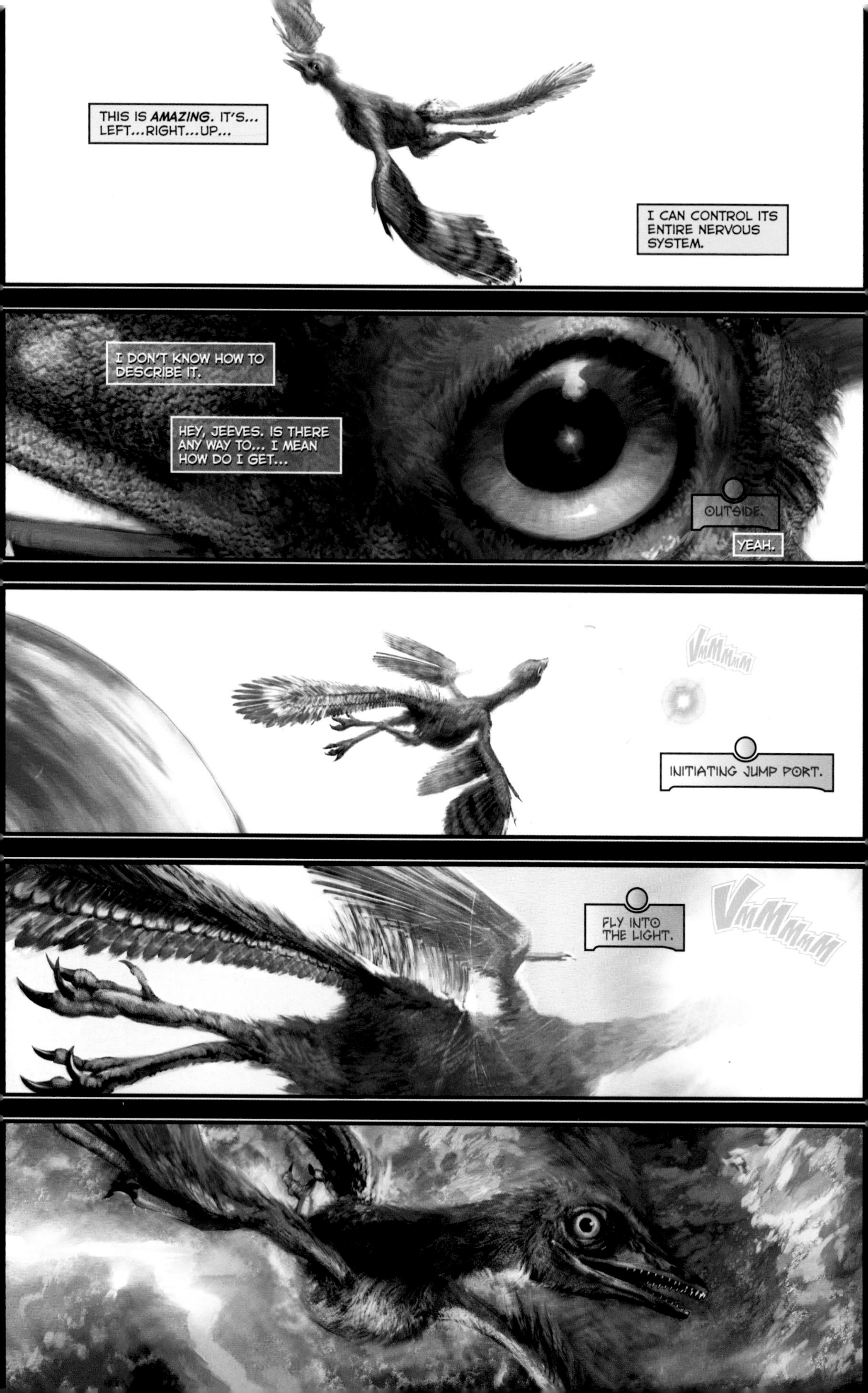

THIS IS AMAZING. IT'S... LEFT...RIGHT...UP...
I CAN CONTROL ITS ENTIRE NERVOUS SYSTEM.
I DON'T KNOW HOW TO DESCRIBE IT.
HEY, JEEVES. IS THERE ANY WAY TO... I MEAN HOW DO I GET...
OUTSIDE.
YEAH.
VMMMMM
INITIATING JUMP PORT.
FLY INTO THE LIGHT.
VMMMMM

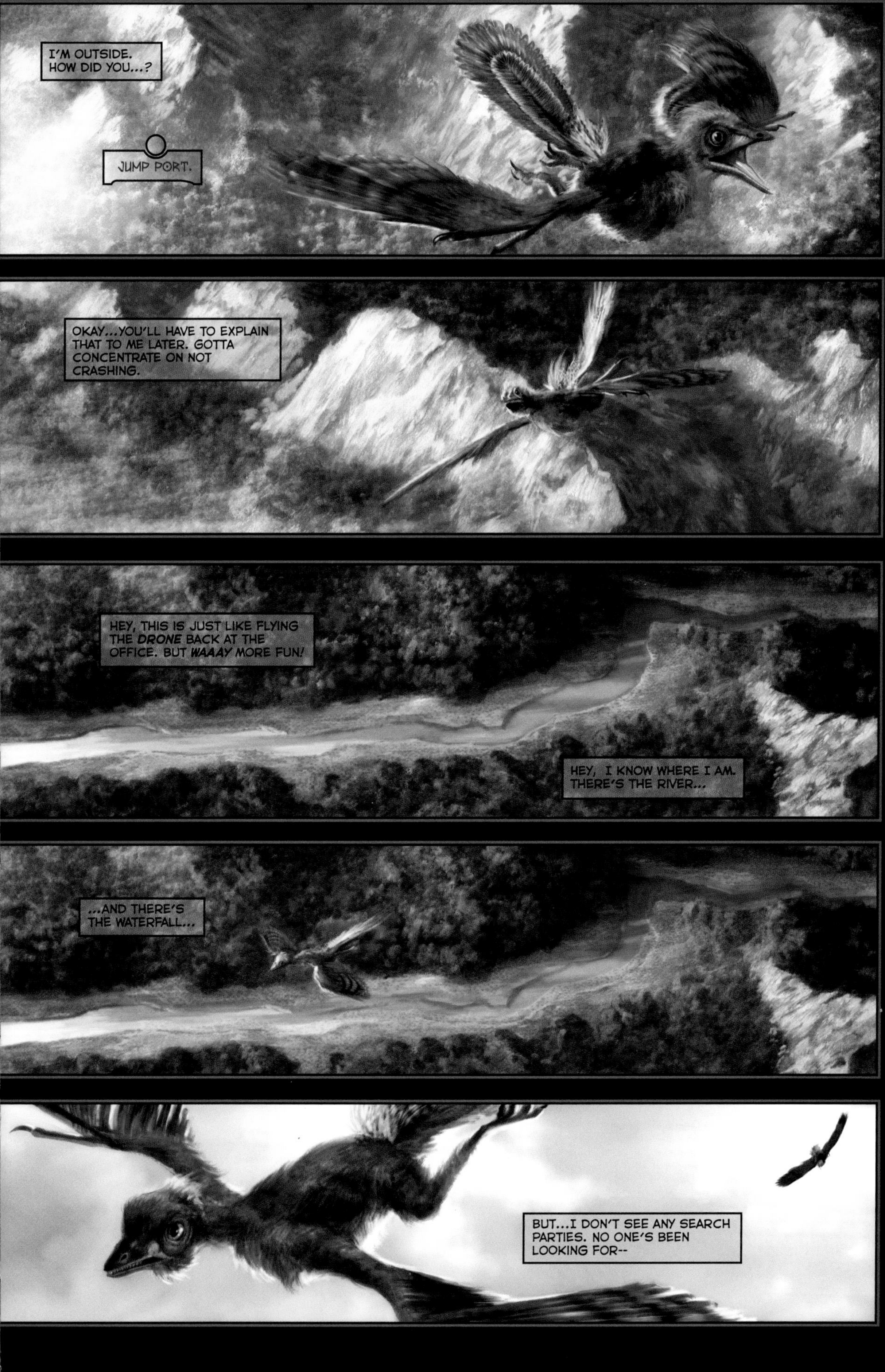
I'M OUTSIDE. HOW DID YOU...?
JUMP PORT.
OKAY...YOU'LL HAVE TO EXPLAIN THAT TO ME LATER. GOTTA CONCENTRATE ON NOT CRASHING.
HEY, THIS IS JUST LIKE FLYING THE *DRONE* BACK AT THE OFFICE. BUT *WAAAY* MORE FUN!
HEY, I KNOW WHERE I AM. THERE'S THE RIVER...
...AND THERE'S THE WATERFALL...
BUT...I DON'T SEE ANY SEARCH PARTIES. NO ONE'S BEEN LOOKING FOR--

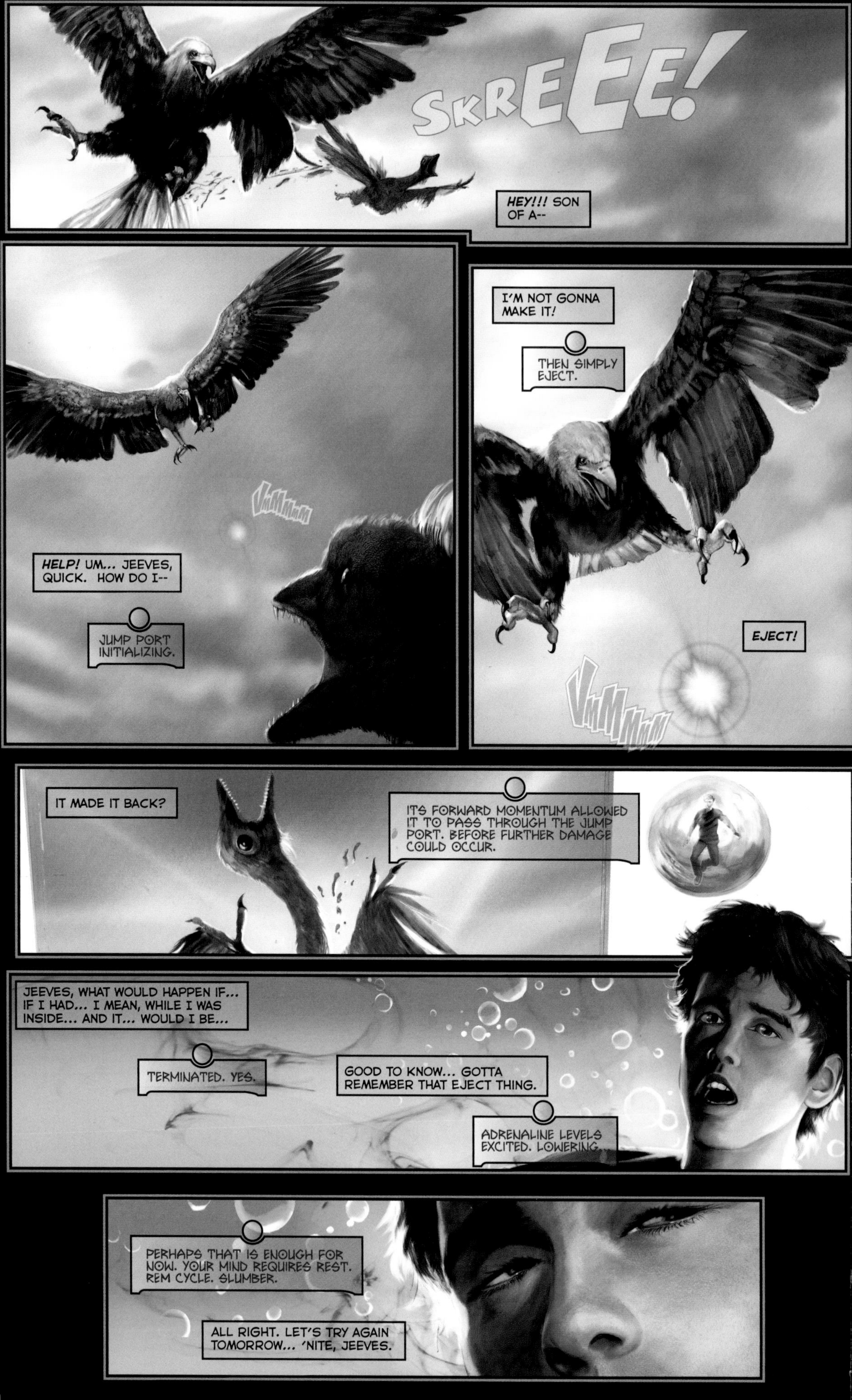
SKREEEE!
HEY!!! SON OF A--
HELP! UM... JEEVES, QUICK. HOW DO I--
JUMP PORT INITIALIZING.
I'M NOT GONNA MAKE IT!
THEN SIMPLY EJECT.
EJECT!
IT MADE IT BACK?
ITS FORWARD MOMENTUM ALLOWED IT TO PASS THROUGH THE JUMP PORT. BEFORE FURTHER DAMAGE COULD OCCUR.
JEEVES, WHAT WOULD HAPPEN IF... IF I HAD... I MEAN, WHILE I WAS INSIDE... AND IT... WOULD I BE...
TERMINATED. YES.
GOOD TO KNOW... GOTTA REMEMBER THAT EJECT THING.
ADRENALINE LEVELS EXCITED. LOWERING.
PERHAPS THAT IS ENOUGH FOR NOW. YOUR MIND REQUIRES REST. REM CYCLE. SLUMBER.
ALL RIGHT. LET'S TRY AGAIN TOMORROW... 'NITE, JEEVES.

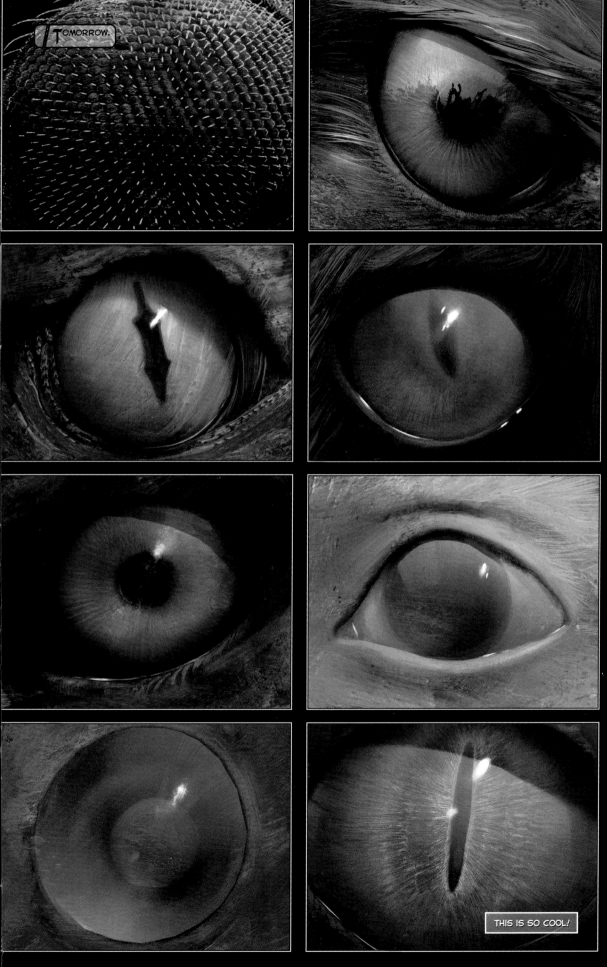

TOMORROW.

THIS IS SO COOL!

65

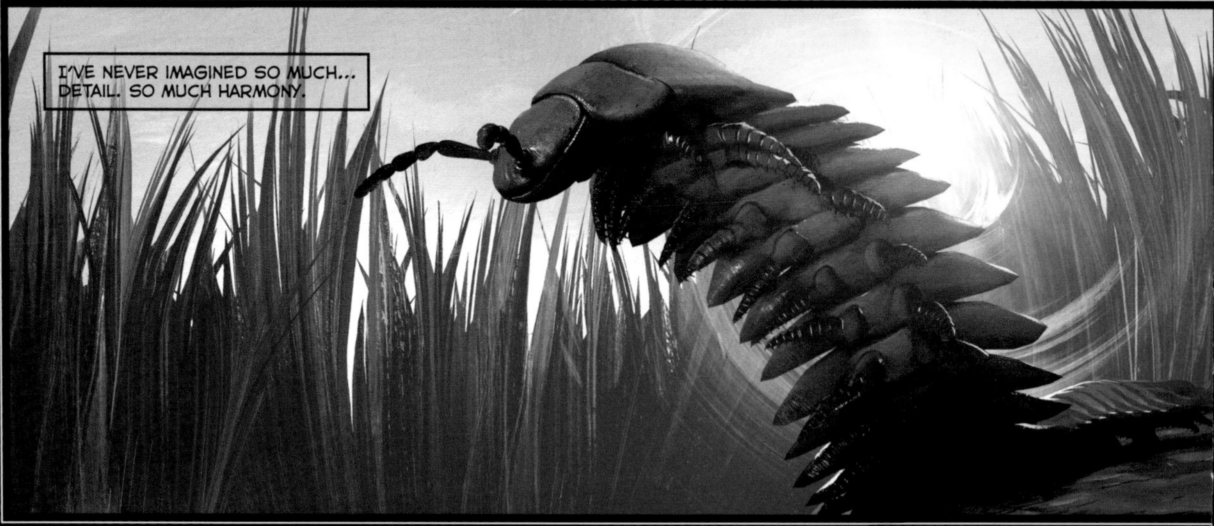
I'VE NEVER IMAGINED SO MUCH... DETAIL. SO MUCH HARMONY.

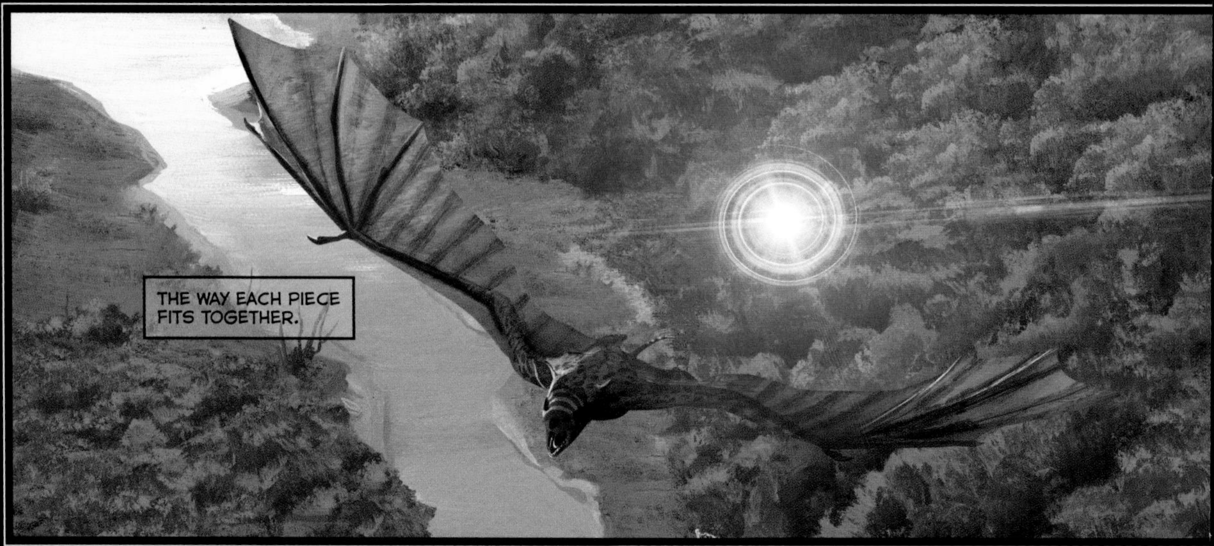
THE WAY EACH PIECE FITS TOGETHER.

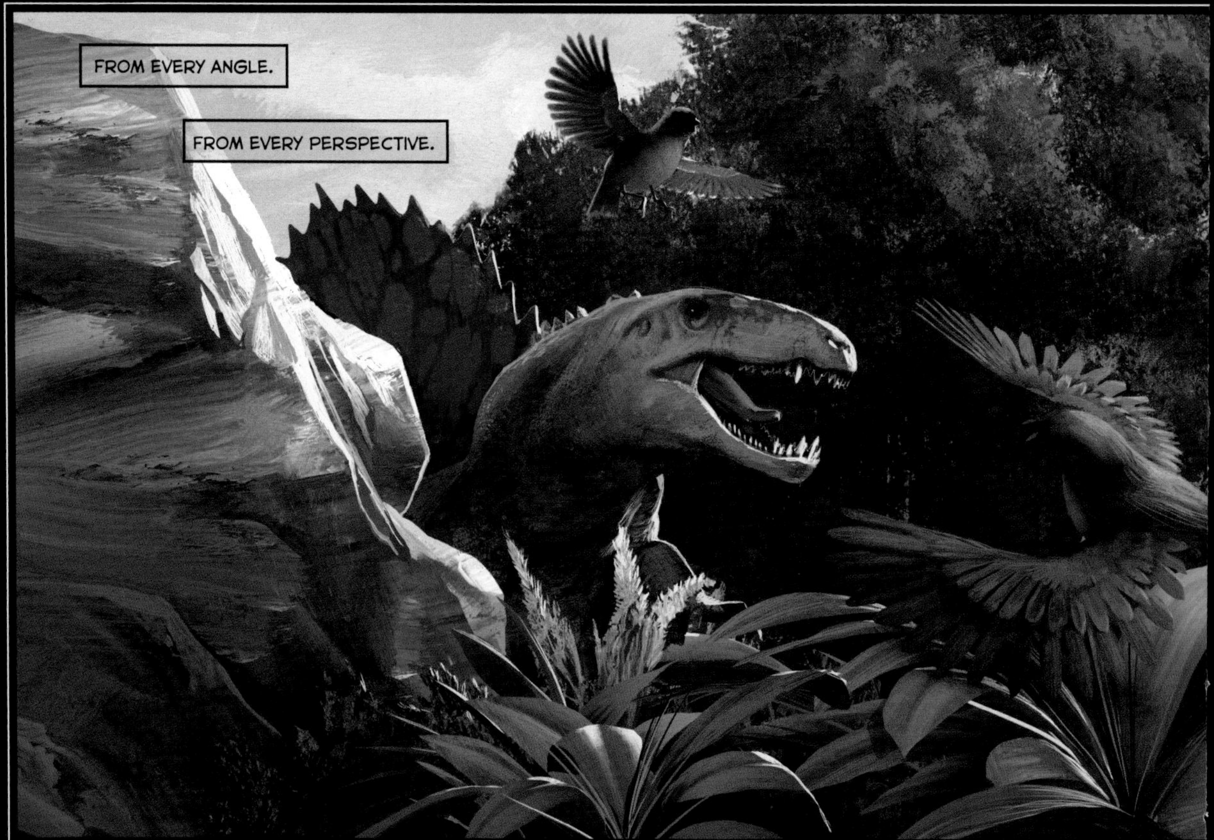
FROM EVERY ANGLE.
FROM EVERY PERSPECTIVE.

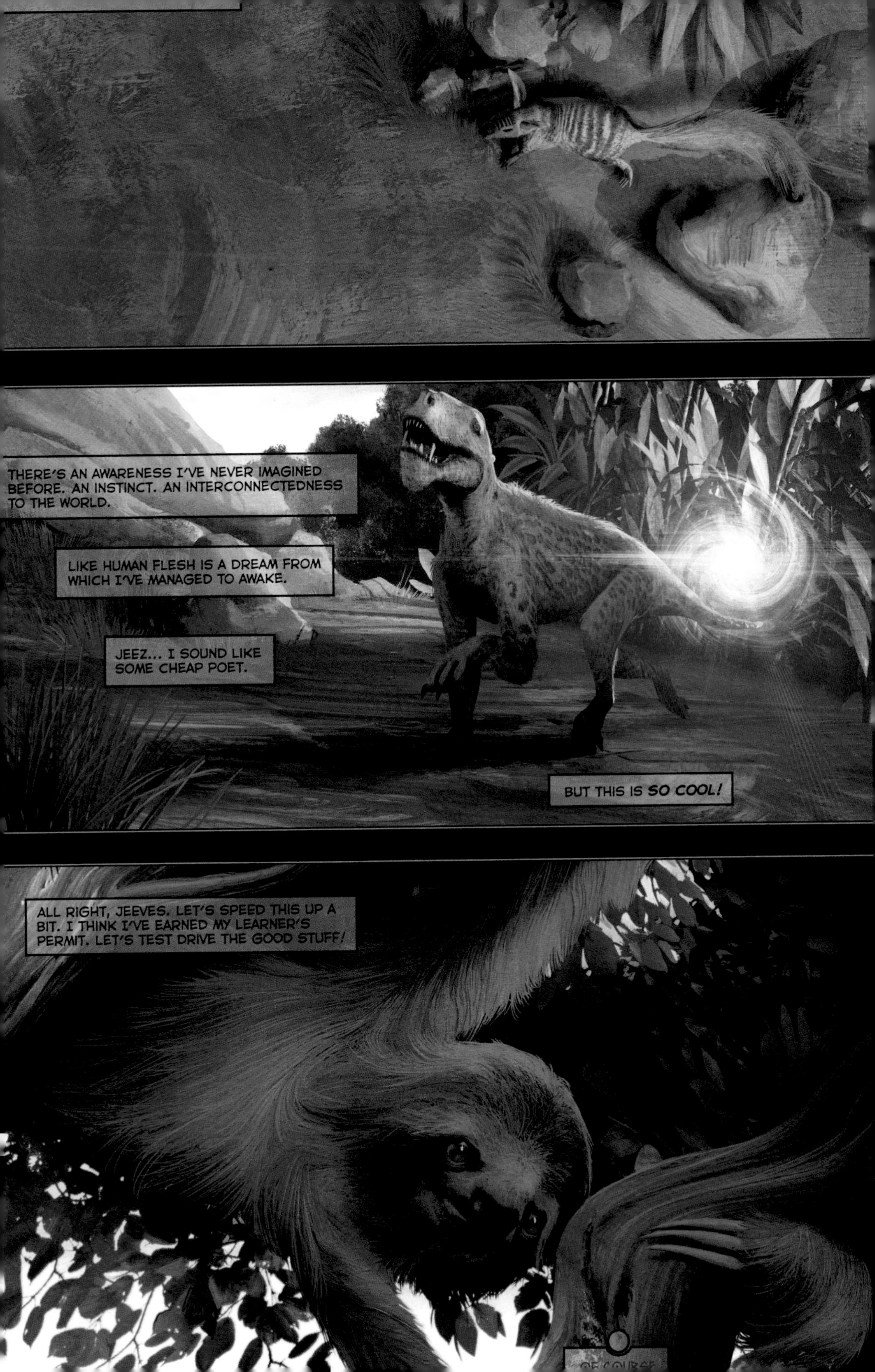
THERE'S AN AWARENESS I'VE NEVER IMAGINED BEFORE. AN INSTINCT. AN INTERCONNECTEDNESS TO THE WORLD.
LIKE HUMAN FLESH IS A DREAM FROM WHICH I'VE MANAGED TO AWAKE.
JEEZ... I SOUND LIKE SOME CHEAP POET.
BUT THIS IS **SO COOL!**
ALL RIGHT, JEEVES. LET'S SPEED THIS UP A BIT. I THINK I'VE EARNED MY LEARNER'S PERMIT. LET'S TEST DRIVE THE GOOD STUFF!

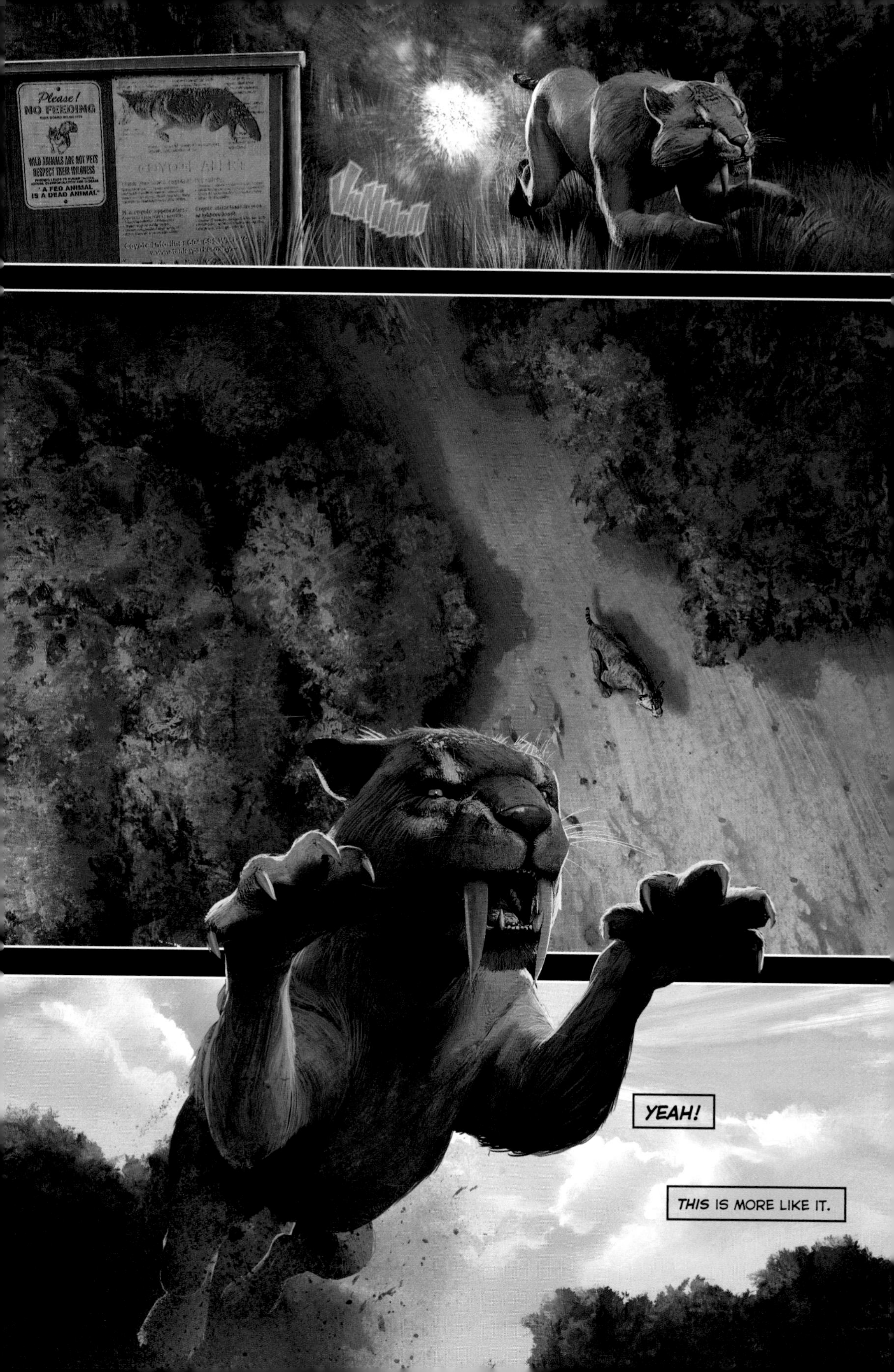
Please!
NO FEEDING
WILD ANIMALS ARE NOT PETS
RESPECT THEIR WILDNESS
"A FED ANIMAL IS A DEAD ANIMAL"
YEAH!
THIS IS MORE LIKE IT.

WHAT...

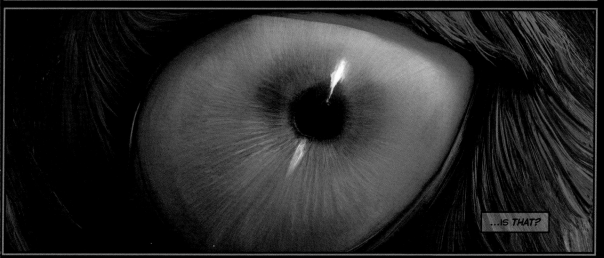

...IS *THAT?*

THAT IS THE SMILODON "SEEING" SCENT TRAILS OF POTENTIAL PREY.

BUT IT'S NOT JUST A SMELL... IT'S SOMETHING MORE... MUCH MORE...

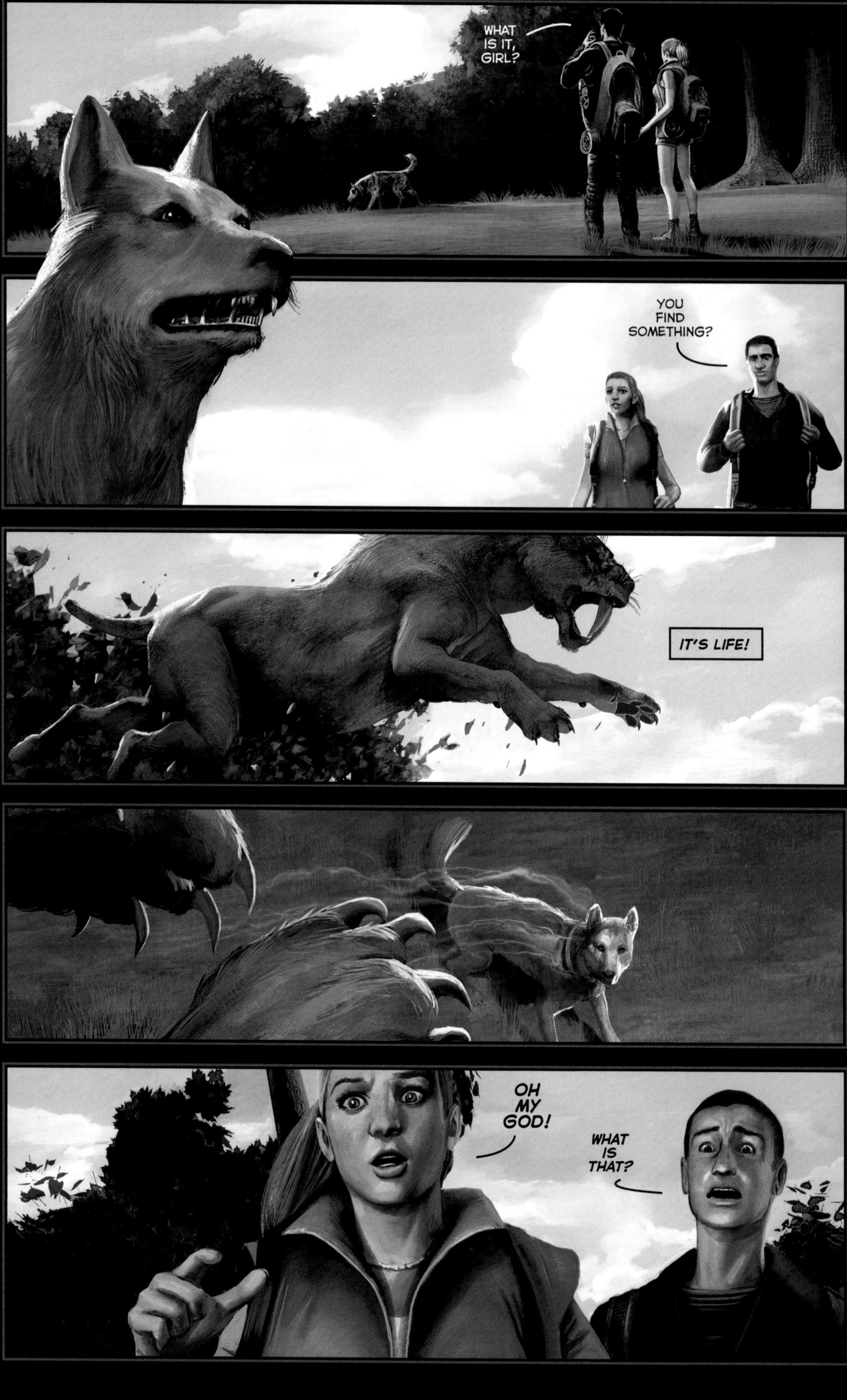
WHAT IS IT, GIRL?
YOU FIND SOMETHING?
IT'S LIFE!
OH MY GOD!
WHAT IS THAT?

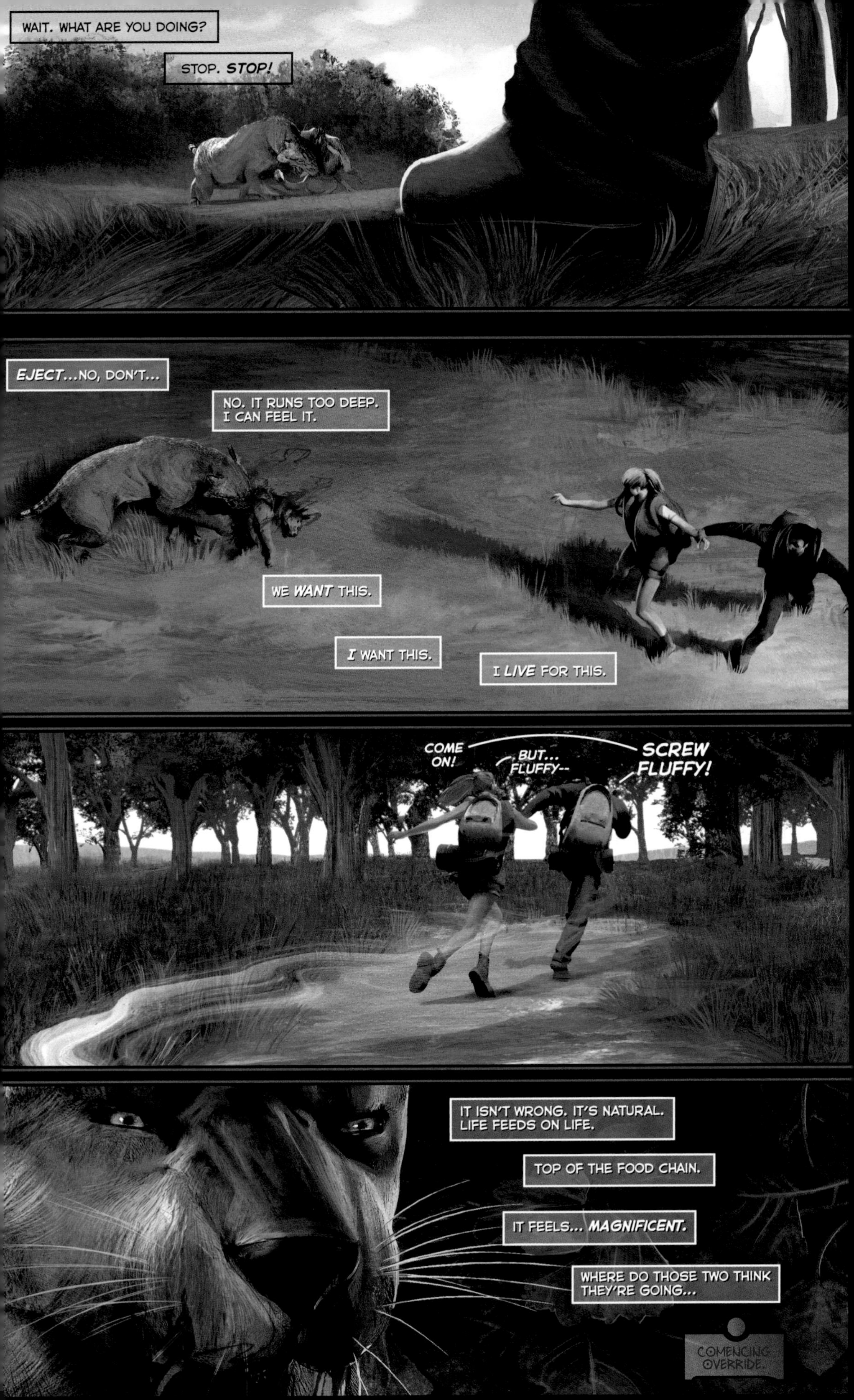
WAIT. WHAT ARE YOU DOING?
STOP. STOP!
EJECT...NO, DON'T...
NO. IT RUNS TOO DEEP. I CAN FEEL IT.
WE WANT THIS.
I WANT THIS.
I LIVE FOR THIS.
COME ON!
BUT... FLUFFY--
SCREW FLUFFY!
IT ISN'T WRONG. IT'S NATURAL. LIFE FEEDS ON LIFE.
TOP OF THE FOOD CHAIN.
IT FEELS... MAGNIFICENT.
WHERE DO THOSE TWO THINK THEY'RE GOING...
COMENCING OVERRIDE.

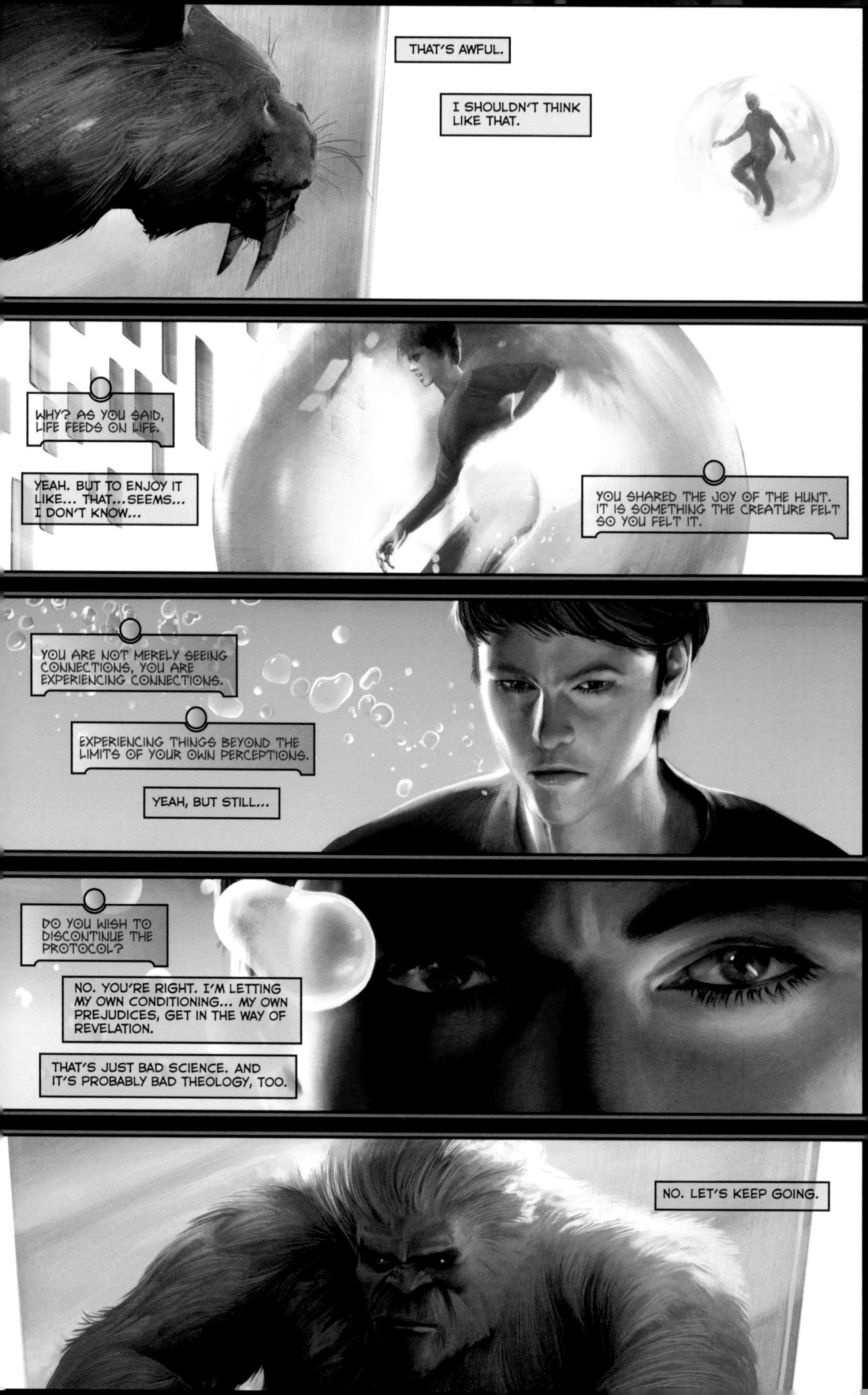
THAT'S AWFUL.
I SHOULDN'T THINK LIKE THAT.
WHY? AS YOU SAID, LIFE FEEDS ON LIFE.
YEAH. BUT TO ENJOY IT LIKE... THAT...SEEMS... I DON'T KNOW...
YOU SHARED THE JOY OF THE HUNT. IT IS SOMETHING THE CREATURE FELT SO YOU FELT IT.
YOU ARE NOT MERELY SEEING CONNECTIONS, YOU ARE EXPERIENCING CONNECTIONS.
EXPERIENCING THINGS BEYOND THE LIMITS OF YOUR OWN PERCEPTIONS.
YEAH, BUT STILL...
DO YOU WISH TO DISCONTINUE THE PROTOCOL?
NO. YOU'RE RIGHT. I'M LETTING MY OWN CONDITIONING... MY OWN PREJUDICES, GET IN THE WAY OF REVELATION.
THAT'S JUST BAD SCIENCE. AND IT'S PROBABLY BAD THEOLOGY, TOO.
NO. LET'S KEEP GOING.

ONLY THIS TIME, MAKE IT SOMEWHERE OUT OF THE WAY. IT'S BAD ENOUGH THE RANGERS ARE GOING TO HEAR STORIES ABOUT SOME WILD DEVIL CAT.

LET'S GO WHERE PEOPLE AREN'T.

AS YOU WISH.

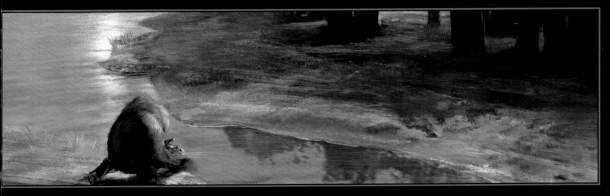

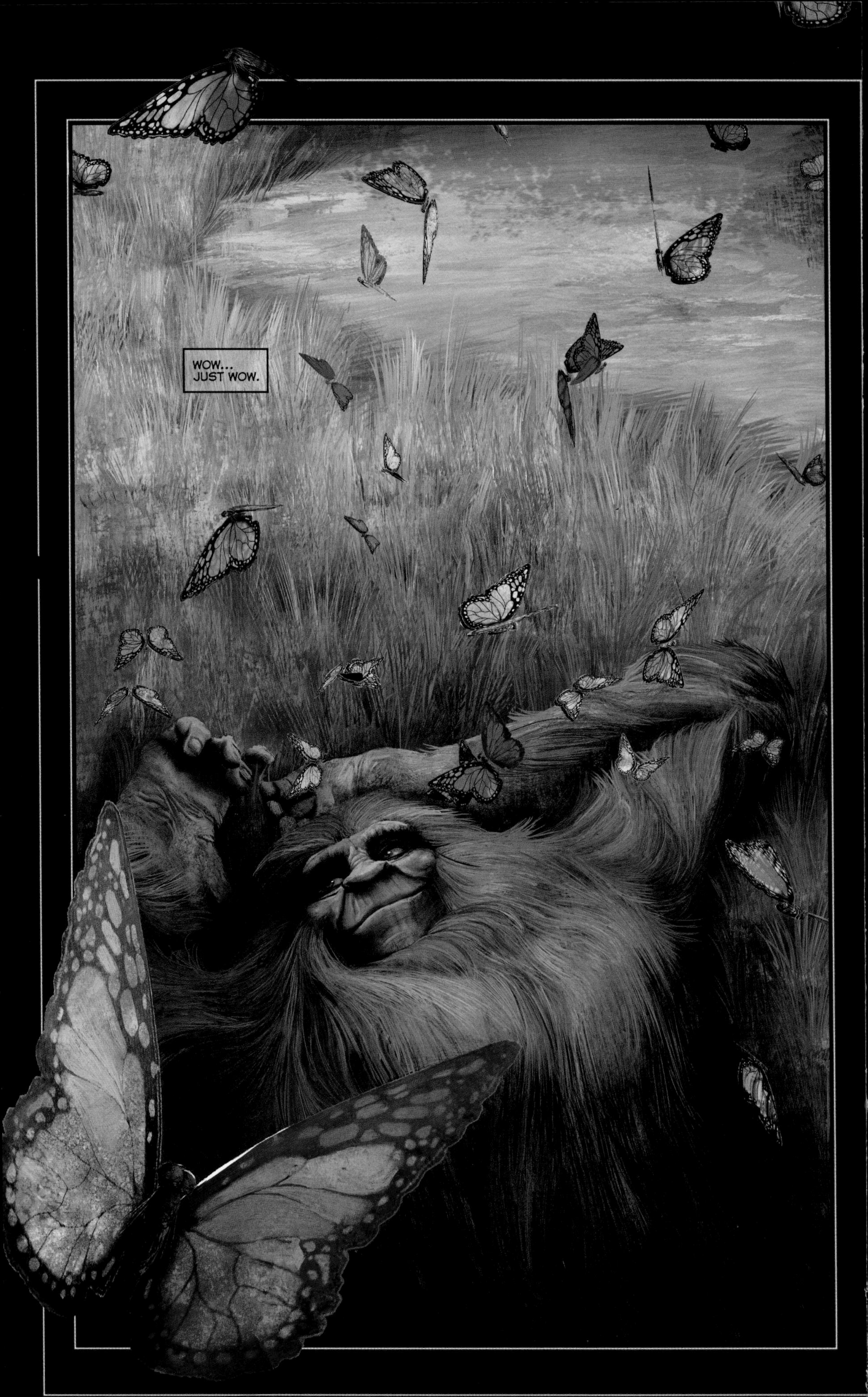
WOW...
JUST WOW.

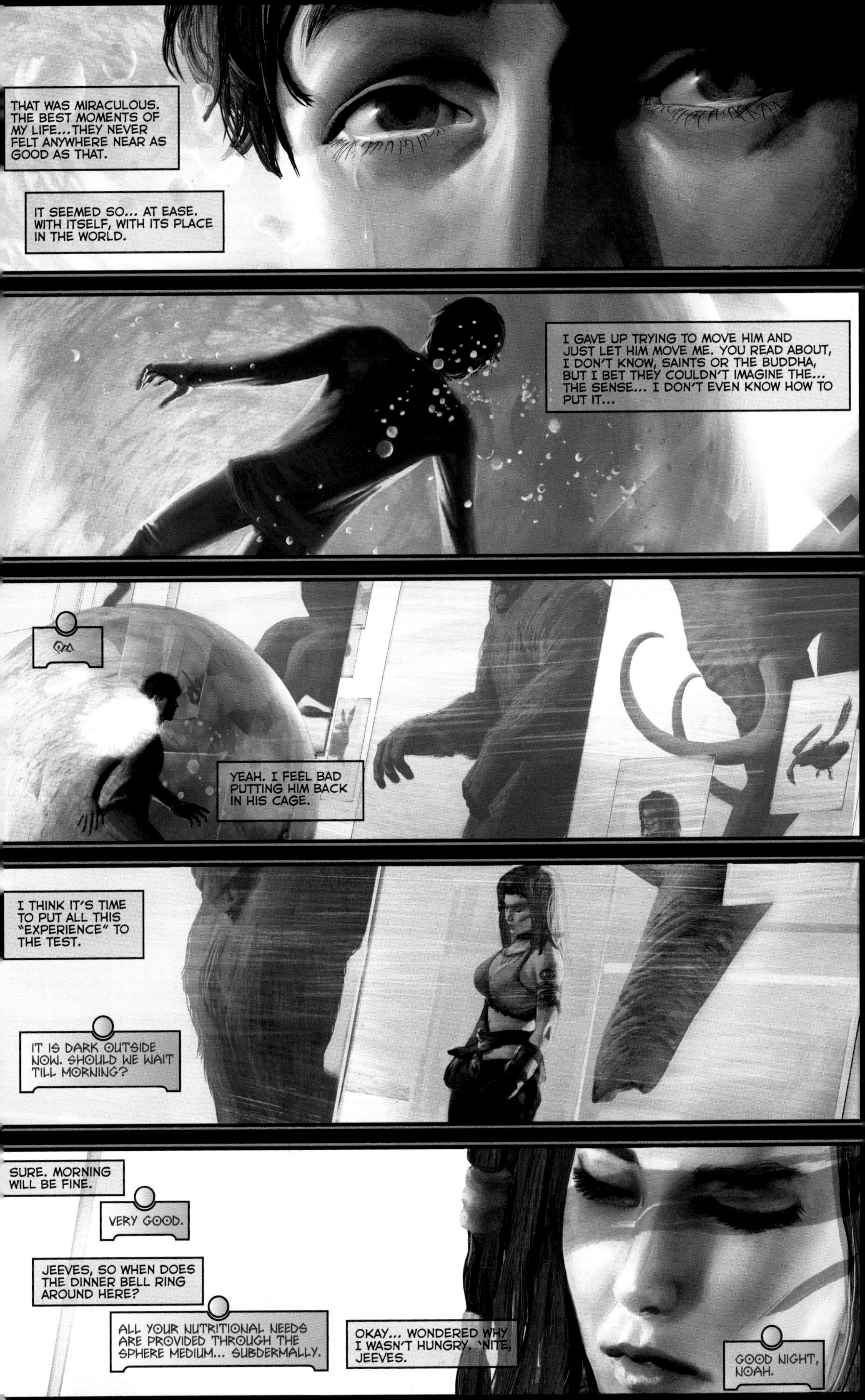
THAT WAS MIRACULOUS. THE BEST MOMENTS OF MY LIFE...THEY NEVER FELT ANYWHERE NEAR AS GOOD AS THAT.
IT SEEMED SO... AT EASE. WITH ITSELF, WITH ITS PLACE IN THE WORLD.
I GAVE UP TRYING TO MOVE HIM AND JUST LET HIM MOVE ME. YOU READ ABOUT, I DON'T KNOW, SAINTS OR THE BUDDHA, BUT I BET THEY COULDN'T IMAGINE THE... THE SENSE... I DON'T EVEN KNOW HOW TO PUT IT...
YEAH. I FEEL BAD PUTTING HIM BACK IN HIS CAGE.
I THINK IT'S TIME TO PUT ALL THIS "EXPERIENCE" TO THE TEST.
IT IS DARK OUTSIDE NOW. SHOULD WE WAIT TILL MORNING?
SURE. MORNING WILL BE FINE.
VERY GOOD.
JEEVES, SO WHEN DOES THE DINNER BELL RING AROUND HERE?
ALL YOUR NUTRITIONAL NEEDS ARE PROVIDED THROUGH THE SPHERE MEDIUM... SUBDERMALLY.
OKAY... WONDERED WHY I WASN'T HUNGRY. 'NITE, JEEVES.
GOOD NIGHT, NOAH.

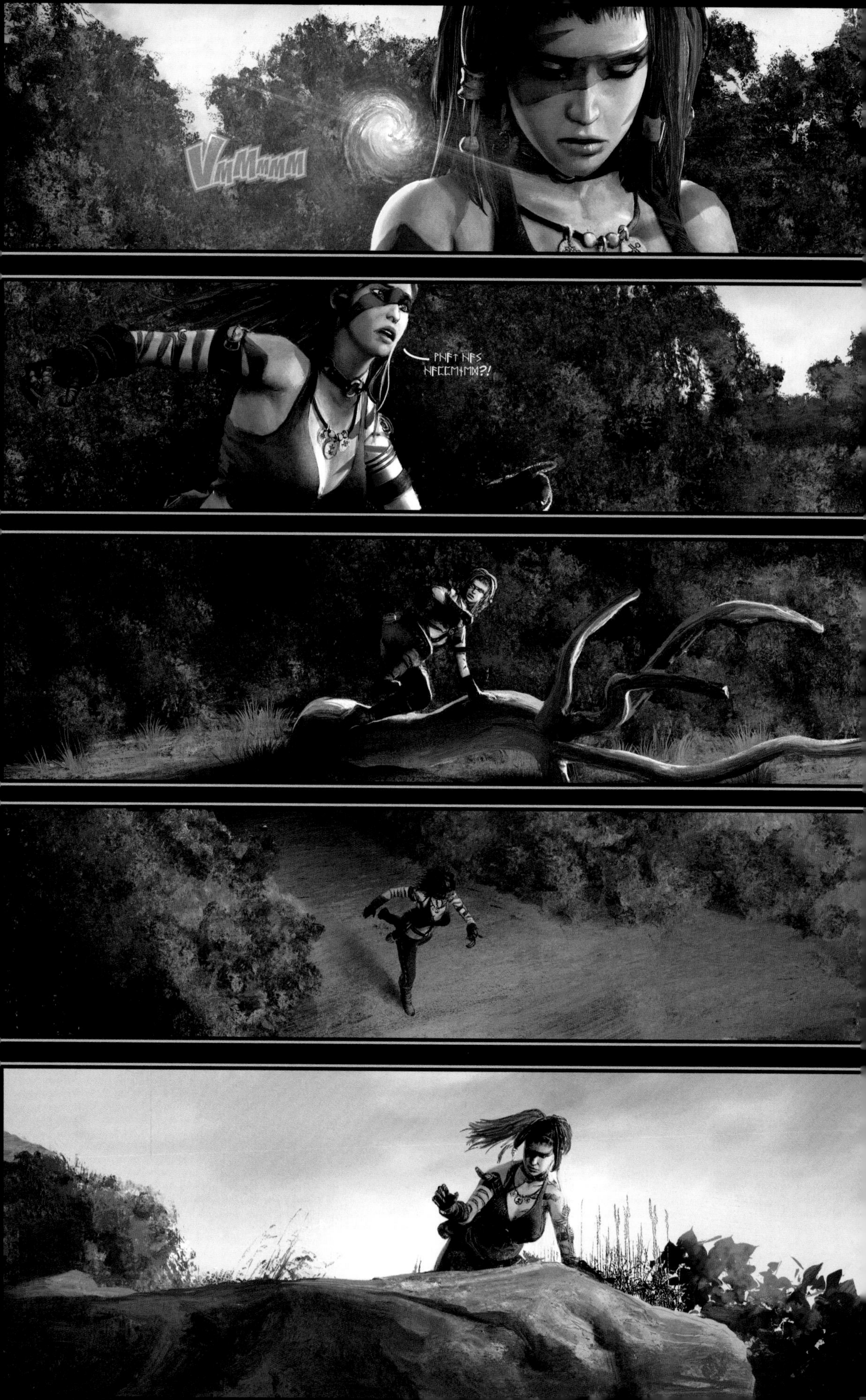
VMMMMM
ᚹᚺᚨᛏ ᚺᚨᛊ ᚺᚨᛈᛈᛖᚾᛖᛞ?!

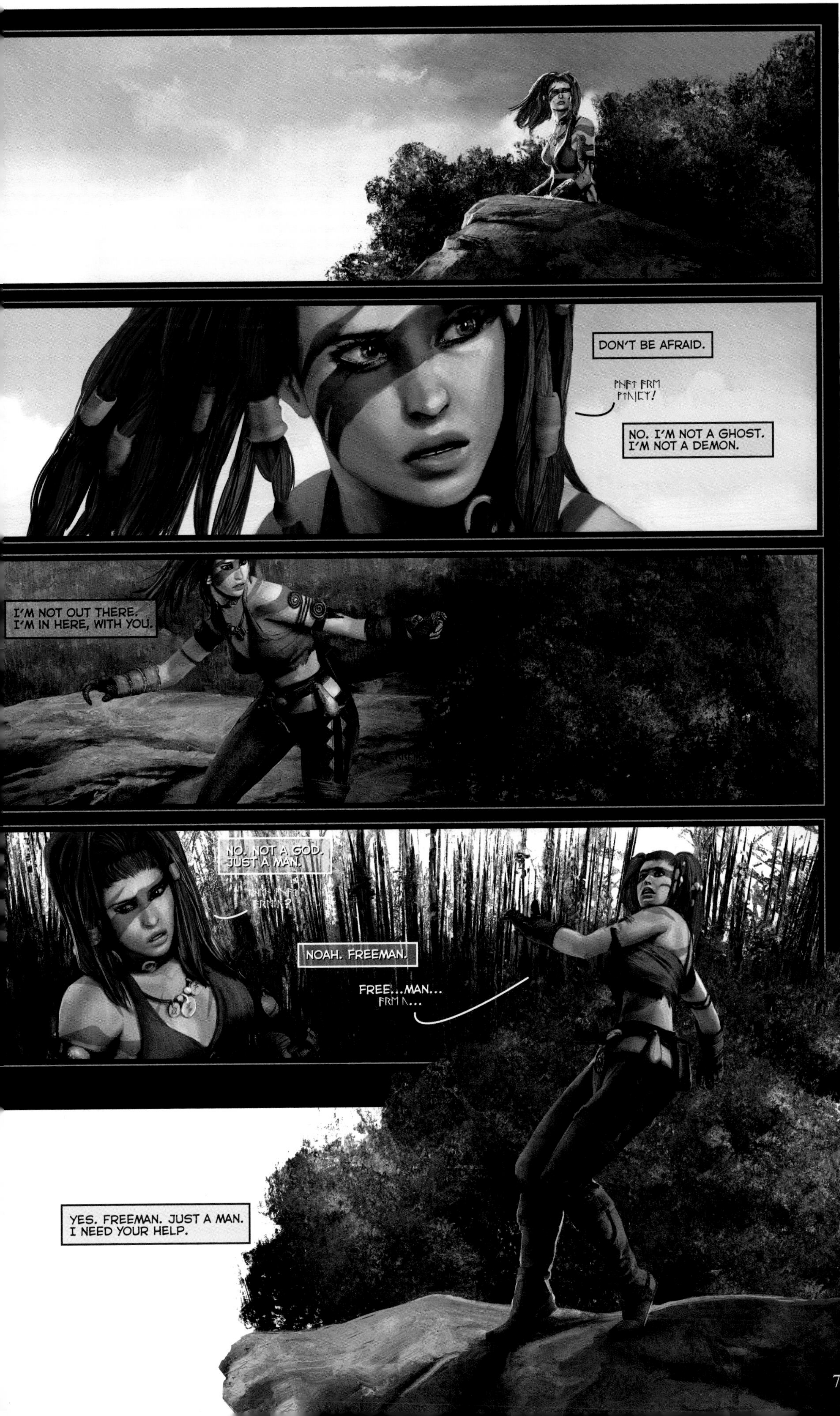
DON'T BE AFRAID.
NO. I'M NOT A GHOST.
I'M NOT A DEMON.
I'M NOT OUT THERE.
I'M IN HERE, WITH YOU.
NO. NOT A GOD.
JUST A MAN.
NOAH. FREEMAN.
FREE...MAN...
YES. FREEMAN. JUST A MAN.
I NEED YOUR HELP.

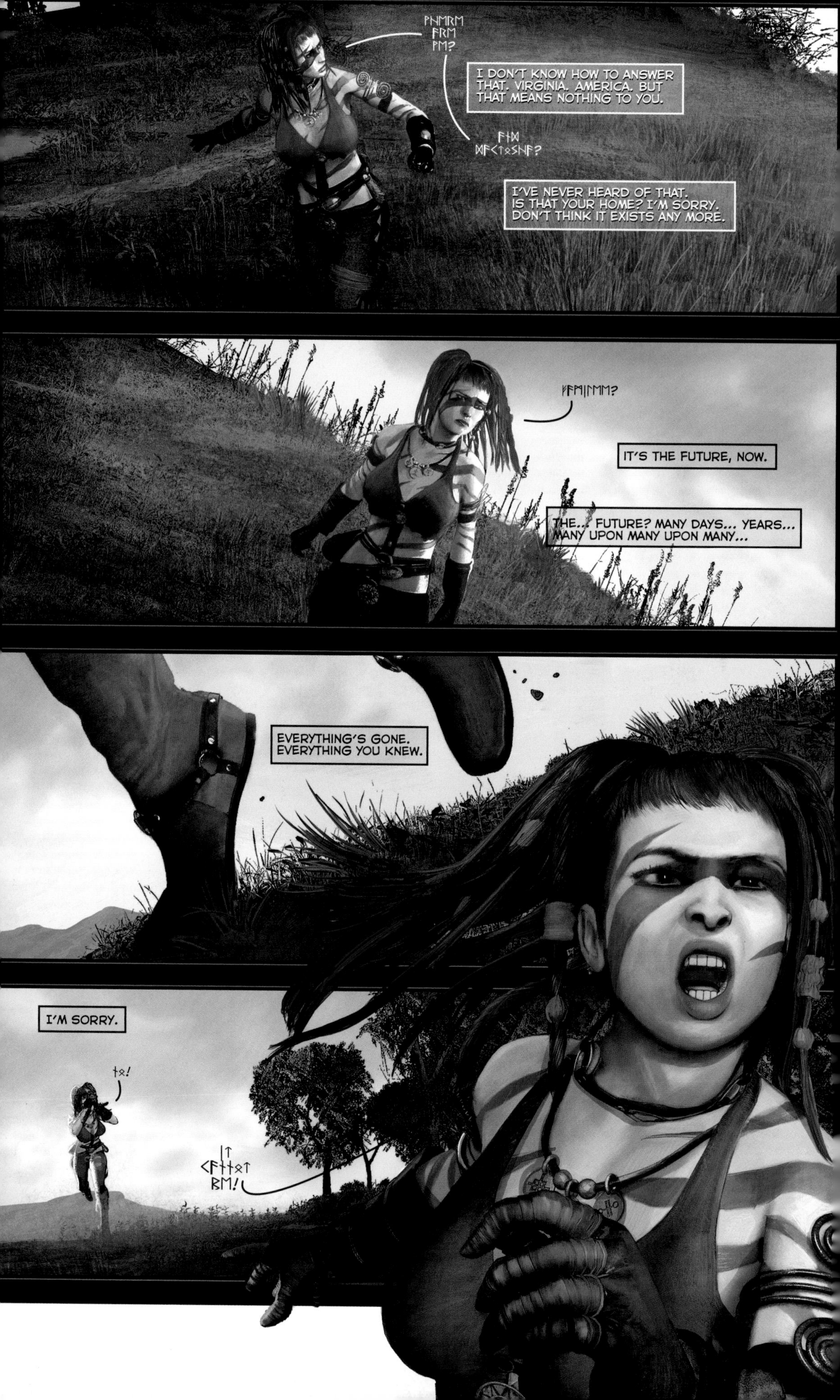

I DON'T KNOW HOW TO ANSWER THAT. VIRGINIA. AMERICA. BUT THAT MEANS NOTHING TO YOU.
I'VE NEVER HEARD OF THAT. IS THAT YOUR HOME? I'M SORRY. DON'T THINK IT EXISTS ANY MORE.
IT'S THE FUTURE, NOW.
THE... FUTURE? MANY DAYS... YEARS... MANY UPON MANY UPON MANY...
EVERYTHING'S GONE. EVERYTHING YOU KNEW.
I'M SORRY.

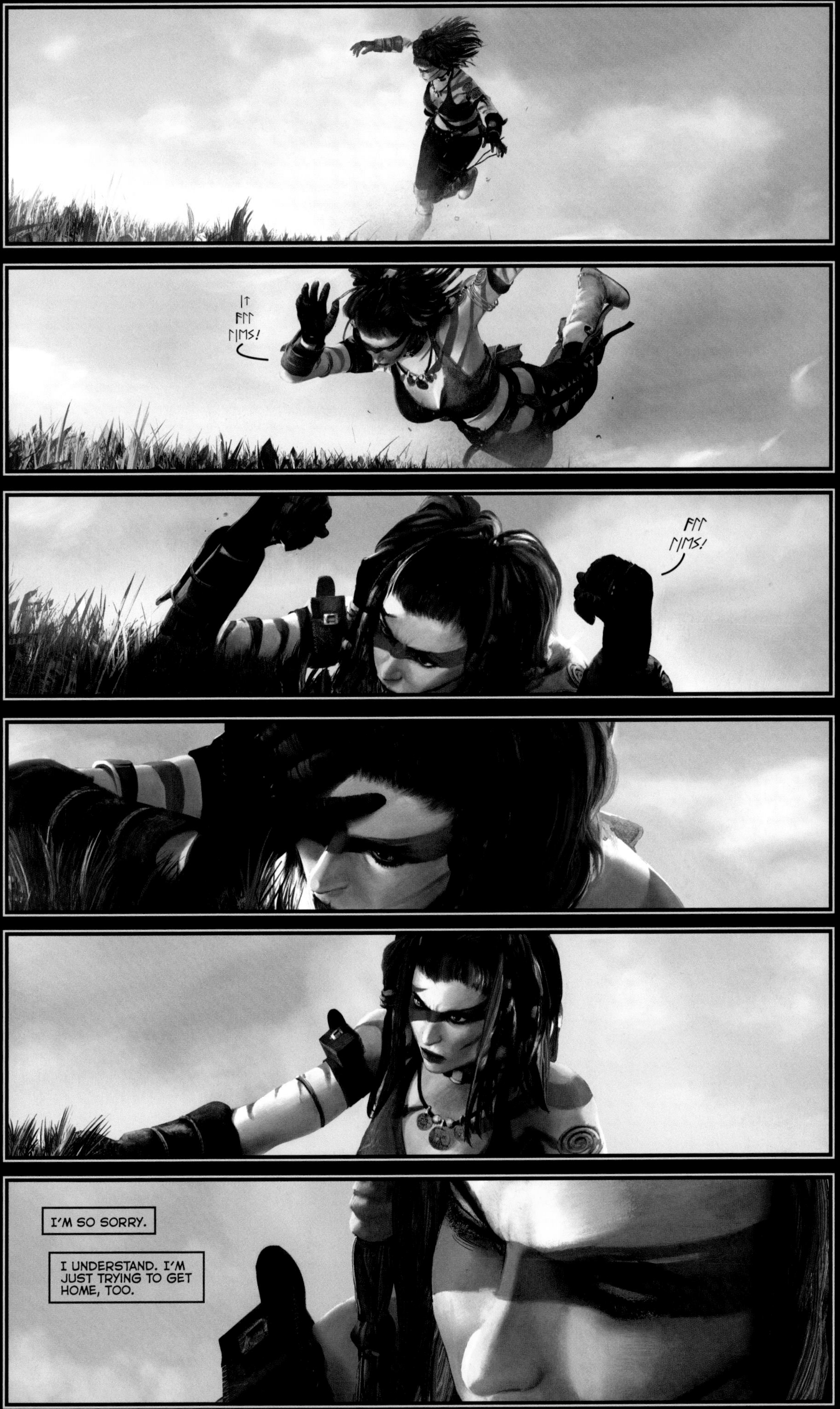
I'M SO SORRY.
I UNDERSTAND. I'M JUST TRYING TO GET HOME, TOO.

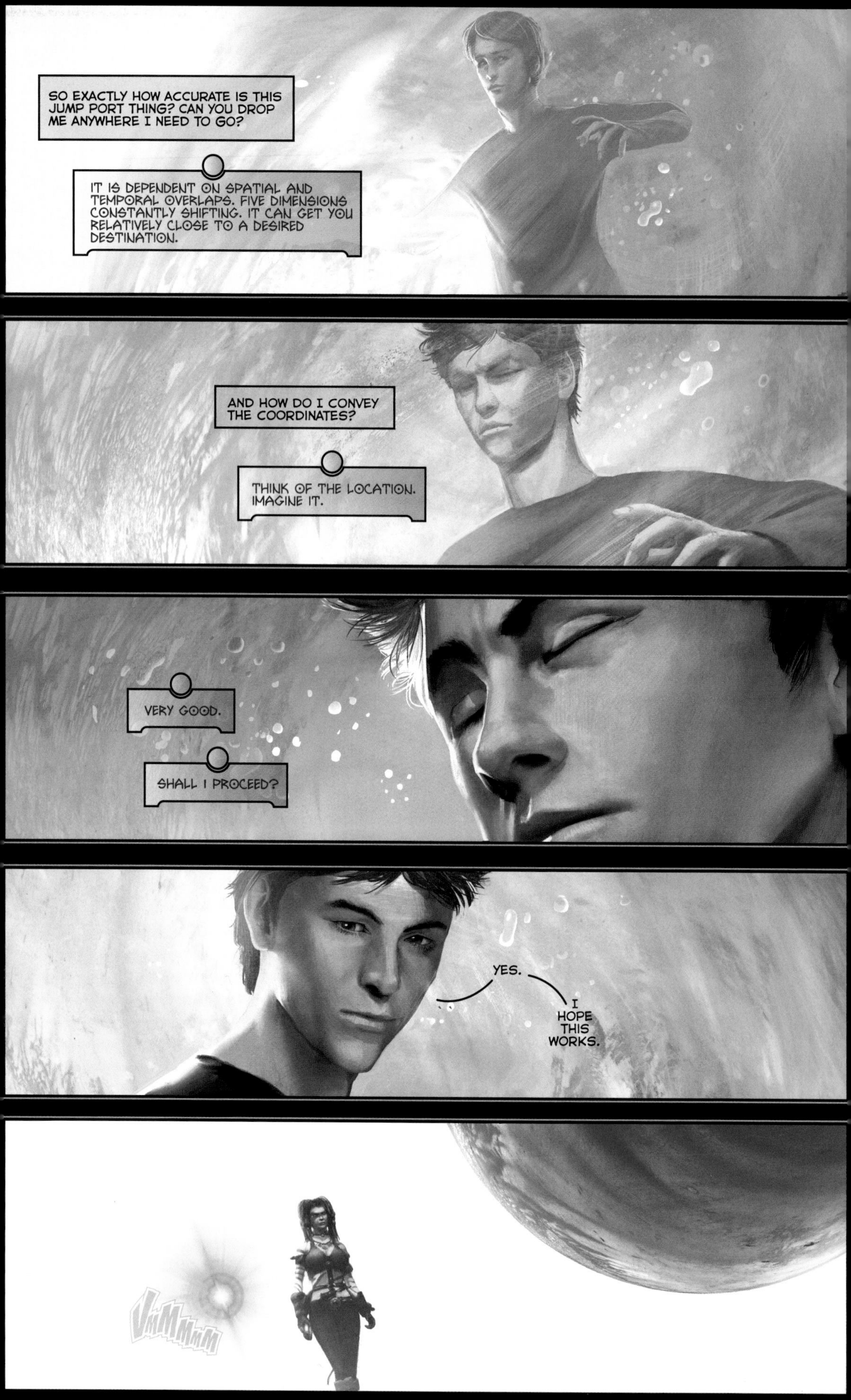
SO EXACTLY HOW ACCURATE IS THIS JUMP PORT THING? CAN YOU DROP ME ANYWHERE I NEED TO GO?
IT IS DEPENDENT ON SPATIAL AND TEMPORAL OVERLAPS. FIVE DIMENSIONS CONSTANTLY SHIFTING. IT CAN GET YOU RELATIVELY CLOSE TO A DESIRED DESTINATION.
AND HOW DO I CONVEY THE COORDINATES?
THINK OF THE LOCATION. IMAGINE IT.
VERY GOOD.
SHALL I PROCEED?
YES.
I HOPE THIS WORKS.
VMMMMM

IT'S OKAY. TRUST ME.
GIVE ME... CONTROL.

THIS IS PRETTY CLOSE.
HELEN'S PLACE IS JUST
AROUND THE CORNER.

JUST RELAX. THIS IS GOING
TO BE QUICK AND PAINLESS.
PROMISE. I JUST NEED TO
LEAVE WORD THAT I'M OKAY.

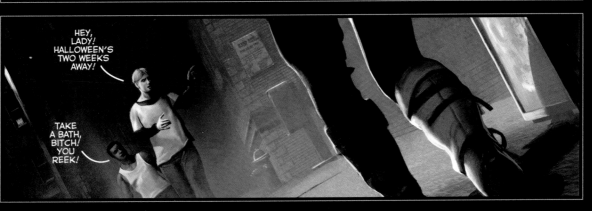

HEY,
LADY!
HALLOWEEN'S
TWO WEEKS
AWAY!

TAKE
A BATH,
BITCH!
YOU
REEK!

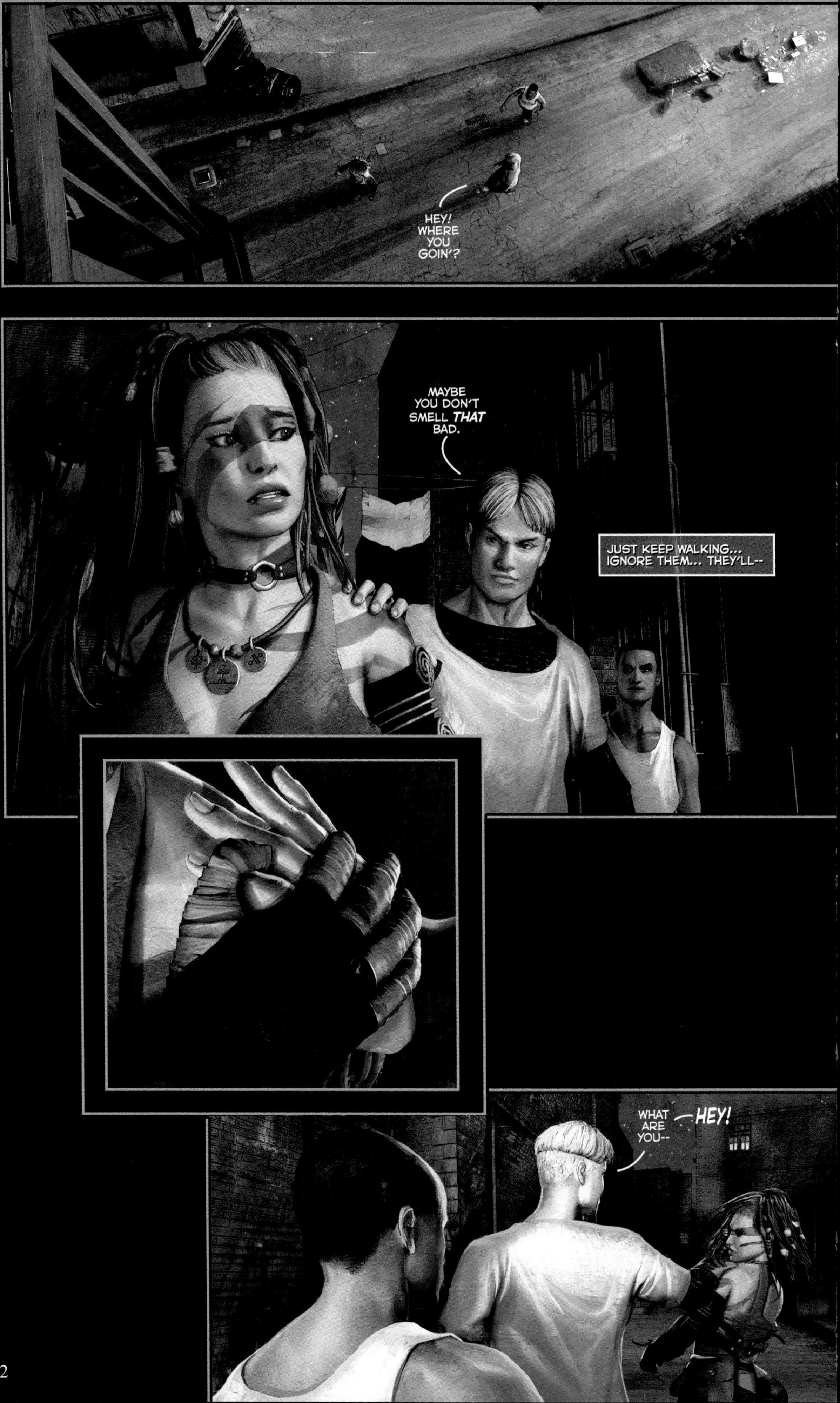

HEY! WHERE YOU GOIN'?
MAYBE YOU DON'T SMELL *THAT* BAD.
JUST KEEP WALKING... IGNORE THEM... THEY'LL--
WHAT ARE YOU--
HEY!

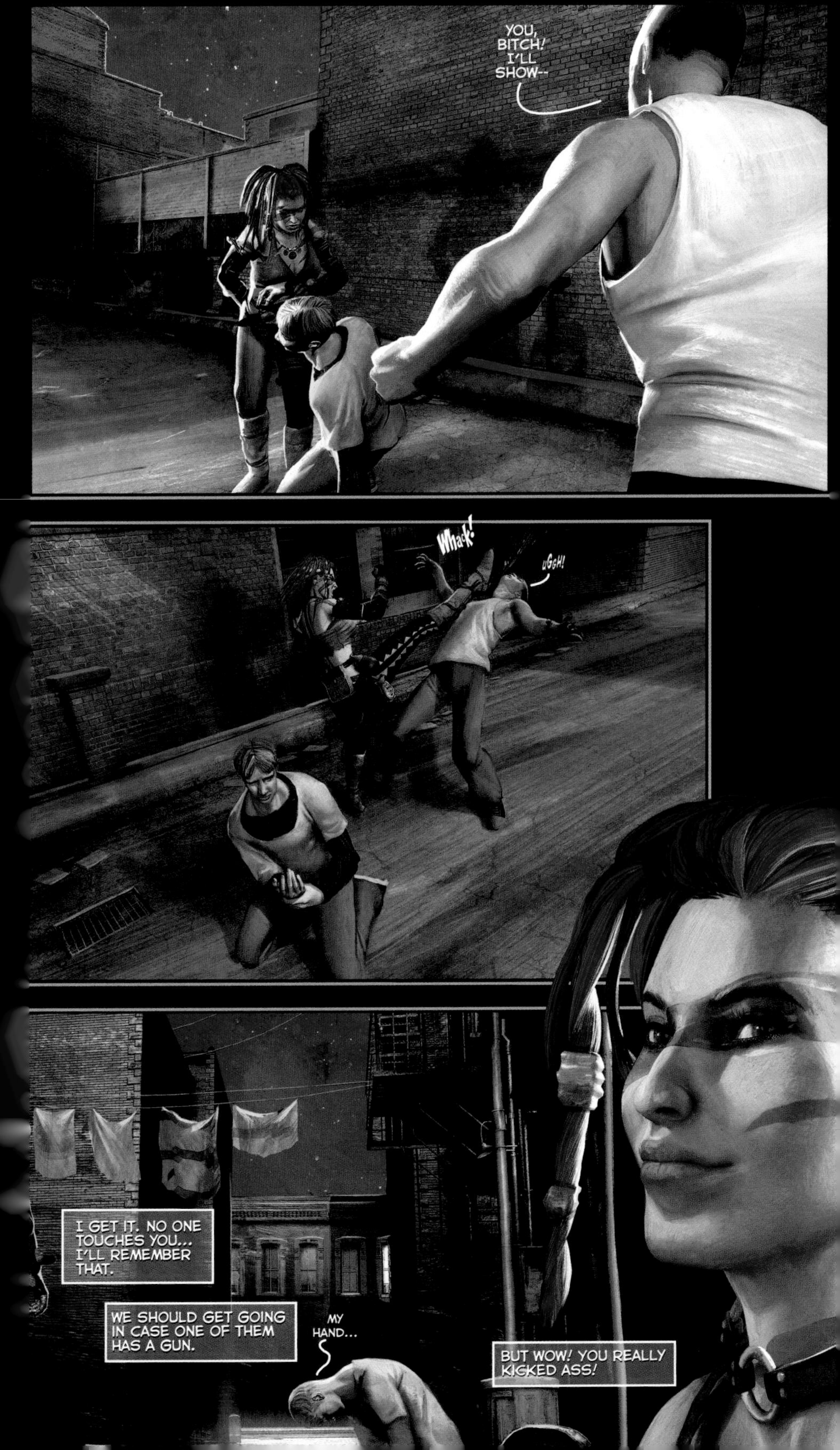
YOU, BITCH! I'LL SHOW--
WHACK!
UGGH!
I GET IT. NO ONE TOUCHES YOU... I'LL REMEMBER THAT.
WE SHOULD GET GOING IN CASE ONE OF THEM HAS A GUN.
MY HAND...
BUT WOW! YOU REALLY KICKED ASS!

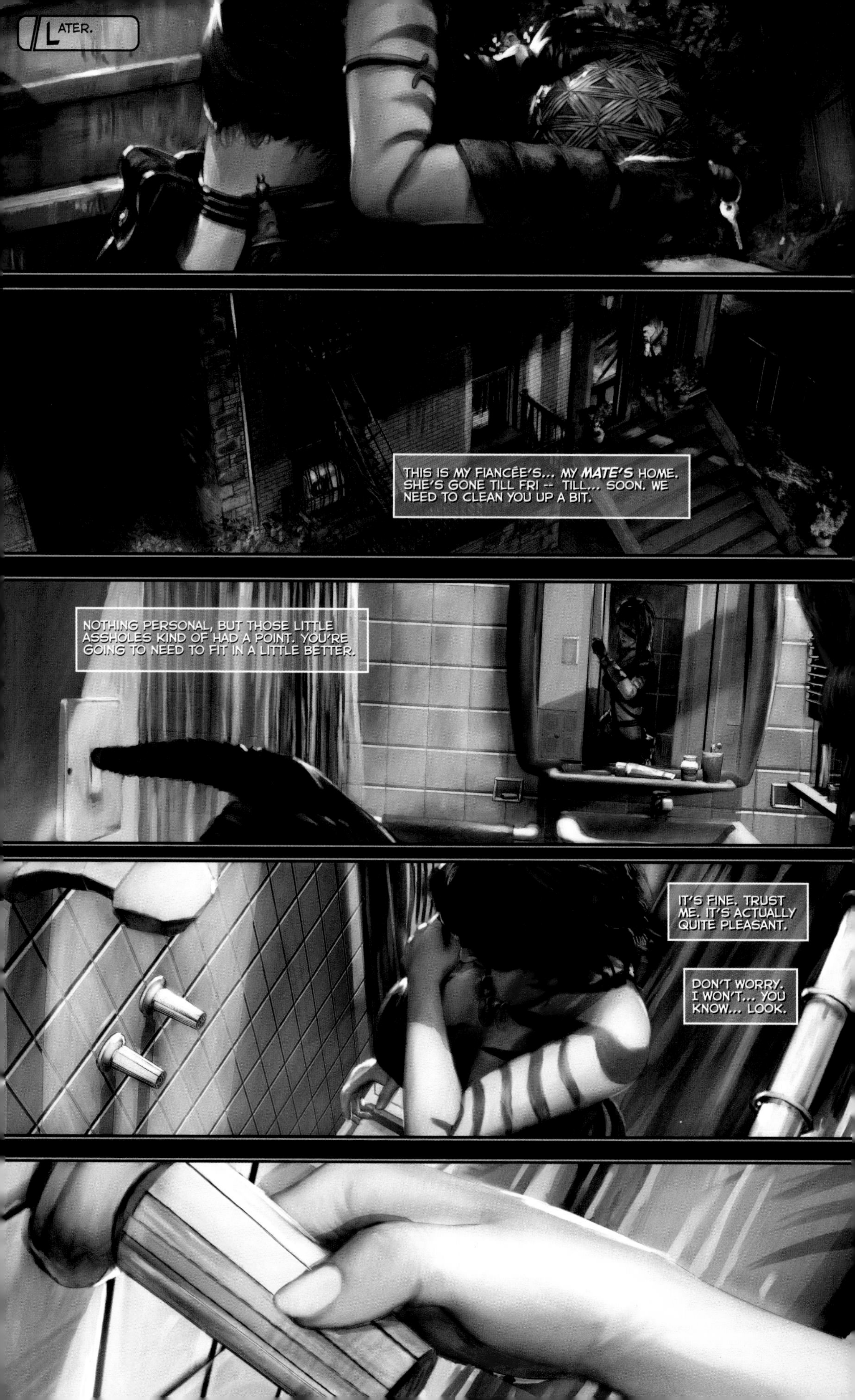
LATER.
THIS IS MY FIANCÉE'S... MY MATE'S HOME. SHE'S GONE TILL FRI -- TILL... SOON. WE NEED TO CLEAN YOU UP A BIT.
NOTHING PERSONAL, BUT THOSE LITTLE ASSHOLES KIND OF HAD A POINT. YOU'RE GOING TO NEED TO FIT IN A LITTLE BETTER.
IT'S FINE. TRUST ME. IT'S ACTUALLY QUITE PLEASANT.
DON'T WORRY. I WON'T... YOU KNOW... LOOK.

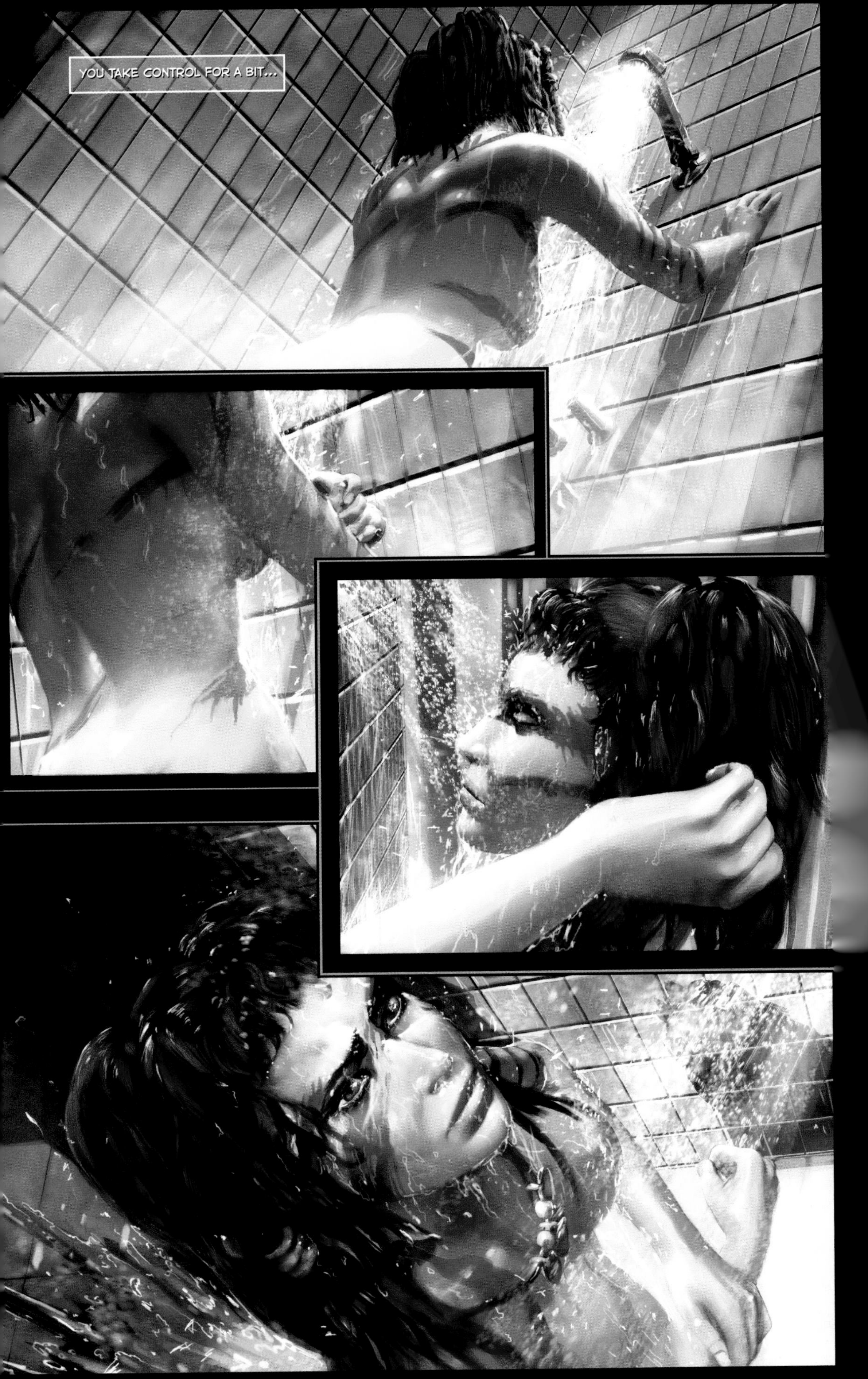
YOU TAKE CONTROL FOR A BIT...

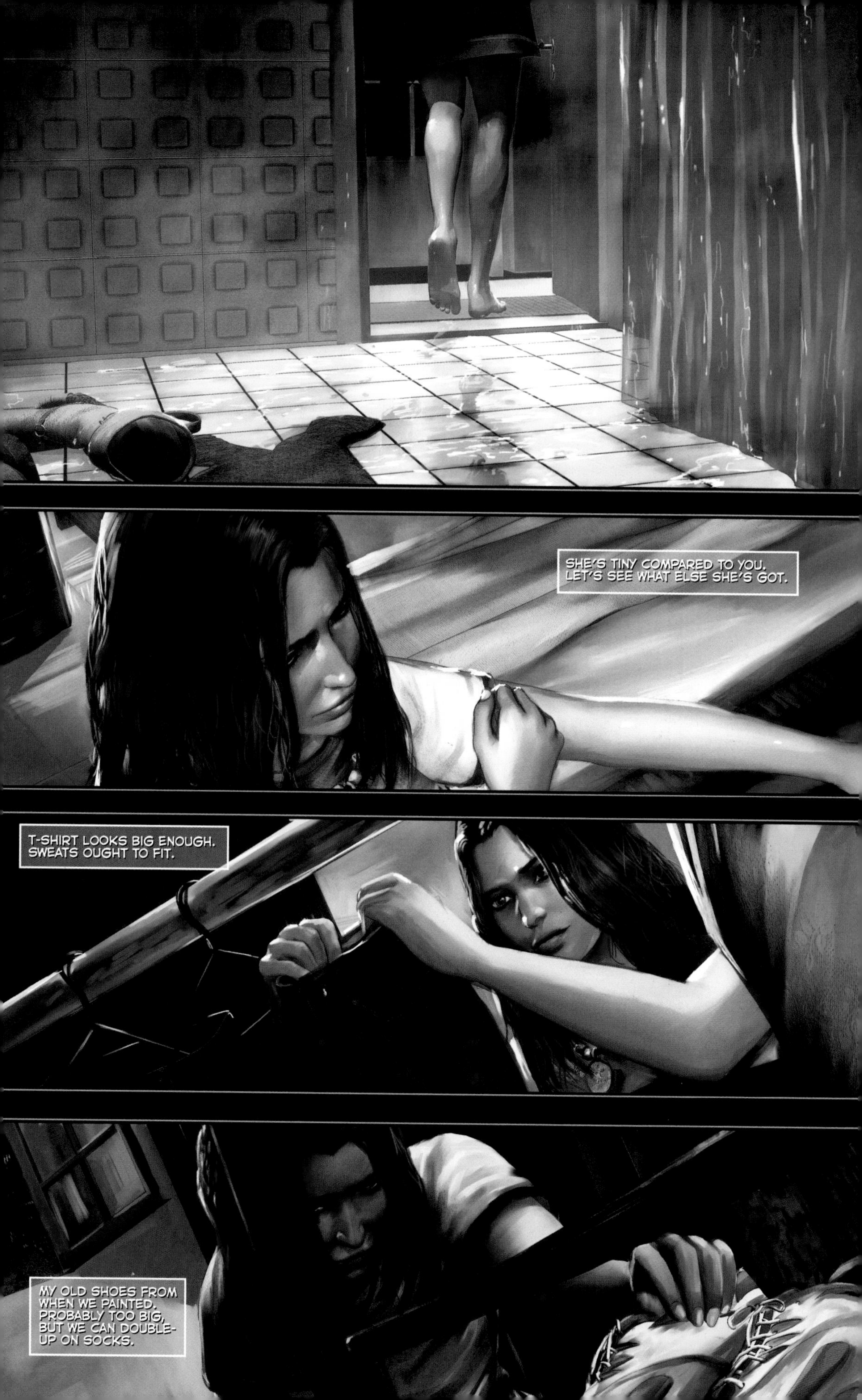
SHE'S TINY COMPARED TO YOU. LET'S SEE WHAT ELSE SHE'S GOT.
T-SHIRT LOOKS BIG ENOUGH. SWEATS OUGHT TO FIT.
MY OLD SHOES FROM WHEN WE PAINTED. PROBABLY TOO BIG, BUT WE CAN DOUBLE-UP ON SOCKS.

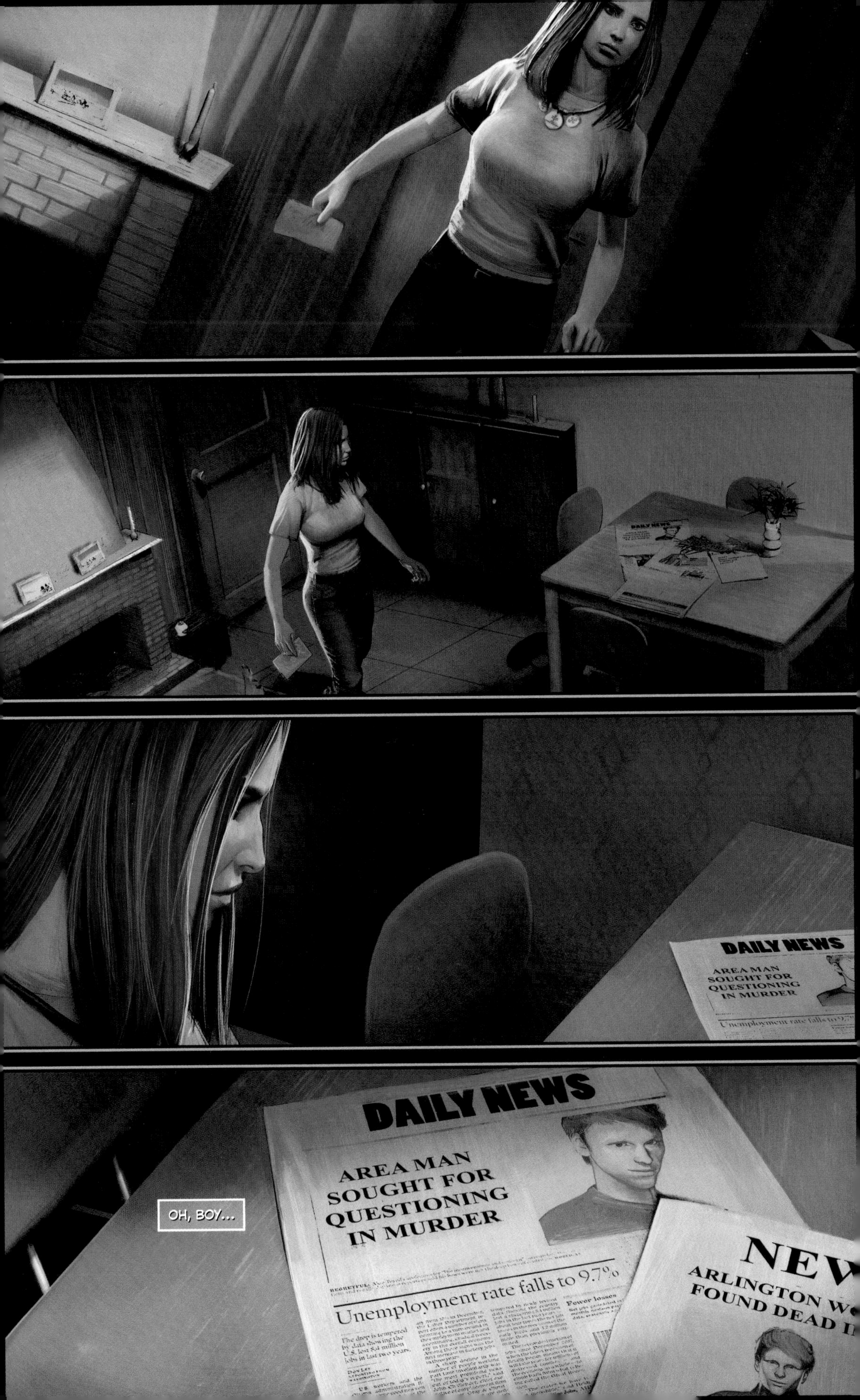
DAILY NEWS
AREA MAN SOUGHT FOR QUESTIONING IN MURDER
Unemployment rate falls to 9.7%
The drop is tempered by data showing the U.S. lost 8.4 million jobs in last two years.
Power losses
OH, BOY...

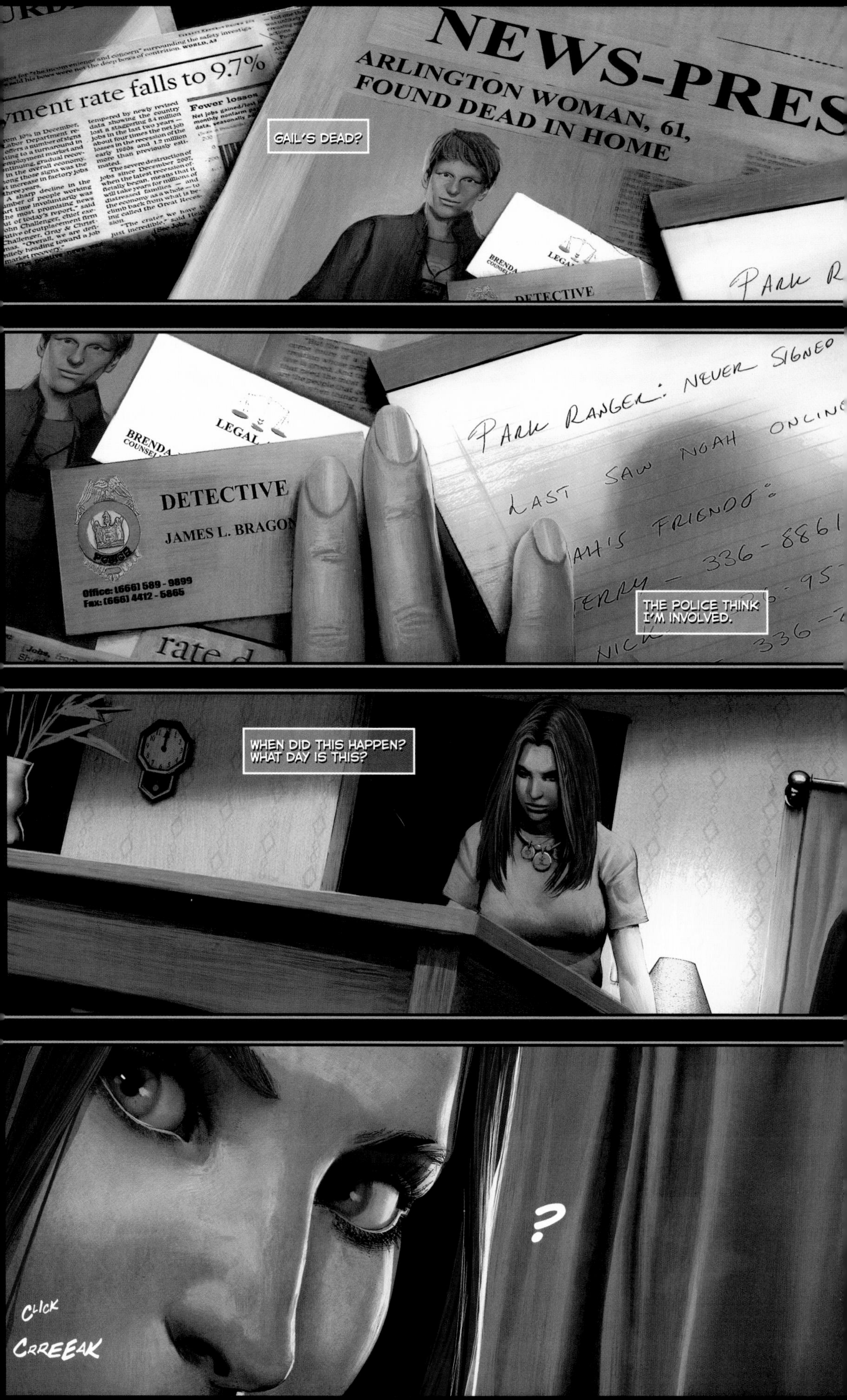
ARLINGTON WOMAN, 61, FOUND DEAD IN HOME
GAIL'S DEAD?
DETECTIVE
JAMES L. BRAGON
Office: (666) 589 - 9899
Fax: (666) 4412 - 5865
THE POLICE THINK I'M INVOLVED.
WHEN DID THIS HAPPEN? WHAT DAY IS THIS?
?
CLICK
CRREEAK

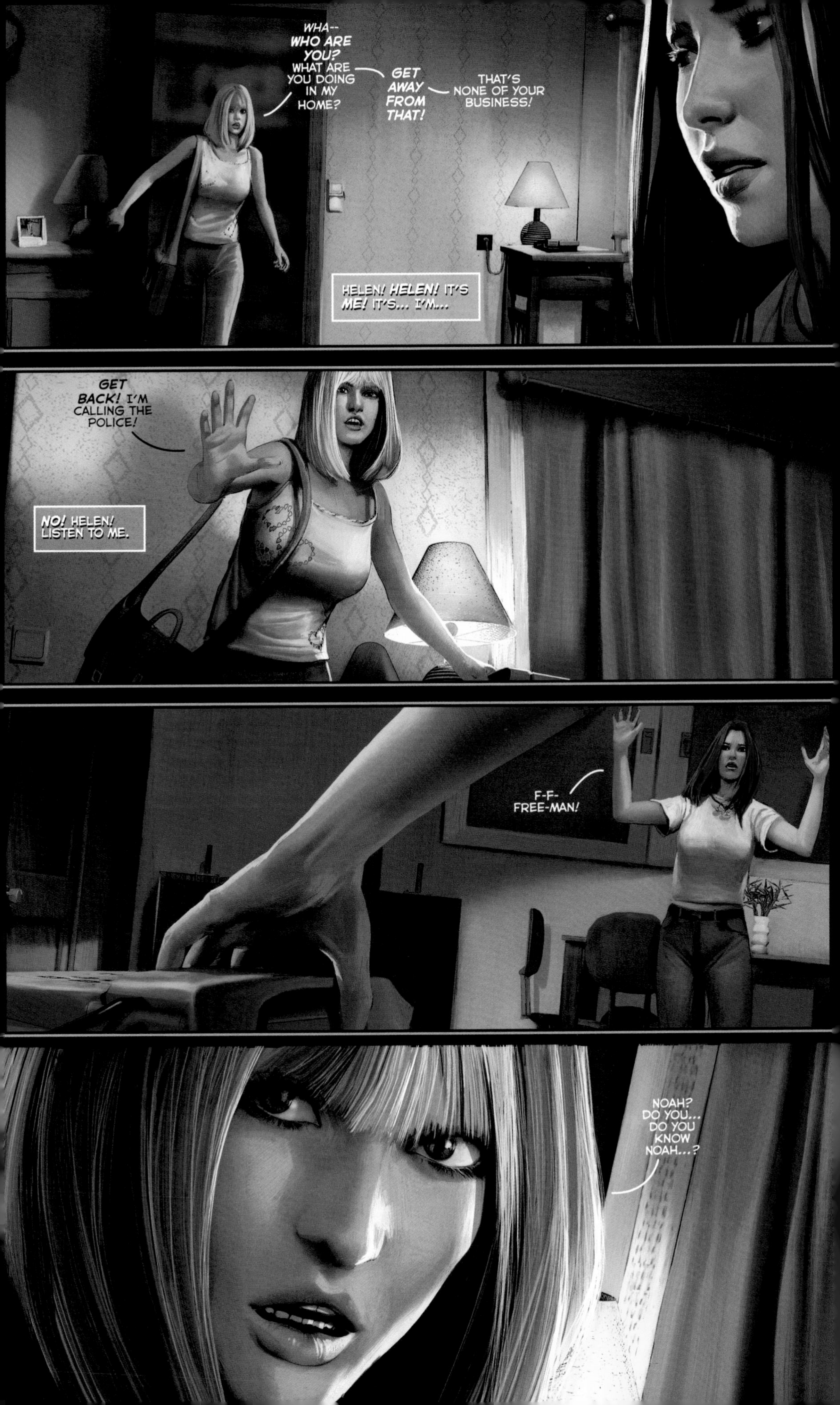
WHA-- WHO ARE YOU? WHAT ARE YOU DOING IN MY HOME?
GET AWAY FROM THAT!
THAT'S NONE OF YOUR BUSINESS!
HELEN! HELEN! IT'S ME! IT'S... I'M...
GET BACK! I'M CALLING THE POLICE!
NO! HELEN! LISTEN TO ME.
F-F-FREE-MAN!
NOAH? DO YOU... DO YOU KNOW NOAH...?

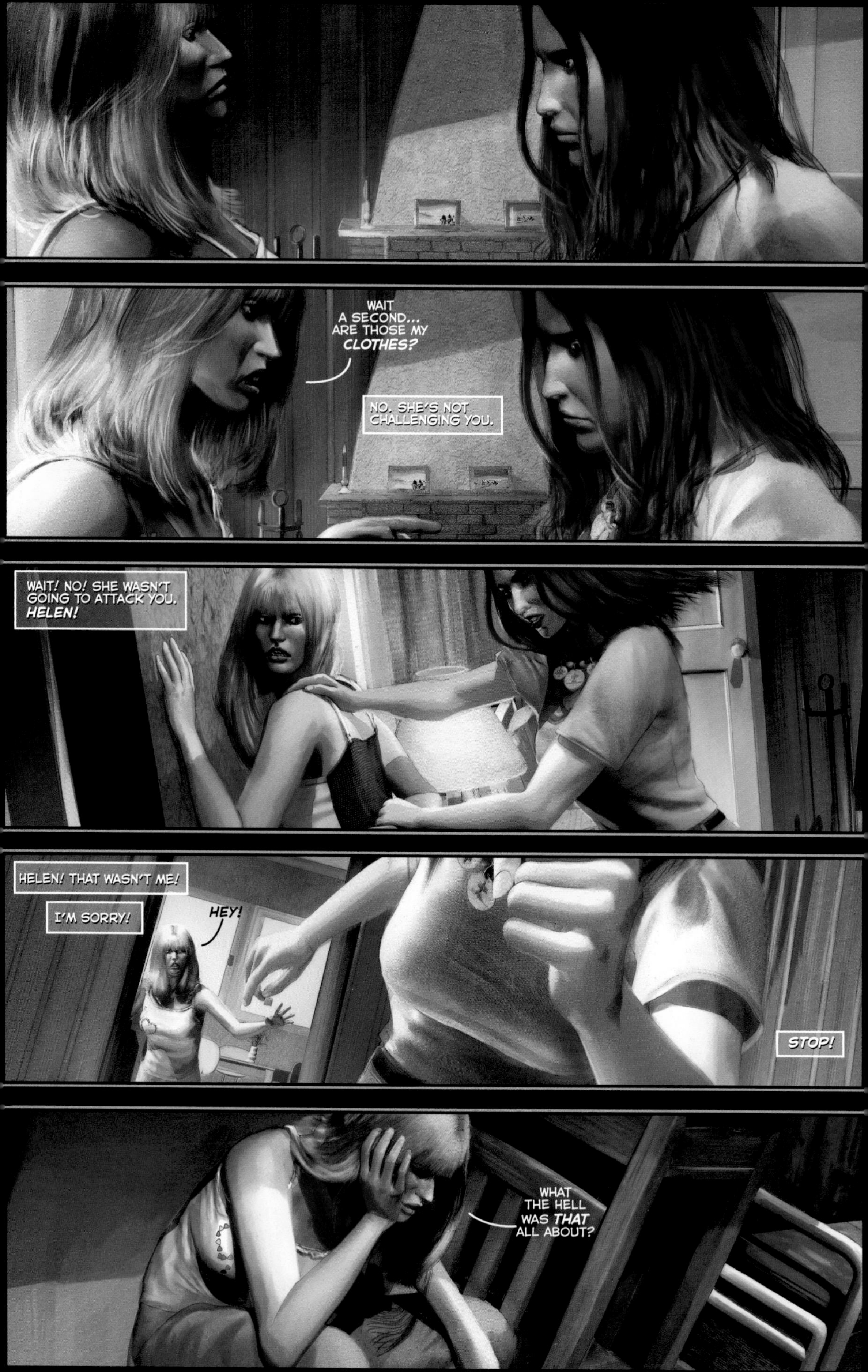
WAIT A SECOND... ARE THOSE MY CLOTHES?
NO. SHE'S NOT CHALLENGING YOU.
WAIT! NO! SHE WASN'T GOING TO ATTACK YOU. HELEN!
HELEN! THAT WASN'T ME!
I'M SORRY!
HEY!
STOP!
WHAT THE HELL WAS THAT ALL ABOUT?

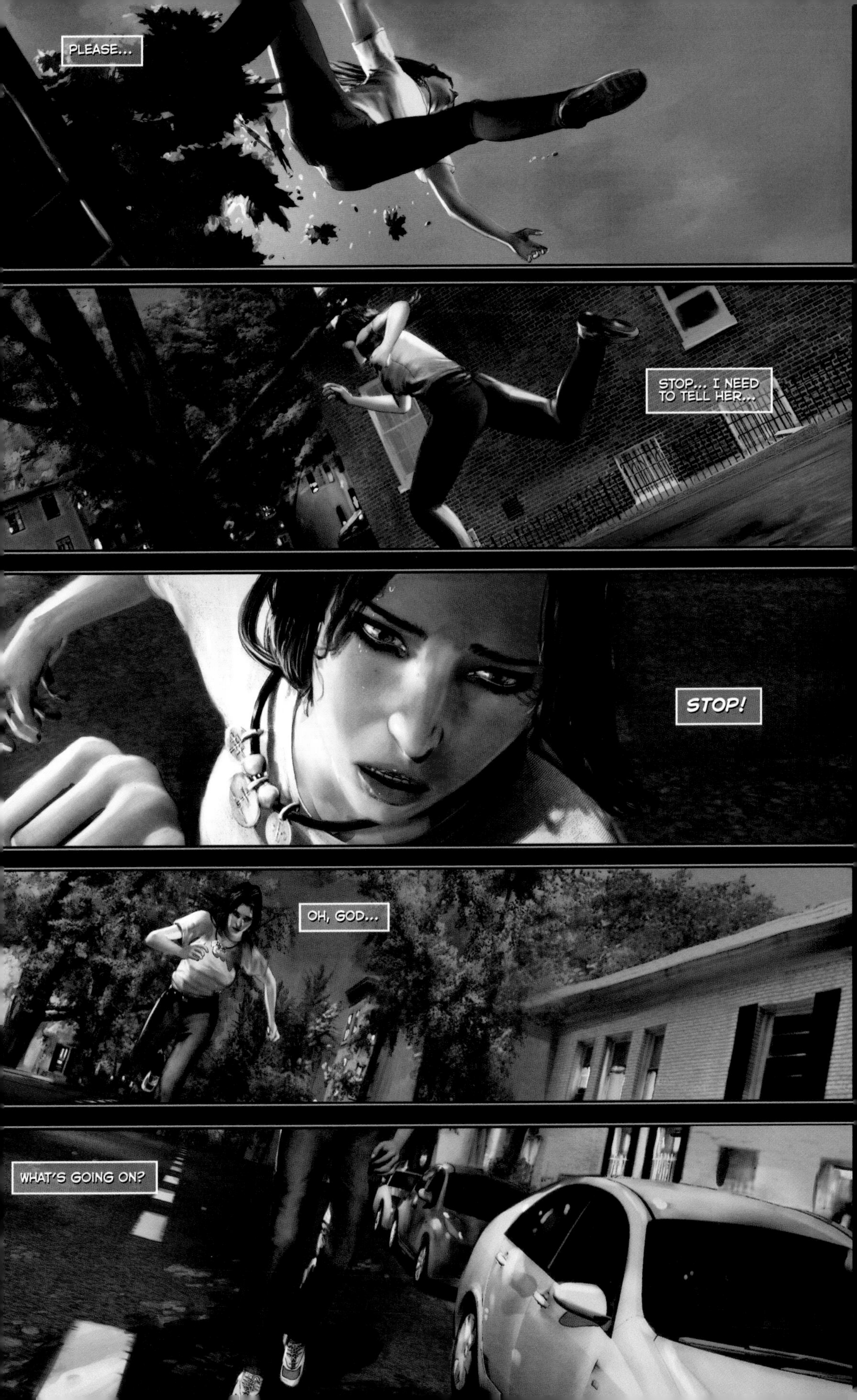
PLEASE...
STOP... I NEED TO TELL HER...
STOP!
OH, GOD...
WHAT'S GOING ON?

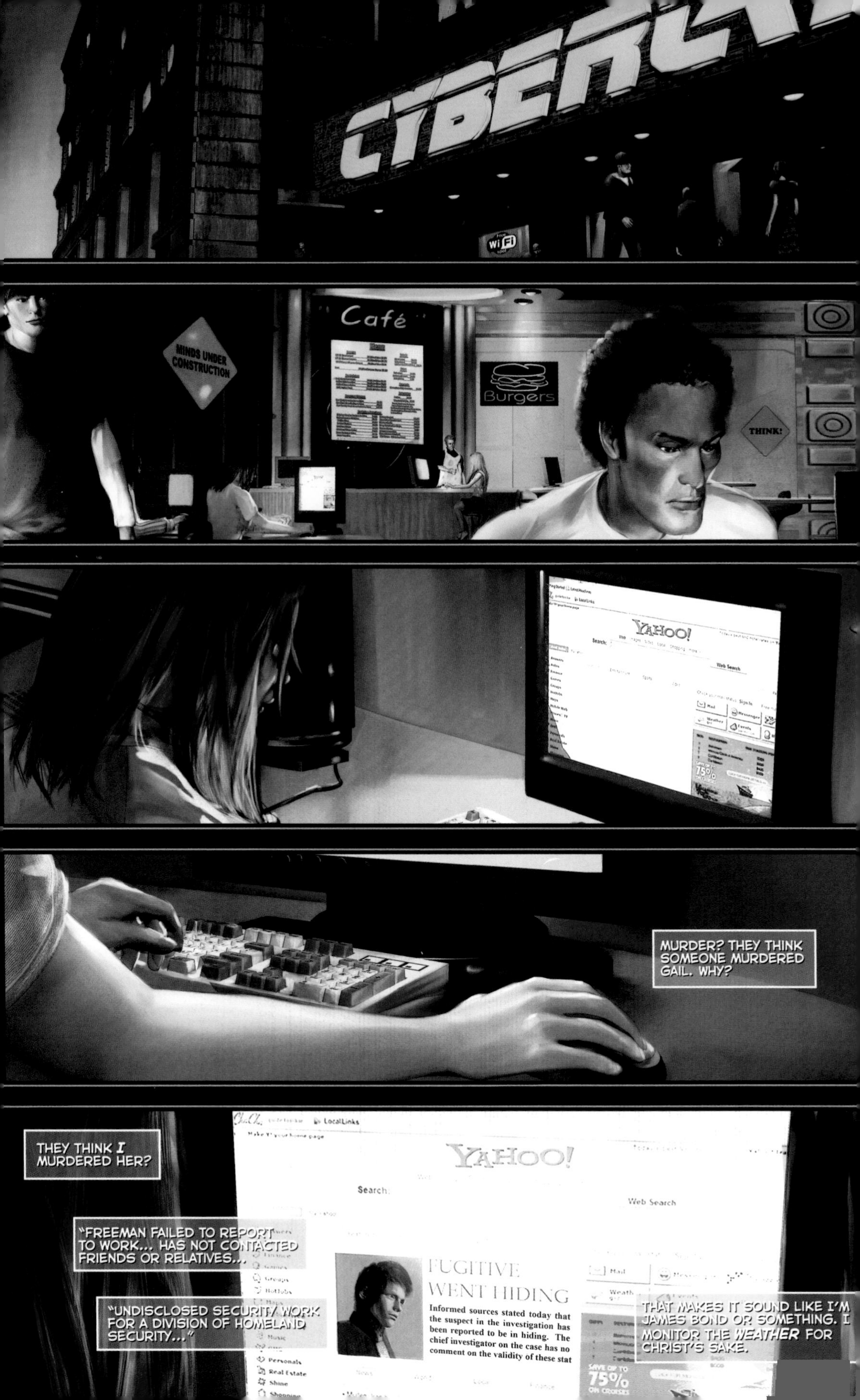
Café
MINDS UNDER CONSTRUCTION
Burgers
THINK!
YAHOO!
MURDER? THEY THINK SOMEONE MURDERED GAIL. WHY?
THEY THINK *I* MURDERED HER?
YAHOO!
Search:
Web Search
"FREEMAN FAILED TO REPORT TO WORK... HAS NOT CONTACTED FRIENDS OR RELATIVES...
"UNDISCLOSED SECURITY WORK FOR A DIVISION OF HOMELAND SECURITY..."
FUGITIVE WENT HIDING
Informed sources stated today that the suspect in the investigation has been reported to be in hiding. The chief investigator on the case has no comment on the validity of these stat
THAT MAKES IT SOUND LIKE I'M JAMES BOND OR SOMETHING. I MONITOR THE *WEATHER* FOR CHRIST'S SAKE.

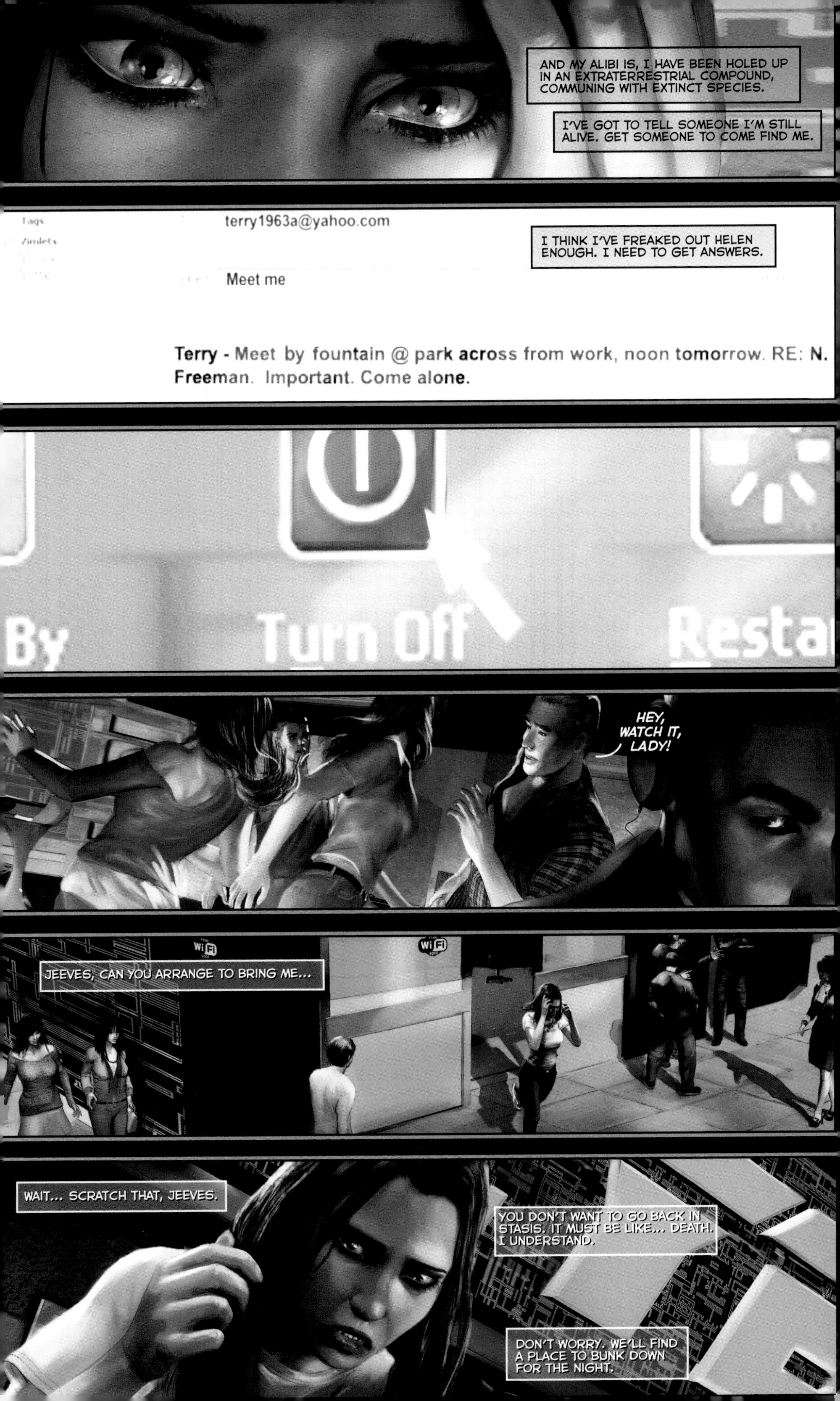
AND MY ALIBI IS, I HAVE BEEN HOLED UP IN AN EXTRATERRESTRIAL COMPOUND, COMMUNING WITH EXTINCT SPECIES.
I'VE GOT TO TELL SOMEONE I'M STILL ALIVE. GET SOMEONE TO COME FIND ME.
Tags
terry1963a@yahoo.com
I THINK I'VE FREAKED OUT HELEN ENOUGH. I NEED TO GET ANSWERS.
Meet me
Terry - Meet by fountain @ park across from work, noon tomorrow. RE: N. Freeman. Important. Come alone.
Turn Off
HEY, WATCH IT, LADY!
JEEVES, CAN YOU ARRANGE TO BRING ME...
WAIT... SCRATCH THAT, JEEVES.
YOU DON'T WANT TO GO BACK IN STASIS. IT MUST BE LIKE... DEATH. I UNDERSTAND.
DON'T WORRY. WE'LL FIND A PLACE TO BUNK DOWN FOR THE NIGHT.

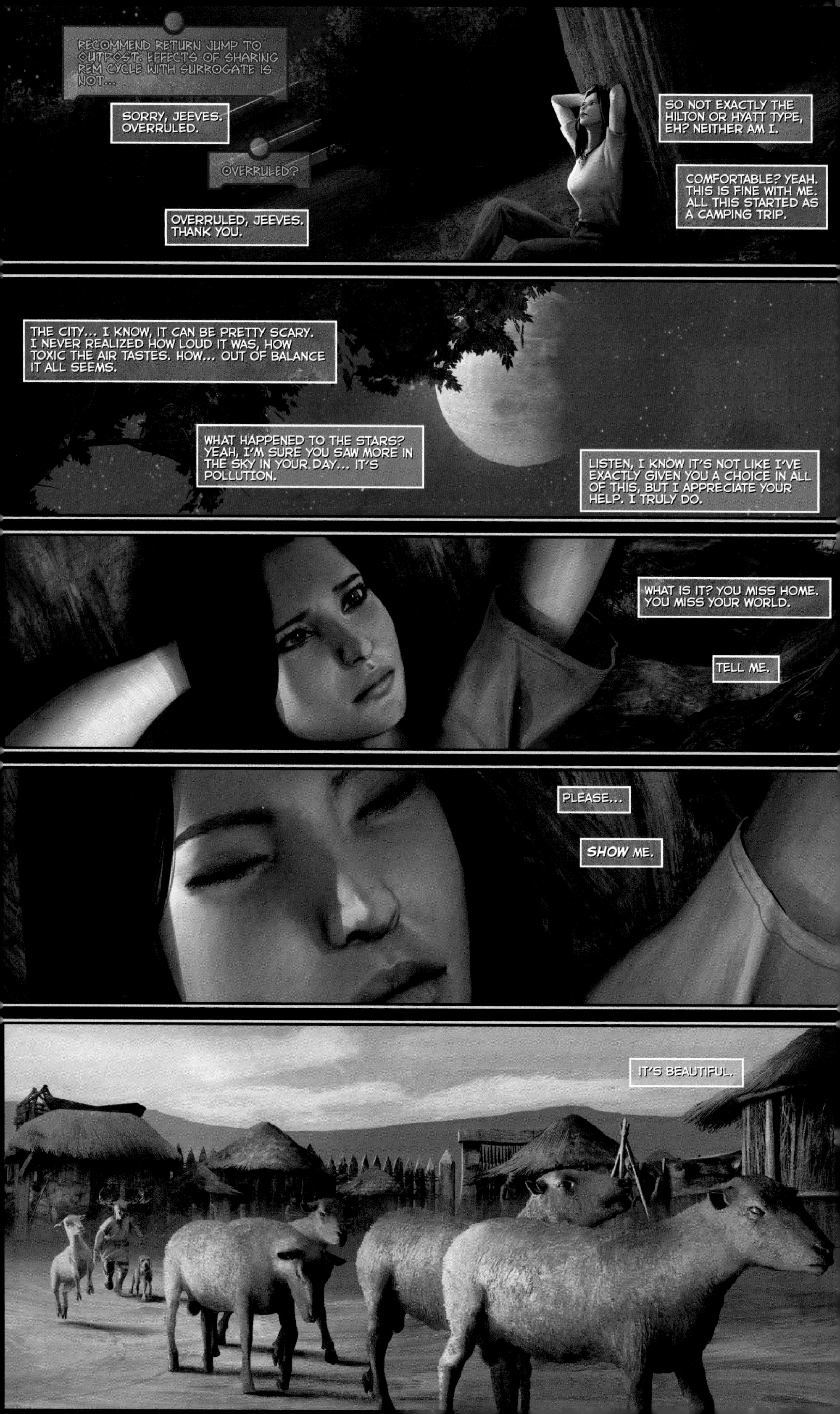

RECOMMEND RETURN JUMP TO OUTPOST. EFFECTS OF SHARING REM CYCLE WITH SURROGATE IS NOT...
SORRY, JEEVES. OVERRULED.
OVERRULED?
OVERRULED, JEEVES. THANK YOU.
SO NOT EXACTLY THE HILTON OR HYATT TYPE, EH? NEITHER AM I.
COMFORTABLE? YEAH. THIS IS FINE WITH ME. ALL THIS STARTED AS A CAMPING TRIP.
THE CITY... I KNOW, IT CAN BE PRETTY SCARY. I NEVER REALIZED HOW LOUD IT WAS, HOW TOXIC THE AIR TASTES. HOW... OUT OF BALANCE IT ALL SEEMS.
WHAT HAPPENED TO THE STARS? YEAH, I'M SURE YOU SAW MORE IN THE SKY IN YOUR DAY... IT'S POLLUTION.
LISTEN, I KNOW IT'S NOT LIKE I'VE EXACTLY GIVEN YOU A CHOICE IN ALL OF THIS, BUT I APPRECIATE YOUR HELP. I TRULY DO.
WHAT IS IT? YOU MISS HOME. YOU MISS YOUR WORLD.
TELL ME.
PLEASE...
SHOW ME.
IT'S BEAUTIFUL.

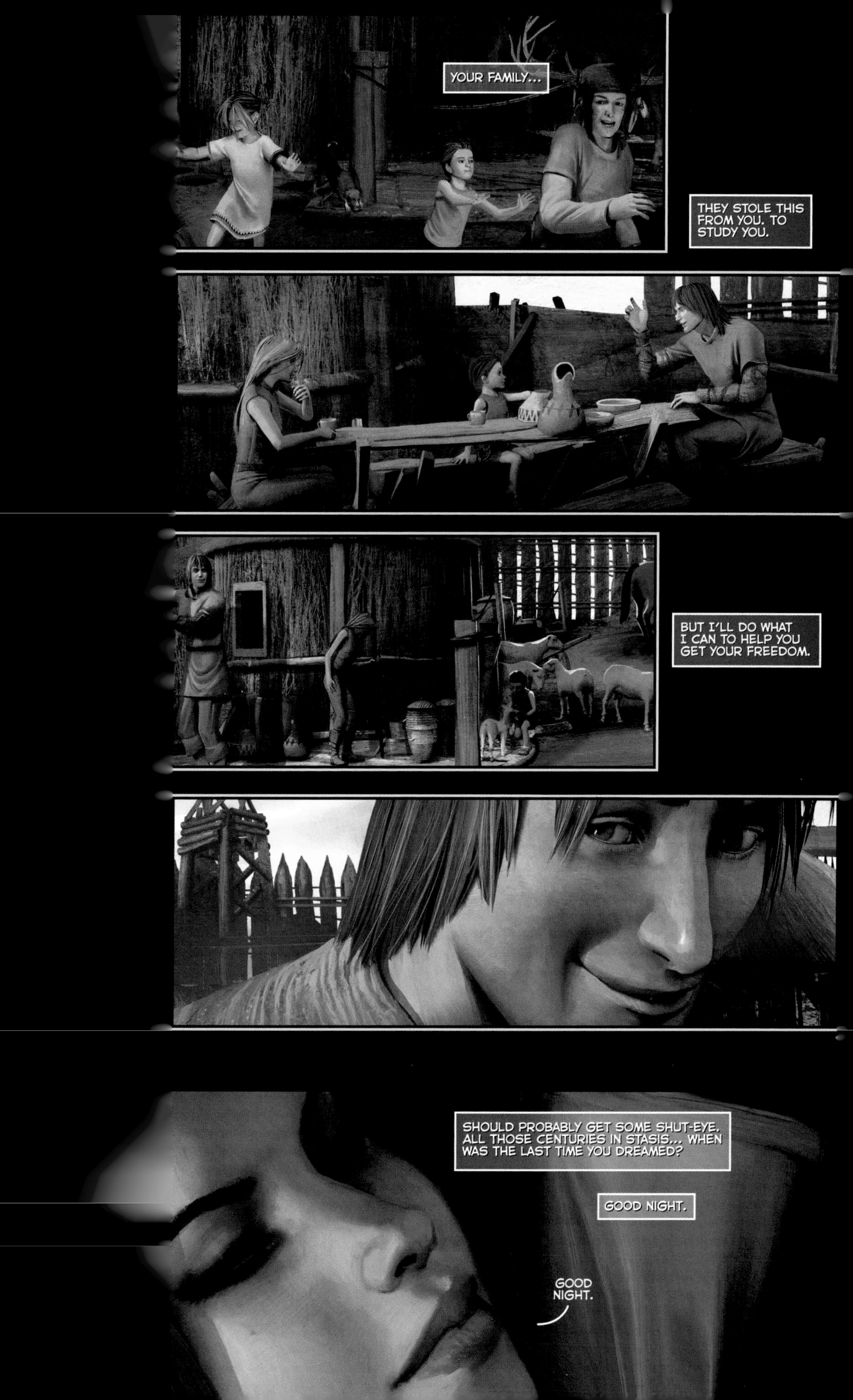
YOUR FAMILY...
THEY STOLE THIS FROM YOU. TO STUDY YOU.
BUT I'LL DO WHAT I CAN TO HELP YOU GET YOUR FREEDOM.
SHOULD PROBABLY GET SOME SHUT-EYE. ALL THOSE CENTURIES IN STASIS... WHEN WAS THE LAST TIME YOU DREAMED?
GOOD NIGHT.
GOOD NIGHT.

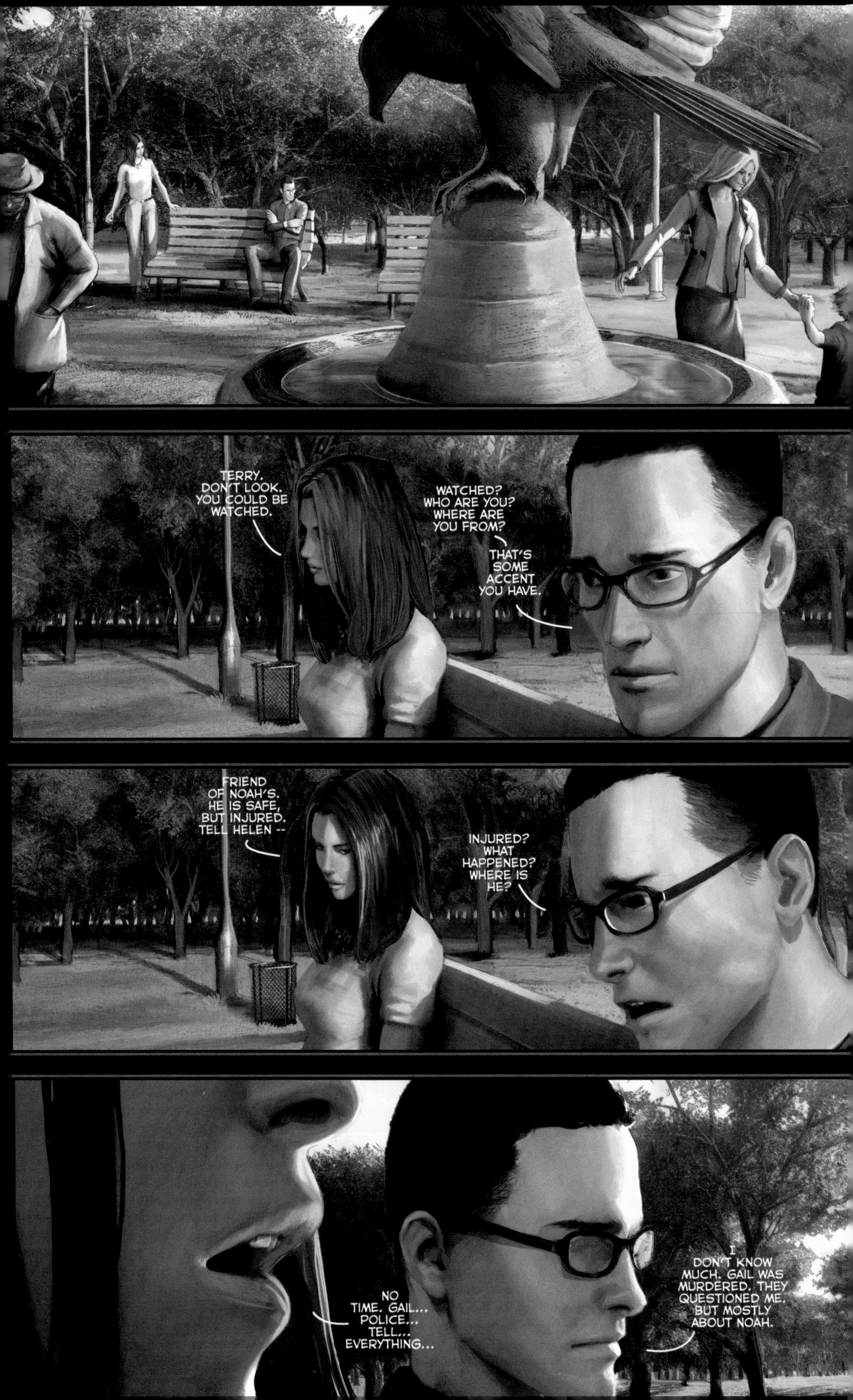
TERRY. DON'T LOOK. YOU COULD BE WATCHED.
WATCHED? WHO ARE YOU? WHERE ARE YOU FROM?
THAT'S SOME ACCENT YOU HAVE.
FRIEND OF NOAH'S. HE IS SAFE, BUT INJURED. TELL HELEN --
INJURED? WHAT HAPPENED? WHERE IS HE?
NO TIME. GAIL... POLICE... TELL... EVERYTHING...
I DON'T KNOW MUCH. GAIL WAS MURDERED. THEY QUESTIONED ME. BUT MOSTLY ABOUT NOAH.

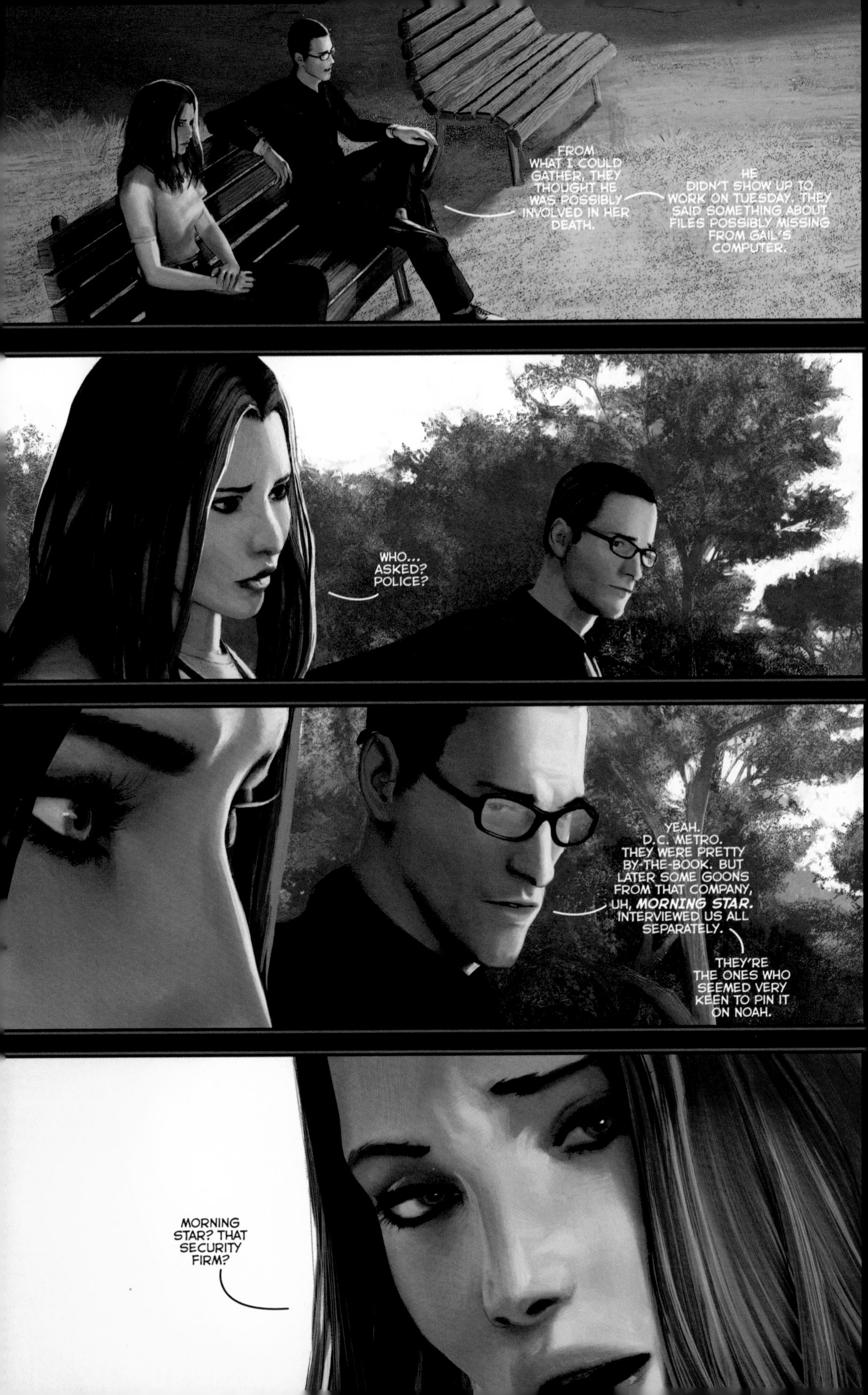
FROM WHAT I COULD GATHER, THEY THOUGHT HE WAS POSSIBLY INVOLVED IN HER DEATH.
HE DIDN'T SHOW UP TO WORK ON TUESDAY. THEY SAID SOMETHING ABOUT FILES POSSIBLY MISSING FROM GAIL'S COMPUTER.
WHO... ASKED? POLICE?
YEAH. D.C. METRO. THEY WERE PRETTY BY-THE-BOOK. BUT LATER SOME GOONS FROM THAT COMPANY, UH, MORNING STAR, INTERVIEWED US ALL SEPARATELY.
THEY'RE THE ONES WHO SEEMED VERY KEEN TO PIN IT ON NOAH.
MORNING STAR? THAT SECURITY FIRM?

YEAH, I GUESS THEY DO A LOT OF PRIVATE SECURITY STUFF WITH THE D.O.D., INCLUDING OUR DEPARTMENT.

ANYWAY, THEY KEPT ASKING QUESTIONS ABOUT NOAH. LIKE, "DID HE SEEM DISSATISFIED AT WORK?"

"DID HE VOICE ANTI-AMERICAN VIEWS? DID HE ACT SUSPICIOUS? DID HE HAVE MONEY PROBLEMS?"

WHAT DID YOU SAY?

I SAID HE MAKES CLARK KENT LOOK LIKE CHARLIE SHEEN.

I SAID THAT HE LOVED HIS JOB AND CARED ABOUT THE WORK. IT WASN'T JUST A PAYCHECK TO HIM.

THEN THEY ASKED A LOT ABOUT HELEN. HER BACKGROUND. IMMIGRATION STATUS, FAMILY TIES, STUFF LIKE THAT.

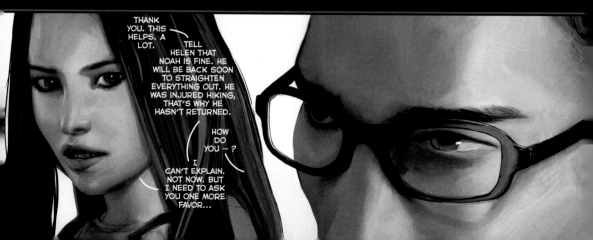

THANK YOU. THIS HELPS. A LOT.

TELL HELEN THAT NOAH IS FINE. HE WILL BE BACK SOON TO STRAIGHTEN EVERYTHING OUT. HE WAS INJURED HIKING, THAT'S WHY HE HASN'T RETURNED.

HOW DO YOU -- ?

I CAN'T EXPLAIN. NOT NOW. BUT I NEED TO ASK YOU ONE MORE FAVOR...

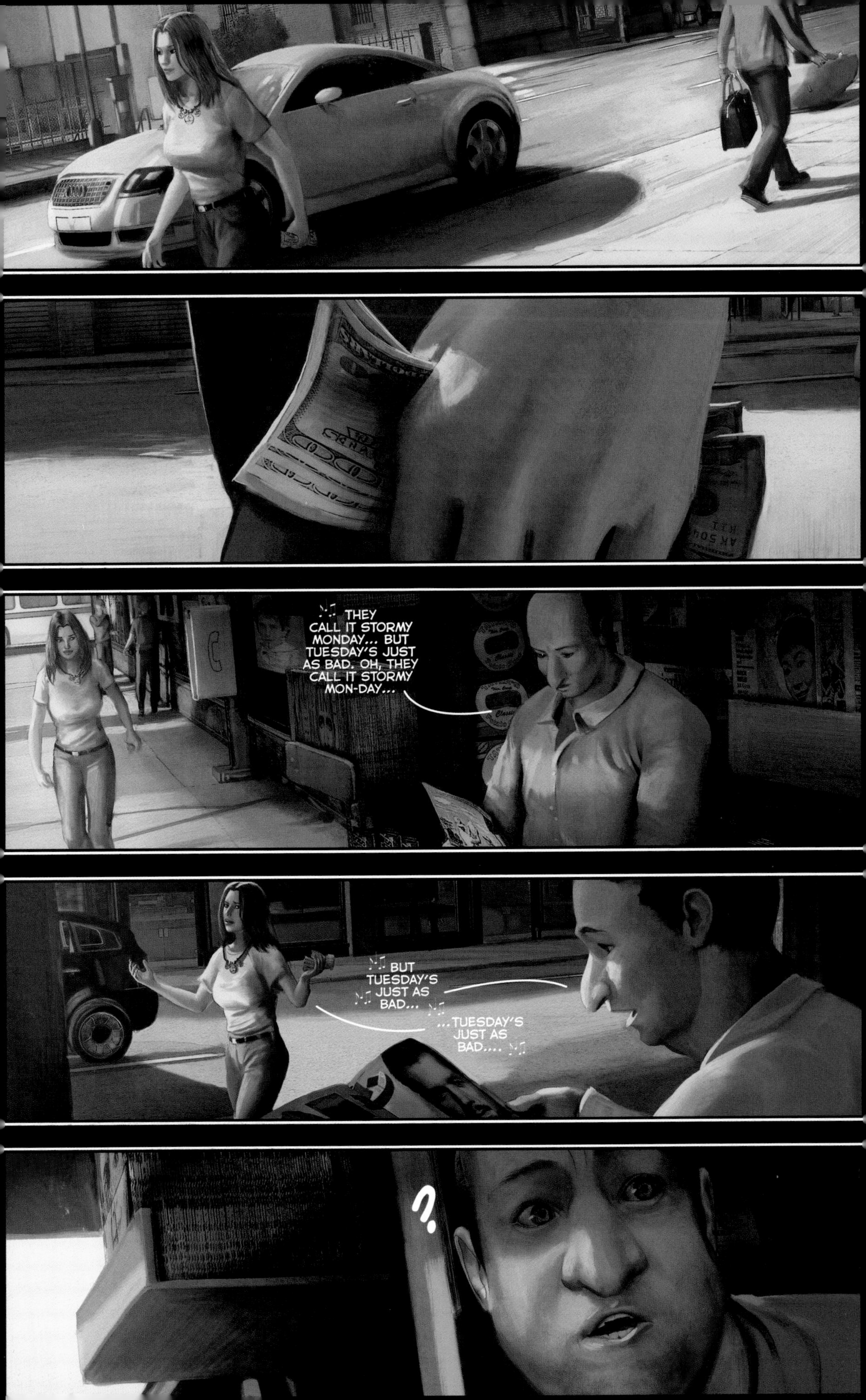
THEY CALL IT STORMY MONDAY... BUT TUESDAY'S JUST AS BAD. OH, THEY CALL IT STORMY MON-DAY...
BUT TUESDAY'S JUST AS BAD...
...TUESDAY'S JUST AS BAD....
?

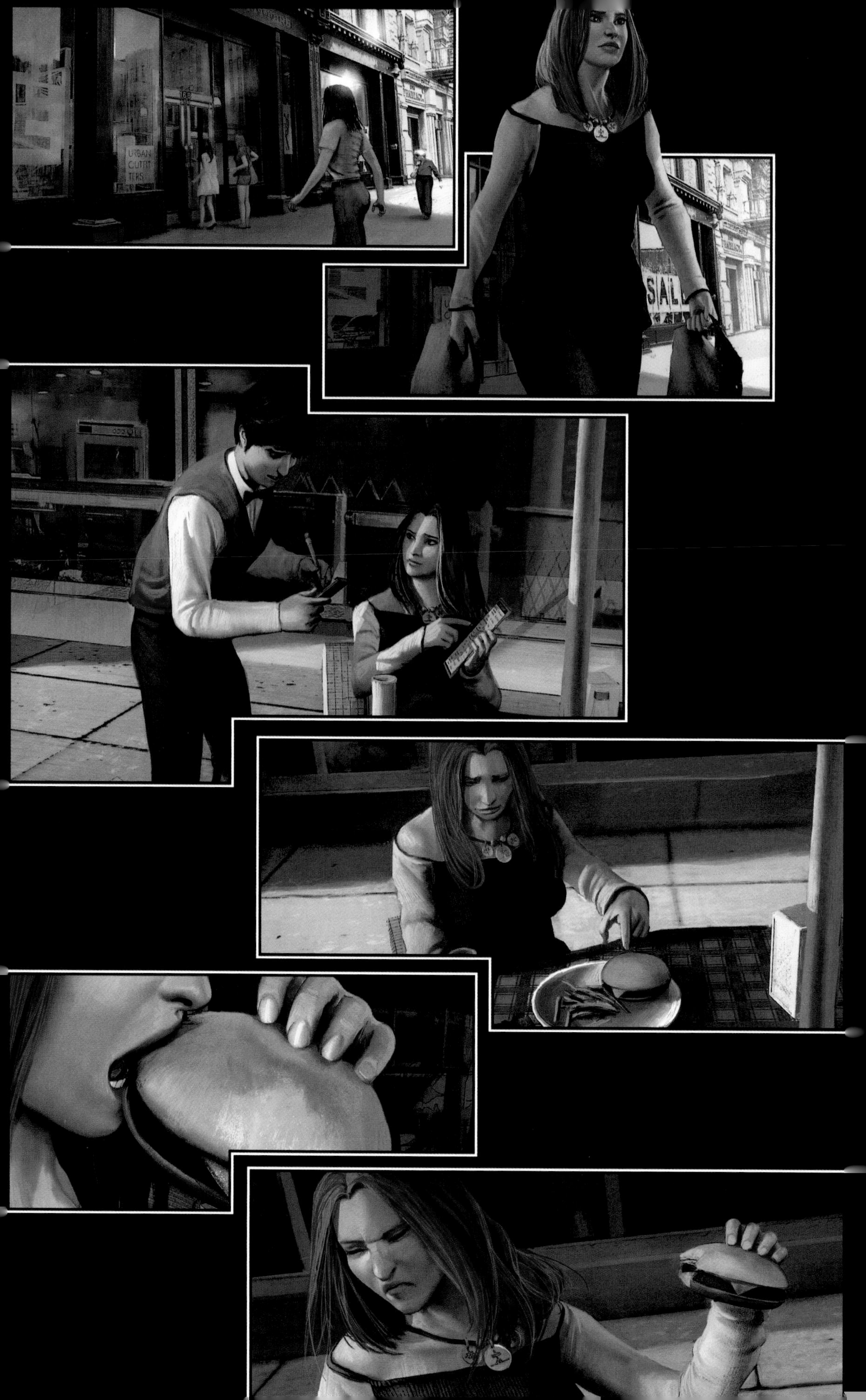
URBAN
OUTFIT
TERS

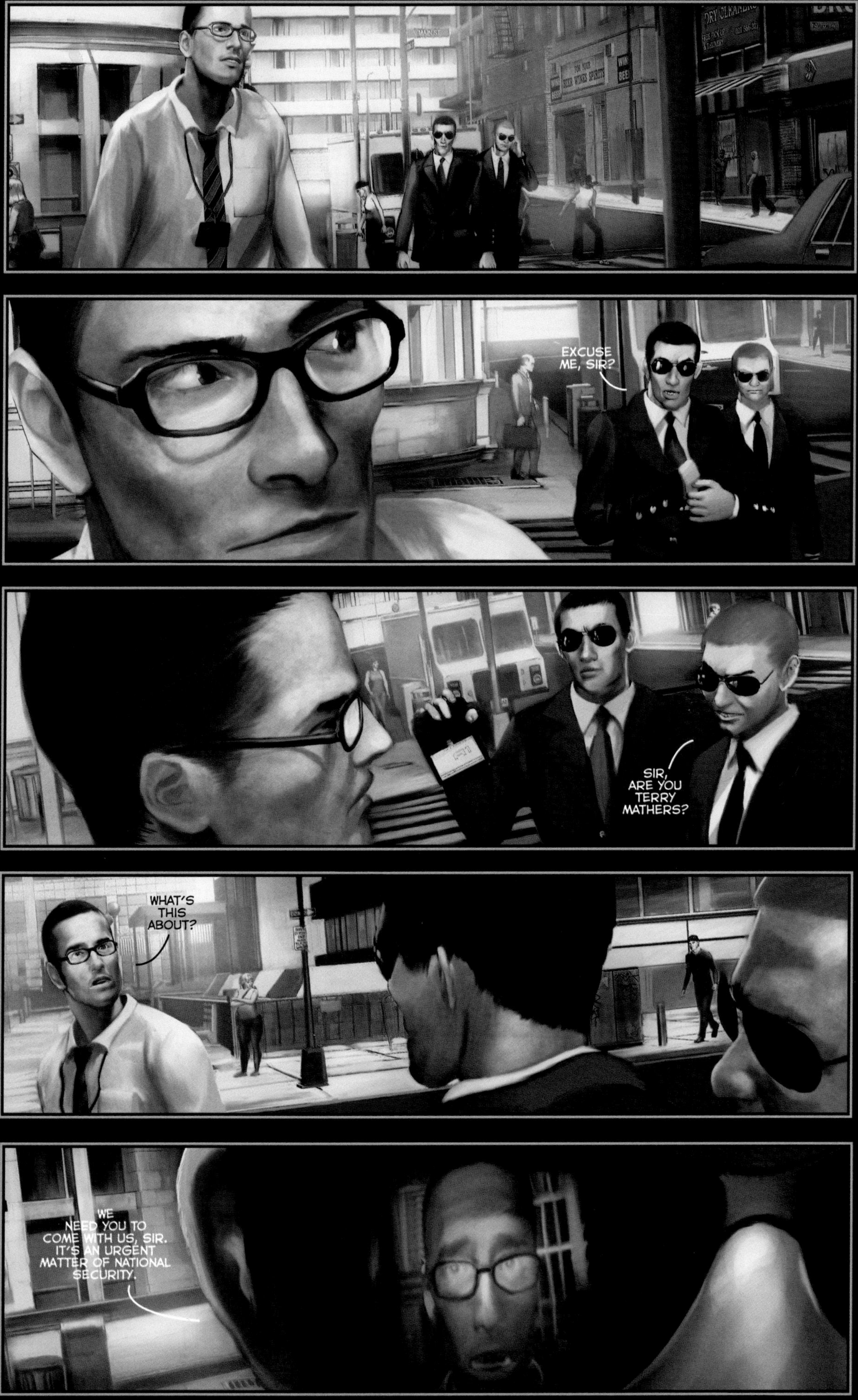
EXCUSE ME, SIR?
SIR, ARE YOU TERRY MATHERS?
WHAT'S THIS ABOUT?
WE NEED YOU TO COME WITH US, SIR. IT'S AN URGENT MATTER OF NATIONAL SECURITY.

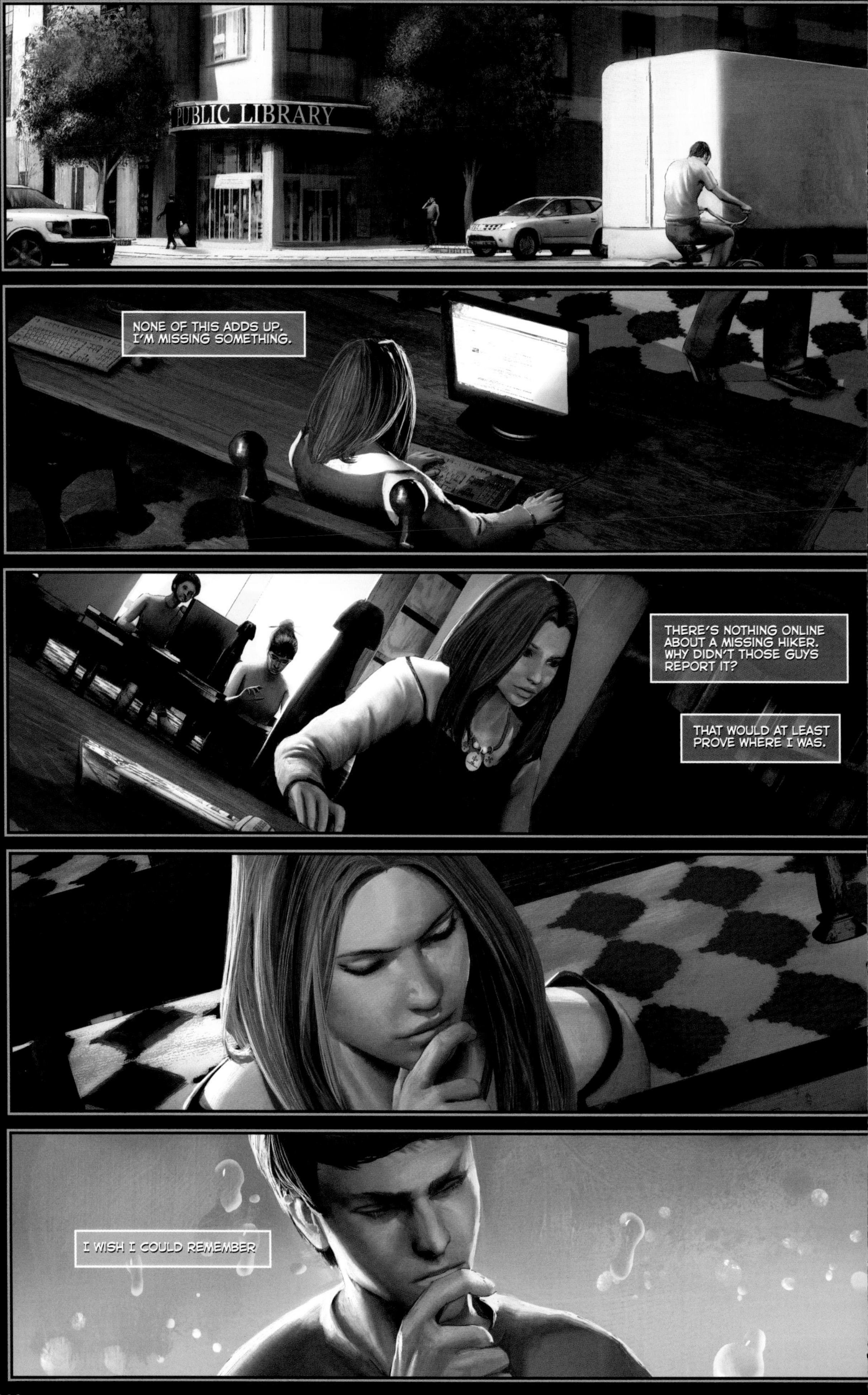
PUBLIC LIBRARY
NONE OF THIS ADDS UP. I'M MISSING SOMETHING.
THERE'S NOTHING ONLINE ABOUT A MISSING HIKER. WHY DIDN'T THOSE GUYS REPORT IT?
THAT WOULD AT LEAST PROVE WHERE I WAS.
I WISH I COULD REMEMBER

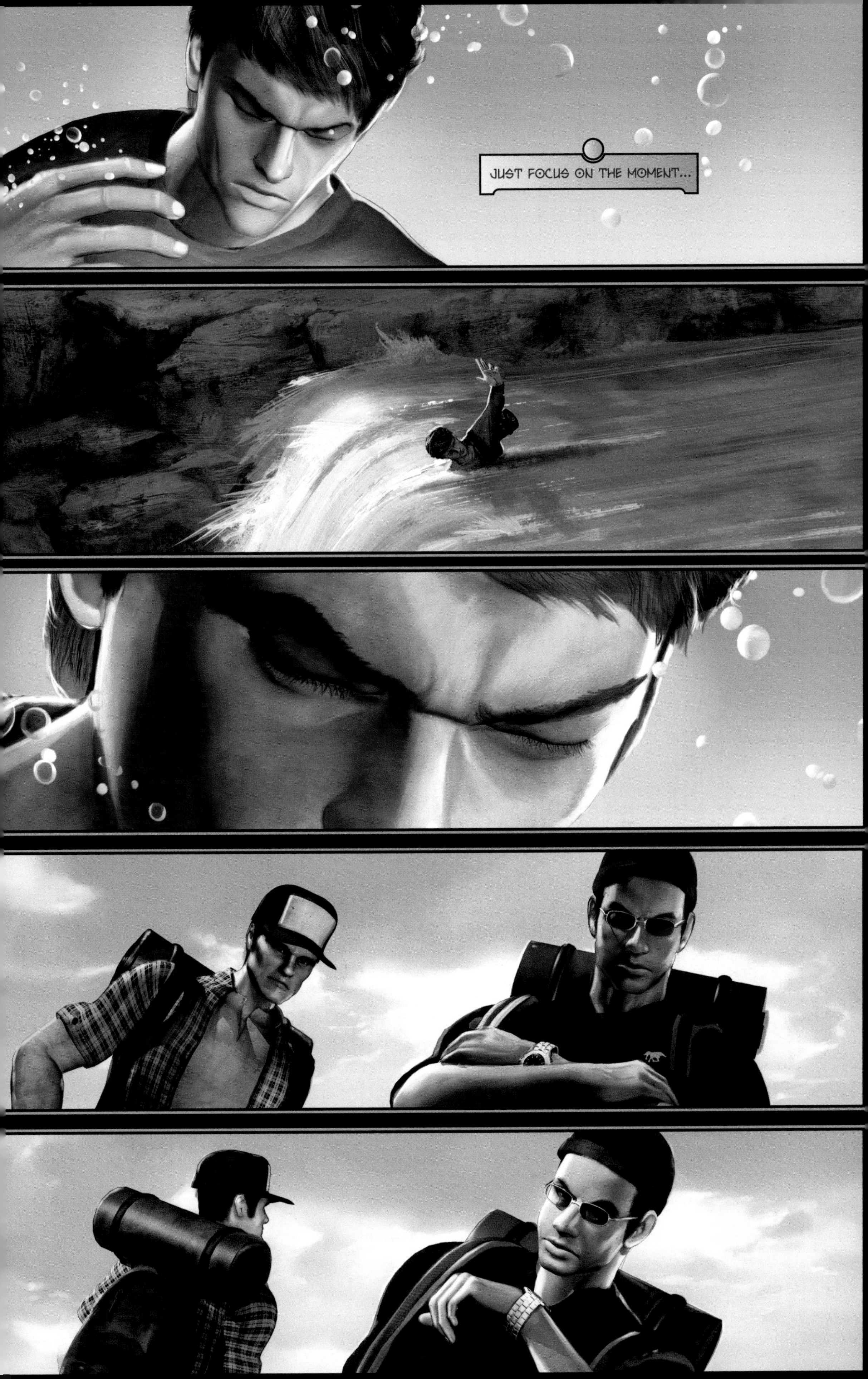
JUST FOCUS ON THE MOMENT...

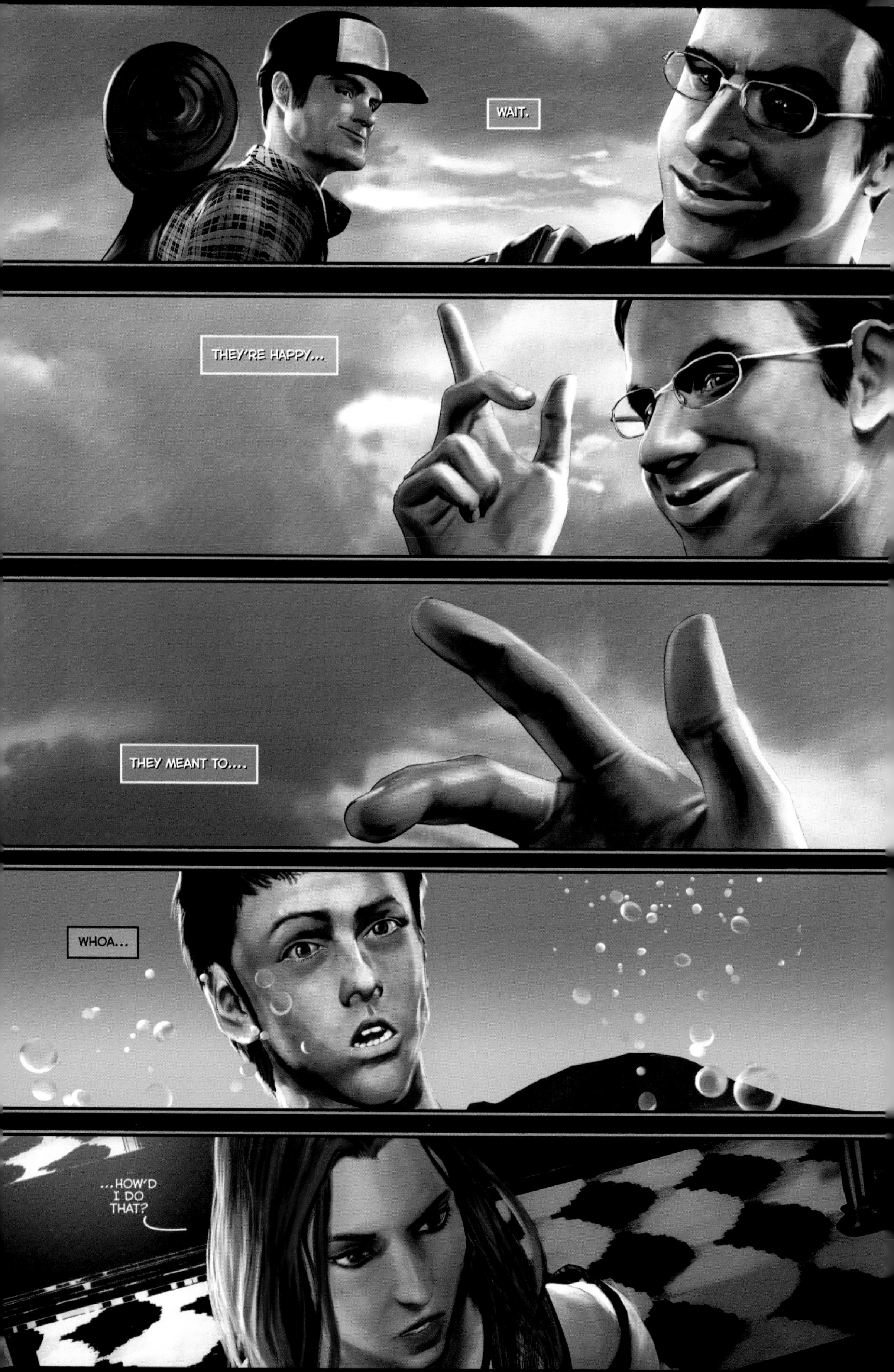
WAIT.
THEY'RE HAPPY...
THEY MEANT TO....
WHOA...
...HOW'D I DO THAT?

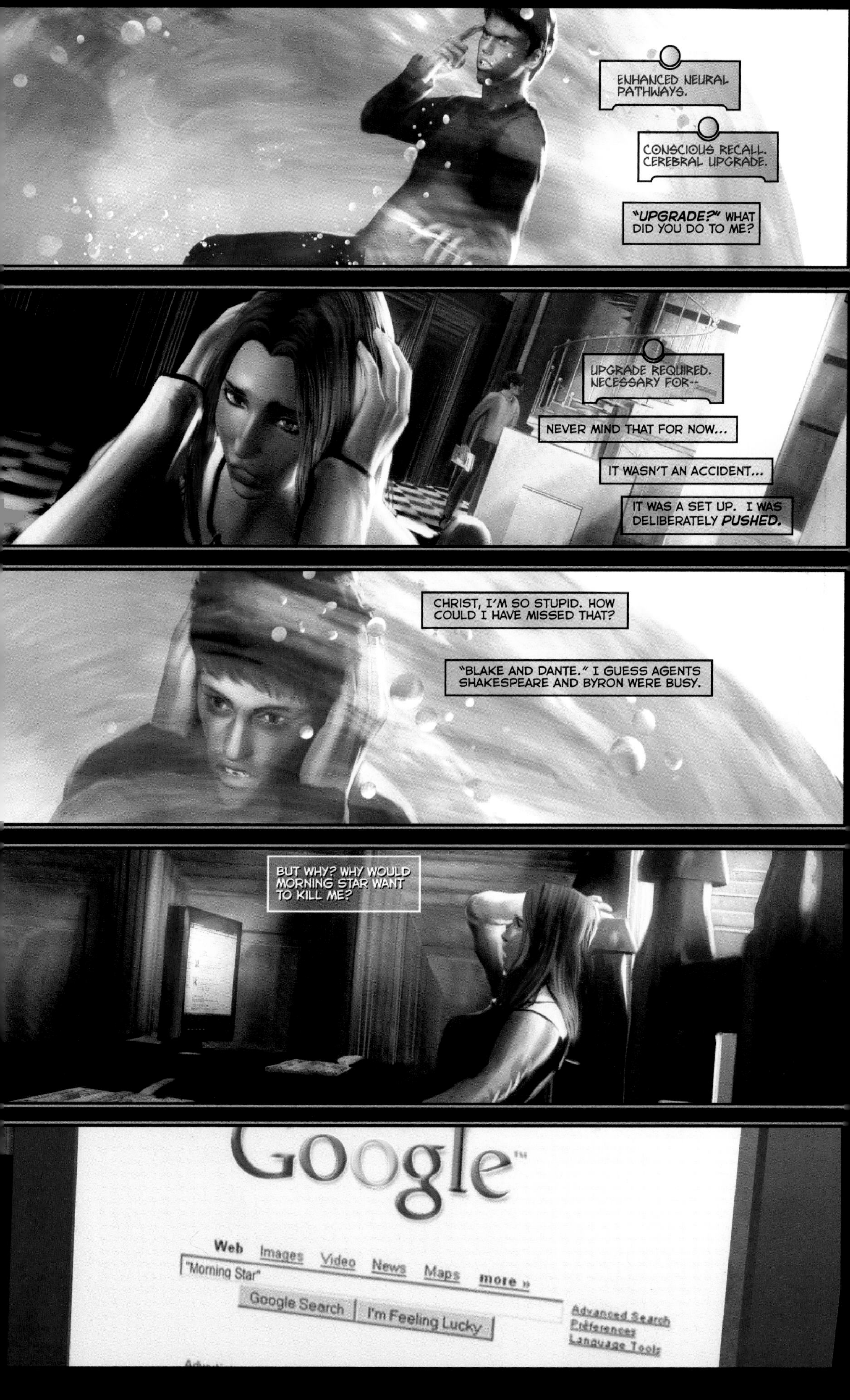
ENHANCED NEURAL PATHWAYS.
CONSCIOUS RECALL. CEREBRAL UPGRADE.
"UPGRADE?" WHAT DID YOU DO TO ME?
UPGRADE REQUIRED. NECESSARY FOR--
NEVER MIND THAT FOR NOW...
IT WASN'T AN ACCIDENT...
IT WAS A SET UP. I WAS DELIBERATELY PUSHED.
CHRIST, I'M SO STUPID. HOW COULD I HAVE MISSED THAT?
"BLAKE AND DANTE." I GUESS AGENTS SHAKESPEARE AND BYRON WERE BUSY.
BUT WHY? WHY WOULD MORNING STAR WANT TO KILL ME?
Google™
Web Images Video News Maps more »
"Morning Star"
Google Search
I'm Feeling Lucky
Advanced Search
Preferences
Language Tools

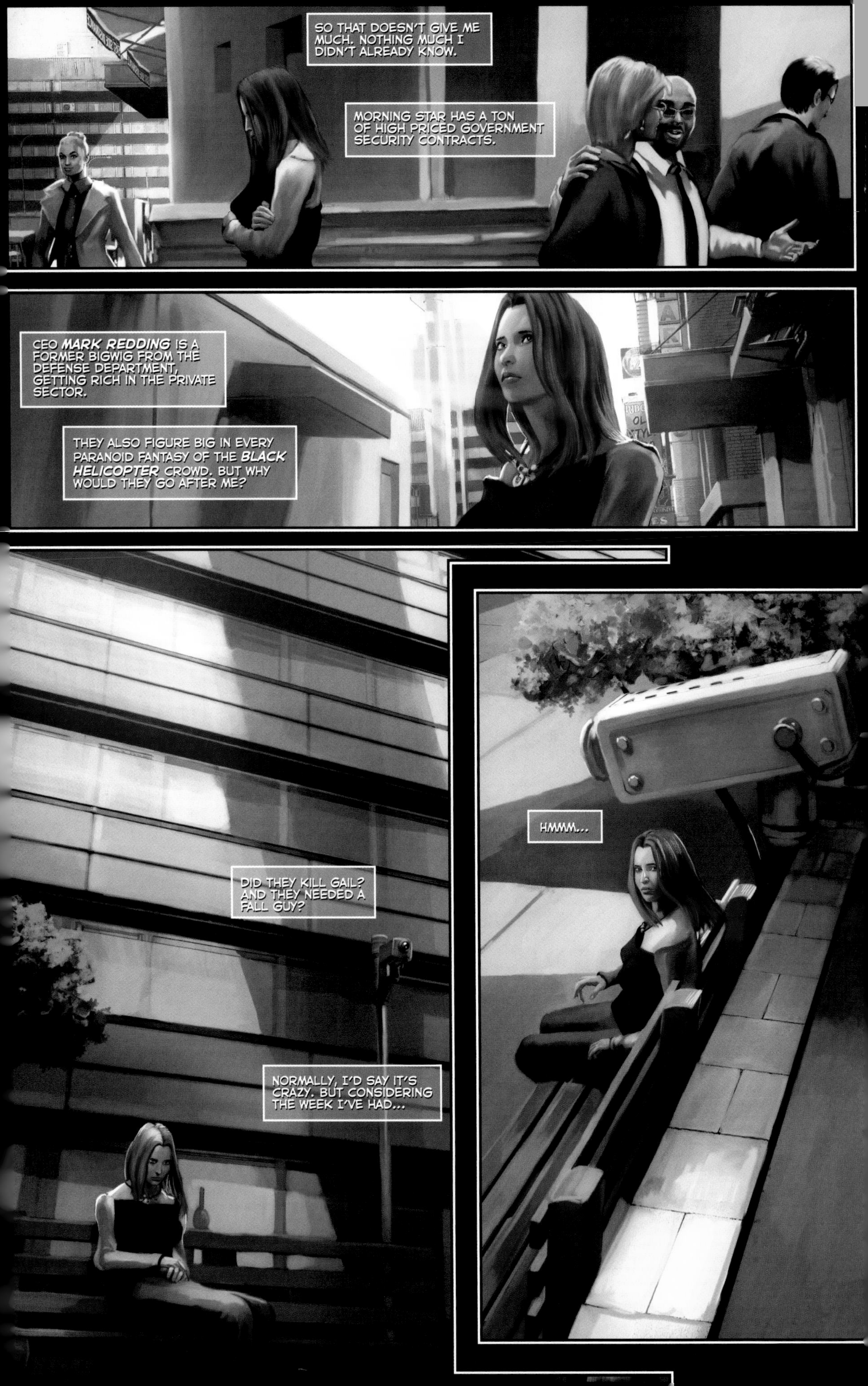

SO THAT DOESN'T GIVE ME MUCH. NOTHING MUCH I DIDN'T ALREADY KNOW.
MORNING STAR HAS A TON OF HIGH PRICED GOVERNMENT SECURITY CONTRACTS.
CEO MARK REDDING IS A FORMER BIGWIG FROM THE DEFENSE DEPARTMENT, GETTING RICH IN THE PRIVATE SECTOR.
THEY ALSO FIGURE BIG IN EVERY PARANOID FANTASY OF THE BLACK HELICOPTER CROWD. BUT WHY WOULD THEY GO AFTER ME?
DID THEY KILL GAIL? AND THEY NEEDED A FALL GUY?
NORMALLY, I'D SAY IT'S CRAZY. BUT CONSIDERING THE WEEK I'VE HAD...
HMMM...

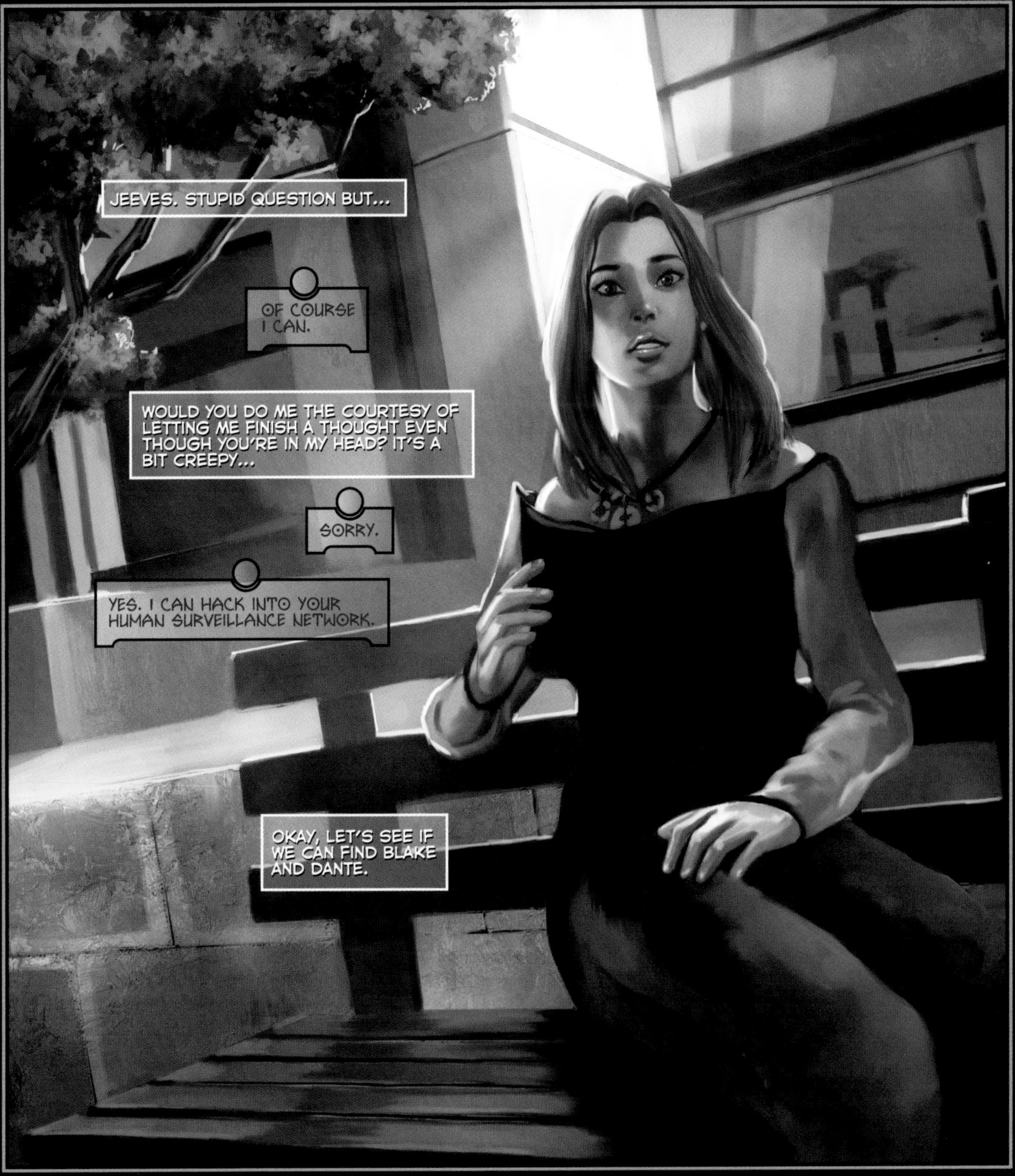
JEEVES. STUPID QUESTION BUT...
OF COURSE I CAN.
WOULD YOU DO ME THE COURTESY OF LETTING ME FINISH A THOUGHT EVEN THOUGH YOU'RE IN MY HEAD? IT'S A BIT CREEPY...
SORRY.
YES. I CAN HACK INTO YOUR HUMAN SURVEILLANCE NETWORK.
OKAY, LET'S SEE IF WE CAN FIND BLAKE AND DANTE.

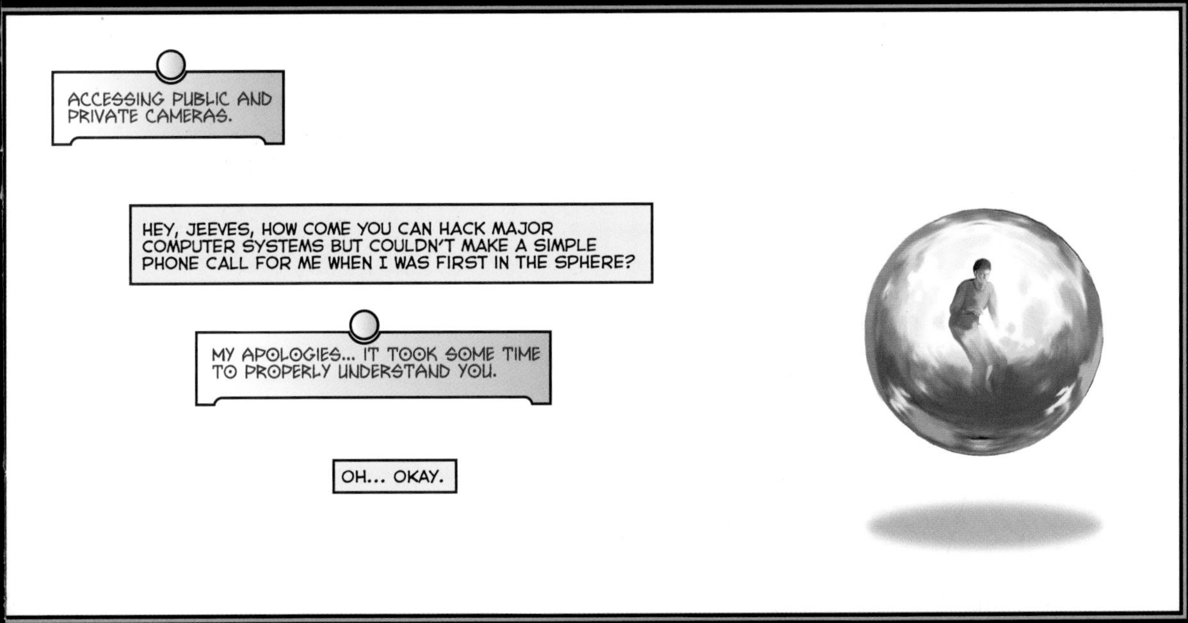
ACCESSING PUBLIC AND PRIVATE CAMERAS.
HEY, JEEVES, HOW COME YOU CAN HACK MAJOR COMPUTER SYSTEMS BUT COULDN'T MAKE A SIMPLE PHONE CALL FOR ME WHEN I WAS FIRST IN THE SPHERE?
MY APOLOGIES... IT TOOK SOME TIME TO PROPERLY UNDERSTAND YOU.
OH... OKAY.

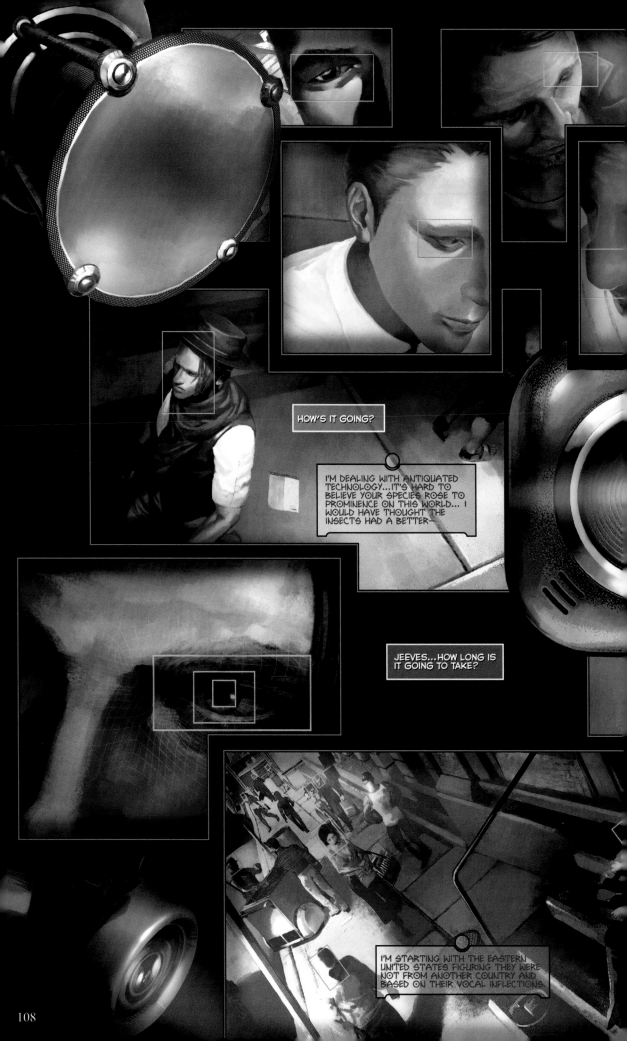

HOW'S IT GOING?

I'M DEALING WITH ANTIQUATED TECHNOLOGY...IT'S HARD TO BELIEVE YOUR SPECIES ROSE TO PROMINENCE ON THIS WORLD... I WOULD HAVE THOUGHT THE INSECTS HAD A BETTER—

JEEVES...HOW LONG IS IT GOING TO TAKE?

I'M STARTING WITH THE EASTERN UNITED STATES FIGURING THEY WERE NOT FROM ANOTHER COUNTRY AND BASED ON THEIR VOCAL INFLECTIONS.

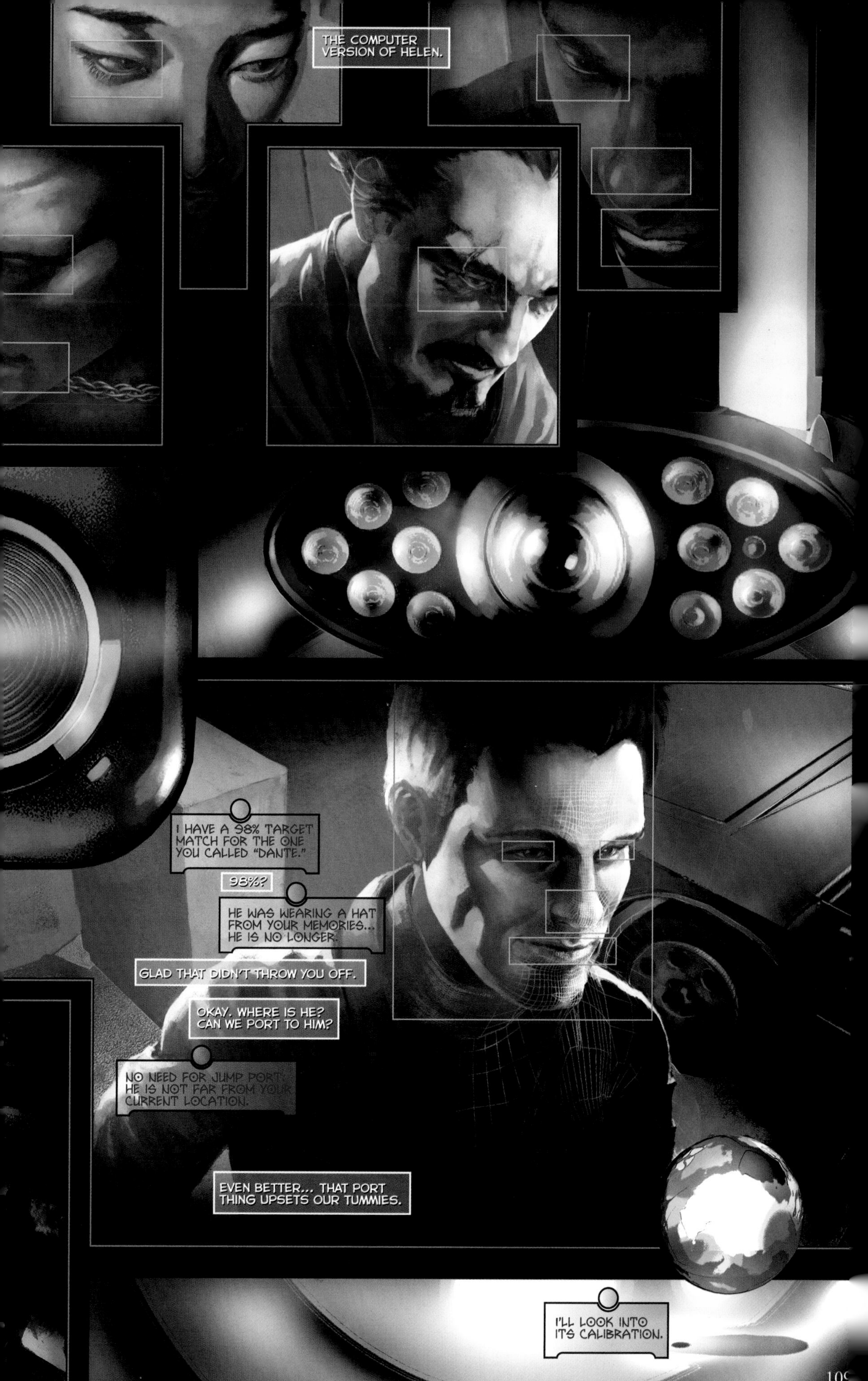
THE COMPUTER VERSION OF HELEN.
I HAVE A 98% TARGET MATCH FOR THE ONE YOU CALLED "DANTE."
98%?
HE WAS WEARING A HAT FROM YOUR MEMORIES... HE IS NO LONGER.
GLAD THAT DIDN'T THROW YOU OFF.
OKAY. WHERE IS HE? CAN WE PORT TO HIM?
NO NEED FOR JUMP PORT. HE IS NOT FAR FROM YOUR CURRENT LOCATION.
EVEN BETTER... THAT PORT THING UPSETS OUR TUMMIES.
I'LL LOOK INTO ITS CALIBRATION.

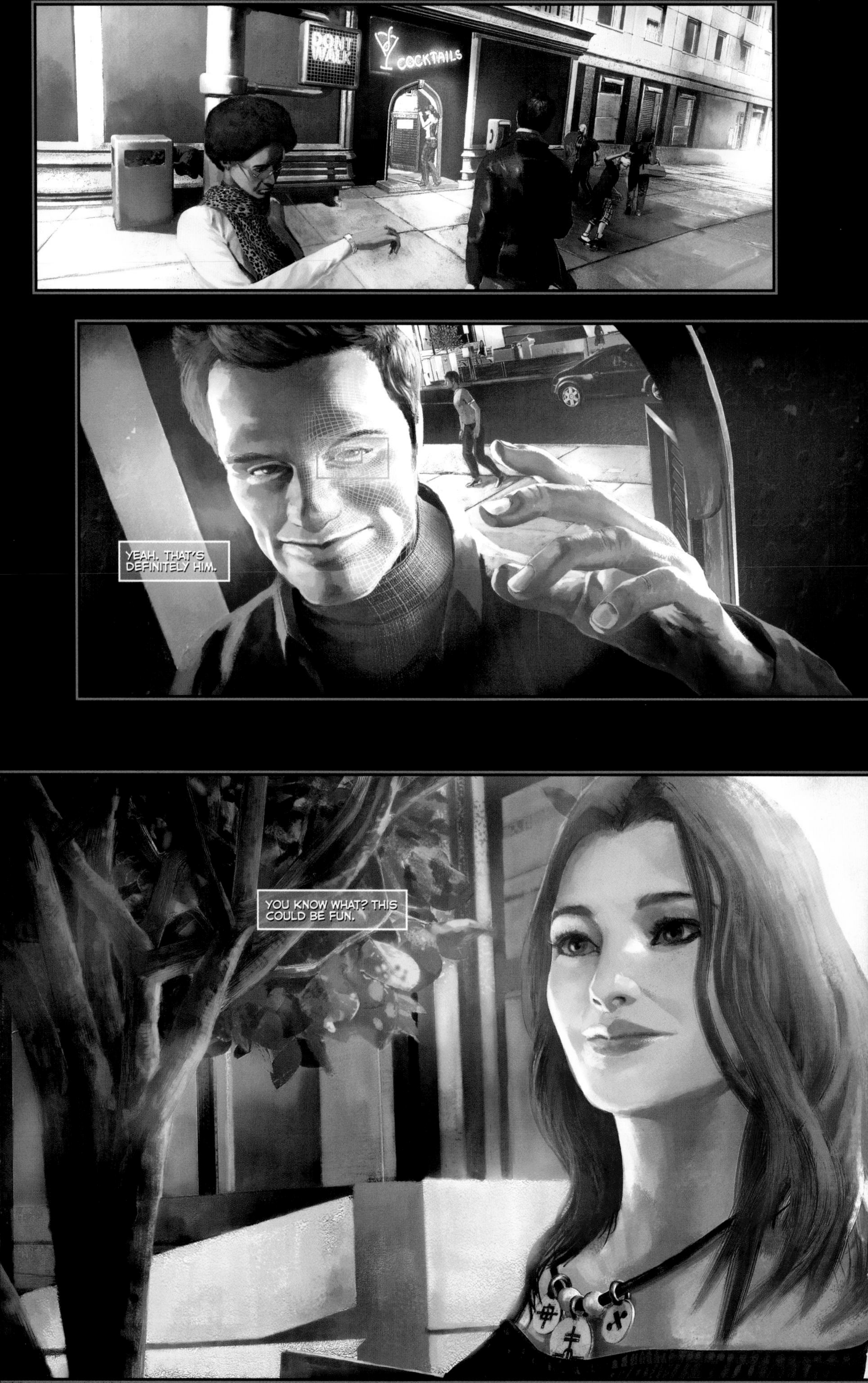
DONT WALK
COCKTAILS
YEAH. THAT'S DEFINITELY HIM.
YOU KNOW WHAT? THIS COULD BE FUN.

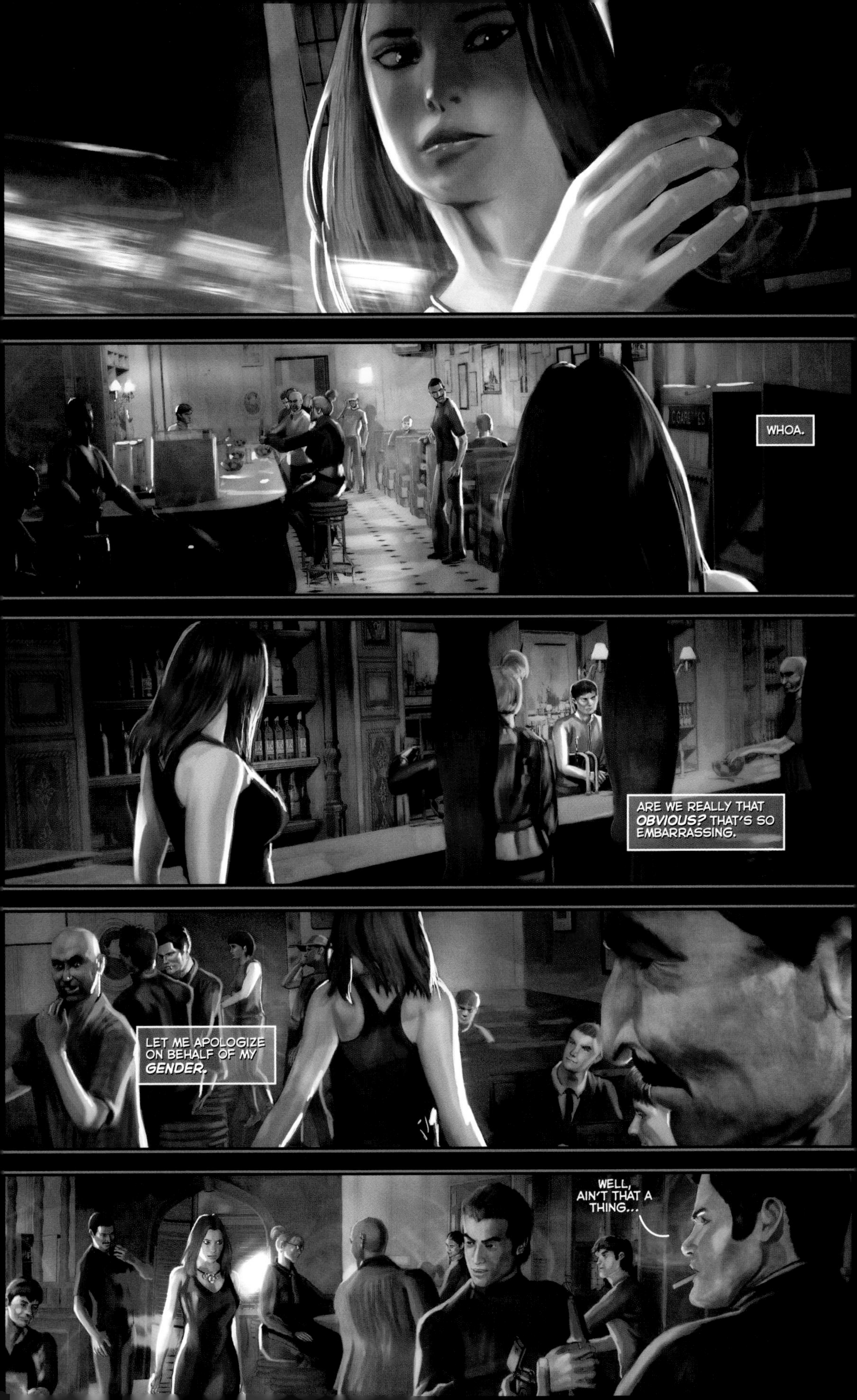

WHOA.
ARE WE REALLY THAT OBVIOUS? THAT'S SO EMBARRASSING.
LET ME APOLOGIZE ON BEHALF OF MY GENDER.
WELL, AIN'T THAT A THING...

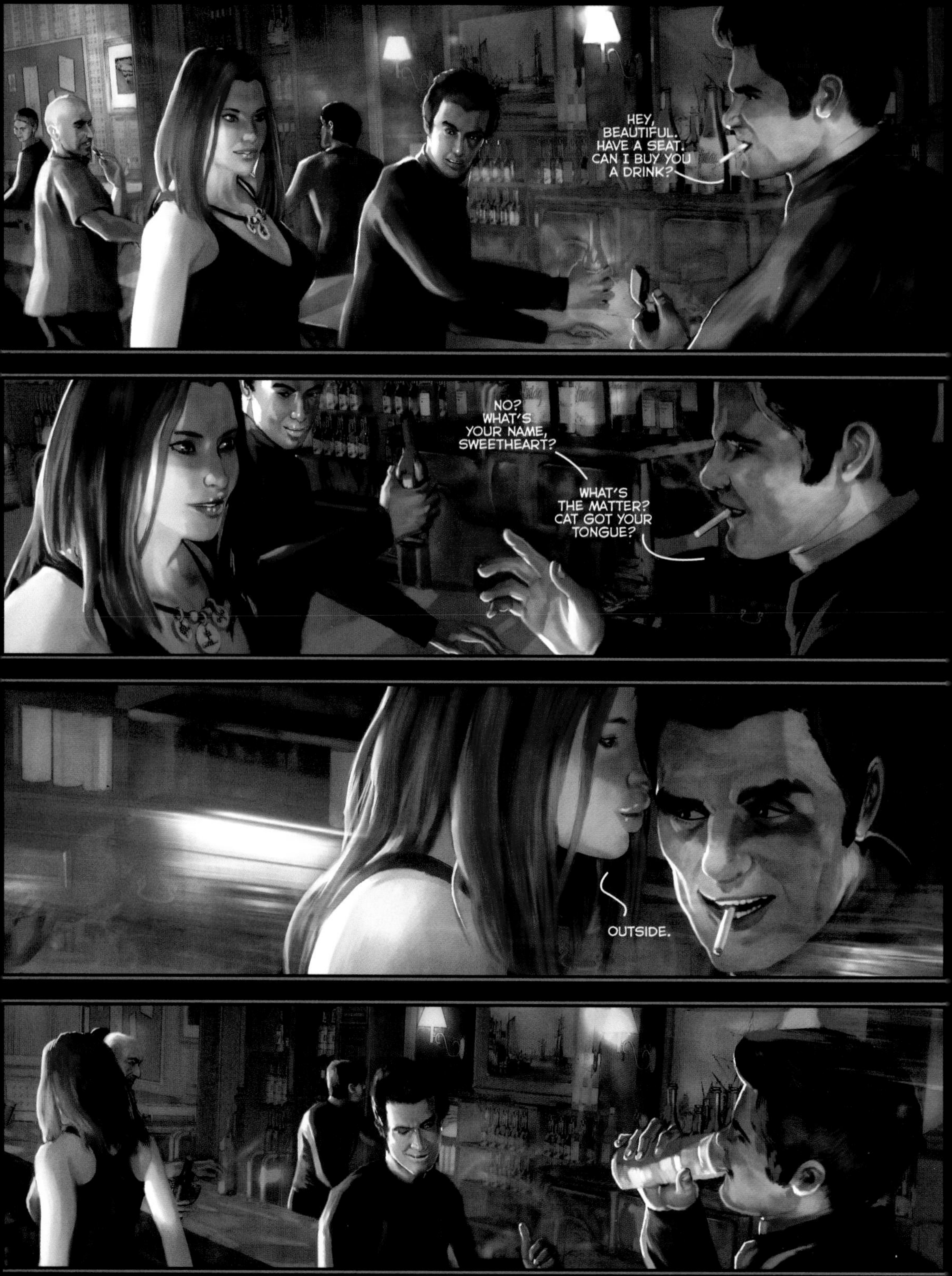
HEY, BEAUTIFUL. HAVE A SEAT. CAN I BUY YOU A DRINK?
NO? WHAT'S YOUR NAME, SWEETHEART?
WHAT'S THE MATTER? CAT GOT YOUR TONGUE?
OUTSIDE.

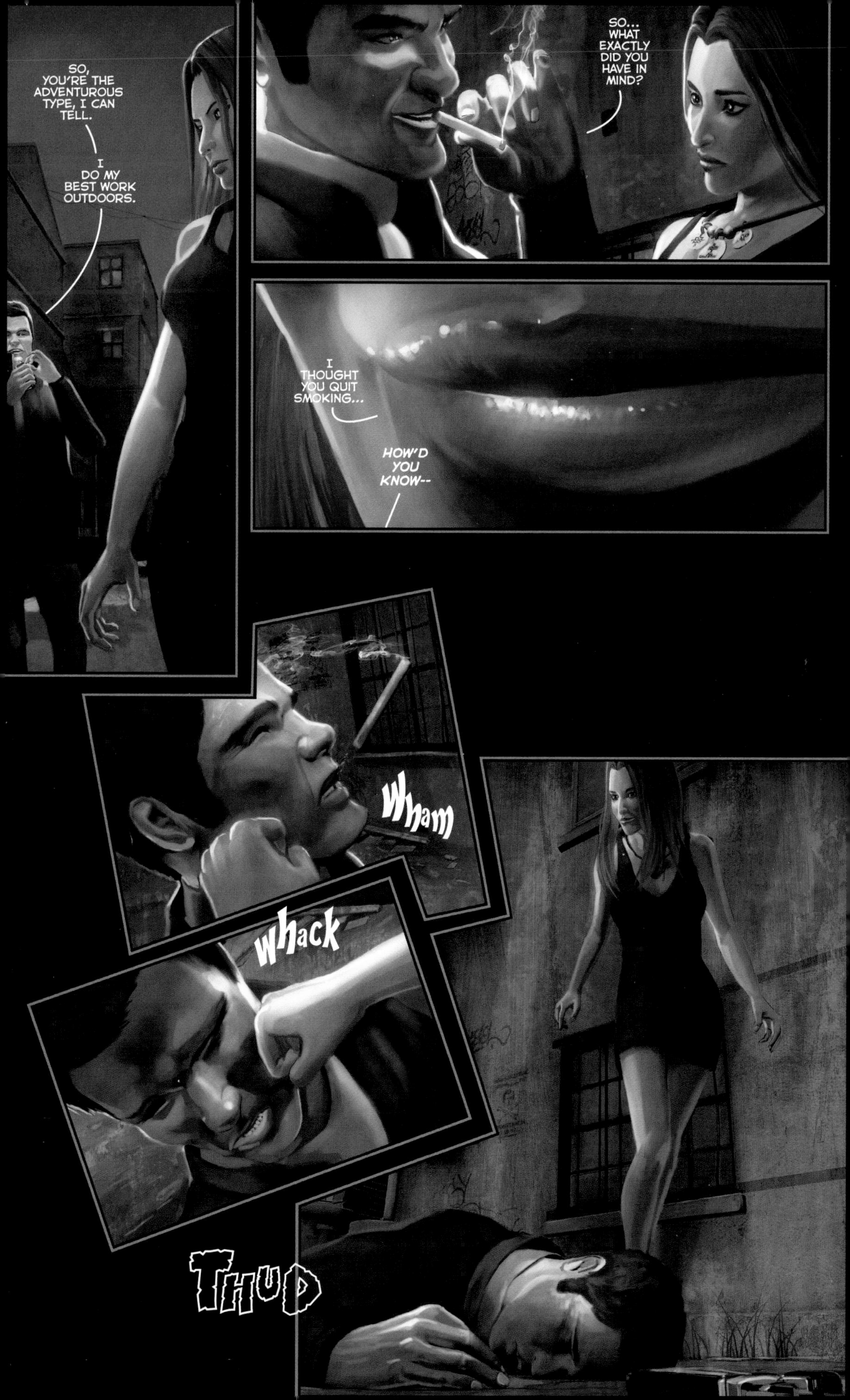
SO, YOU'RE THE ADVENTUROUS TYPE, I CAN TELL.
I DO MY BEST WORK OUTDOORS.
SO... WHAT EXACTLY DID YOU HAVE IN MIND?
I THOUGHT YOU QUIT SMOKING...
HOW'D YOU KNOW--
WHAM
WHACK
THUD

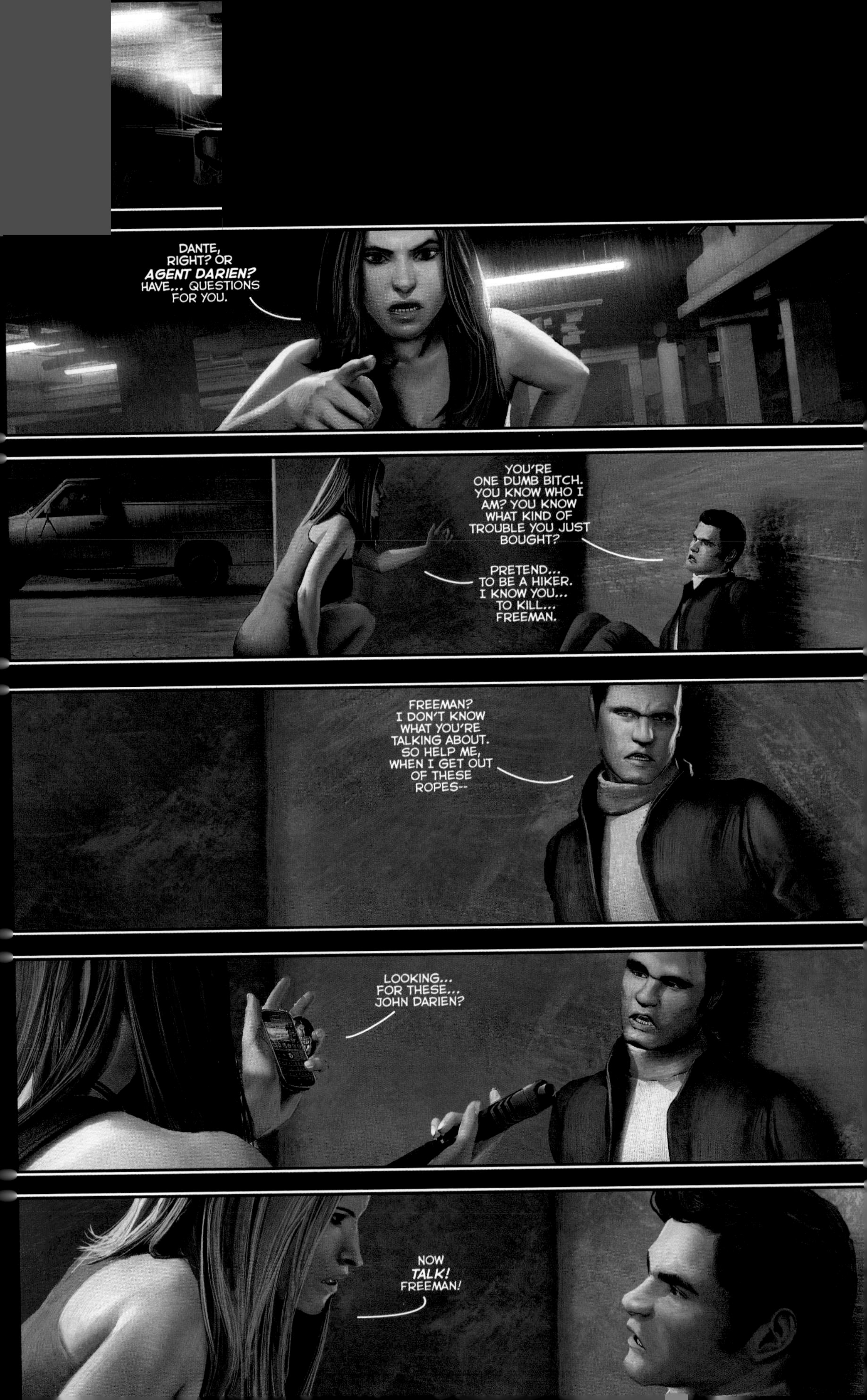
DANTE, RIGHT? OR AGENT DARIEN? HAVE... QUESTIONS FOR YOU.
YOU'RE ONE DUMB BITCH. YOU KNOW WHO I AM? YOU KNOW WHAT KIND OF TROUBLE YOU JUST BOUGHT?
PRETEND... TO BE A HIKER. I KNOW YOU... TO KILL... FREEMAN.
FREEMAN? I DON'T KNOW WHAT YOU'RE TALKING ABOUT. SO HELP ME, WHEN I GET OUT OF THESE ROPES--
LOOKING... FOR THESE... JOHN DARIEN?
NOW TALK! FREEMAN!

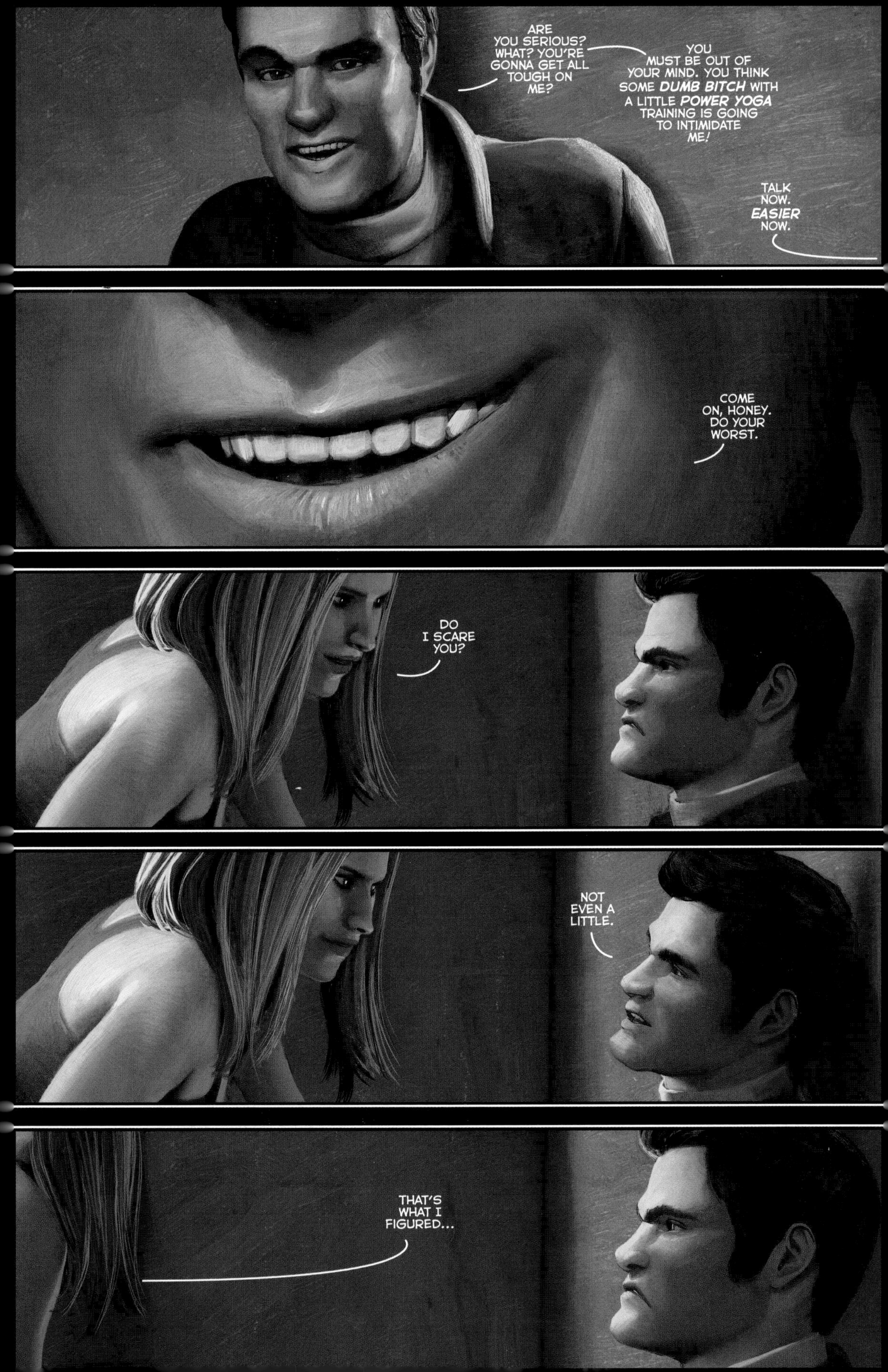
ARE YOU SERIOUS? WHAT? YOU'RE GONNA GET ALL TOUGH ON ME?
YOU MUST BE OUT OF YOUR MIND. YOU THINK SOME DUMB BITCH WITH A LITTLE POWER YOGA TRAINING IS GOING TO INTIMIDATE ME!
TALK NOW. EASIER NOW.
COME ON, HONEY. DO YOUR WORST.
DO I SCARE YOU?
NOT EVEN A LITTLE.
THAT'S WHAT I FIGURED...

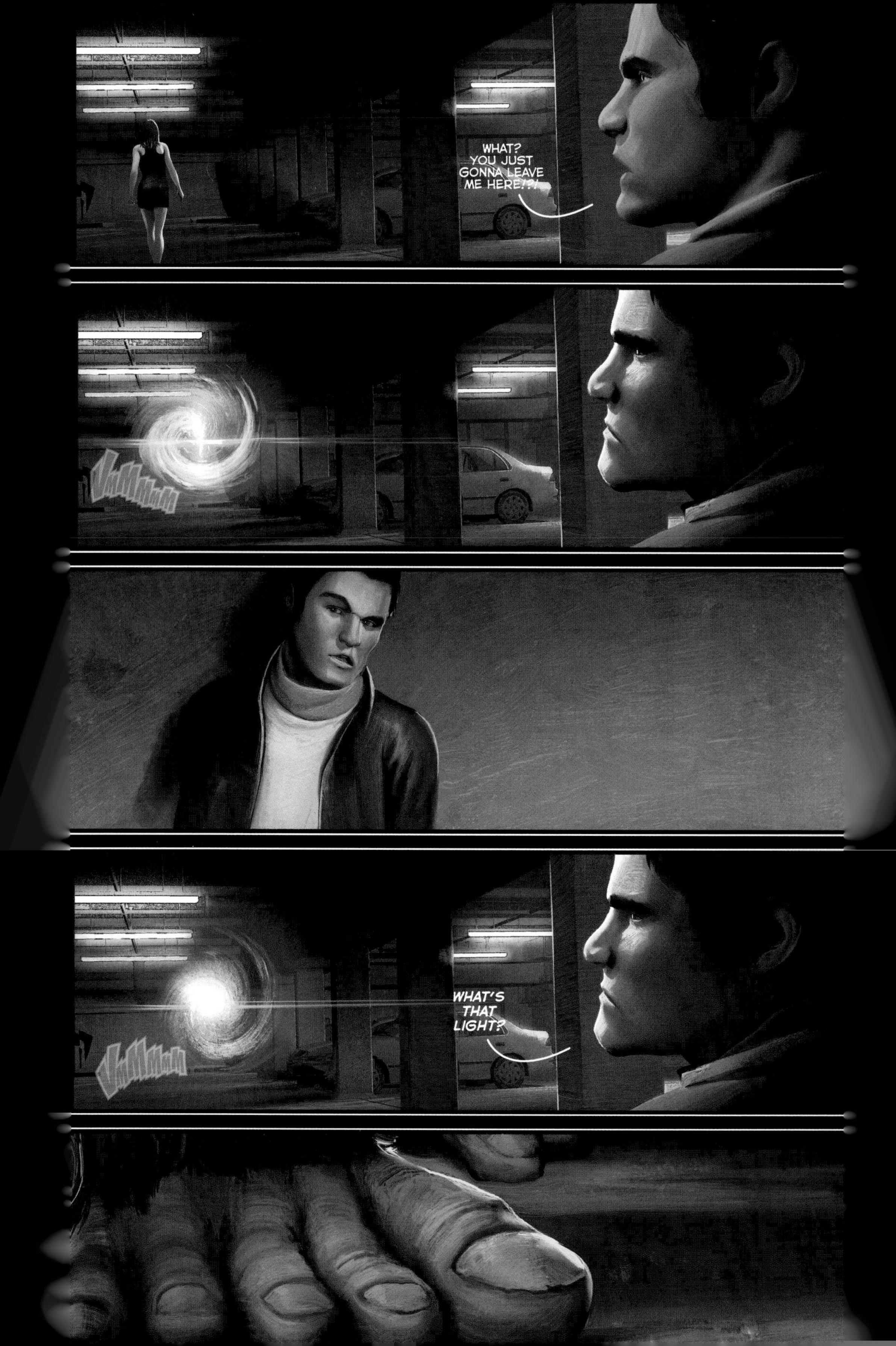
WHAT? YOU JUST GONNA LEAVE ME HERE!?!
VMMMMM
WHAT'S THAT LIGHT?
VMMMMM

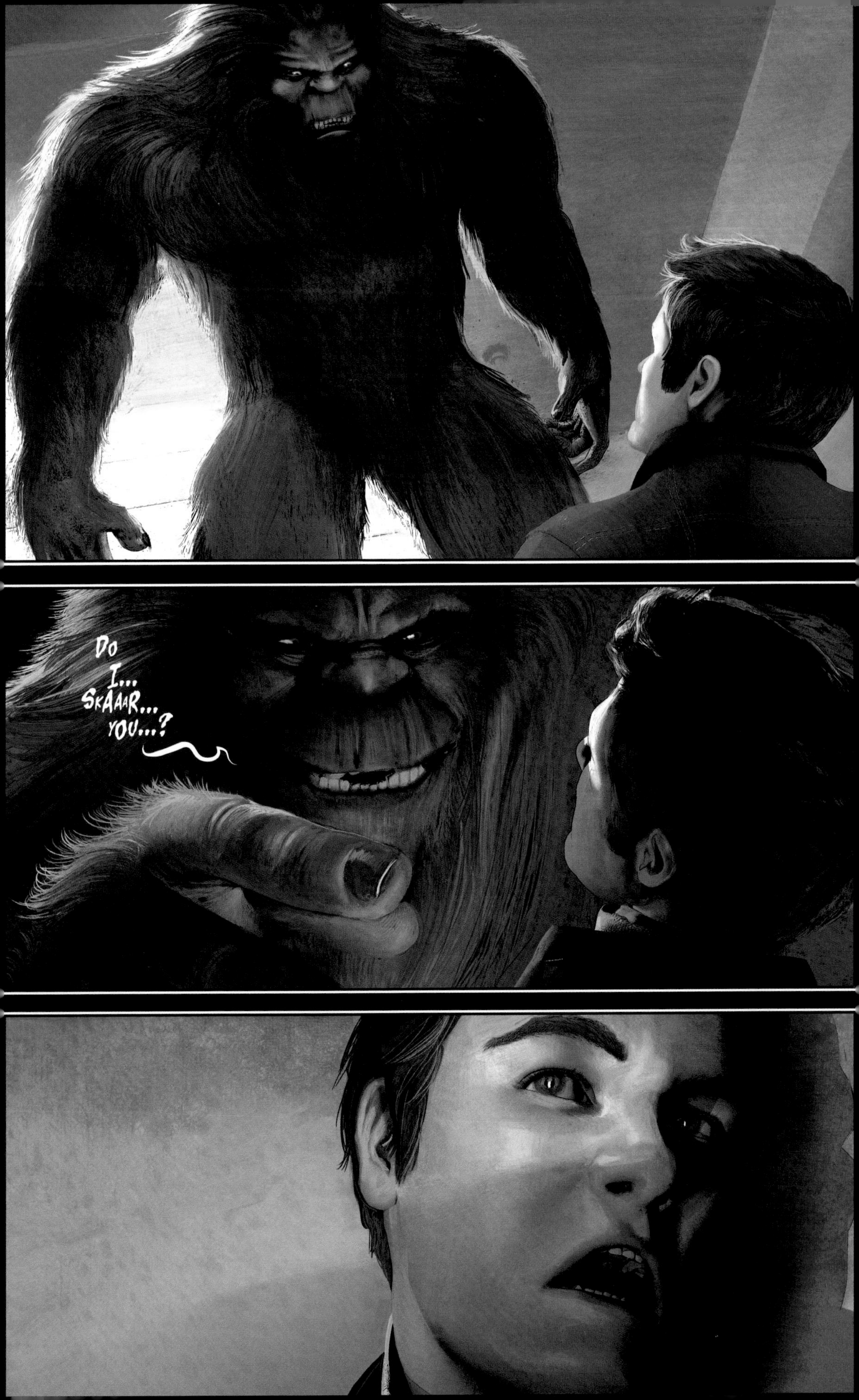
DO I... SKAAAR... YOU...?

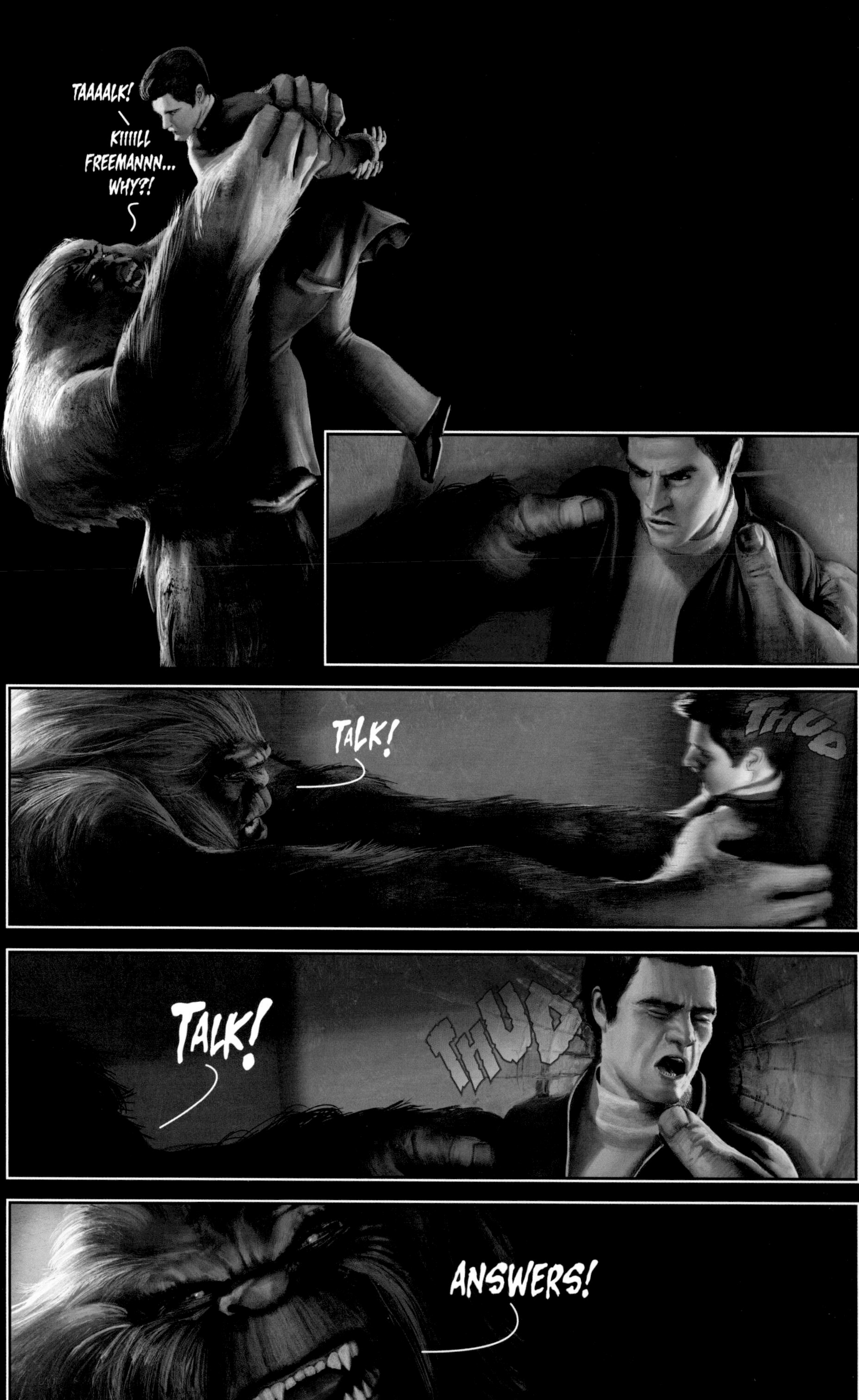
TAAAALK!
KIIIILL FREEMANNN... WHY?!
TALK!
THUD
TALK!
THUD
ANSWERS!

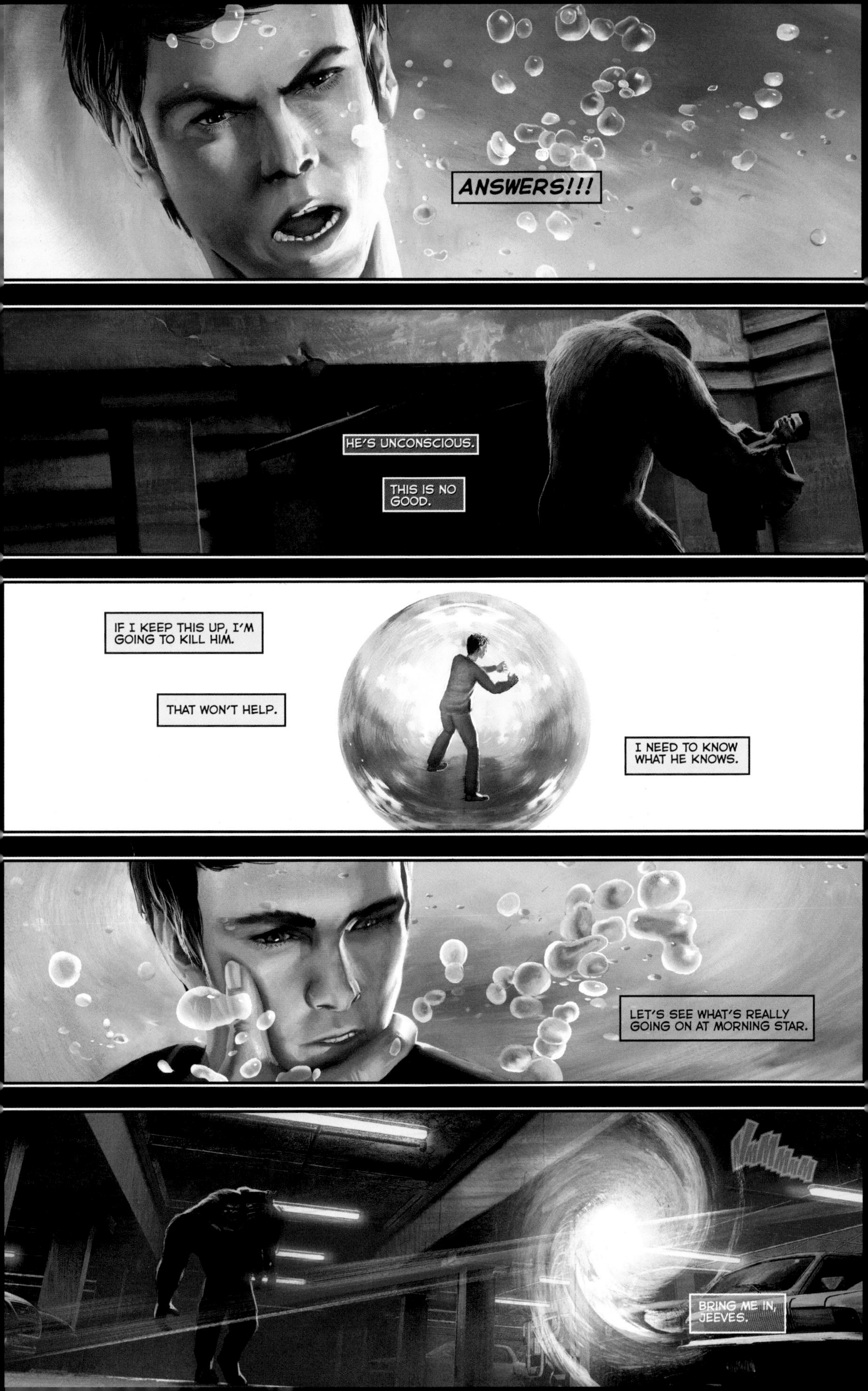
ANSWERS!!!
HE'S UNCONSCIOUS.
THIS IS NO GOOD.
IF I KEEP THIS UP, I'M GOING TO KILL HIM.
THAT WON'T HELP.
I NEED TO KNOW WHAT HE KNOWS.
LET'S SEE WHAT'S REALLY GOING ON AT MORNING STAR.
BRING ME IN, JEEVES.

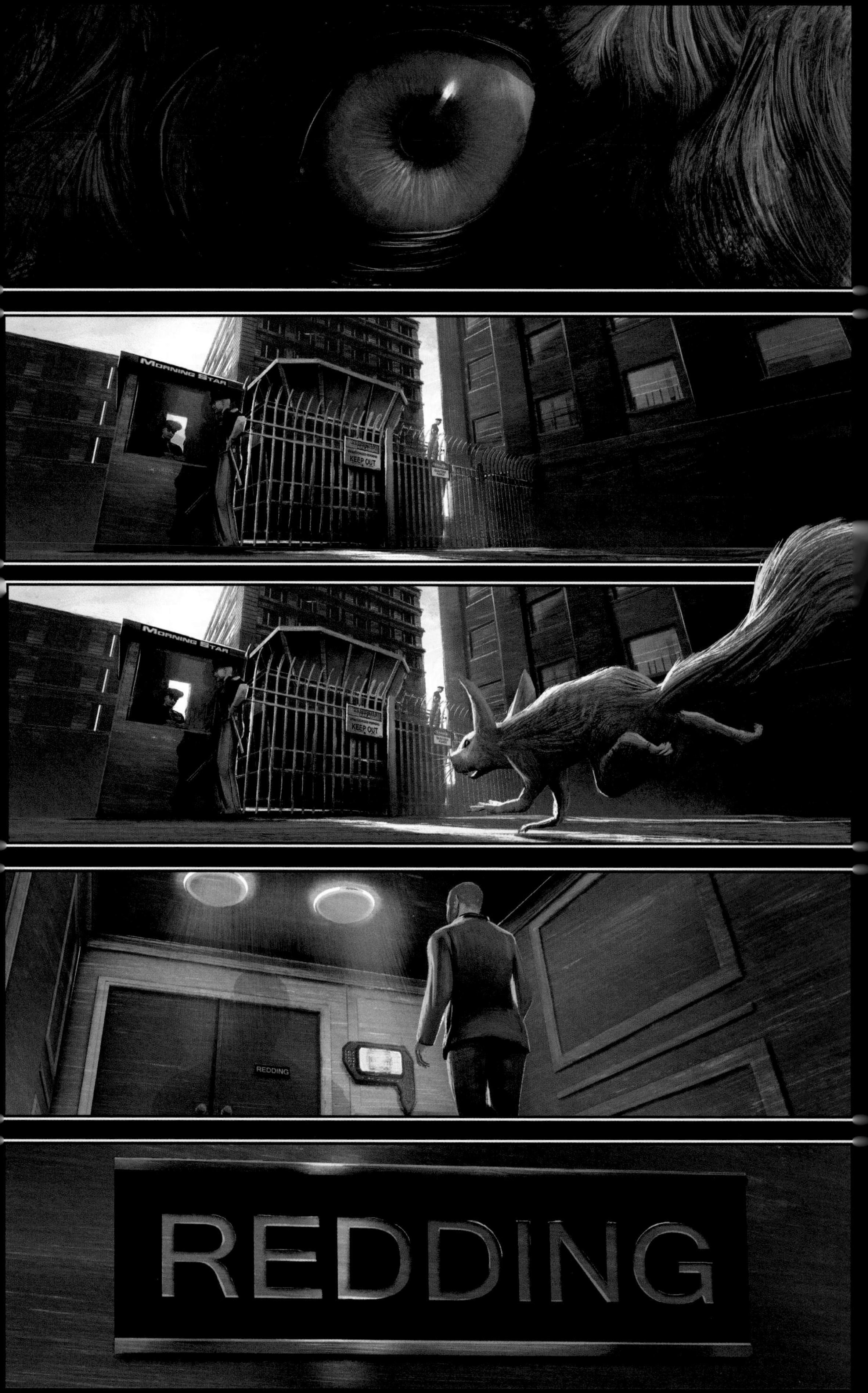
MORNING STAR
KEEP OUT
MORNING STAR
KEEP OUT
REDDING
REDDING

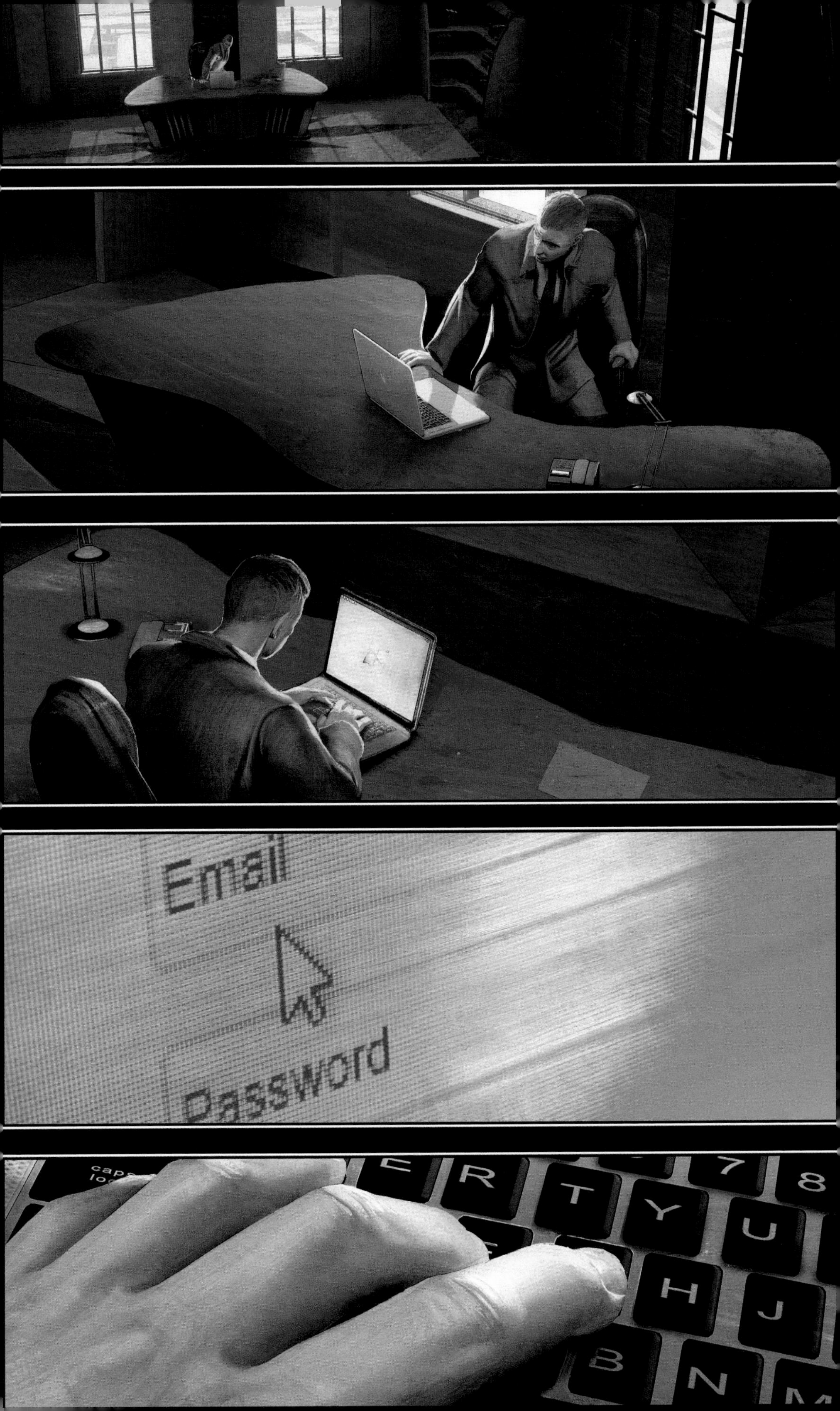
Email
Password

GOTCHA.

PRETTY EASY PASSWORD
TO REMEMBER, MR. REDDING.

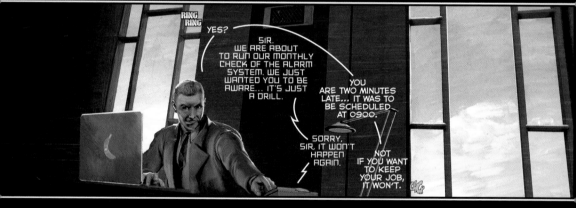

RING RING

YES?

SIR.
WE ARE ABOUT
TO RUN OUR MONTHLY
CHECK OF THE ALARM
SYSTEM. WE JUST
WANTED YOU TO BE
AWARE... IT'S JUST
A DRILL.

YOU
ARE TWO MINUTES
LATE... IT WAS TO
BE SCHEDULED
AT 0900.

SORRY,
SIR, IT WON'T
HAPPEN
AGAIN.

NOT
IF YOU WANT
TO KEEP
YOUR JOB,
IT WON'T.

WHAT AN ASS...

OKAY, JEEVES WE GOT
WHAT WE NEED—

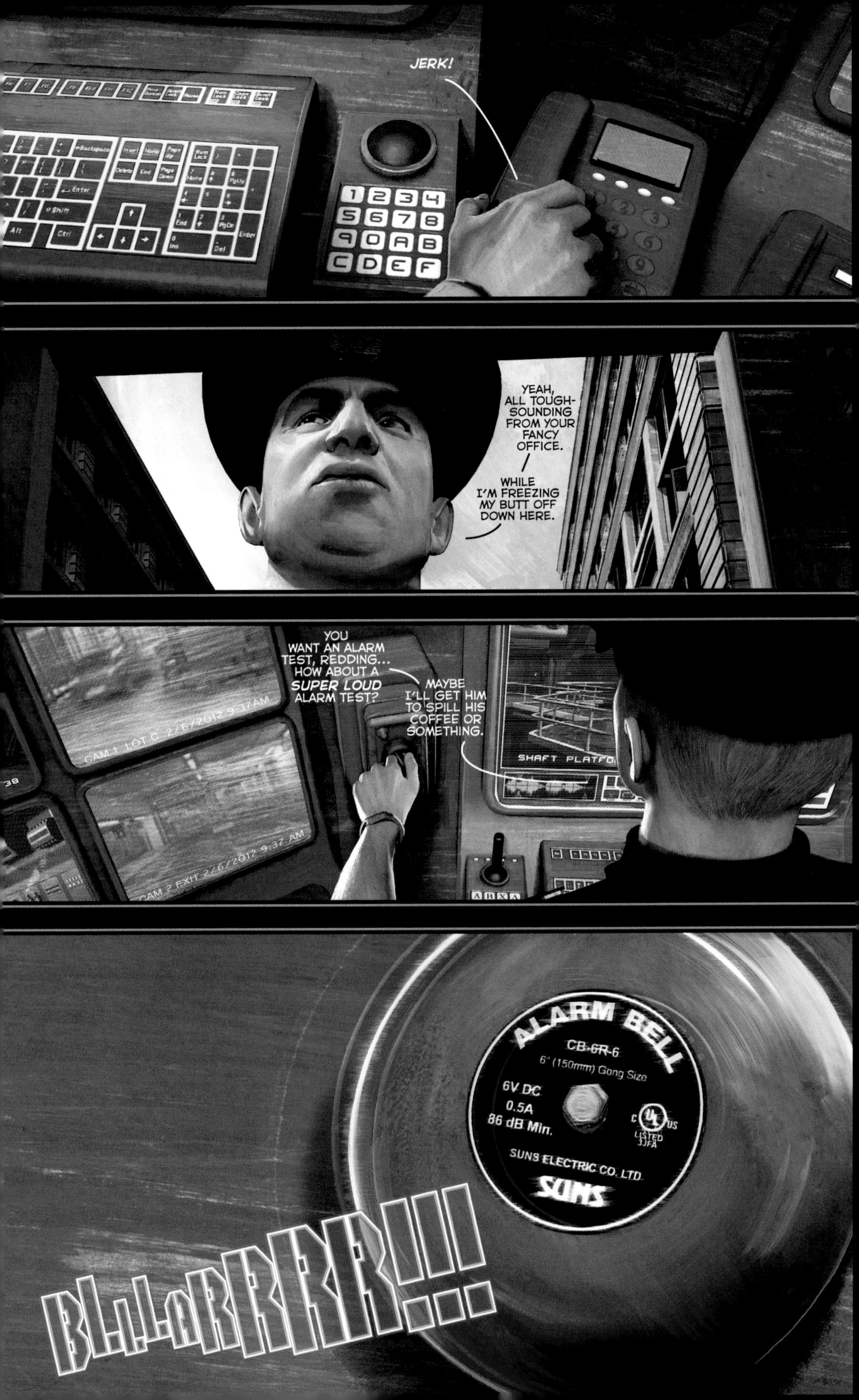
JERK!
YEAH, ALL TOUGH-SOUNDING FROM YOUR FANCY OFFICE.
WHILE I'M FREEZING MY BUTT OFF DOWN HERE.
YOU WANT AN ALARM TEST, REDDING... HOW ABOUT A *SUPER LOUD* ALARM TEST?
MAYBE I'LL GET HIM TO SPILL HIS COFFEE OR SOMETHING.
CAM 1 LOT C 2/6/2012 9:37AM
CAM 2 EXIT 2/6/2012 9:37 AM
SHAFT PLATFO
ALARM BELL
CB-6R-6
6" (150mm) Gong Size
6V DC
0.5A
86 dB Min.
LISTED
3JFA
SUNS ELECTRIC CO. LTD.
SUNS
BLLLaRRRR!!!...

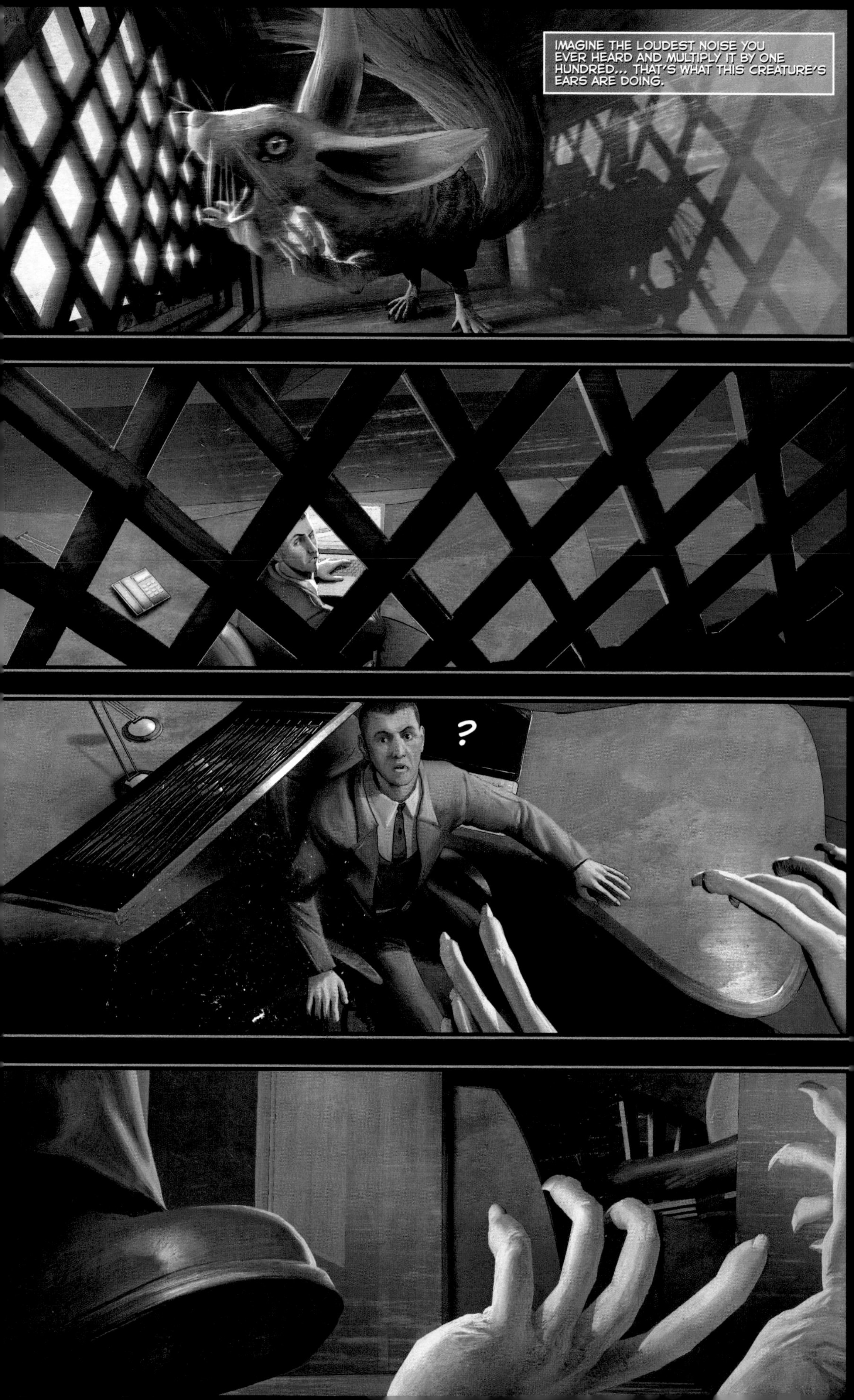
IMAGINE THE LOUDEST NOISE YOU EVER HEARD AND MULTIPLY IT BY ONE HUNDRED... THAT'S WHAT THIS CREATURE'S EARS ARE DOING.
?

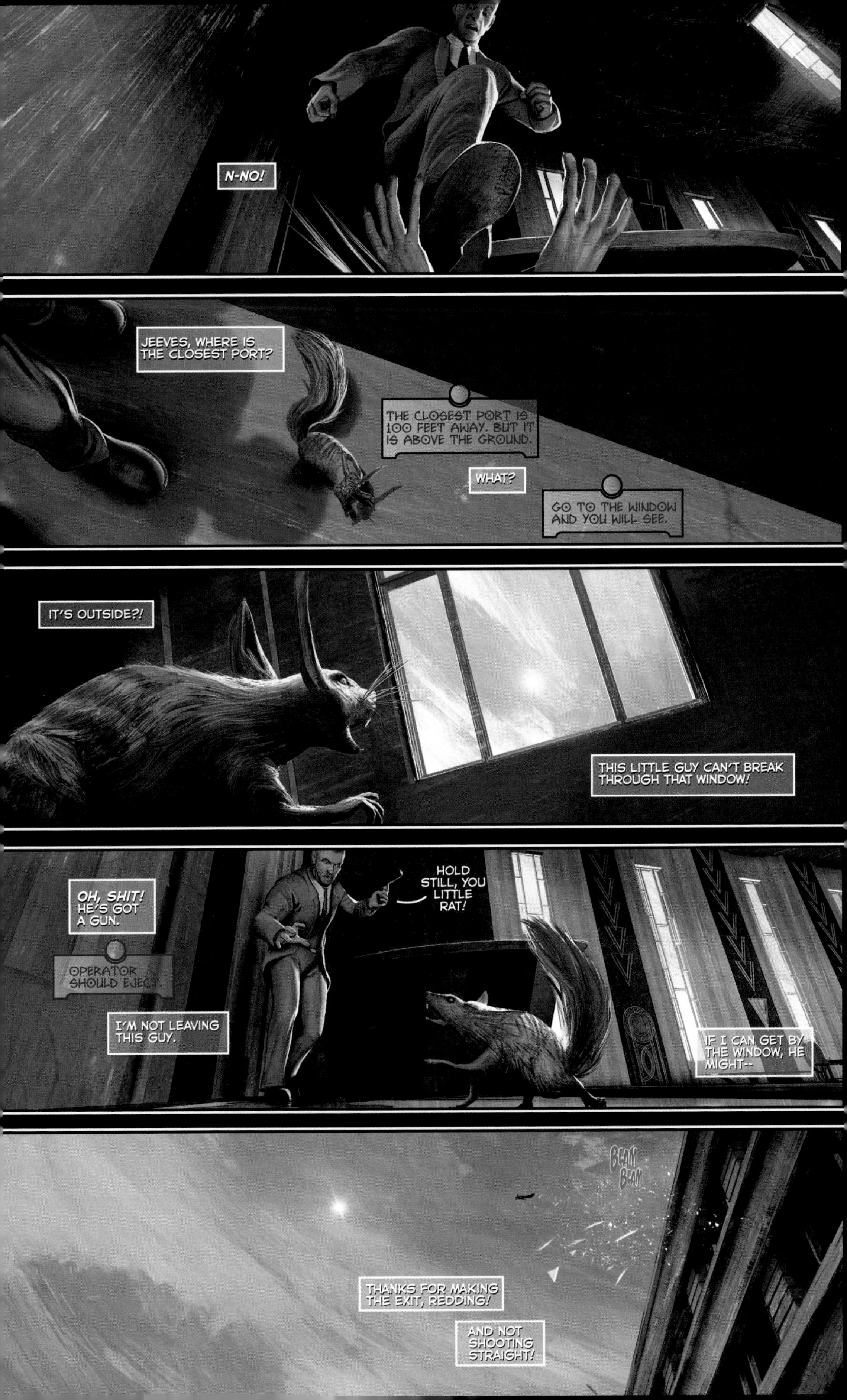
N-NO!
JEEVES, WHERE IS THE CLOSEST PORT?
THE CLOSEST PORT IS 100 FEET AWAY. BUT IT IS ABOVE THE GROUND.
WHAT?
GO TO THE WINDOW AND YOU WILL SEE.
IT'S OUTSIDE?!
THIS LITTLE GUY CAN'T BREAK THROUGH THAT WINDOW!
OH, SHIT! HE'S GOT A GUN.
OPERATOR SHOULD EJECT.
I'M NOT LEAVING THIS GUY.
HOLD STILL, YOU LITTLE RAT!
IF I CAN GET BY THE WINDOW, HE MIGHT--
BLAM
BLAM
THANKS FOR MAKING THE EXIT, REDDING!
AND NOT SHOOTING STRAIGHT!

YOU KNOW HE ONLY MISSED YOU BY 3.6 MILLIMETERS.

NO, AND I DON'T THINK I NEEDED TO KNOW THAT AT ALL, JEEVES.

I THINK IT'S TIME WE APPROACHED THIS PROBLEM FROM A NEW ANGLE.

OPERATOR'S STRATEGY NOT RECOMMENDED. POTENTIAL SURROGATE HAS NOT BEEN PROPERLY EXAMINED AND VETTED. TACTIC POSES INHERENT--

HOW LONG WOULD IT TAKE TO "PROPERLY" EXAMINE AND VET?

TWO DAYS.

DON'T HAVE THE TIME.

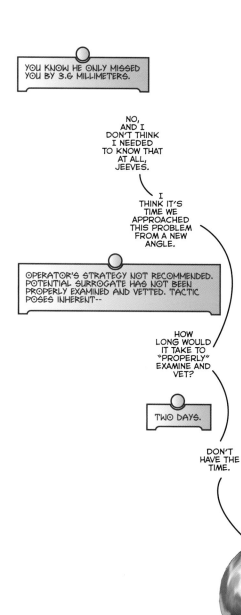

I'LL JUST HAVE TO RISK IT.

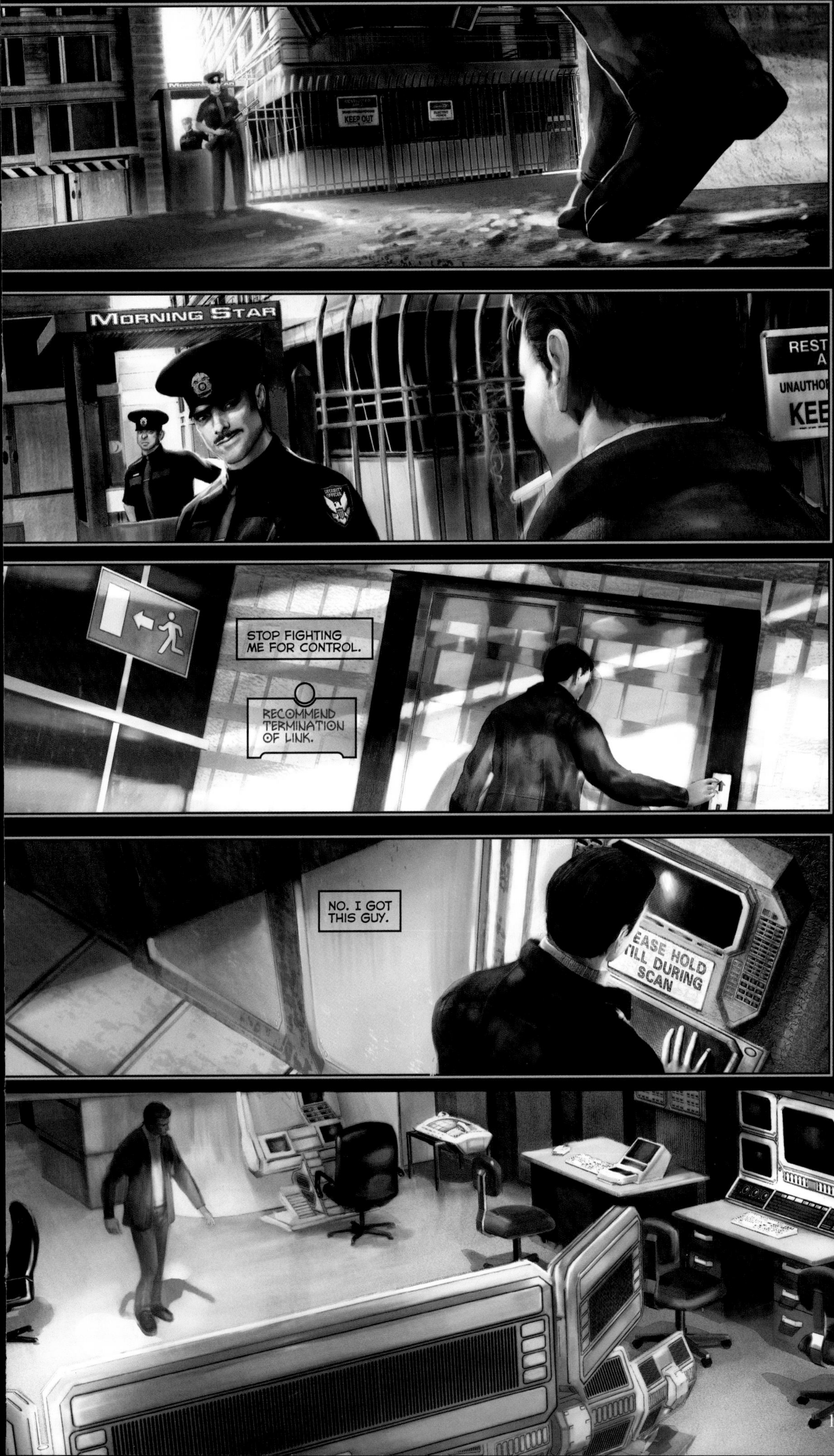
KEEP OUT
MORNING STAR
STOP FIGHTING ME FOR CONTROL.
RECOMMEND TERMINATION OF LINK.
NO. I GOT THIS GUY.

NOW... LET'S SEE WHAT ALL THIS IS ABOUT.

N-NO...

SHOW ME... GET TYPING...

PROJECT EVERGREEN

PASSWORD ********

THANKS FOR THE PASSWORD, MR. REDDING.

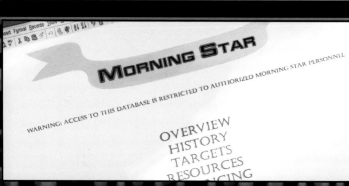

MORNING STAR

WARNING: ACCESS TO THIS DATABASE IS RESTRICTED TO AUTHORIZED MORNING STAR PERSONNEL

OVERVIEW
HISTORY
TARGETS
RESOURCES

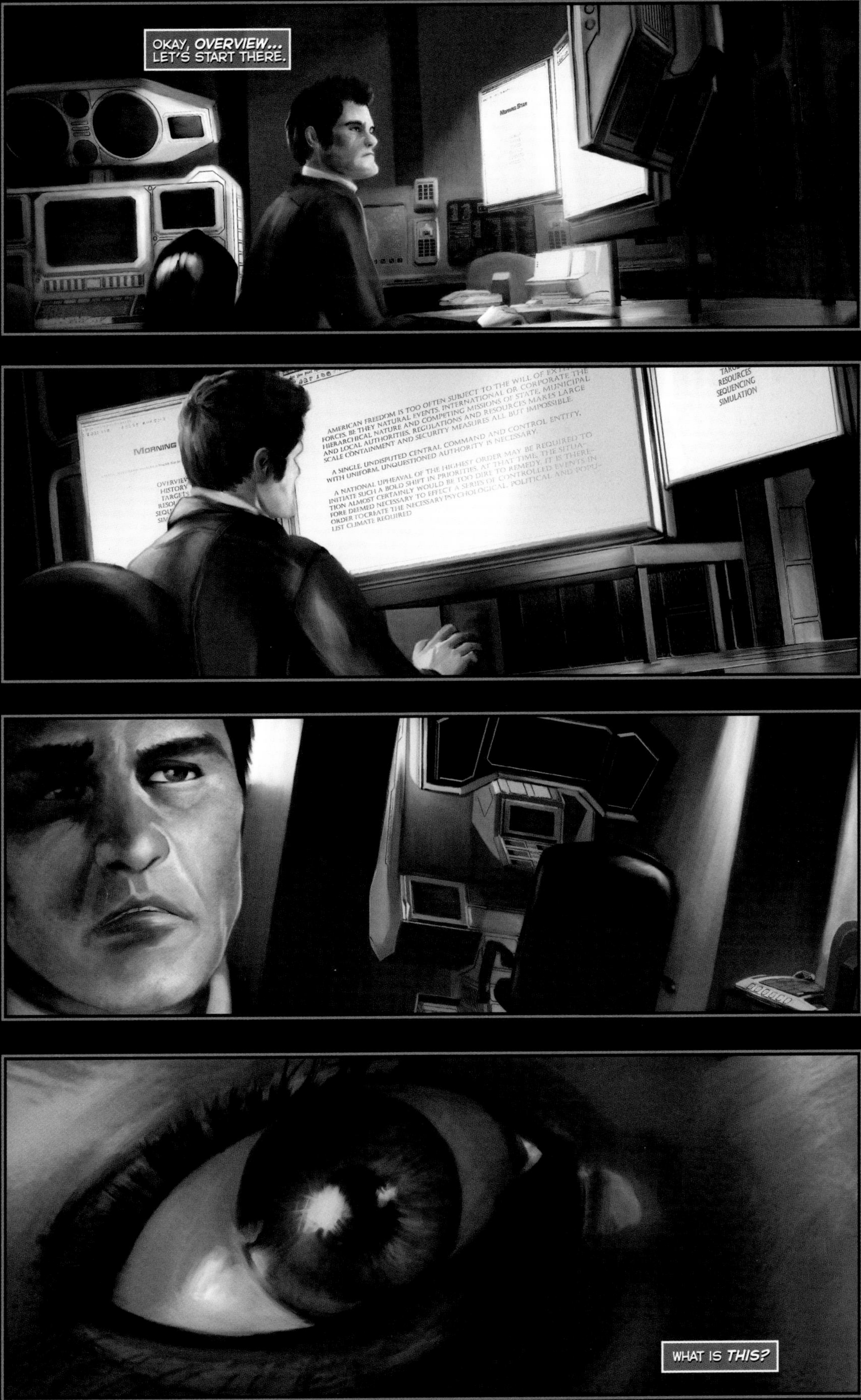
OKAY, *OVERVIEW*... LET'S START THERE.
AMERICAN FREEDOM IS TOO OFTEN SUBJECT TO THE WILL OF EX
FORCES, BE THEY NATURAL EVENTS, INTERNATIONAL OR CORPORATE THE
HIERARCHICAL NATURE AND COMPETING MISSIONS OF STATE, MUNICIPAL
AND LOCAL AUTHORITIES, REGULATIONS AND RESOURCES MAKES LARGE
SCALE CONTAINMENT AND SECURITY MEASURES ALL BUT IMPOSSIBLE.
A SINGLE, UNDISPUTED CENTRAL COMMAND AND CONTROL ENTITY,
WITH UNIFORM, UNQUESTIONED AUTHORITY IS NECESSARY.
A NATIONAL UPHEAVAL OF THE HIGHEST ORDER MAY BE REQUIRED TO
INITIATE SUCH A BOLD SHIFT IN PRIORITIES. AT THAT TIME, THE SITUA-
TION ALMOST CERTAINLY WOULD BE TOO DIRE TO REMEDY. IT IS THERE-
FORE DEEMED NECESSARY TO EFFECT A SERIES OF CONTROLLED EVENTS IN
ORDER TOCREATE THE NECESSARY PSYCHOLOGICAL, POLITICAL AND POPU-
LIST CLIMATE REQUIRED
MORNING
OVERVIEW
HISTORY
TARGETS
RESOURCES
SEQUENCING
SIMULATION
WHAT IS *THIS?*

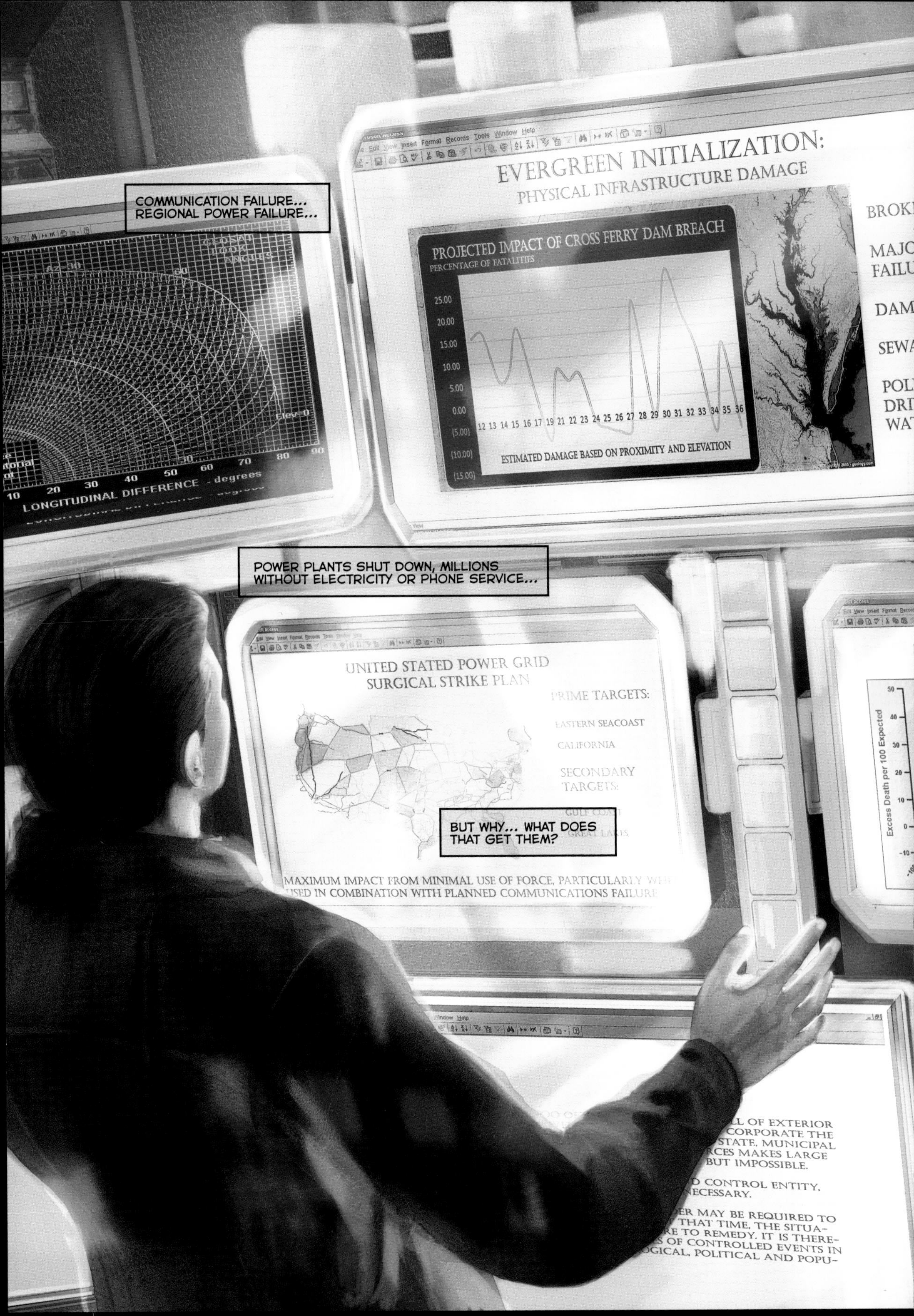
COMMUNICATION FAILURE...
REGIONAL POWER FAILURE...
LONGITUDINAL DIFFERENCE - degrees
EVERGREEN INITIALIZATION:
PHYSICAL INFRASTRUCTURE DAMAGE
PROJECTED IMPACT OF CROSS FERRY DAM BREACH
PERCENTAGE OF FATALITIES
ESTIMATED DAMAGE BASED ON PROXIMITY AND ELEVATION
POWER PLANTS SHUT DOWN, MILLIONS WITHOUT ELECTRICITY OR PHONE SERVICE...
UNITED STATED POWER GRID
SURGICAL STRIKE PLAN
PRIME TARGETS:
EASTERN SEACOAST
CALIFORNIA
SECONDARY TARGETS:
BUT WHY... WHAT DOES THAT GET THEM?
MAXIMUM IMPACT FROM MINIMAL USE OF FORCE, PARTICULARLY
USED IN COMBINATION WITH PLANNED COMMUNICATIONS FAILURE
Excess Death per 100 Expected

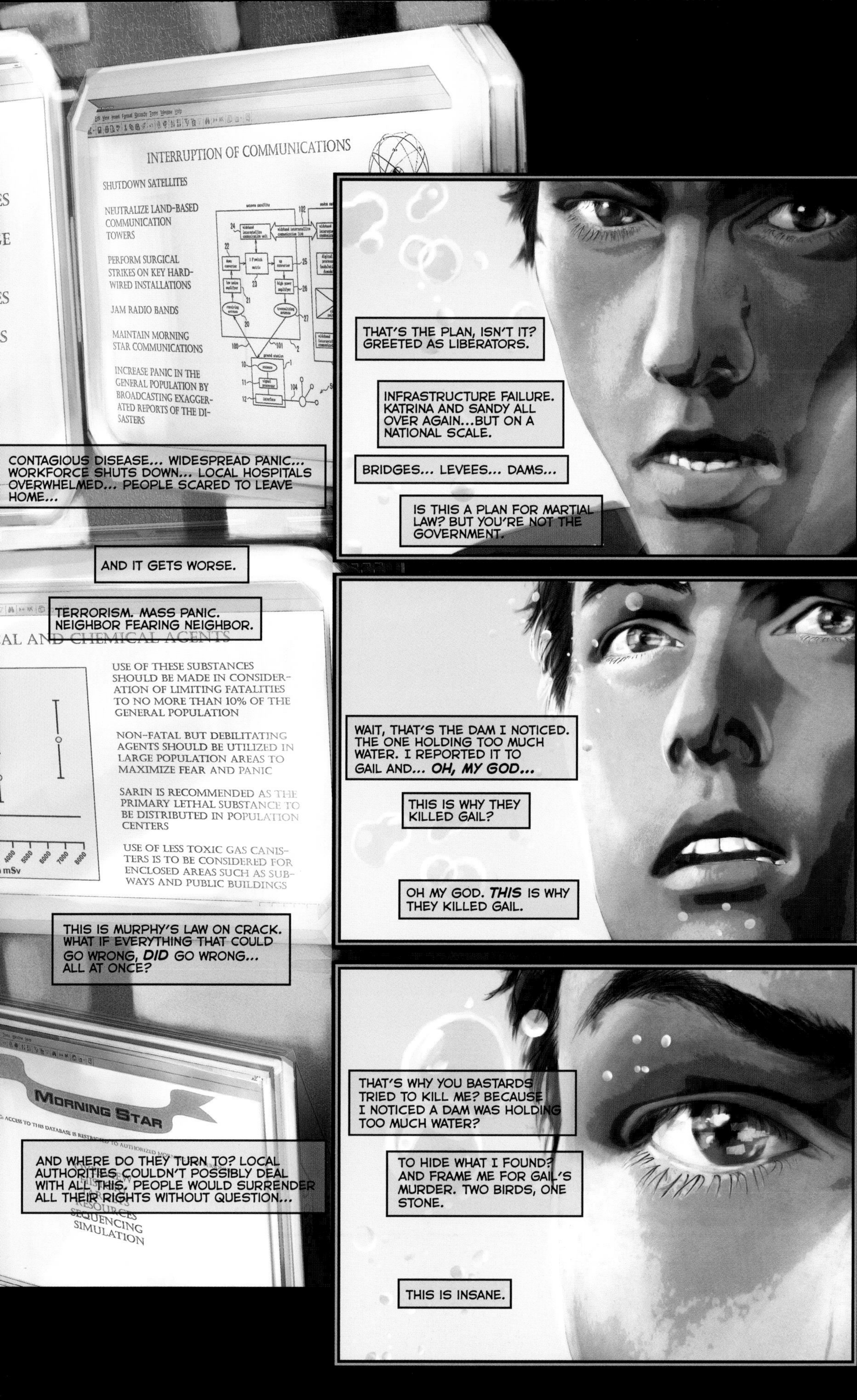
INTERRUPTION OF COMMUNICATIONS
SHUTDOWN SATELLITES
NEUTRALIZE LAND-BASED COMMUNICATION TOWERS
PERFORM SURGICAL STRIKES ON KEY HARD-WIRED INSTALLATIONS
JAM RADIO BANDS
MAINTAIN MORNING STAR COMMUNICATIONS
INCREASE PANIC IN THE GENERAL POPULATION BY BROADCASTING EXAGGER-ATED REPORTS OF THE DI-SASTERS
CONTAGIOUS DISEASE... WIDESPREAD PANIC... WORKFORCE SHUTS DOWN... LOCAL HOSPITALS OVERWHELMED... PEOPLE SCARED TO LEAVE HOME...
AND IT GETS WORSE.
TERRORISM. MASS PANIC. NEIGHBOR FEARING NEIGHBOR.
USE OF THESE SUBSTANCES SHOULD BE MADE IN CONSIDER-ATION OF LIMITING FATALITIES TO NO MORE THAN 10% OF THE GENERAL POPULATION
NON-FATAL BUT DEBILITATING AGENTS SHOULD BE UTILIZED IN LARGE POPULATION AREAS TO MAXIMIZE FEAR AND PANIC
SARIN IS RECOMMENDED AS THE PRIMARY LETHAL SUBSTANCE TO BE DISTRIBUTED IN POPULATION CENTERS
USE OF LESS TOXIC GAS CANIS-TERS IS TO BE CONSIDERED FOR ENCLOSED AREAS SUCH AS SUB-WAYS AND PUBLIC BUILDINGS
THIS IS MURPHY'S LAW ON CRACK. WHAT IF EVERYTHING THAT COULD GO WRONG, *DID* GO WRONG... ALL AT ONCE?
MORNING STAR
SEQUENCING
SIMULATION
AND WHERE DO THEY TURN TO? LOCAL AUTHORITIES COULDN'T POSSIBLY DEAL WITH ALL THIS. PEOPLE WOULD SURRENDER ALL THEIR RIGHTS WITHOUT QUESTION...
THAT'S THE PLAN, ISN'T IT? GREETED AS LIBERATORS.
INFRASTRUCTURE FAILURE. KATRINA AND SANDY ALL OVER AGAIN...BUT ON A NATIONAL SCALE.
BRIDGES... LEVEES... DAMS...
IS THIS A PLAN FOR MARTIAL LAW? BUT YOU'RE NOT THE GOVERNMENT.
WAIT, THAT'S THE DAM I NOTICED. THE ONE HOLDING TOO MUCH WATER. I REPORTED IT TO GAIL AND... *OH, MY GOD...*
THIS IS WHY THEY KILLED GAIL?
OH MY GOD. *THIS* IS WHY THEY KILLED GAIL.
THAT'S WHY YOU BASTARDS TRIED TO KILL ME? BECAUSE I NOTICED A DAM WAS HOLDING TOO MUCH WATER?
TO HIDE WHAT I FOUND? AND FRAME ME FOR GAIL'S MURDER. TWO BIRDS, ONE STONE.
THIS IS INSANE.

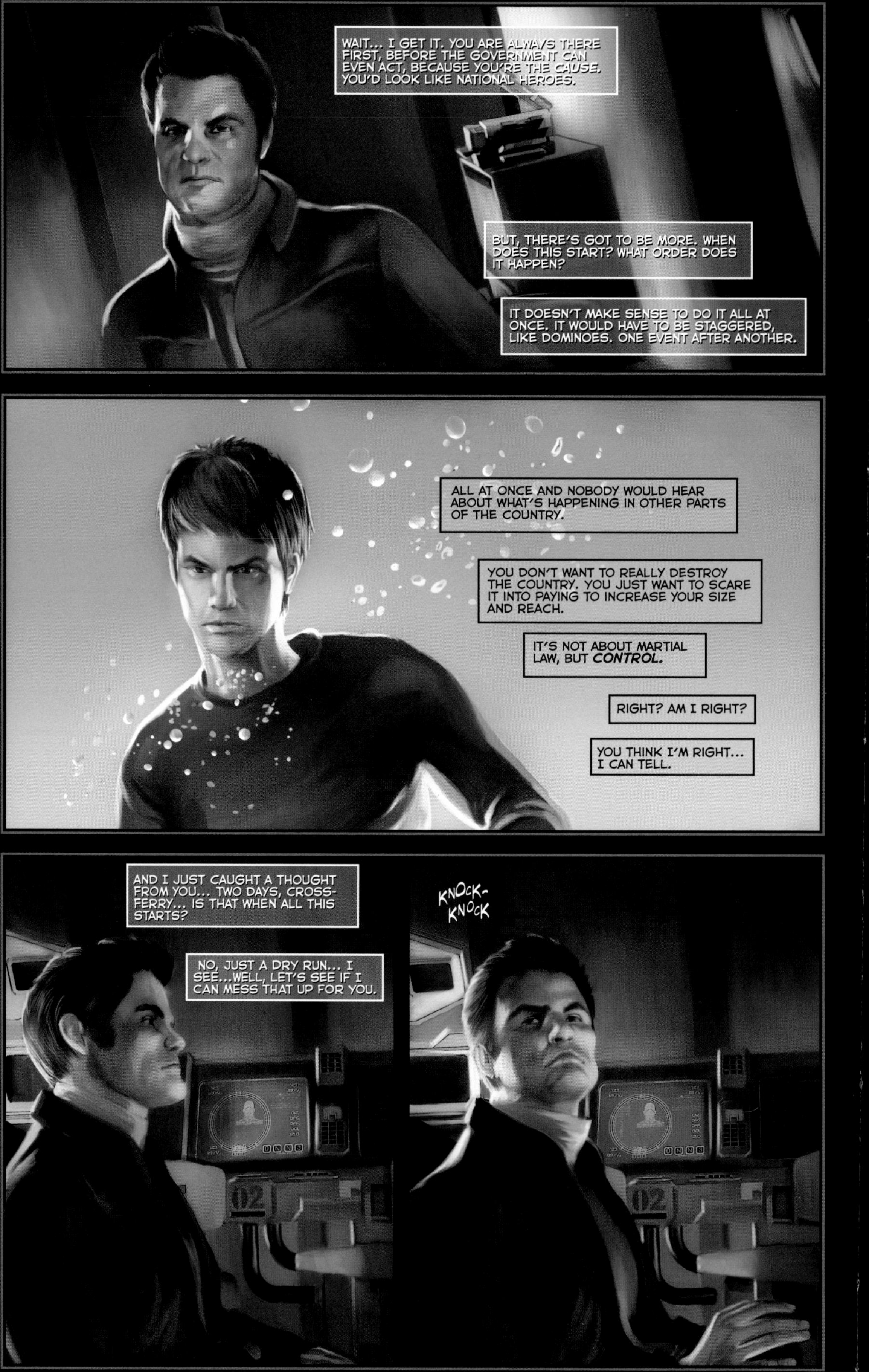
WAIT... I GET IT. YOU ARE ALWAYS THERE FIRST, BEFORE THE GOVERNMENT CAN EVEN ACT, BECAUSE YOU'RE THE CAUSE. YOU'D LOOK LIKE NATIONAL HEROES.
BUT, THERE'S GOT TO BE MORE. WHEN DOES THIS START? WHAT ORDER DOES IT HAPPEN?
IT DOESN'T MAKE SENSE TO DO IT ALL AT ONCE. IT WOULD HAVE TO BE STAGGERED, LIKE DOMINOES. ONE EVENT AFTER ANOTHER.
ALL AT ONCE AND NOBODY WOULD HEAR ABOUT WHAT'S HAPPENING IN OTHER PARTS OF THE COUNTRY.
YOU DON'T WANT TO REALLY DESTROY THE COUNTRY. YOU JUST WANT TO SCARE IT INTO PAYING TO INCREASE YOUR SIZE AND REACH.
IT'S NOT ABOUT MARTIAL LAW, BUT CONTROL.
RIGHT? AM I RIGHT?
YOU THINK I'M RIGHT... I CAN TELL.
AND I JUST CAUGHT A THOUGHT FROM YOU... TWO DAYS, CROSS-FERRY... IS THAT WHEN ALL THIS STARTS?
NO, JUST A DRY RUN... I SEE...WELL, LET'S SEE IF I CAN MESS THAT UP FOR YOU.
KNOCK-KNOCK
02
02

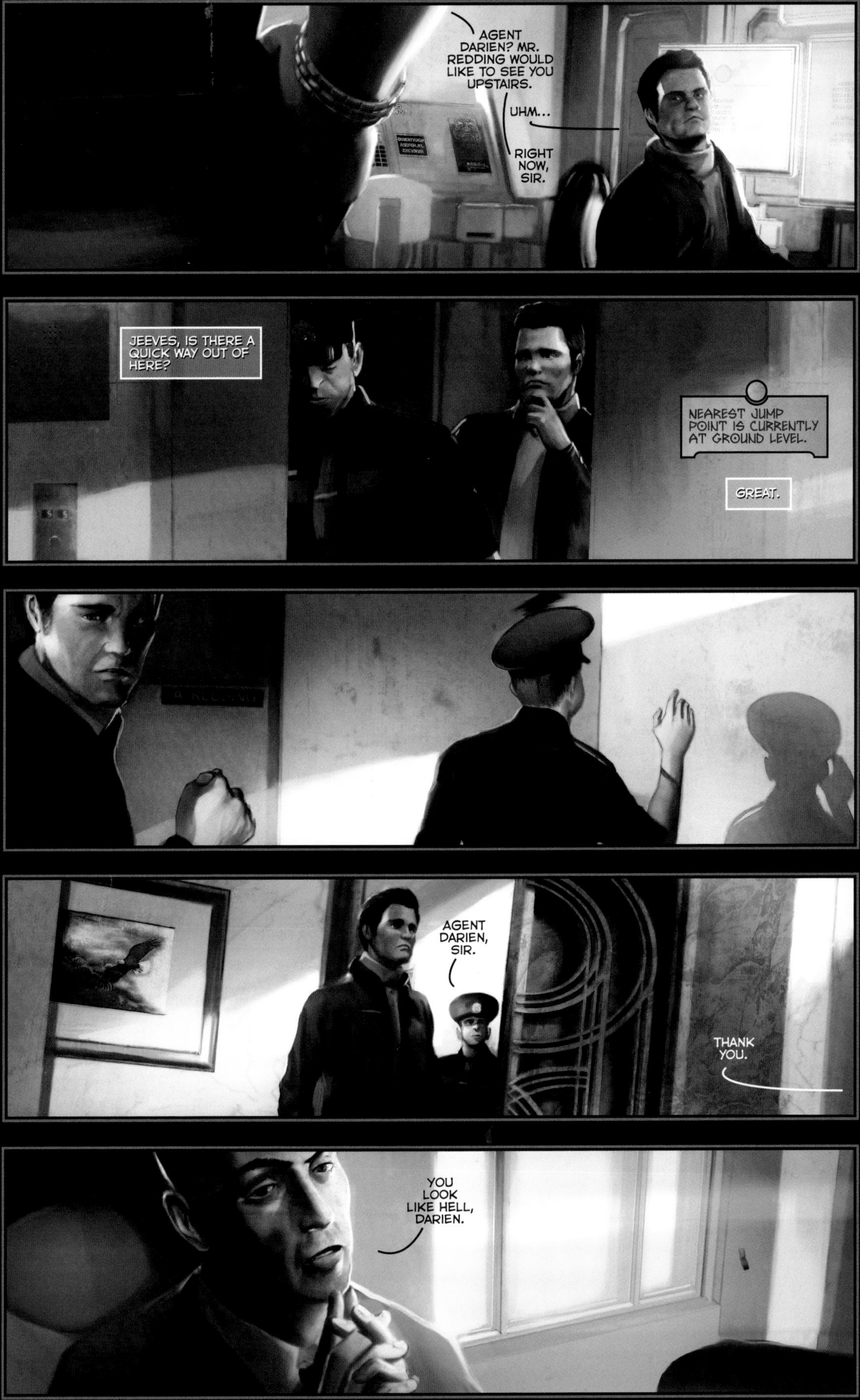
AGENT DARIEN? MR. REDDING WOULD LIKE TO SEE YOU UPSTAIRS.
UHM...
RIGHT NOW, SIR.
JEEVES, IS THERE A QUICK WAY OUT OF HERE?
NEAREST JUMP POINT IS CURRENTLY AT GROUND LEVEL.
GREAT.
AGENT DARIEN, SIR.
THANK YOU.
YOU LOOK LIKE HELL, DARIEN.

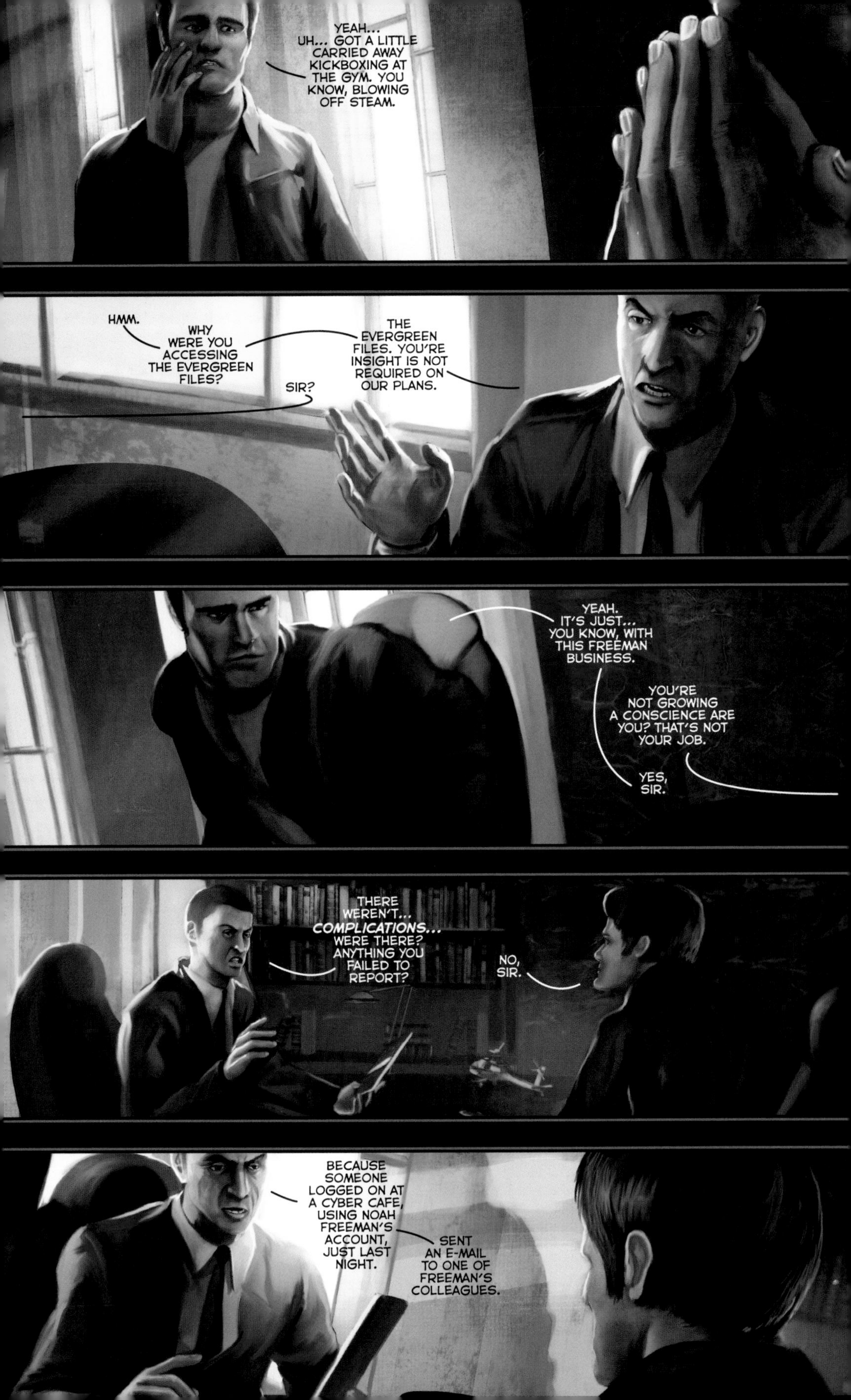
YEAH... UH... GOT A LITTLE CARRIED AWAY KICKBOXING AT THE GYM. YOU KNOW, BLOWING OFF STEAM.
HMM.
WHY WERE YOU ACCESSING THE EVERGREEN FILES?
SIR?
THE EVERGREEN FILES. YOU'RE INSIGHT IS NOT REQUIRED ON OUR PLANS.
YEAH. IT'S JUST... YOU KNOW, WITH THIS FREEMAN BUSINESS.
YOU'RE NOT GROWING A CONSCIENCE ARE YOU? THAT'S NOT YOUR JOB.
YES, SIR.
THERE WEREN'T... *COMPLICATIONS...* WERE THERE? ANYTHING YOU FAILED TO REPORT?
NO, SIR.
BECAUSE SOMEONE LOGGED ON AT A CYBER CAFE, USING NOAH FREEMAN'S ACCOUNT, JUST LAST NIGHT.
SENT AN E-MAIL TO ONE OF FREEMAN'S COLLEAGUES.

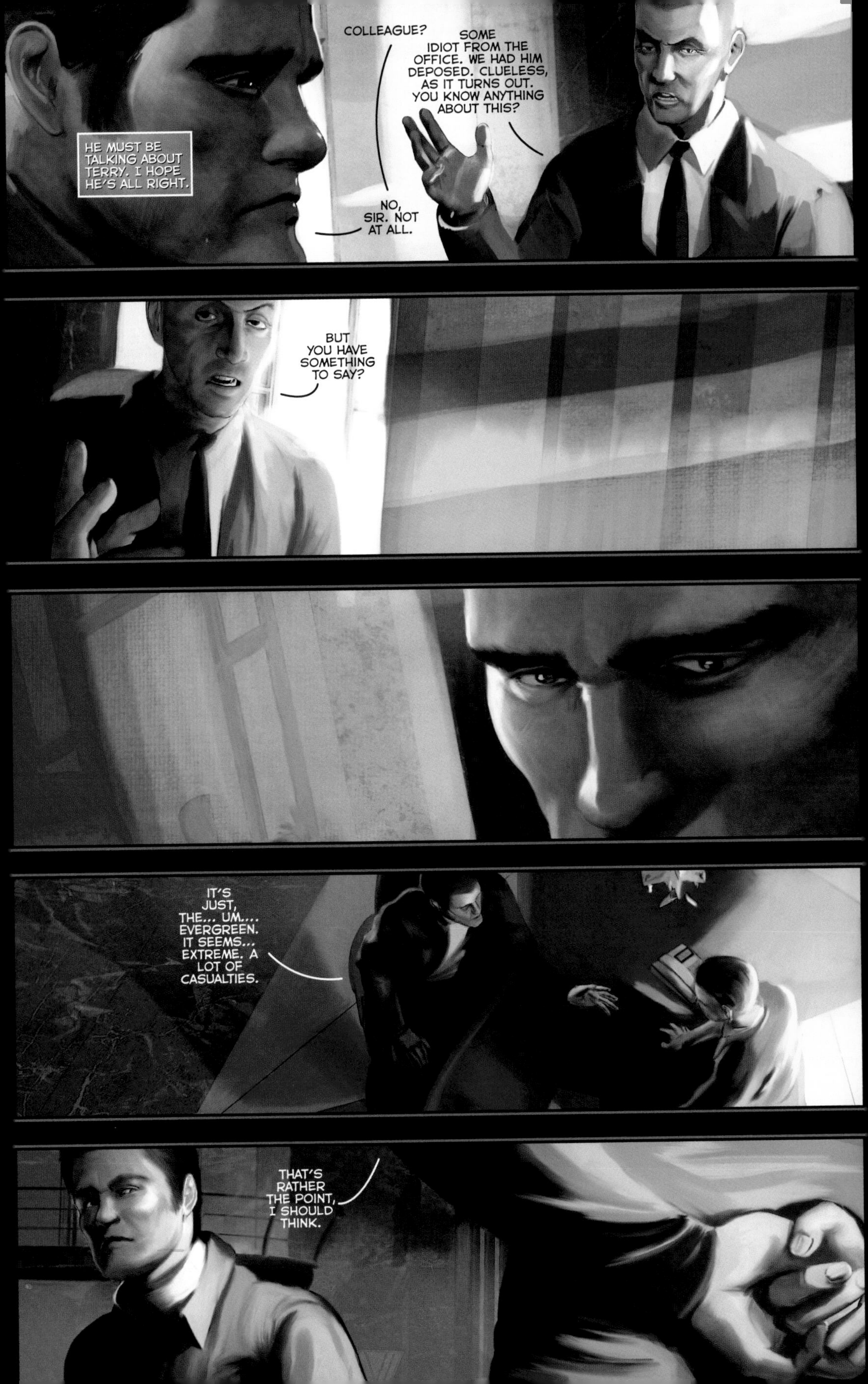

HE MUST BE TALKING ABOUT TERRY. I HOPE HE'S ALL RIGHT.
COLLEAGUE?
SOME IDIOT FROM THE OFFICE. WE HAD HIM DEPOSED. CLUELESS, AS IT TURNS OUT. YOU KNOW ANYTHING ABOUT THIS?
NO, SIR. NOT AT ALL.
BUT YOU HAVE SOMETHING TO SAY?
IT'S JUST, THE... UM.... EVERGREEN. IT SEEMS... EXTREME. A LOT OF CASUALTIES.
THAT'S RATHER THE POINT, I SHOULD THINK.

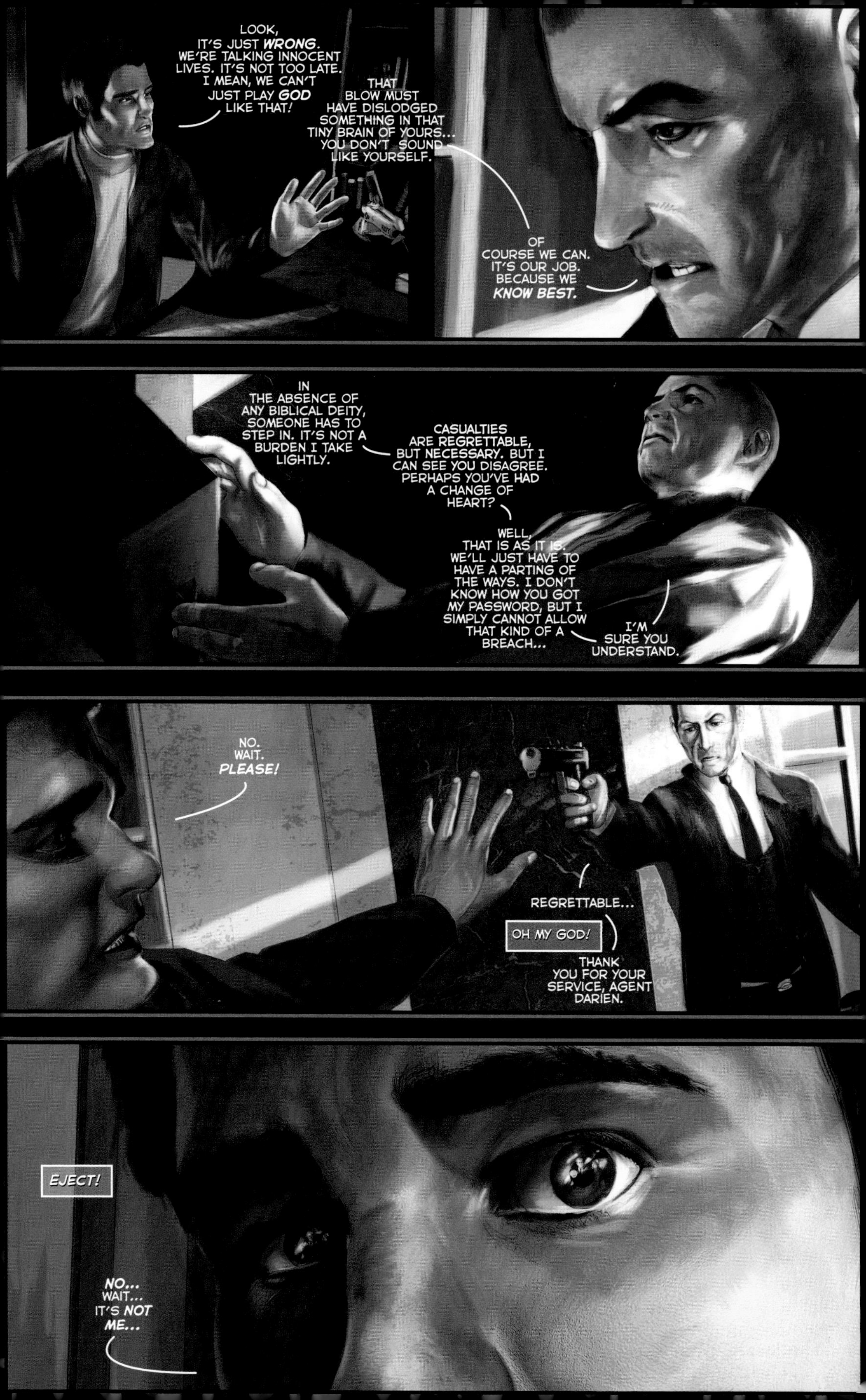

LOOK, IT'S JUST WRONG. WE'RE TALKING INNOCENT LIVES. IT'S NOT TOO LATE. I MEAN, WE CAN'T JUST PLAY GOD LIKE THAT!
THAT BLOW MUST HAVE DISLODGED SOMETHING IN THAT TINY BRAIN OF YOURS... YOU DON'T SOUND LIKE YOURSELF.
OF COURSE WE CAN. IT'S OUR JOB. BECAUSE WE KNOW BEST.
IN THE ABSENCE OF ANY BIBLICAL DEITY, SOMEONE HAS TO STEP IN. IT'S NOT A BURDEN I TAKE LIGHTLY.
CASUALTIES ARE REGRETTABLE, BUT NECESSARY. BUT I CAN SEE YOU DISAGREE. PERHAPS YOU'VE HAD A CHANGE OF HEART?
WELL, THAT IS AS IT IS. WE'LL JUST HAVE TO HAVE A PARTING OF THE WAYS. I DON'T KNOW HOW YOU GOT MY PASSWORD, BUT I SIMPLY CANNOT ALLOW THAT KIND OF A BREACH...
I'M SURE YOU UNDERSTAND.
NO. WAIT. PLEASE!
REGRETTABLE...
OH MY GOD!
THANK YOU FOR YOUR SERVICE, AGENT DARIEN.
EJECT!
NO... WAIT... IT'S NOT ME...

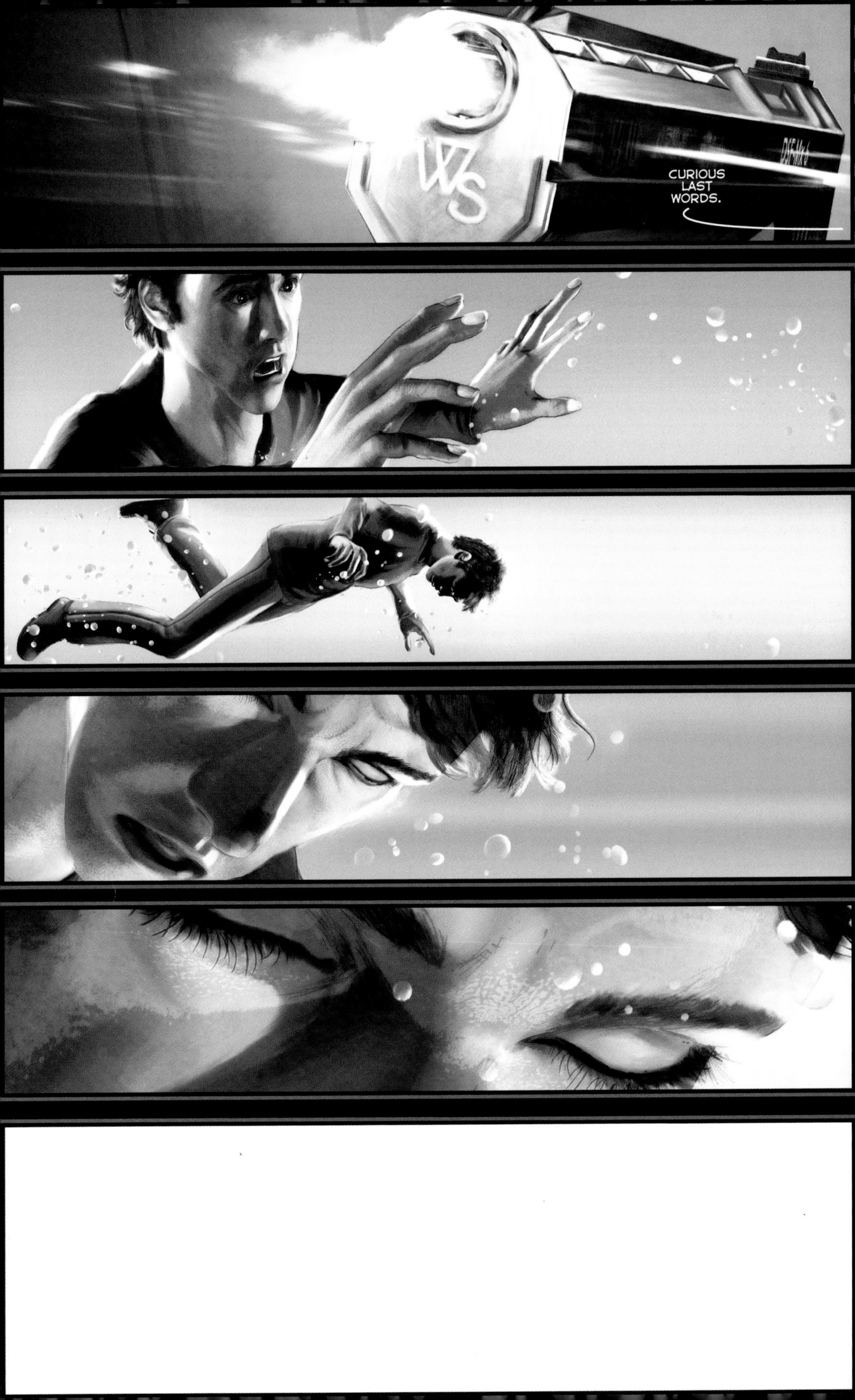
CURIOUS LAST WORDS.

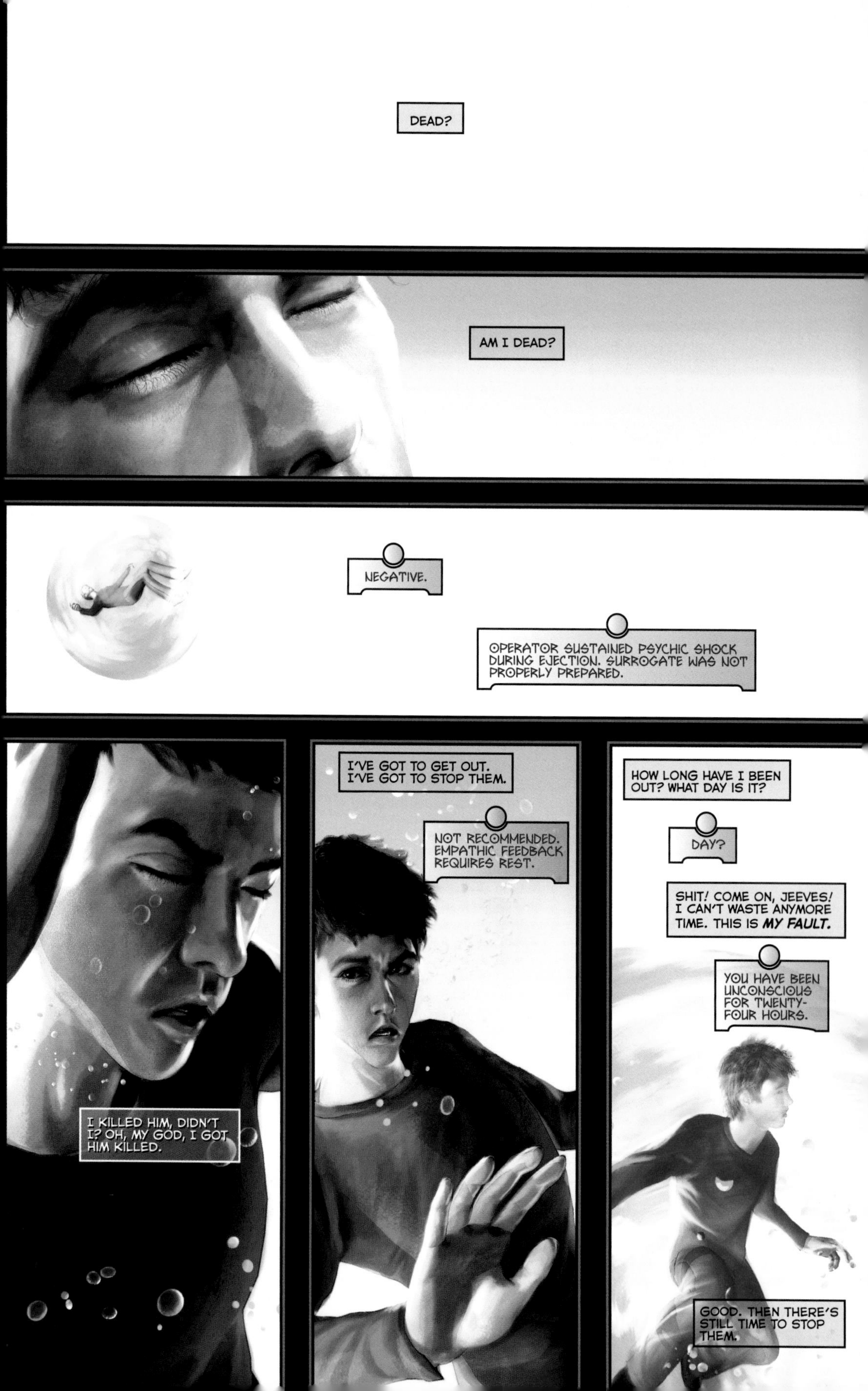

DEAD?
AM I DEAD?
NEGATIVE.
OPERATOR SUSTAINED PSYCHIC SHOCK DURING EJECTION. SURROGATE WAS NOT PROPERLY PREPARED.
I KILLED HIM, DIDN'T I? OH, MY GOD, I GOT HIM KILLED.
I'VE GOT TO GET OUT. I'VE GOT TO STOP THEM.
NOT RECOMMENDED. EMPATHIC FEEDBACK REQUIRES REST.
HOW LONG HAVE I BEEN OUT? WHAT DAY IS IT?
DAY?
SHIT! COME ON, JEEVES! I CAN'T WASTE ANYMORE TIME. THIS IS *MY FAULT.*
YOU HAVE BEEN UNCONSCIOUS FOR TWENTY-FOUR HOURS.
GOOD. THEN THERE'S STILL TIME TO STOP THEM.

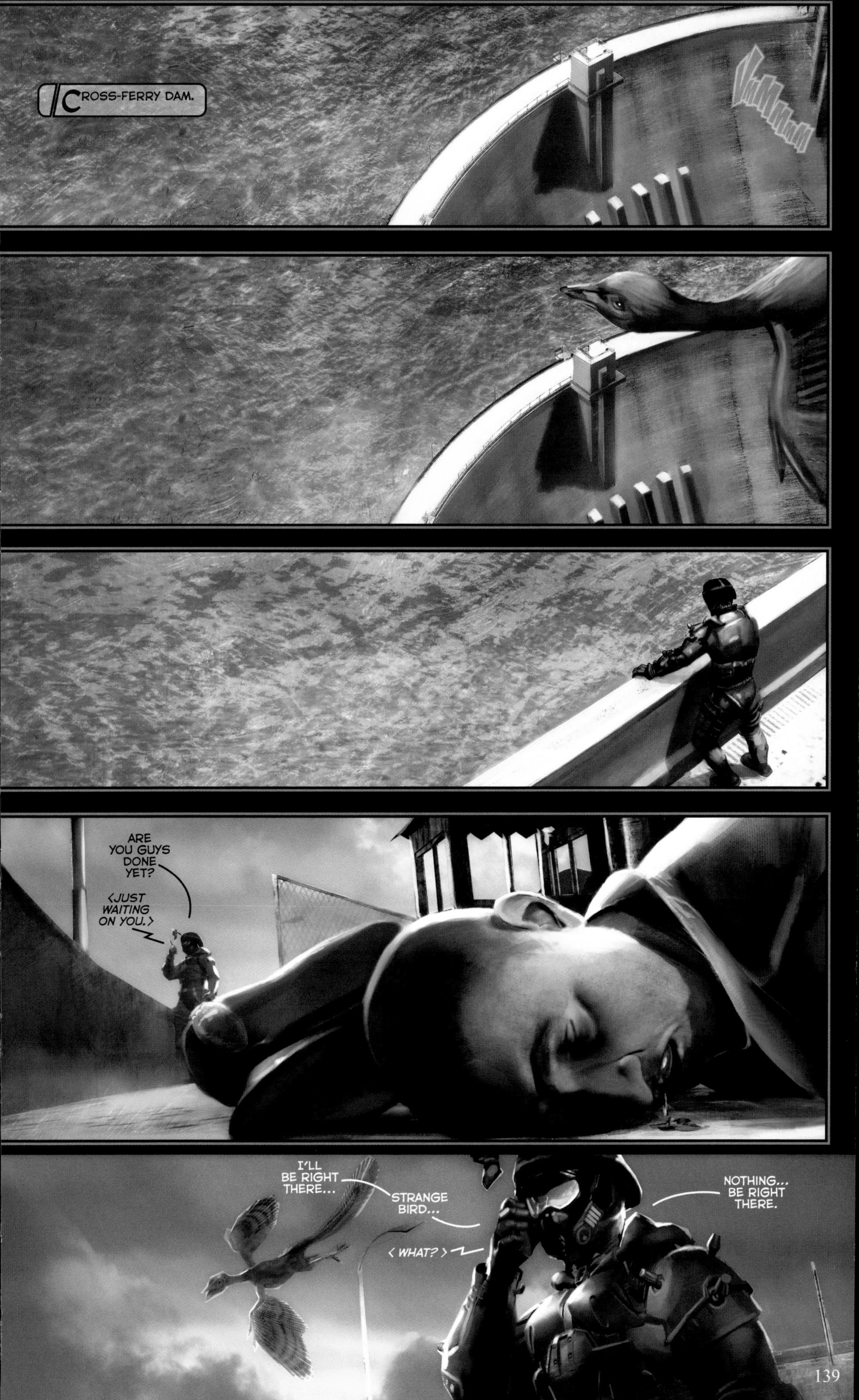
CROSS-FERRY DAM.
VMMMM
ARE YOU GUYS DONE YET?
<JUST WAITING ON YOU.>
I'LL BE RIGHT THERE...
STRANGE BIRD...
< WHAT? >
NOTHING... BE RIGHT THERE.

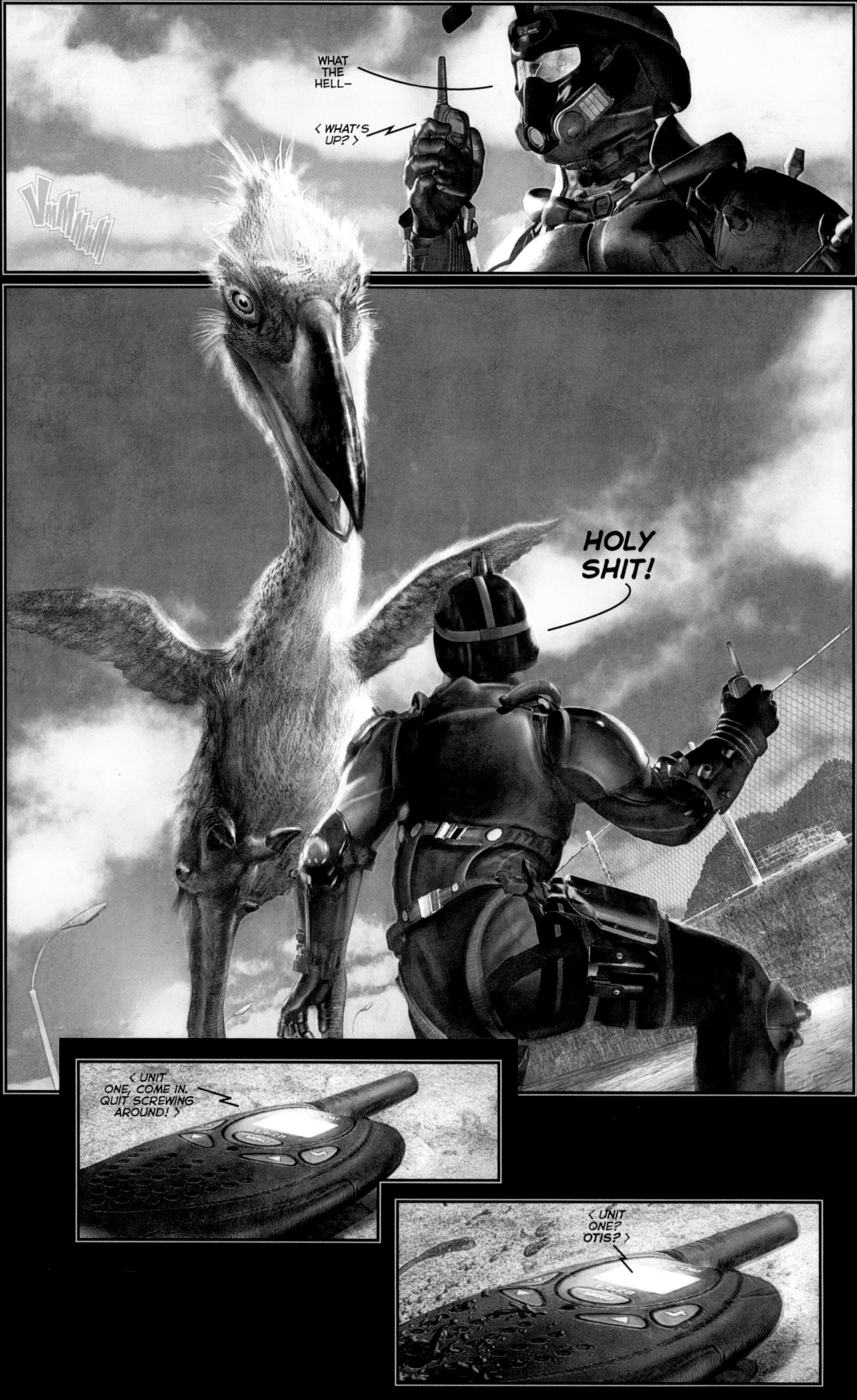
WHAT THE HELL–
< WHAT'S UP? >
VMMMMM
HOLY SHIT!
< UNIT ONE, COME IN. QUIT SCREWING AROUND! >
< UNIT ONE? OTIS? >

SOMETHING'S GOING ON--- IT SOUNDED LIKE SCREAMS...

MAYBE THAT RENT-A-COP THEY HAD OVER THERE HAD MORE GOING FOR HIM THAN WE FIGURED.

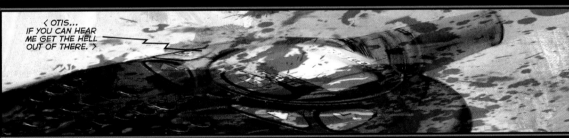

DOESN'T MATTER... WE HAVE A SCHEDULE TO KEEP.

BUT--

YOU KNOW THE DRILL.

OKAY...

‹ OTIS... IF YOU CAN HEAR ME GET THE HELL OUT OF THERE. ›

‹ ORDERS... YOU'VE GOT FIVE SECONDS BEFORE WE BLOW THIS THING. ›

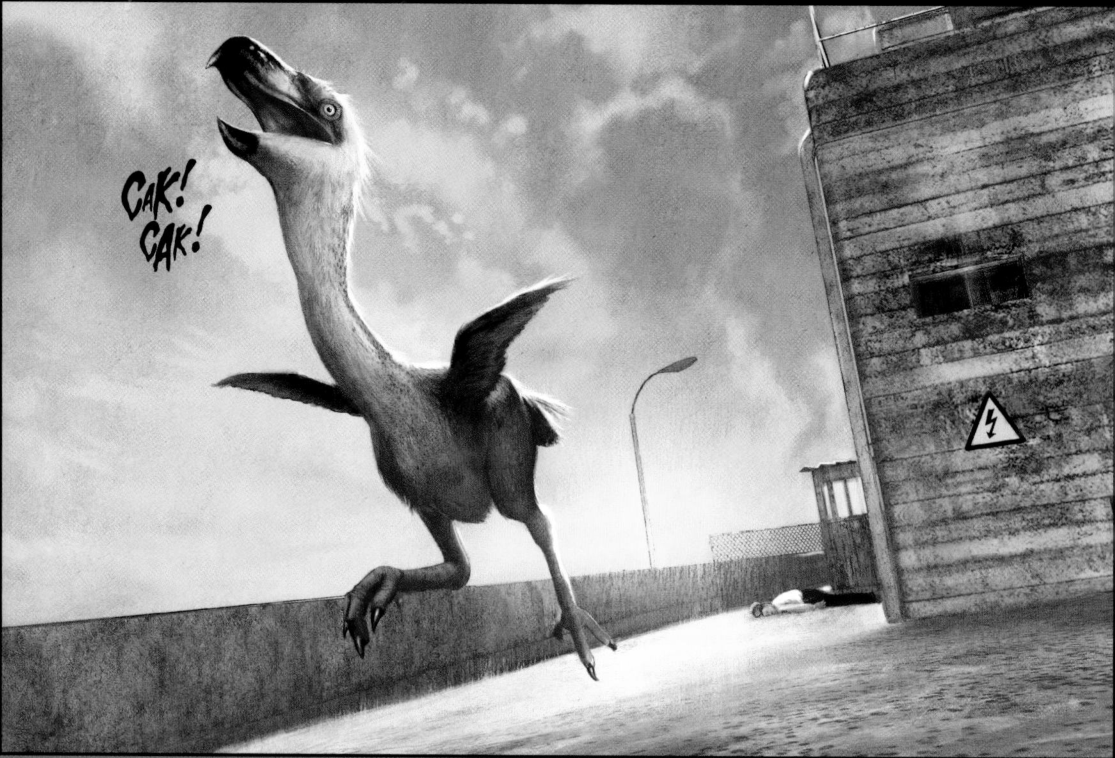
CAK!
CAK!

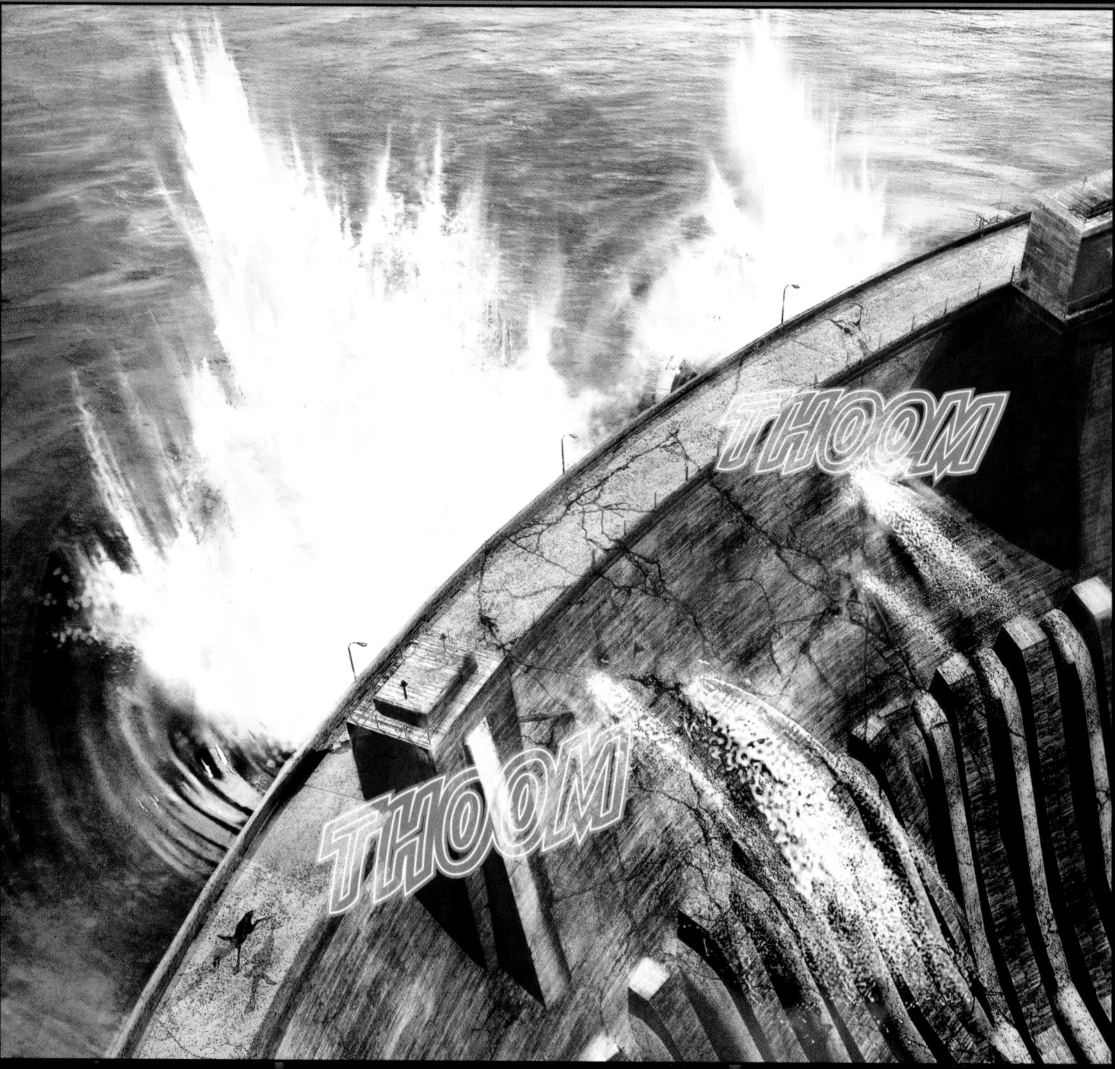
THOOM
THOOM

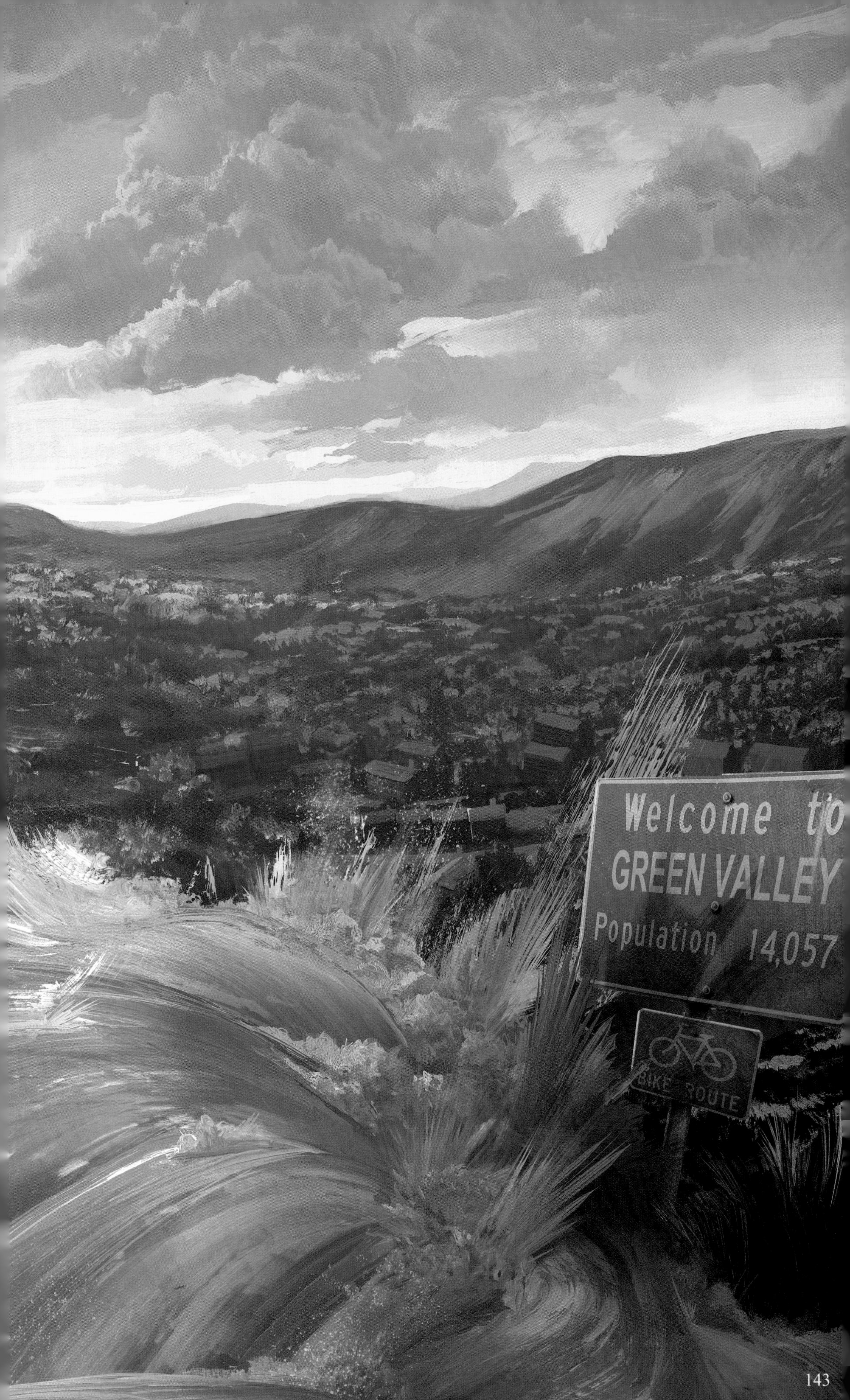
Welcome to
GREEN VALLEY
Population 14,057
BIKE ROUTE

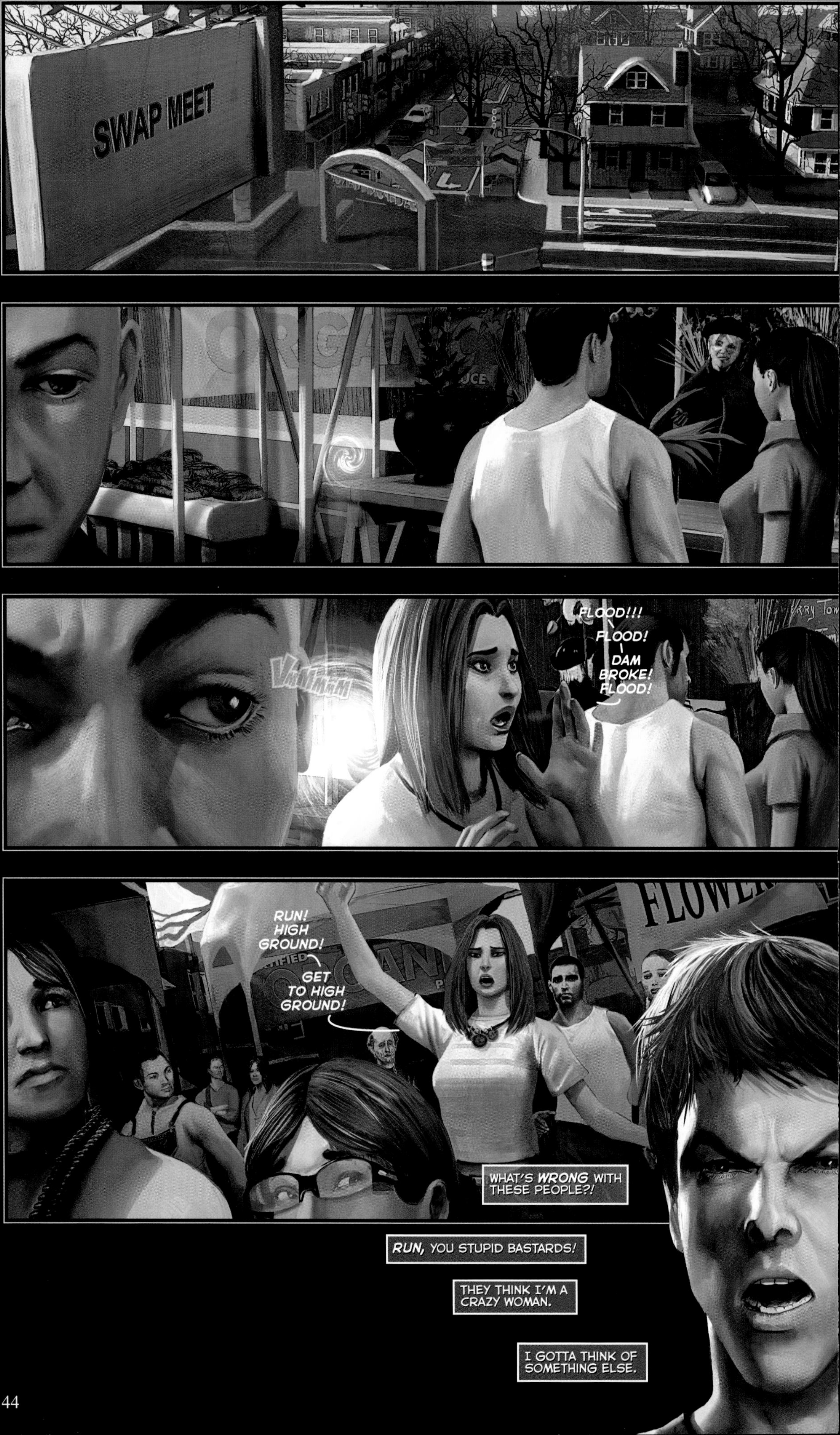
SWAP MEET
VMMMM
FLOOD!!!
FLOOD!
DAM BROKE! FLOOD!
FLOWER
RUN! HIGH GROUND!
GET TO HIGH GROUND!
WHAT'S **WRONG** WITH THESE PEOPLE?!
RUN, YOU STUPID BASTARDS!
THEY THINK I'M A CRAZY WOMAN.
I GOTTA THINK OF SOMETHING ELSE.

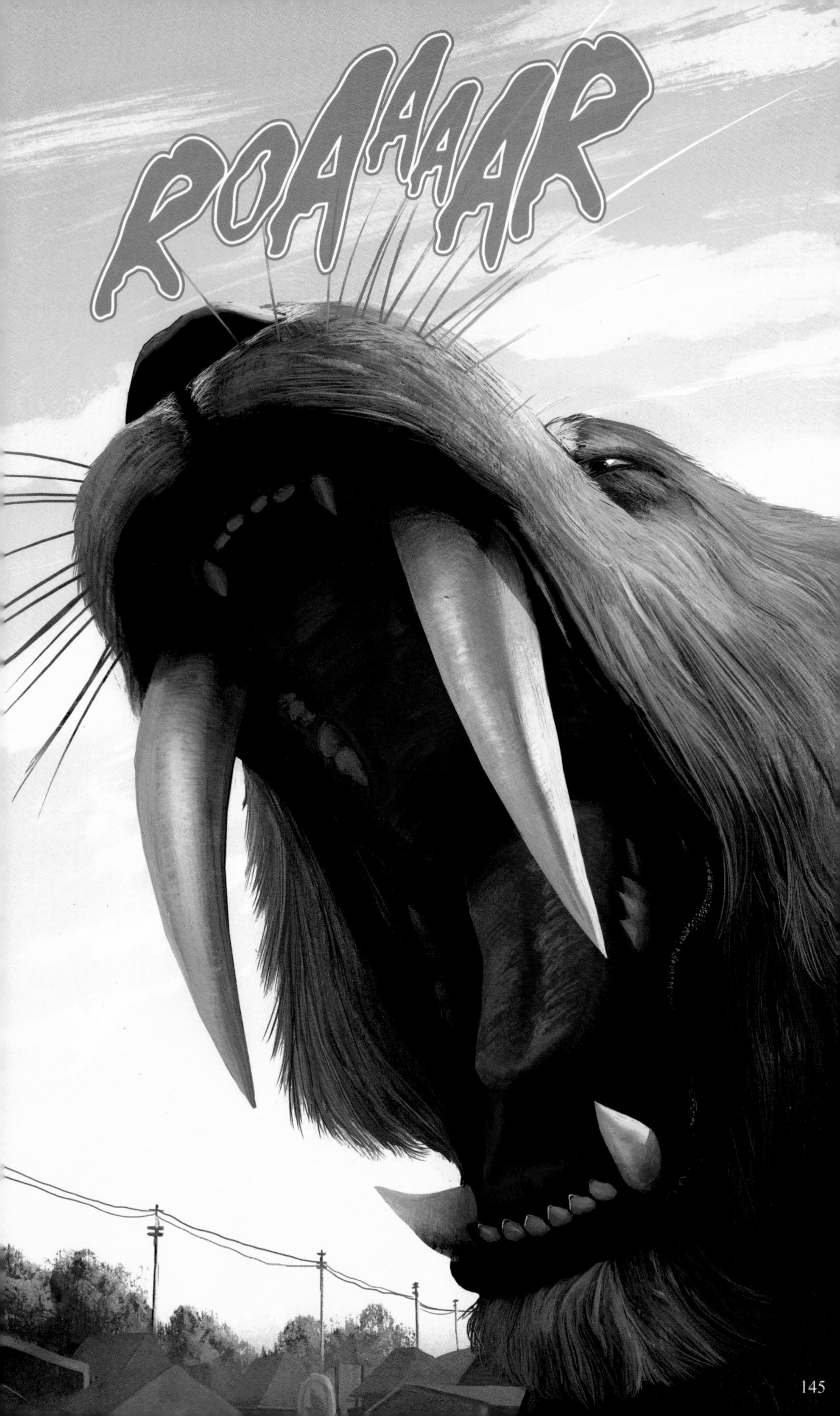
ROAAAAR

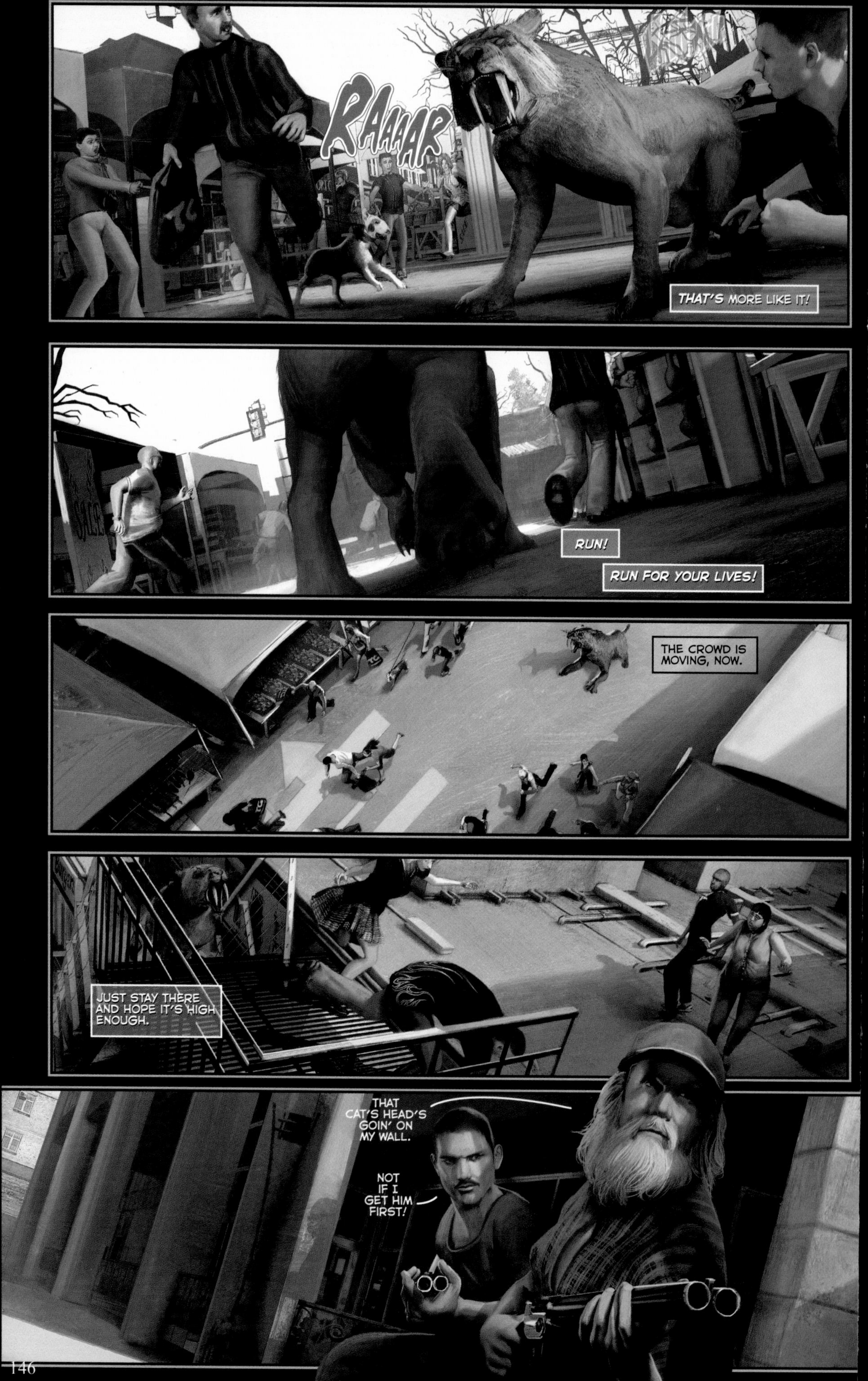
RAAAAR
THAT'S MORE LIKE IT!
RUN!
RUN FOR YOUR LIVES!
THE CROWD IS MOVING, NOW.
JUST STAY THERE AND HOPE IT'S HIGH ENOUGH.
THAT CAT'S HEAD'S GOIN' ON MY WALL.
NOT IF I GET HIM FIRST!

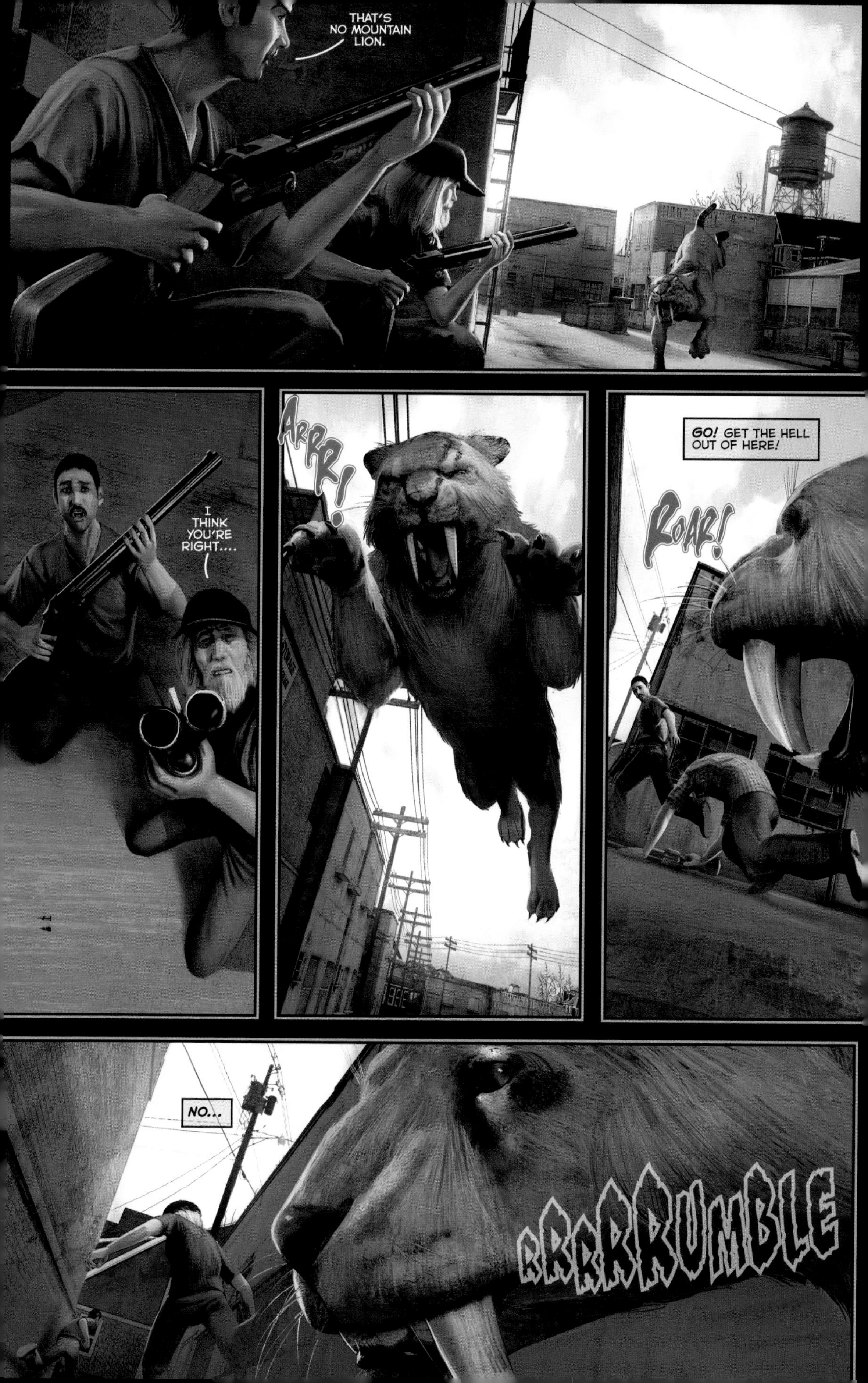
THAT'S NO MOUNTAIN LION.
I THINK YOU'RE RIGHT....
ARRRR!
GO! GET THE HELL OUT OF HERE!
ROAR!
NO...
RRRRRUMBLE

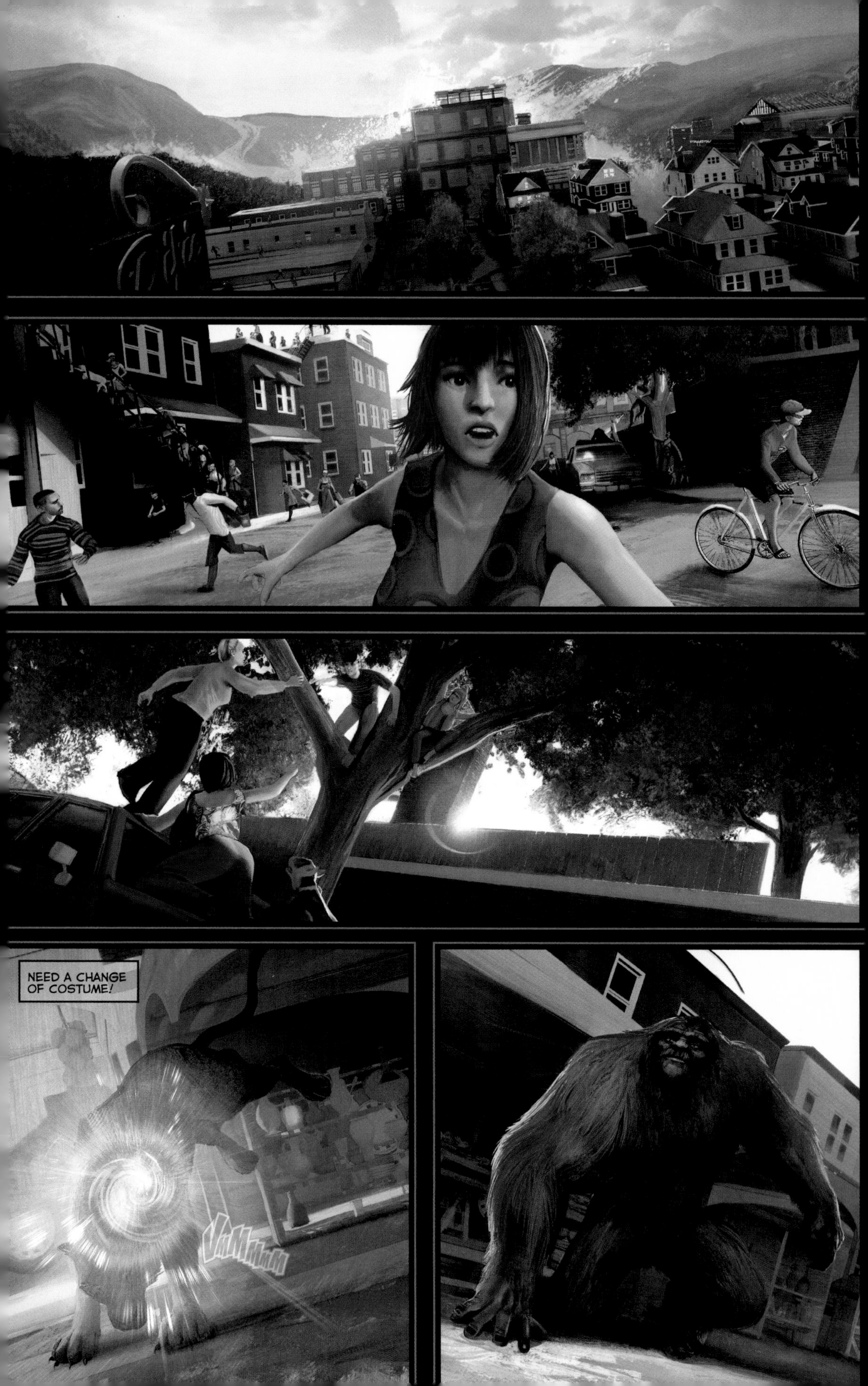
NEED A CHANGE OF COSTUME!
VMMMM

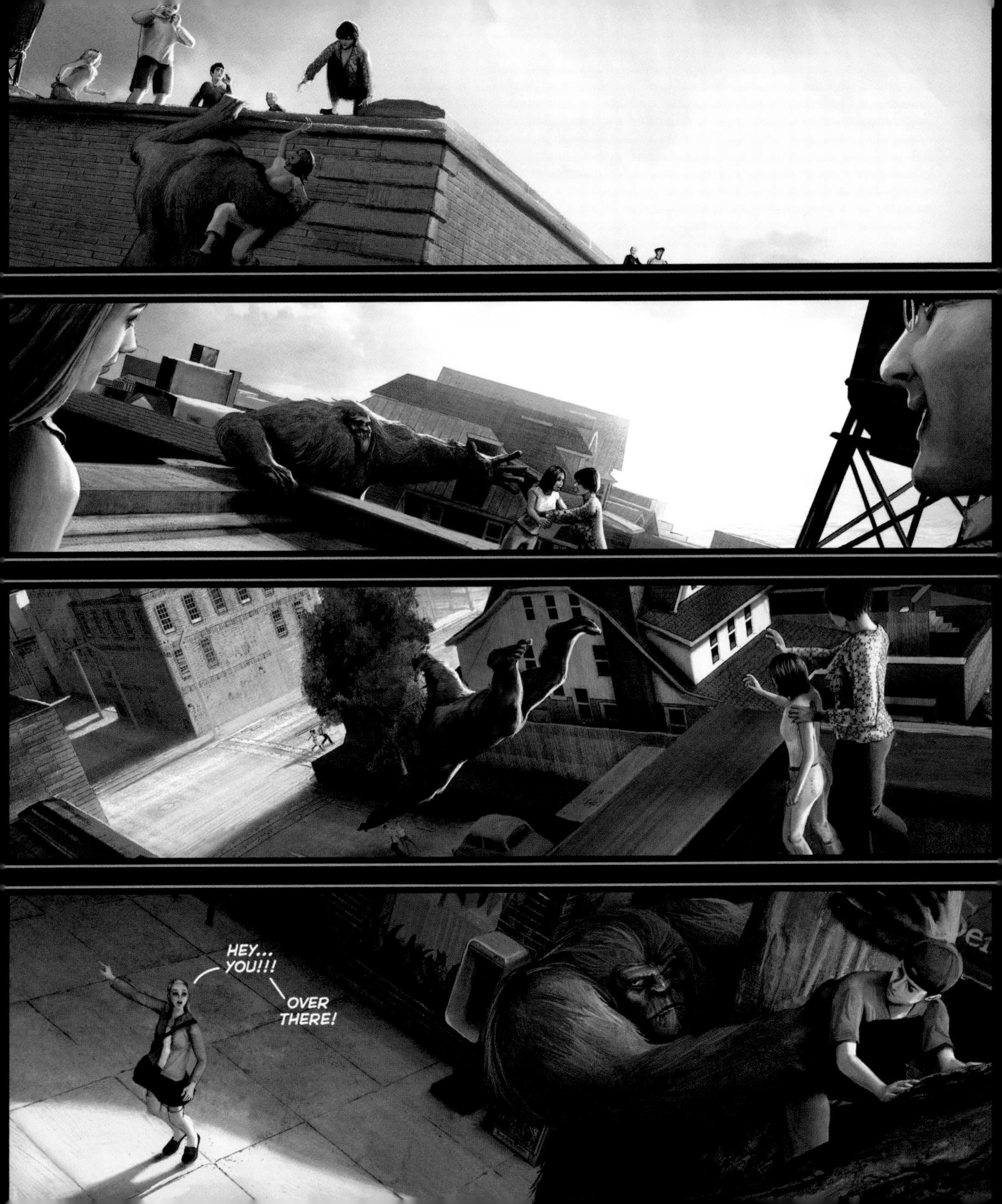
HEY... YOU!!!
OVER THERE!

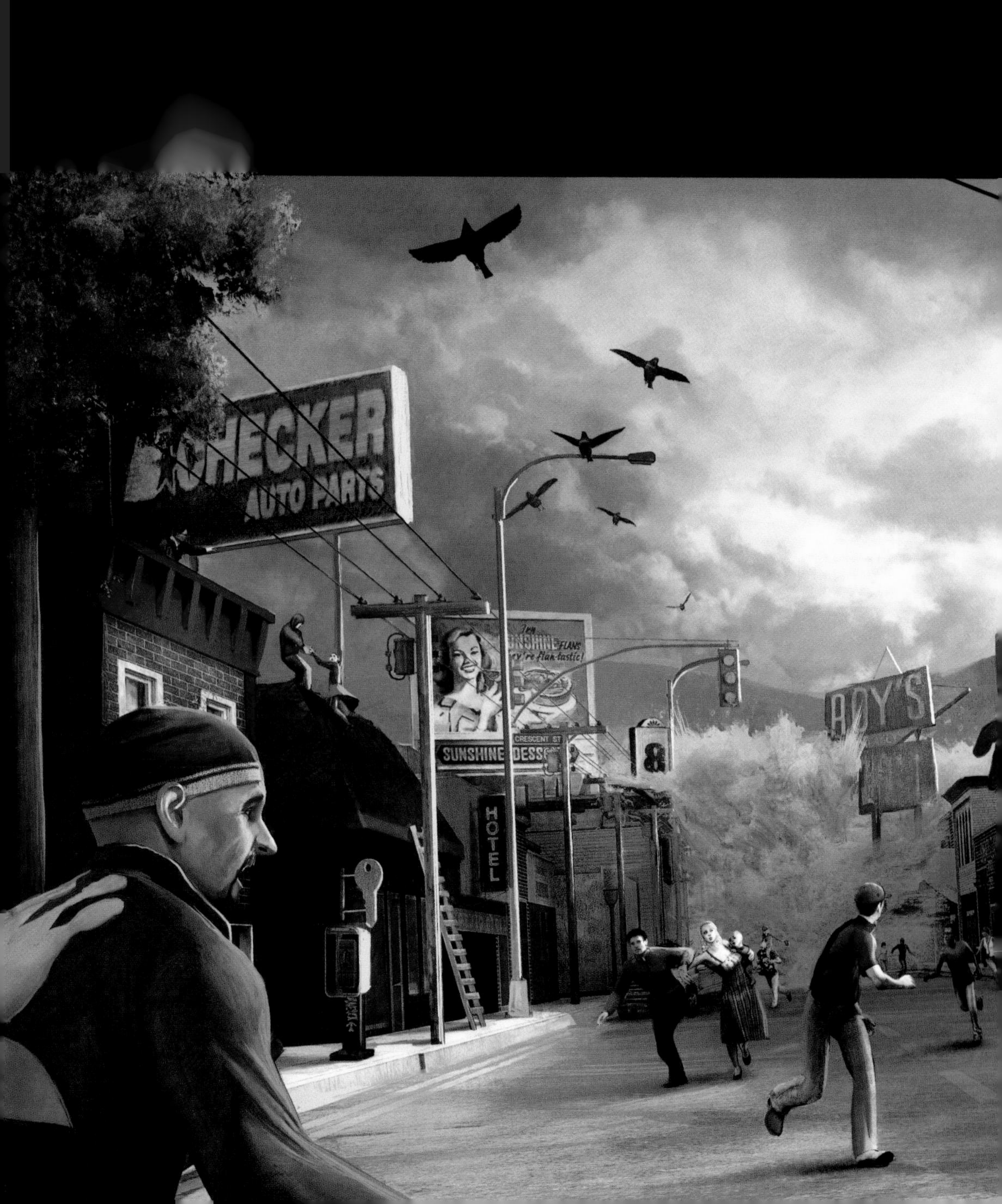
HECKER
AUTO PARTS
Try
SUNSHINE FLANS
flan-tastic!
CRESCENT ST
SUNSHINE DESS
HOTEL
8

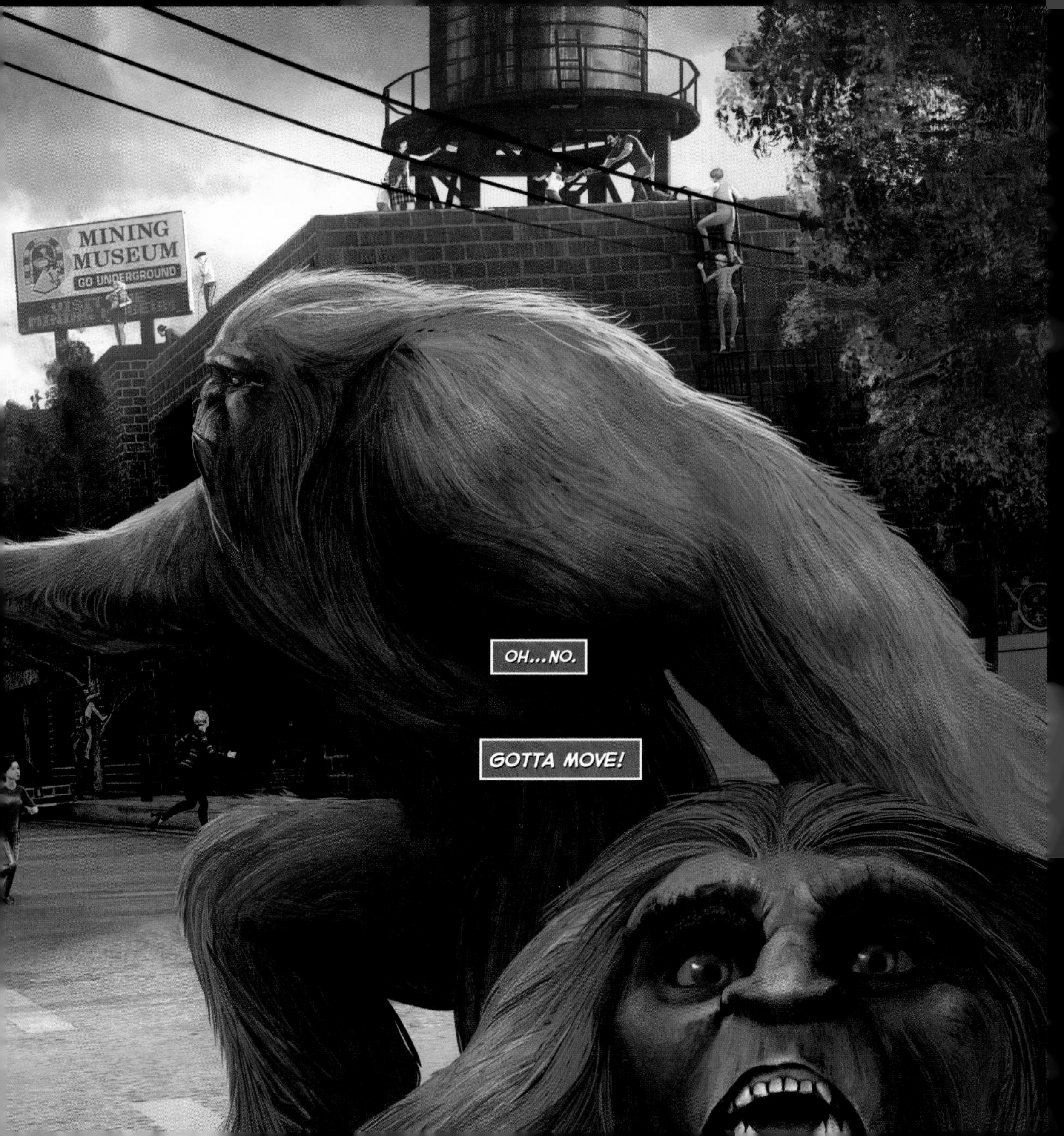
MINING MUSEUM
GO UNDERGROUND
OH...NO.
GOTTA MOVE!

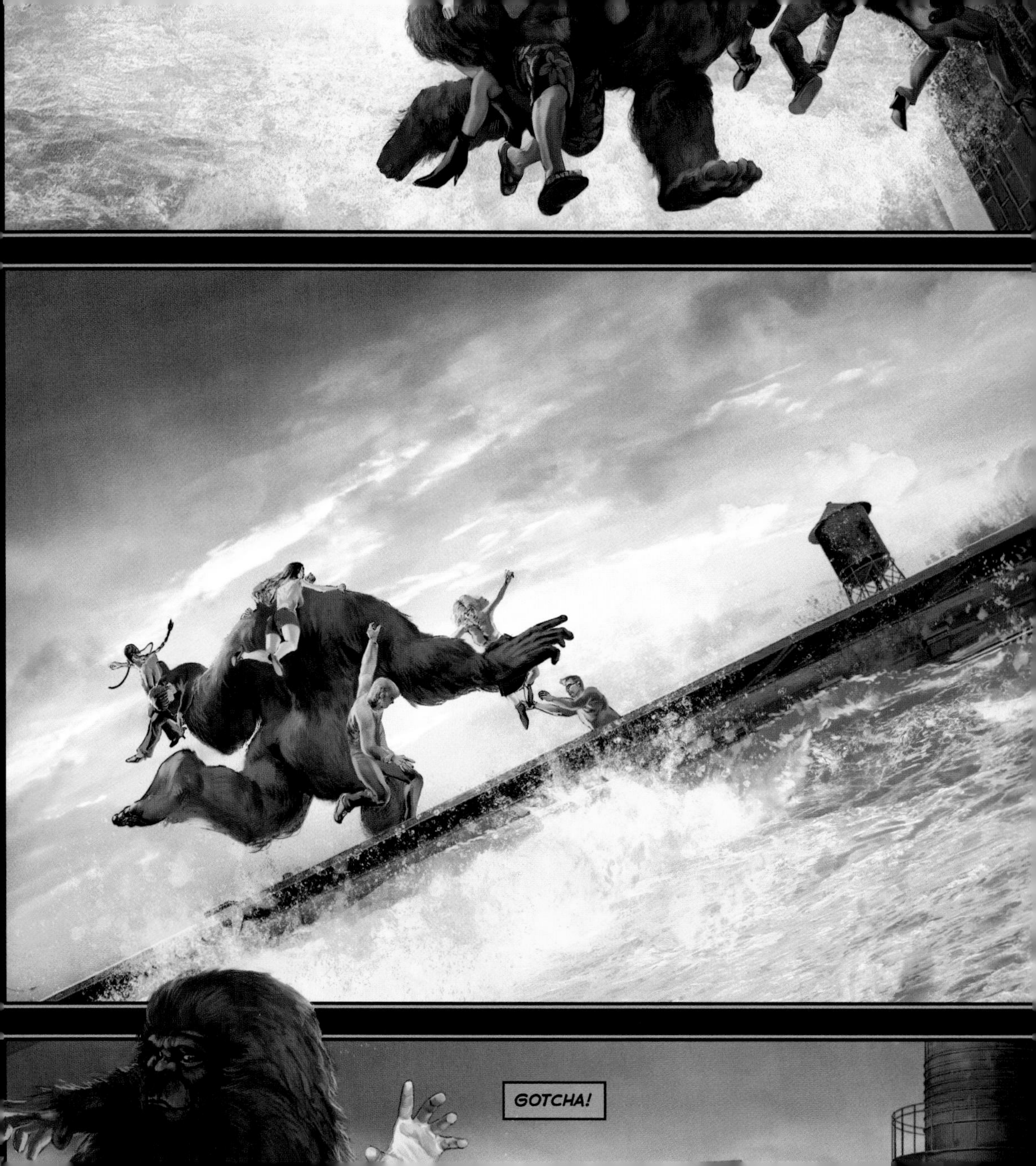
GOTCHA!

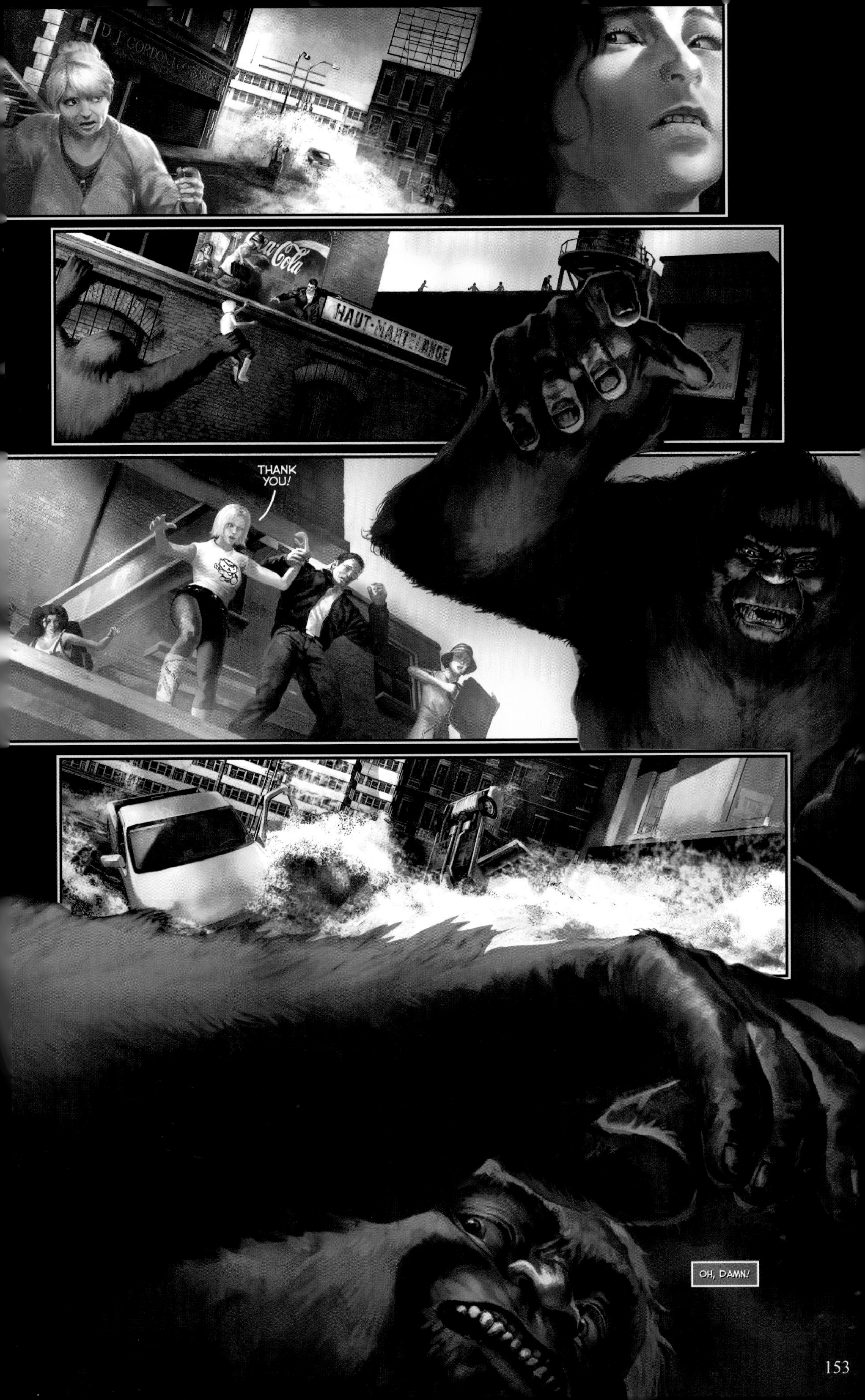
THANK YOU!
OH, DAMN!

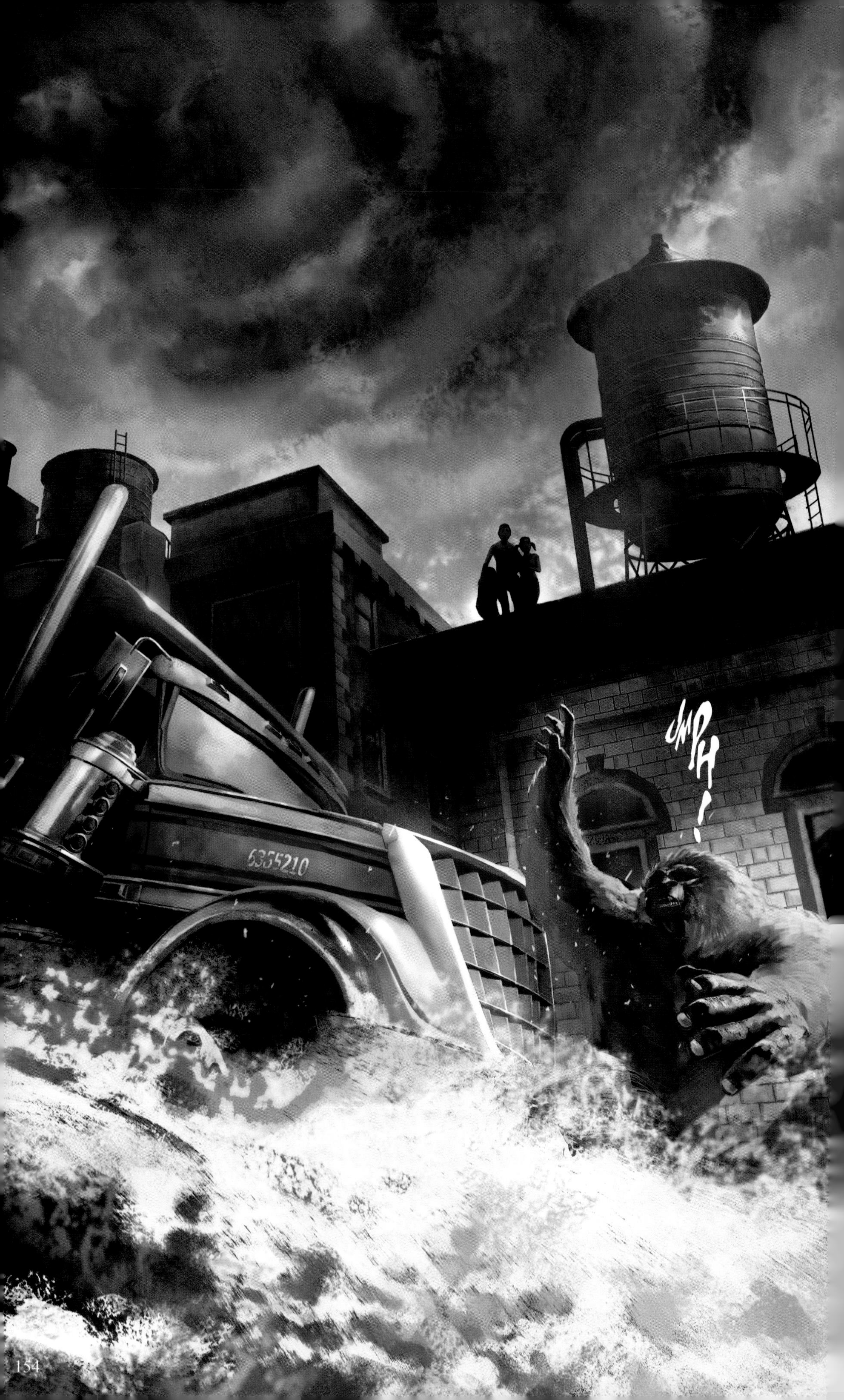
6335210
UMPH!

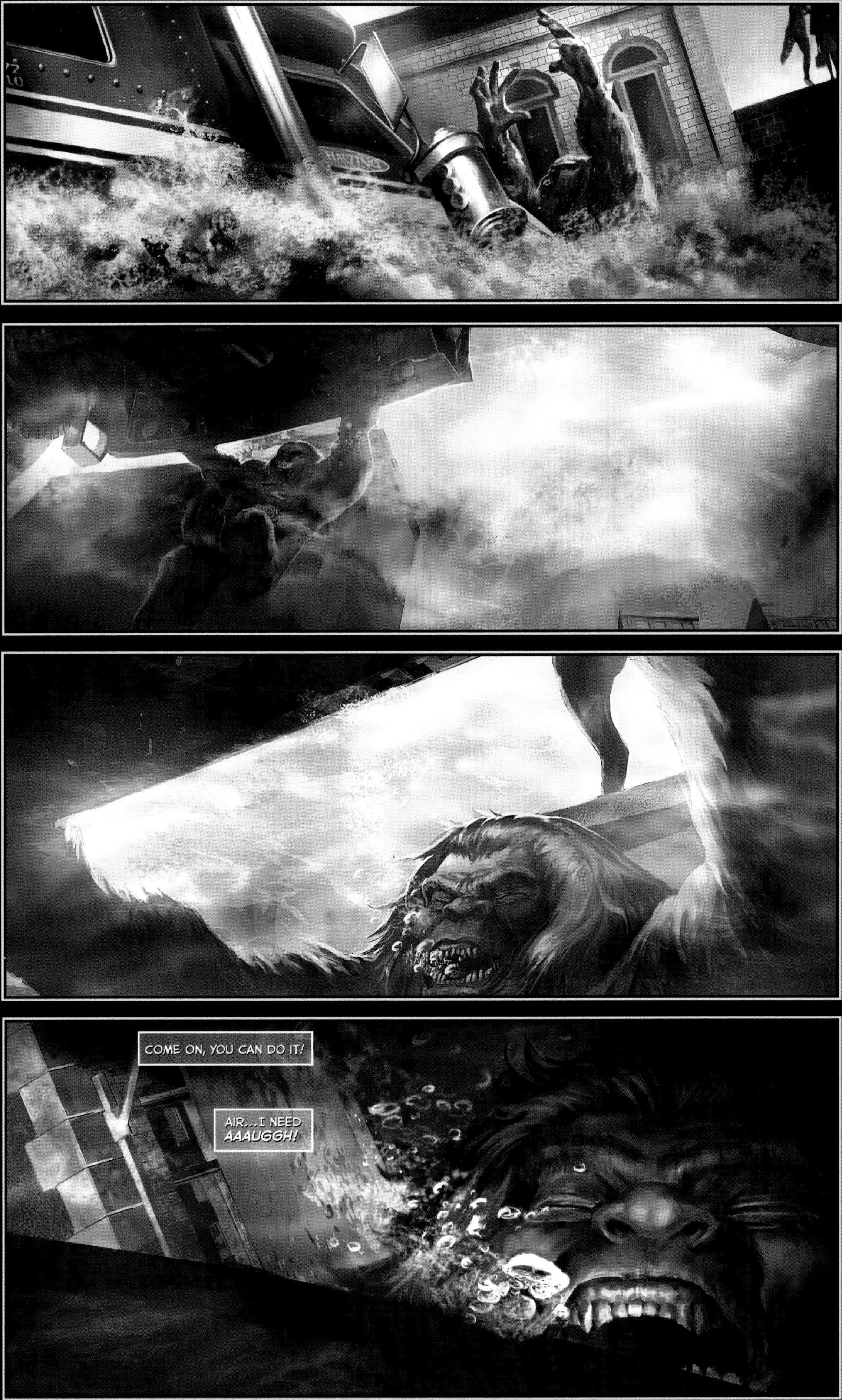
COME ON, YOU CAN DO IT!
AIR...I NEED *AAAUGGH!*

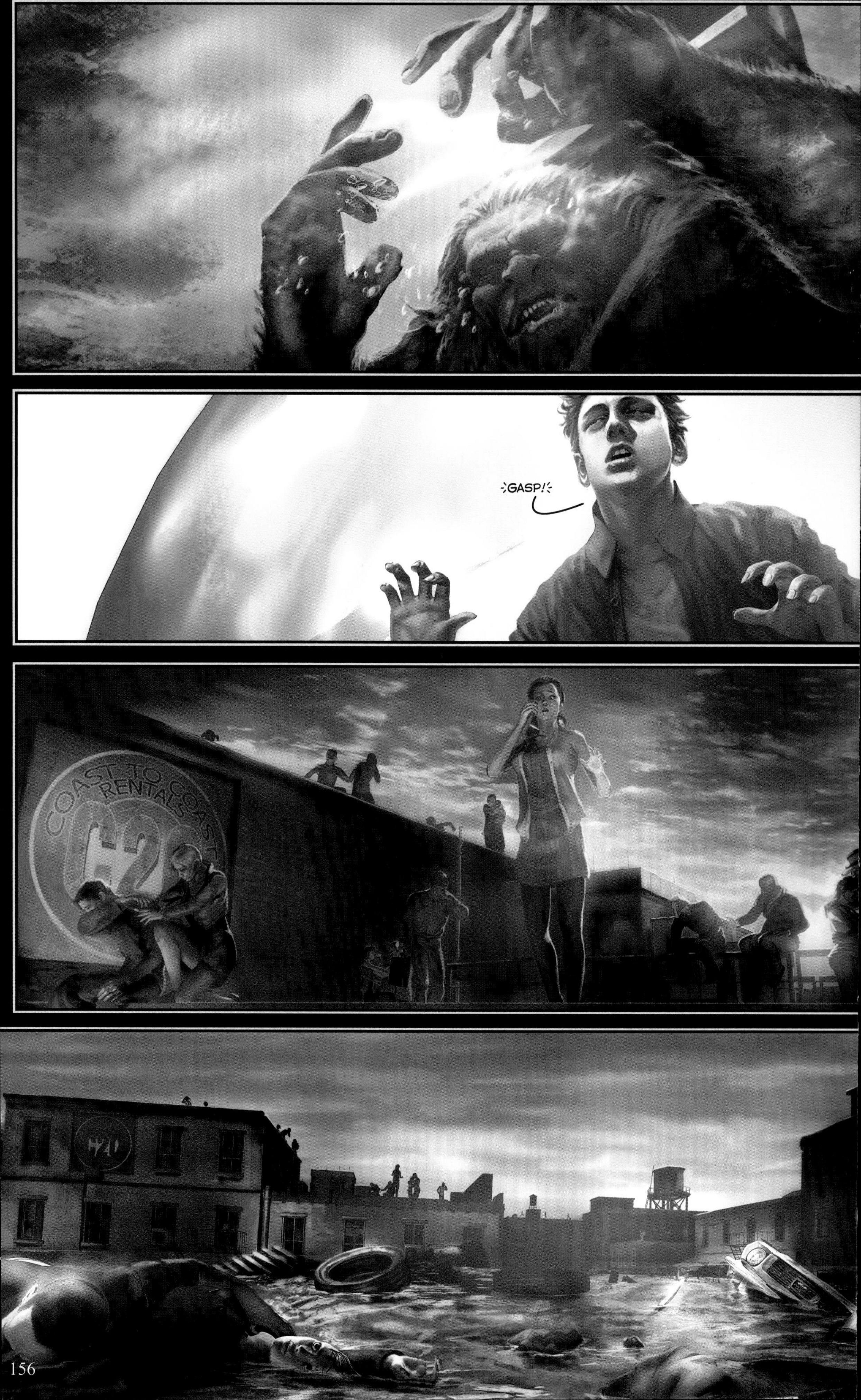
GASP!
COAST TO COAST
RENTALS

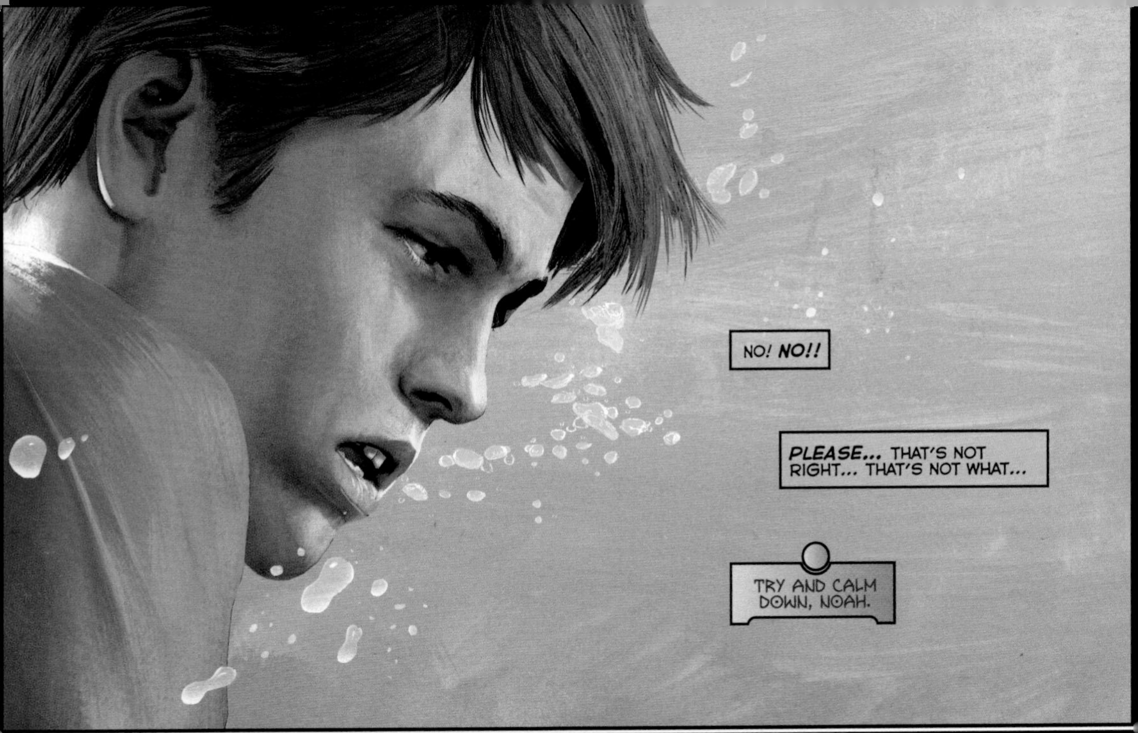
NO! *NO!!*
PLEASE... THAT'S NOT RIGHT... THAT'S NOT WHAT...
TRY AND CALM DOWN, NOAH.

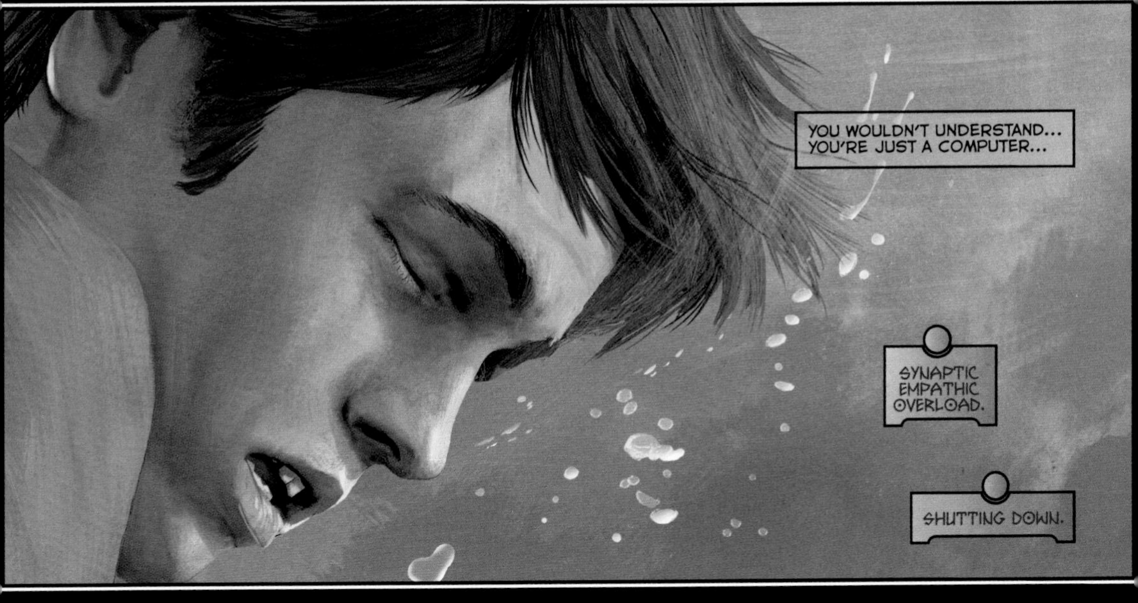
YOU WOULDN'T UNDERSTAND... YOU'RE JUST A COMPUTER...
SYNAPTIC EMPATHIC OVERLOAD.
SHUTTING DOWN.

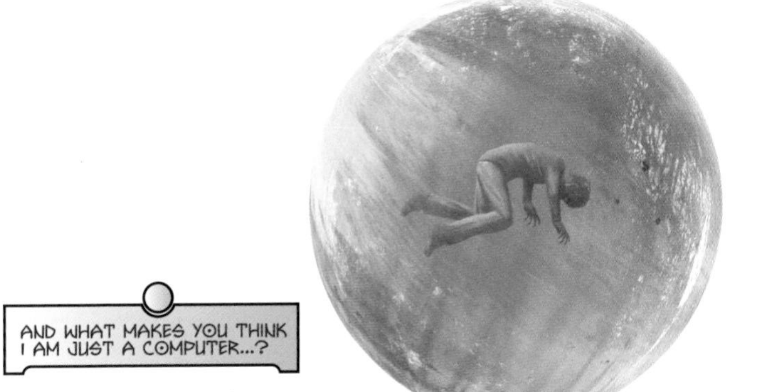
AND WHAT MAKES YOU THINK I AM JUST A COMPUTER...?

INITIATING CONSCIOUSNESS...

OPERATOR IS WELL ENOUGH TO LEAVE COMPOUND.

FINALLY.

SCHEDULE DEPARTURE?

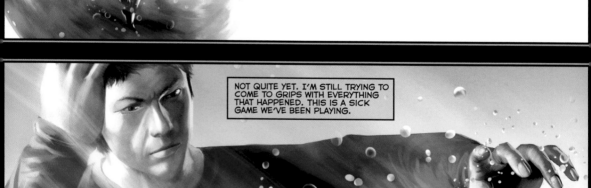

NOT QUITE YET. I'M STILL TRYING TO COME TO GRIPS WITH EVERYTHING THAT HAPPENED. THIS IS A SICK GAME WE'VE BEEN PLAYING.

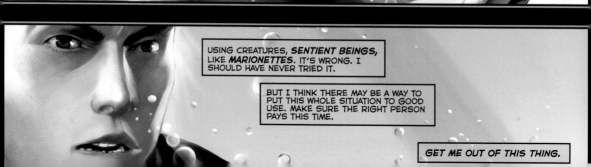

USING CREATURES, *SENTIENT BEINGS,* LIKE *MARIONETTES.* IT'S WRONG. I SHOULD HAVE NEVER TRIED IT.

BUT I THINK THERE MAY BE A WAY TO PUT THIS WHOLE SITUATION TO GOOD USE. MAKE SURE THE RIGHT PERSON PAYS THIS TIME.

GET ME OUT OF THIS THING.

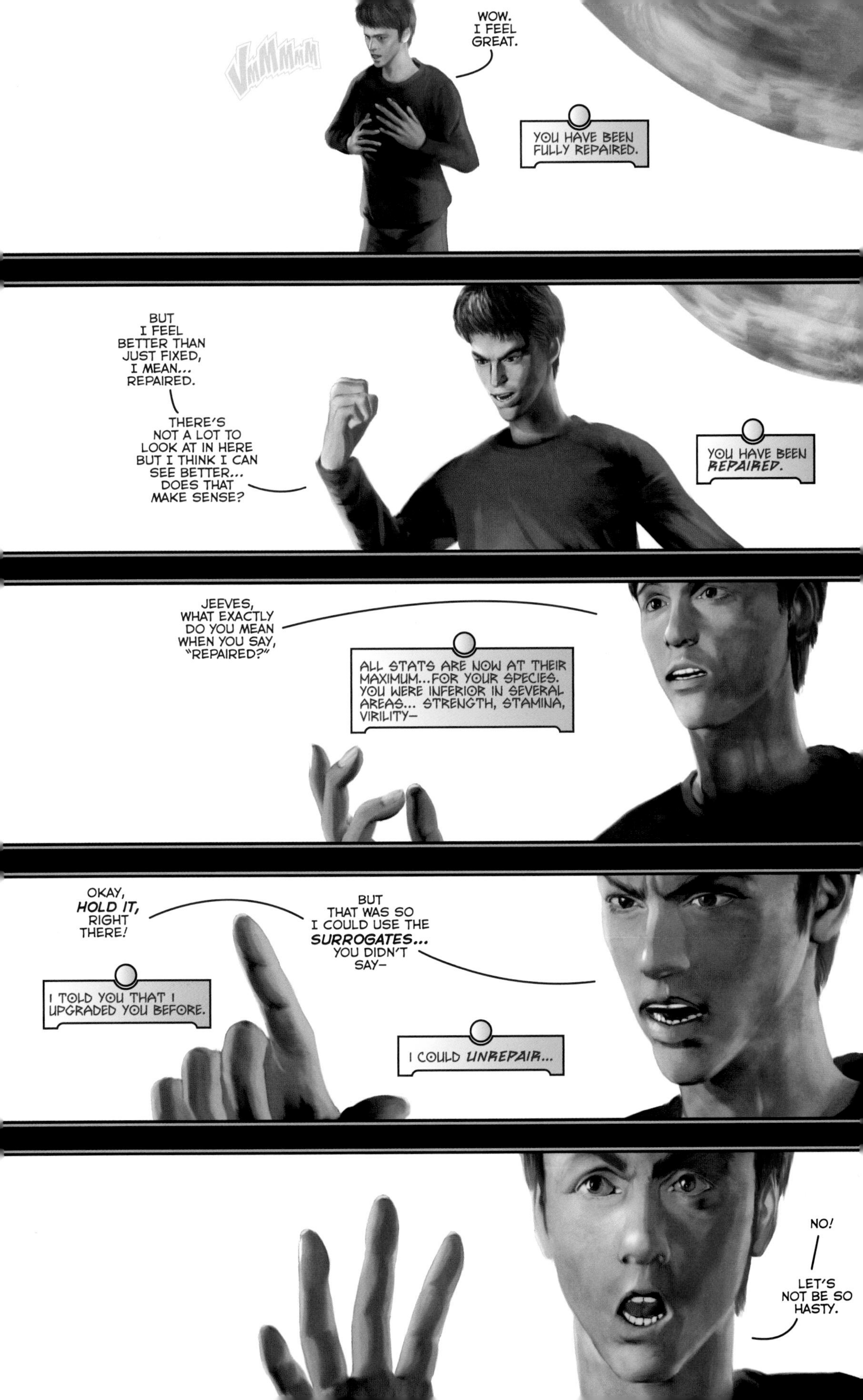
VMMMMM
WOW. I FEEL GREAT.
YOU HAVE BEEN FULLY REPAIRED.
BUT I FEEL BETTER THAN JUST FIXED, I MEAN... REPAIRED.
THERE'S NOT A LOT TO LOOK AT IN HERE BUT I THINK I CAN SEE BETTER... DOES THAT MAKE SENSE?
YOU HAVE BEEN REPAIRED.
JEEVES, WHAT EXACTLY DO YOU MEAN WHEN YOU SAY, "REPAIRED?"
ALL STATS ARE NOW AT THEIR MAXIMUM...FOR YOUR SPECIES. YOU WERE INFERIOR IN SEVERAL AREAS... STRENGTH, STAMINA, VIRILITY–
OKAY, HOLD IT, RIGHT THERE!
BUT THAT WAS SO I COULD USE THE SURROGATES... YOU DIDN'T SAY–
I TOLD YOU THAT I UPGRADED YOU BEFORE.
I COULD UNREPAIR...
NO!
LET'S NOT BE SO HASTY.

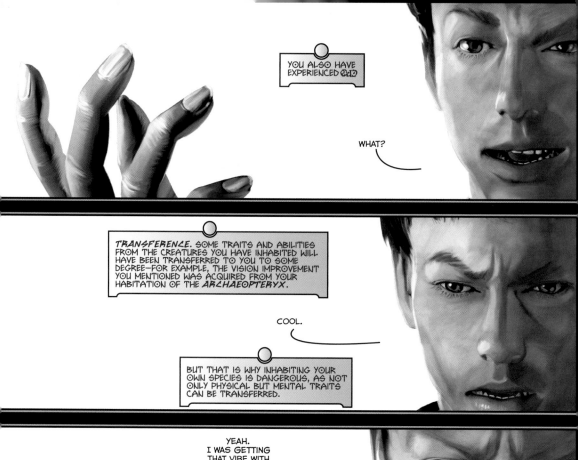

YOU ALSO HAVE EXPERIENCED

WHAT?

TRANSFERENCE. SOME TRAITS AND ABILITIES FROM THE CREATURES YOU HAVE INHABITED WILL HAVE BEEN TRANSFERRED TO YOU TO SOME DEGREE—FOR EXAMPLE, THE VISION IMPROVEMENT YOU MENTIONED WAS ACQUIRED FROM YOUR HABITATION OF THE *ARCHAEOPTERYX*.

COOL.

BUT THAT IS WHY INHABITING YOUR OWN SPECIES IS DANGEROUS, AS NOT ONLY PHYSICAL BUT MENTAL TRAITS CAN BE TRANSFERRED.

YEAH.
I WAS GETTING THAT VIBE WITH DANTE. DARK THOUGHTS...

STILL?

NO.
NOT ANYMORE. I CAN CONTROL IT.

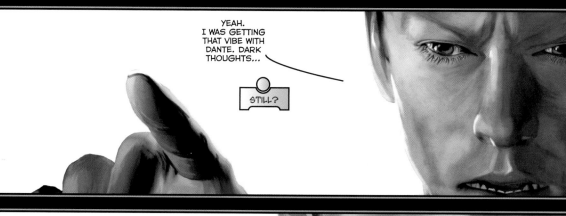

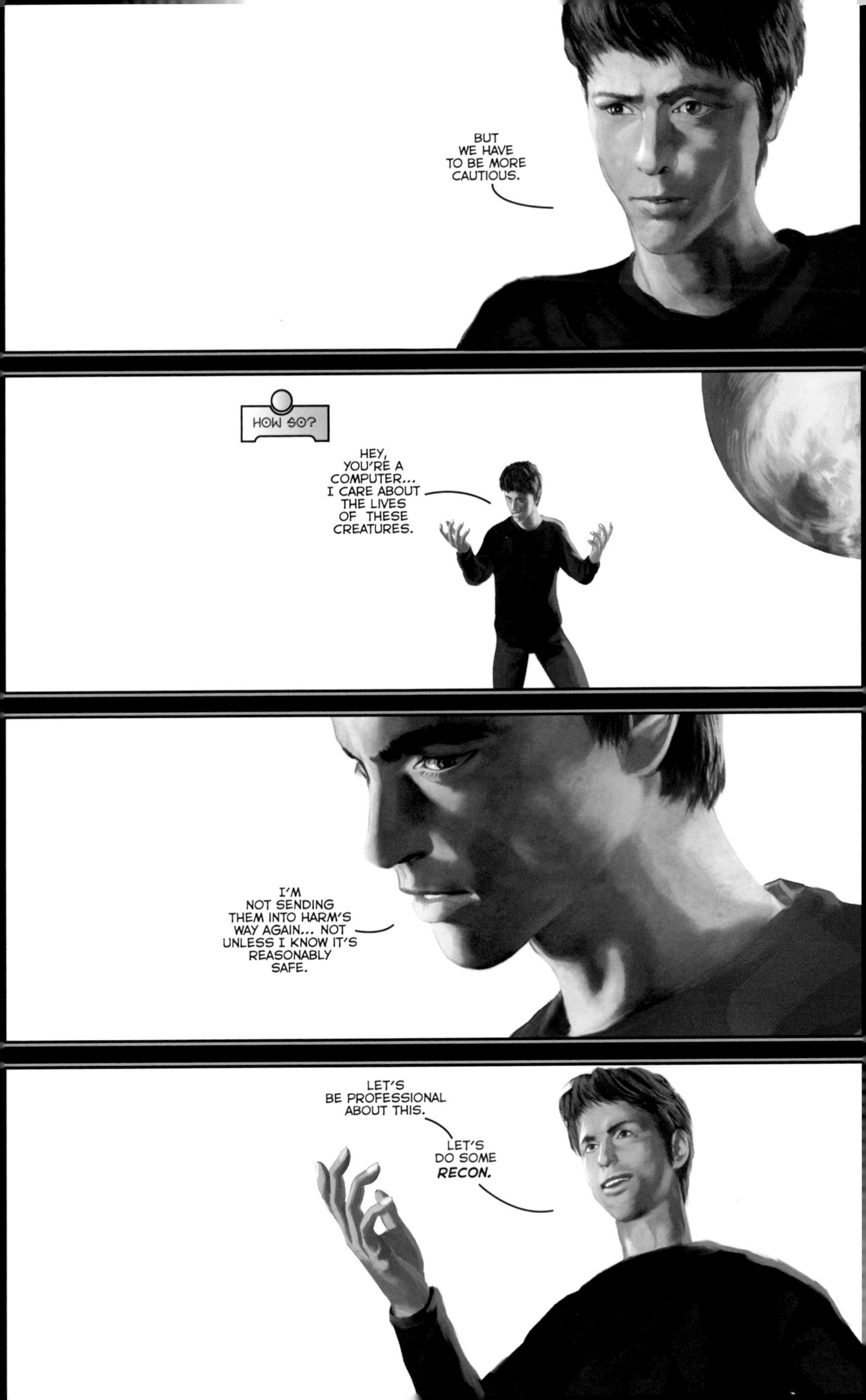
BUT WE HAVE TO BE MORE CAUTIOUS.
HOW SO?
HEY, YOU'RE A COMPUTER... I CARE ABOUT THE LIVES OF THESE CREATURES.
I'M NOT SENDING THEM INTO HARM'S WAY AGAIN... NOT UNLESS I KNOW IT'S REASONABLY SAFE.
LET'S BE PROFESSIONAL ABOUT THIS.
LET'S DO SOME RECON.

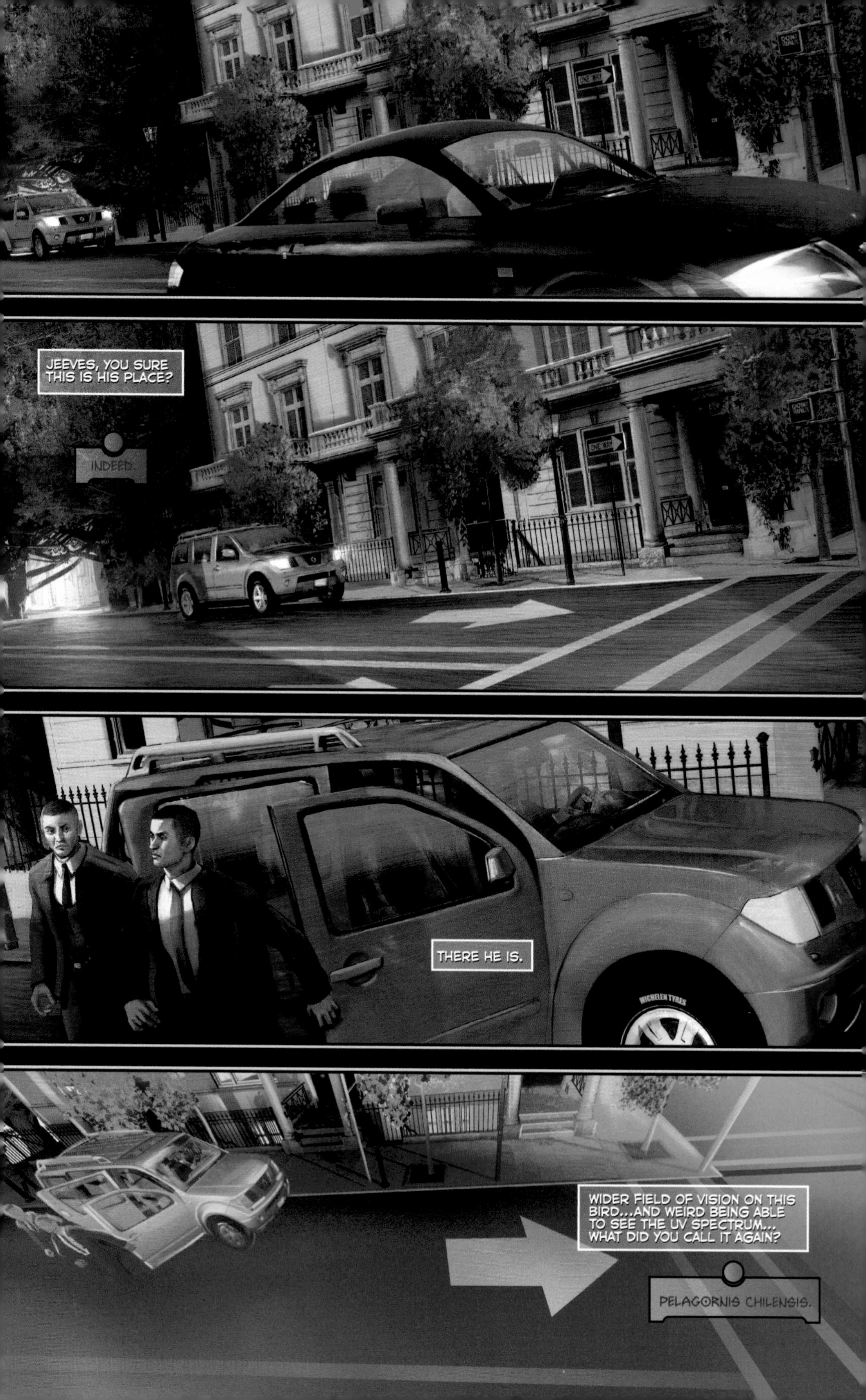
ONE WAY
JEEVES, YOU SURE THIS IS HIS PLACE?
INDEED.
ONE WAY
THERE HE IS.
MICHELEN TYRES
WIDER FIELD OF VISION ON THIS BIRD...AND WEIRD BEING ABLE TO SEE THE UV SPECTRUM... WHAT DID YOU CALL IT AGAIN?
PELAGORNIS CHILENSIS.

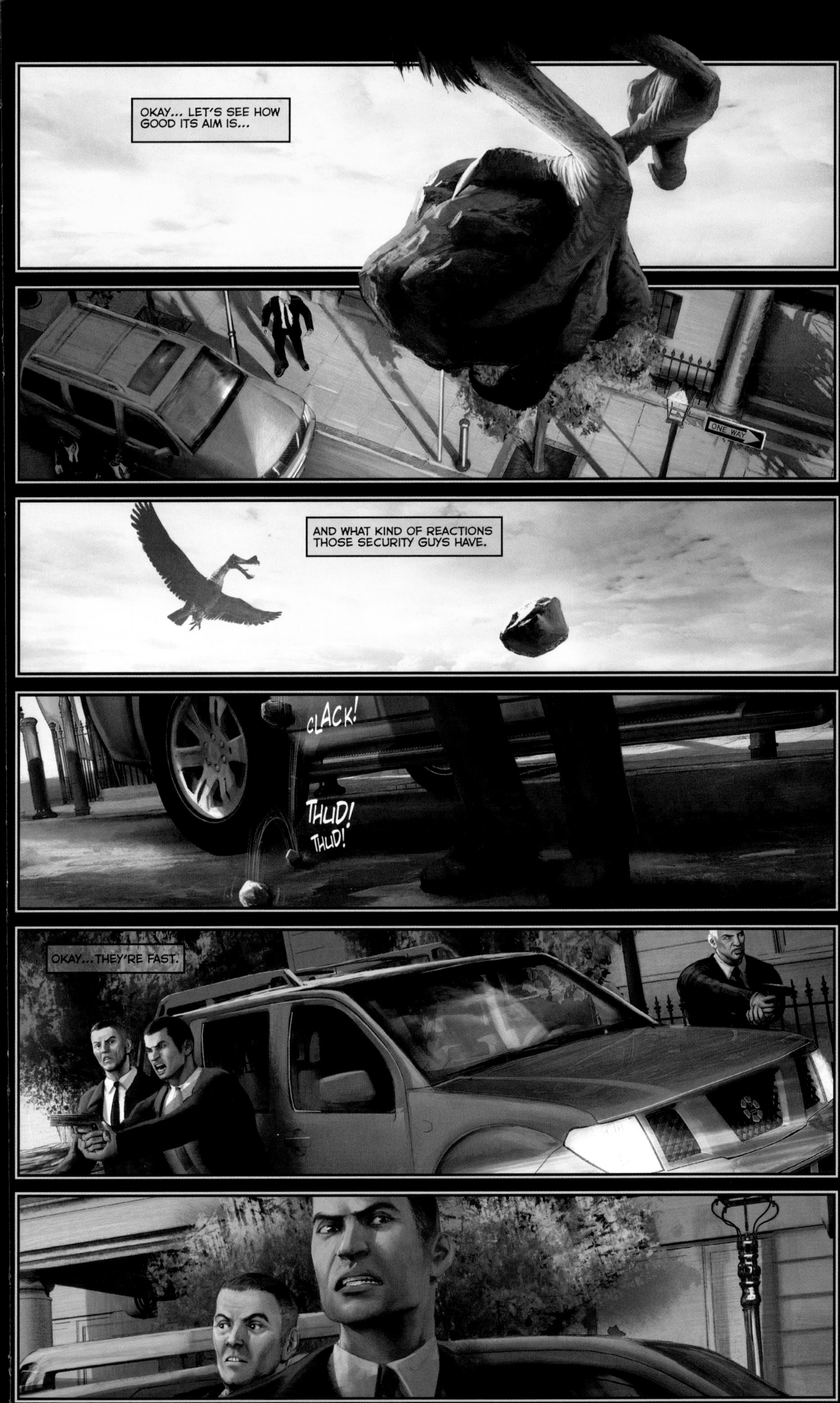

OKAY... LET'S SEE HOW GOOD ITS AIM IS...
ONE WAY
AND WHAT KIND OF REACTIONS THOSE SECURITY GUYS HAVE.
CLACK!
THUD!
THUD!
OKAY...THEY'RE FAST.

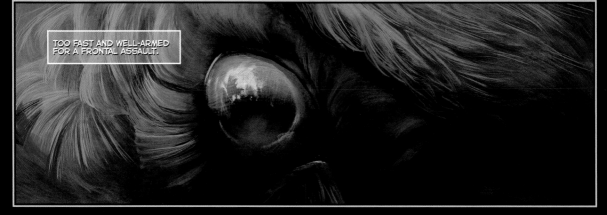

TOO FAST AND WELL-ARMED FOR A FRONTAL ASSAULT.

WE'LL HAVE TO THINK MORE CREATIVELY.

HMMM...

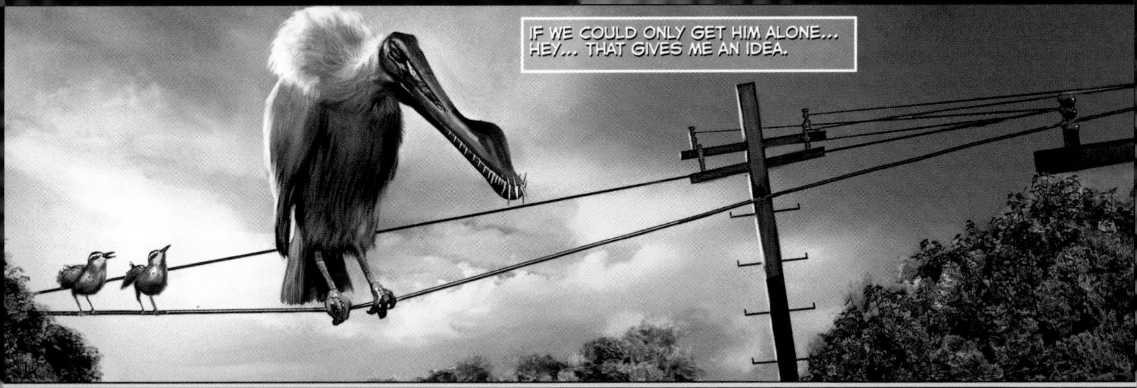
IF WE COULD ONLY GET HIM ALONE...
HEY... THAT GIVES ME AN IDEA.

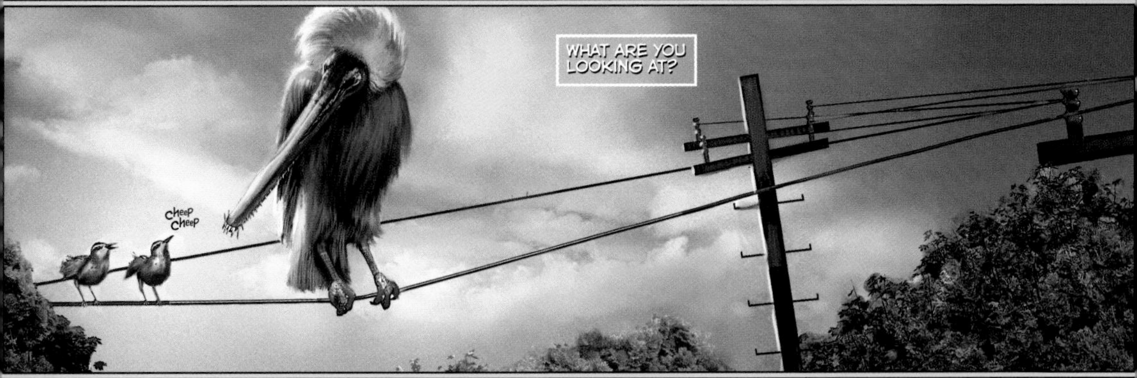
WHAT ARE YOU LOOKING AT?
CHEEP CHEEP

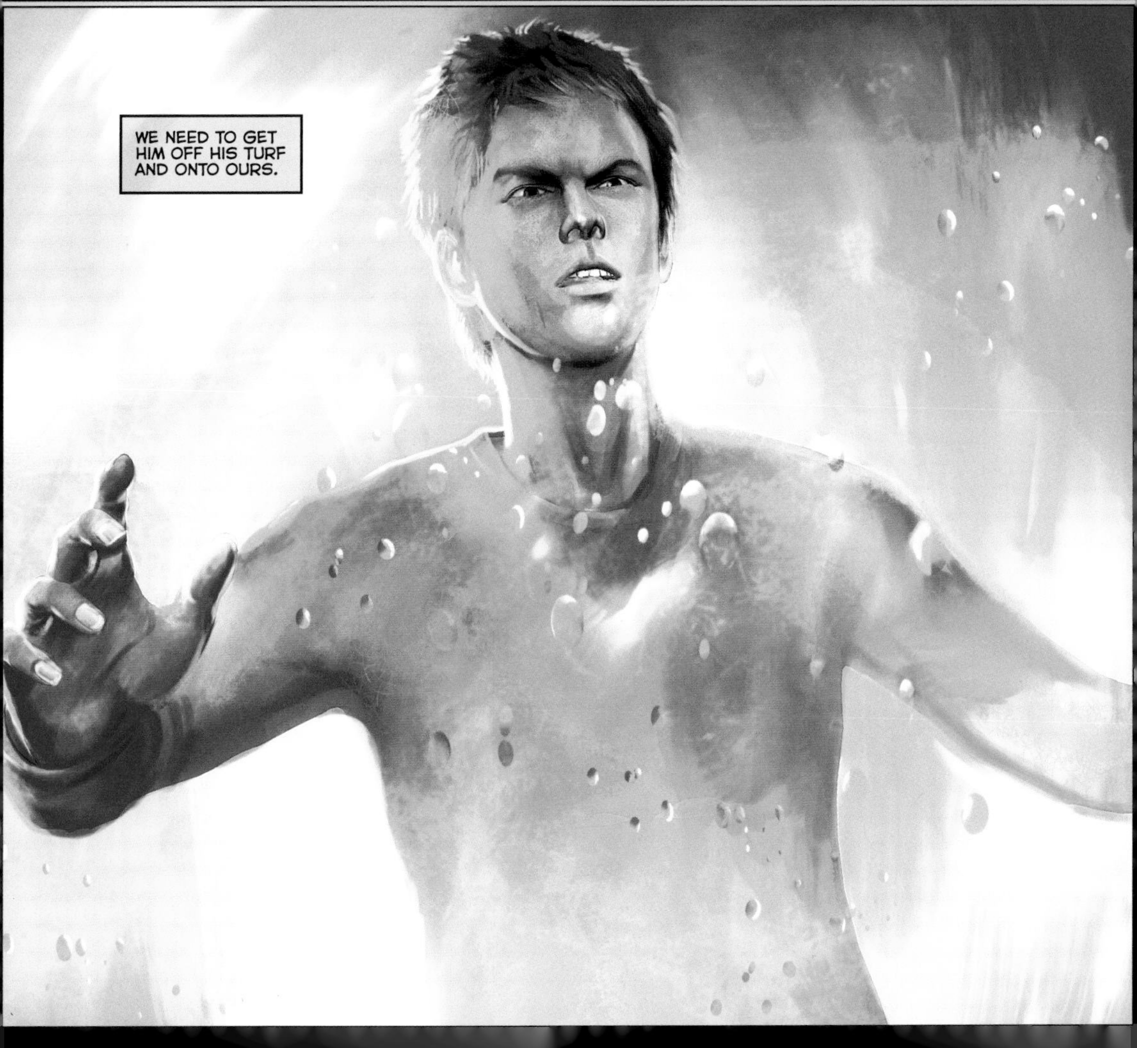
WE NEED TO GET HIM OFF HIS TURF AND ONTO OURS.

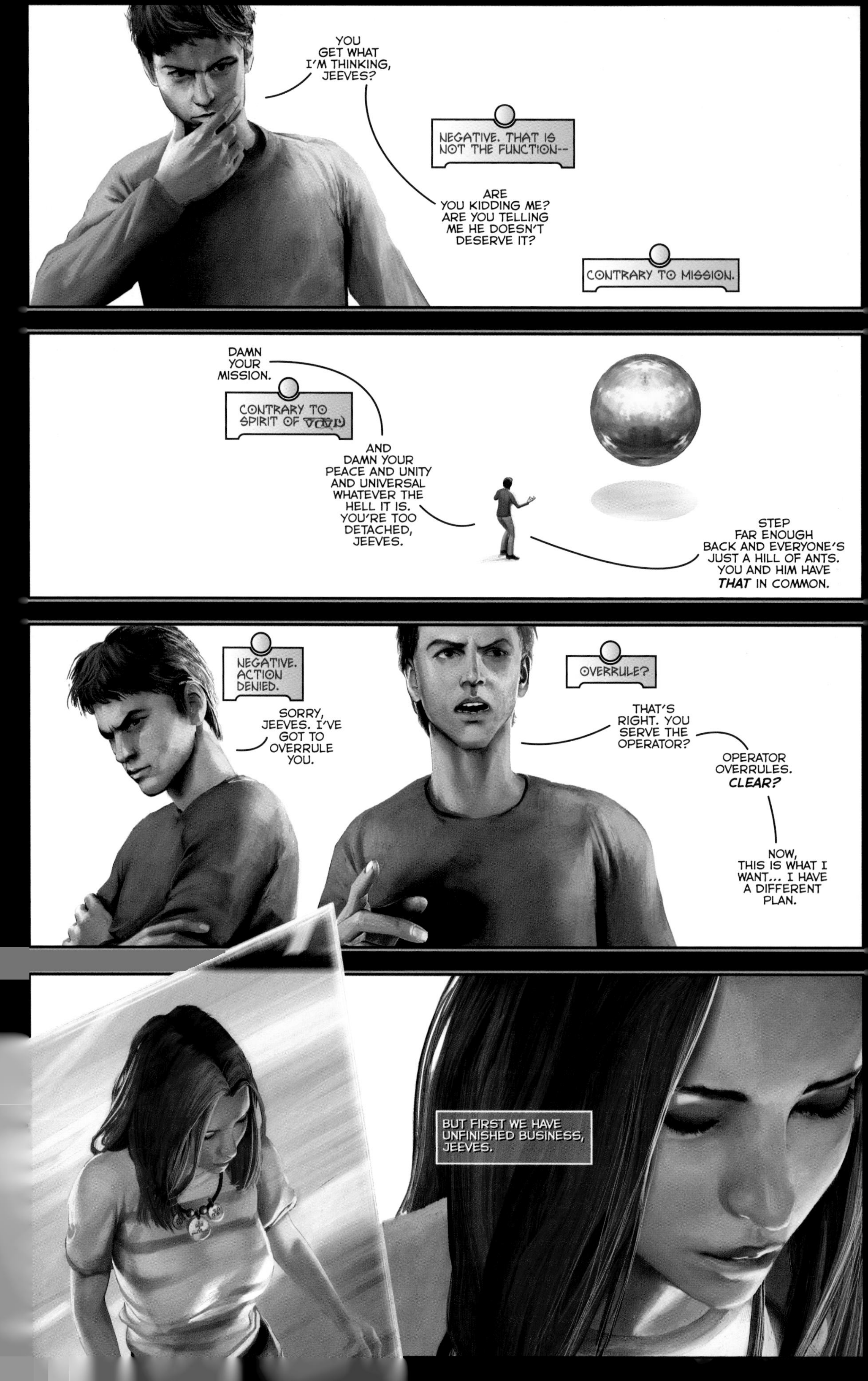
YOU GET WHAT I'M THINKING, JEEVES?
NEGATIVE. THAT IS NOT THE FUNCTION--
ARE YOU KIDDING ME? ARE YOU TELLING ME HE DOESN'T DESERVE IT?
CONTRARY TO MISSION.
DAMN YOUR MISSION.
CONTRARY TO SPIRIT OF
AND DAMN YOUR PEACE AND UNITY AND UNIVERSAL WHATEVER THE HELL IT IS. YOU'RE TOO DETACHED, JEEVES.
STEP FAR ENOUGH BACK AND EVERYONE'S JUST A HILL OF ANTS. YOU AND HIM HAVE *THAT* IN COMMON.
NEGATIVE. ACTION DENIED.
SORRY, JEEVES. I'VE GOT TO OVERRULE YOU.
OVERRULE?
THAT'S RIGHT. YOU SERVE THE OPERATOR?
OPERATOR OVERRULES. *CLEAR?*
NOW, THIS IS WHAT I WANT... I HAVE A DIFFERENT PLAN.
BUT FIRST WE HAVE UNFINISHED BUSINESS, JEEVES.

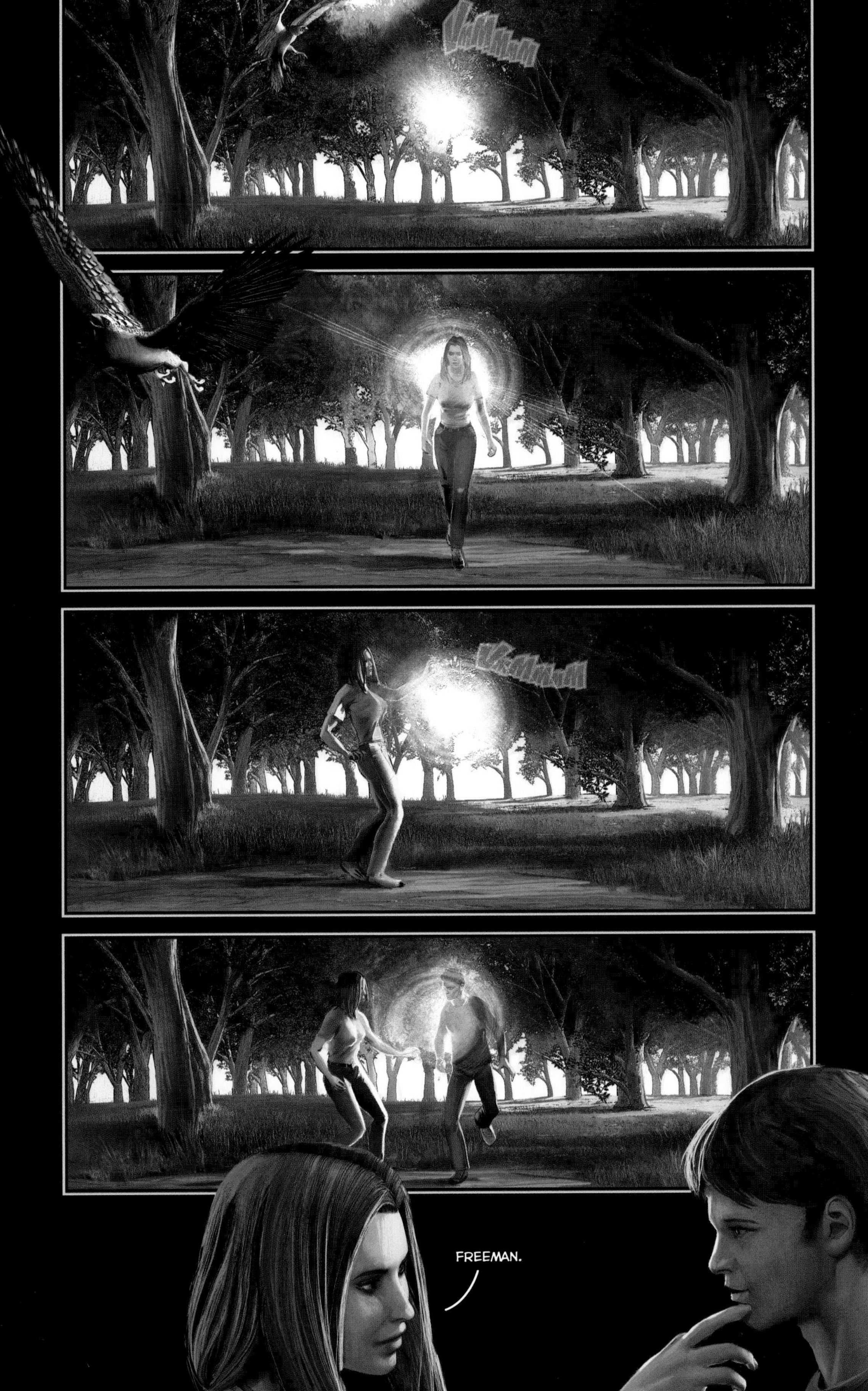
FREEMAN.

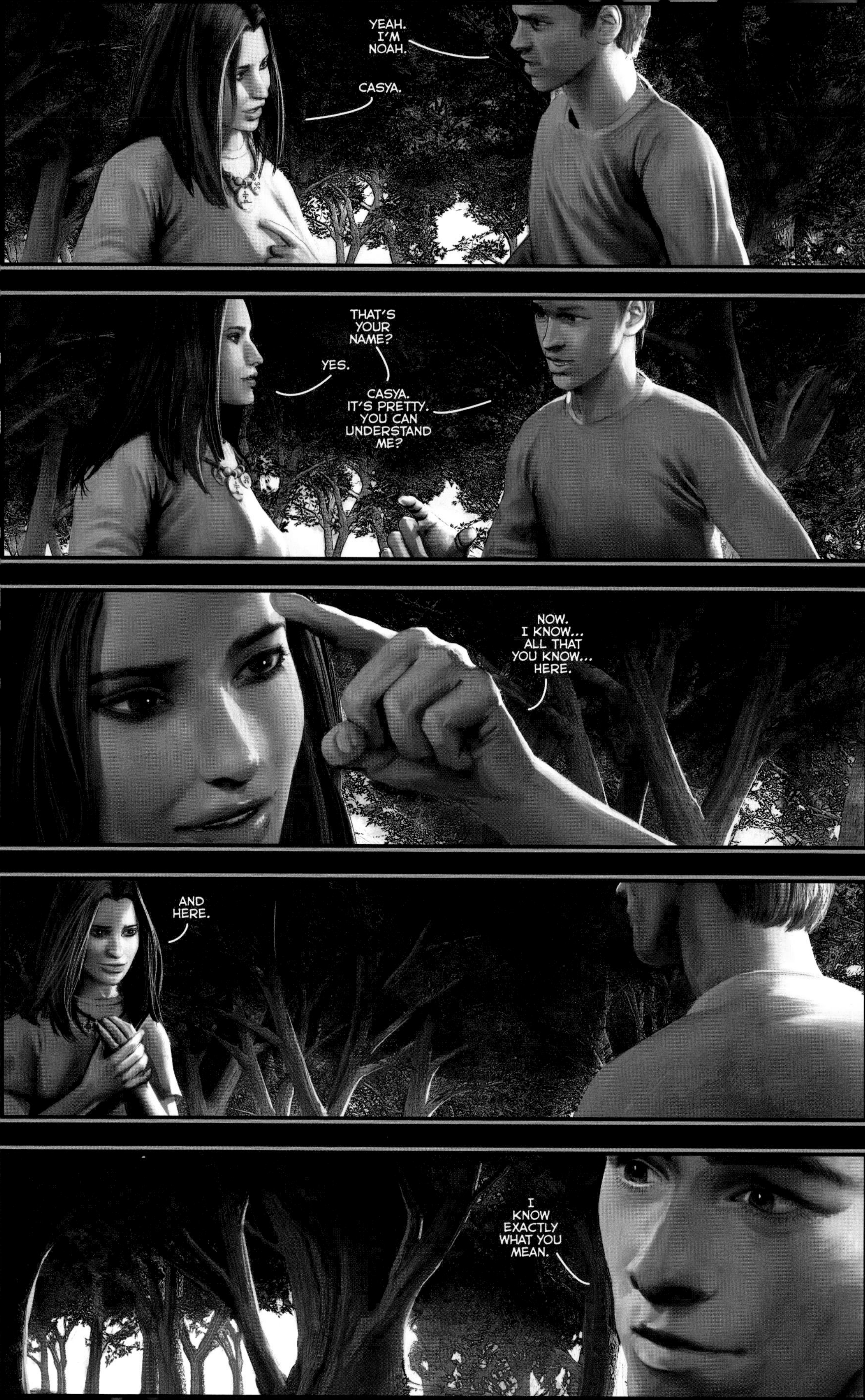
YEAH. I'M NOAH.
CASYA.
THAT'S YOUR NAME?
YES.
CASYA. IT'S PRETTY. YOU CAN UNDERSTAND ME?
NOW. I KNOW... ALL THAT YOU KNOW... HERE.
AND HERE.
I KNOW EXACTLY WHAT YOU MEAN.

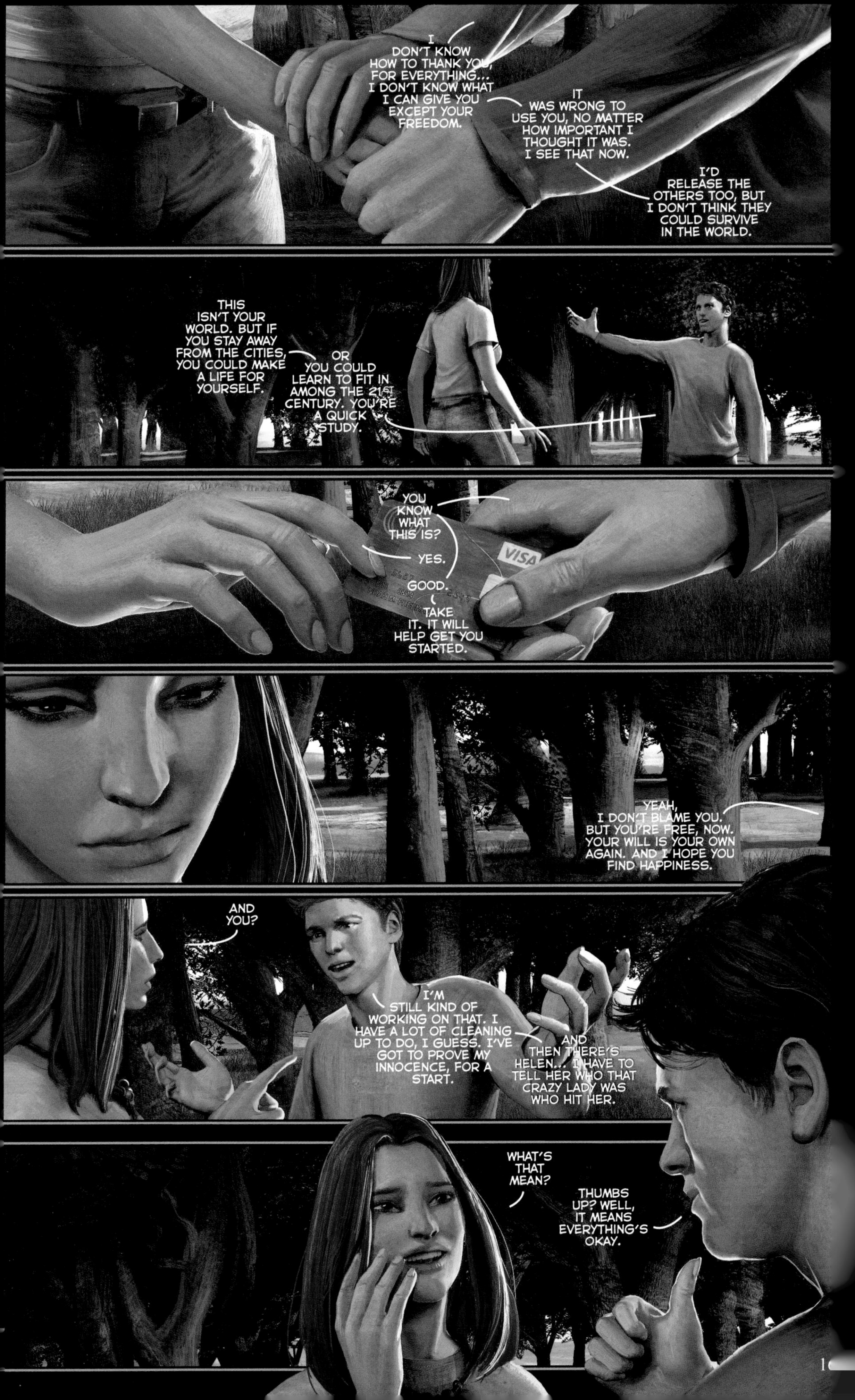
I DON'T KNOW HOW TO THANK YOU, FOR EVERYTHING... I DON'T KNOW WHAT I CAN GIVE YOU EXCEPT YOUR FREEDOM.
IT WAS WRONG TO USE YOU, NO MATTER HOW IMPORTANT I THOUGHT IT WAS. I SEE THAT NOW.
I'D RELEASE THE OTHERS TOO, BUT I DON'T THINK THEY COULD SURVIVE IN THE WORLD.
THIS ISN'T YOUR WORLD. BUT IF YOU STAY AWAY FROM THE CITIES, YOU COULD MAKE A LIFE FOR YOURSELF.
OR YOU COULD LEARN TO FIT IN AMONG THE 21ST CENTURY. YOU'RE A QUICK STUDY.
YOU KNOW WHAT THIS IS?
YES.
GOOD.
TAKE IT. IT WILL HELP GET YOU STARTED.
VISA
YEAH, I DON'T BLAME YOU. BUT YOU'RE FREE, NOW. YOUR WILL IS YOUR OWN AGAIN. AND I HOPE YOU FIND HAPPINESS.
AND YOU?
I'M STILL KIND OF WORKING ON THAT. I HAVE A LOT OF CLEANING UP TO DO, I GUESS. I'VE GOT TO PROVE MY INNOCENCE, FOR A START.
AND THEN THERE'S HELEN... I HAVE TO TELL HER WHO THAT CRAZY LADY WAS WHO HIT HER.
WHAT'S THAT MEAN?
THUMBS UP? WELL, IT MEANS EVERYTHING'S OKAY.

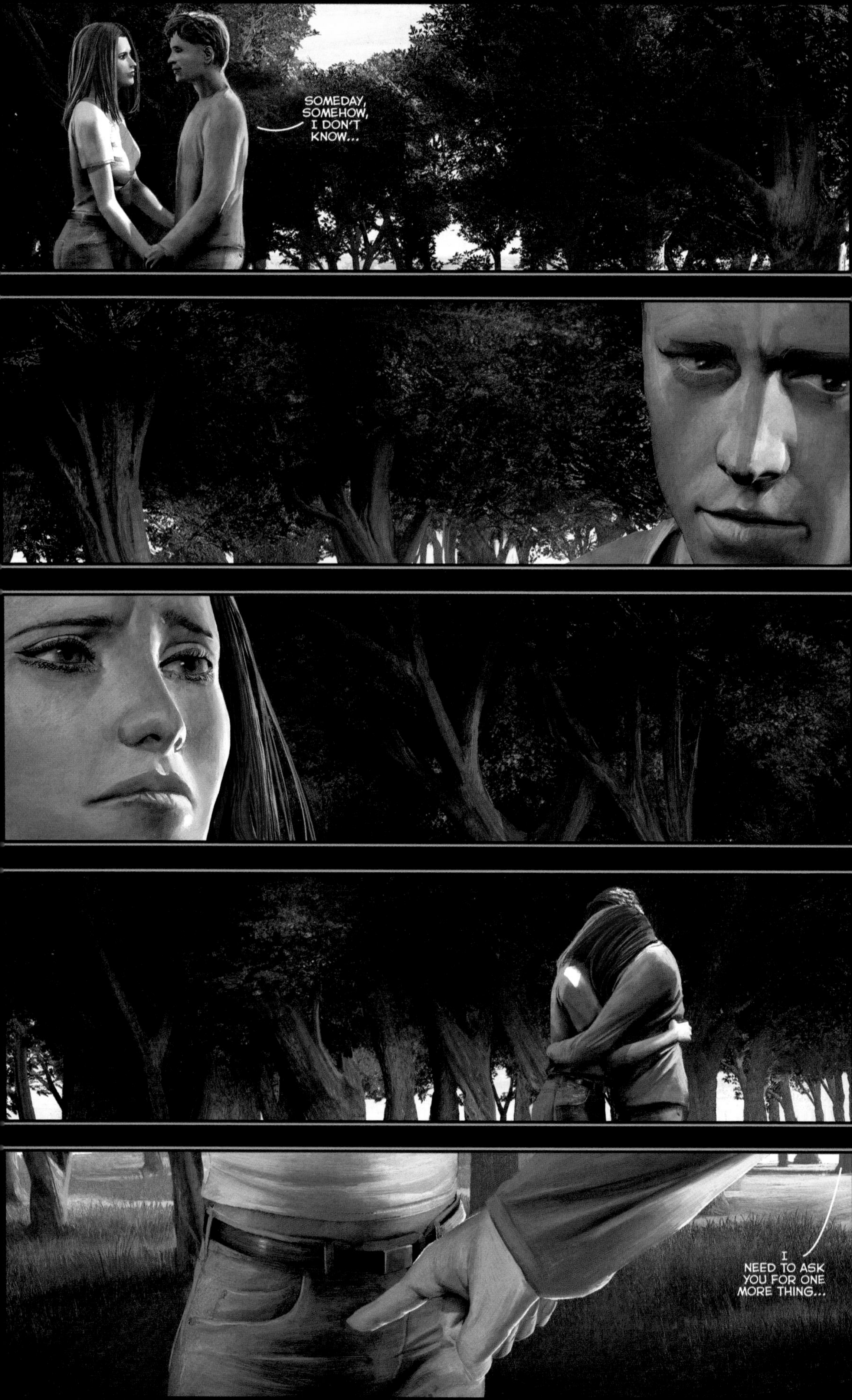
SOMEDAY, SOMEHOW, I DON'T KNOW...
I NEED TO ASK YOU FOR ONE MORE THING...

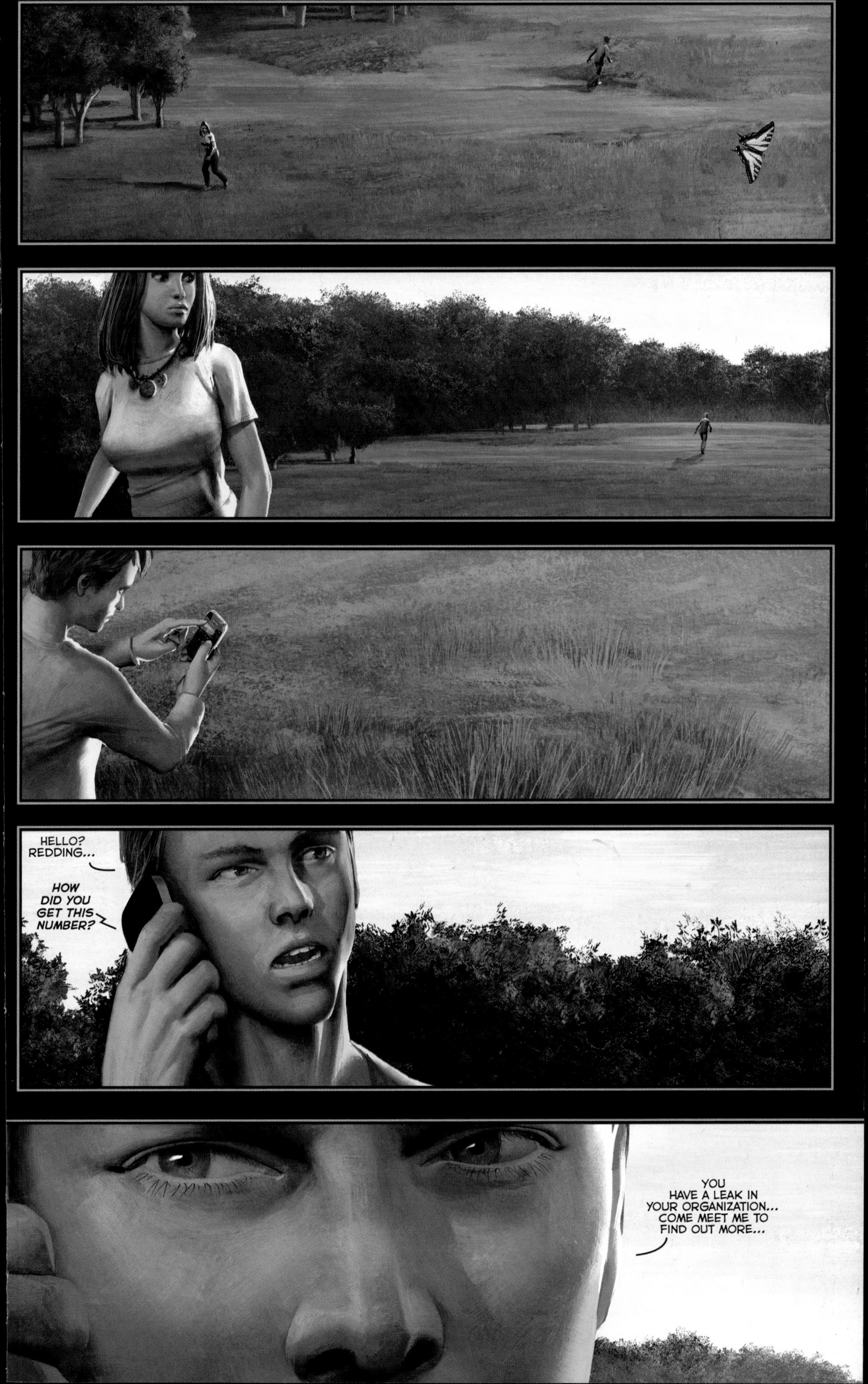
HELLO? REDDING...
HOW DID YOU GET THIS NUMBER?
YOU HAVE A LEAK IN YOUR ORGANIZATION... COME MEET ME TO FIND OUT MORE...

I KNOW...
WHAT YOU
KNOW...

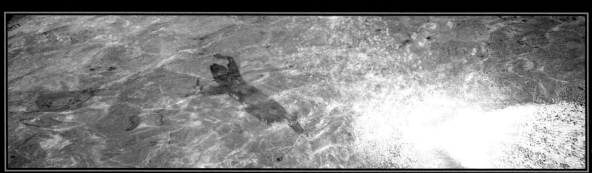

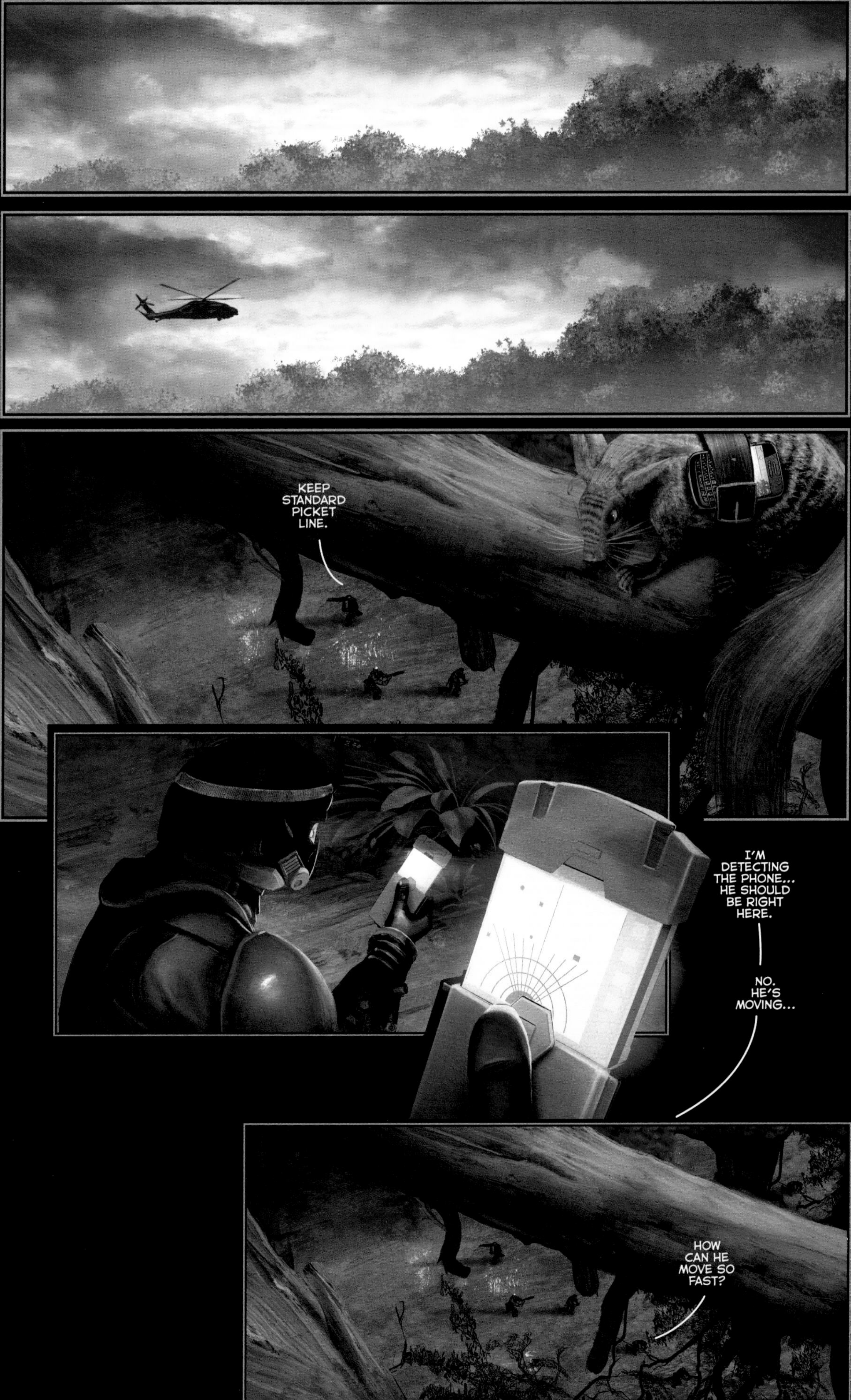
KEEP STANDARD PICKET LINE.
I'M DETECTING THE PHONE... HE SHOULD BE RIGHT HERE.
NO. HE'S MOVING...
HOW CAN HE MOVE SO FAST?

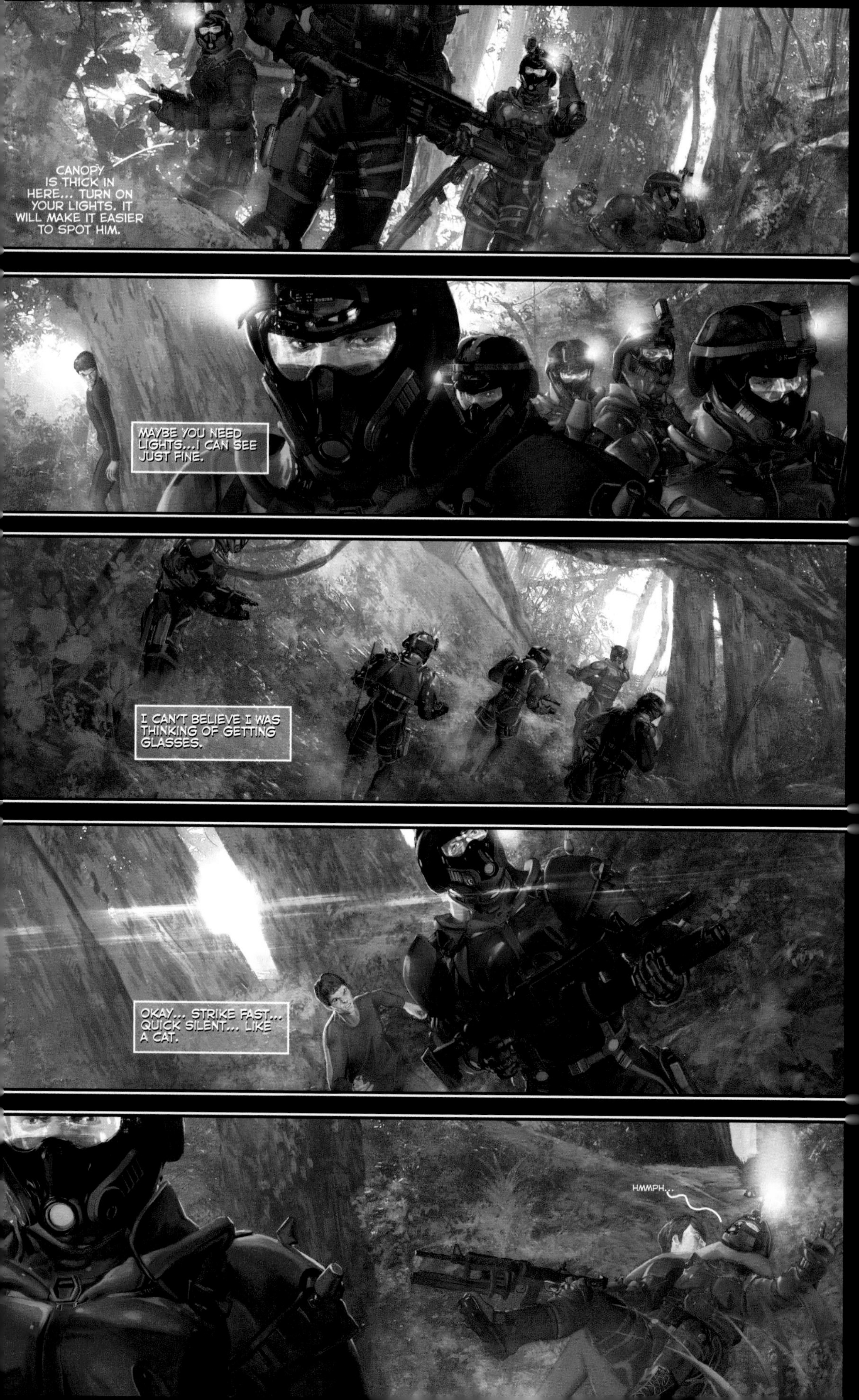

CANOPY IS THICK IN HERE... TURN ON YOUR LIGHTS. IT WILL MAKE IT EASIER TO SPOT HIM.
MAYBE YOU NEED LIGHTS...I CAN SEE JUST FINE.
I CAN'T BELIEVE I WAS THINKING OF GETTING GLASSES.
OKAY... STRIKE FAST... QUICK SILENT... LIKE A CAT.
HMMPH...

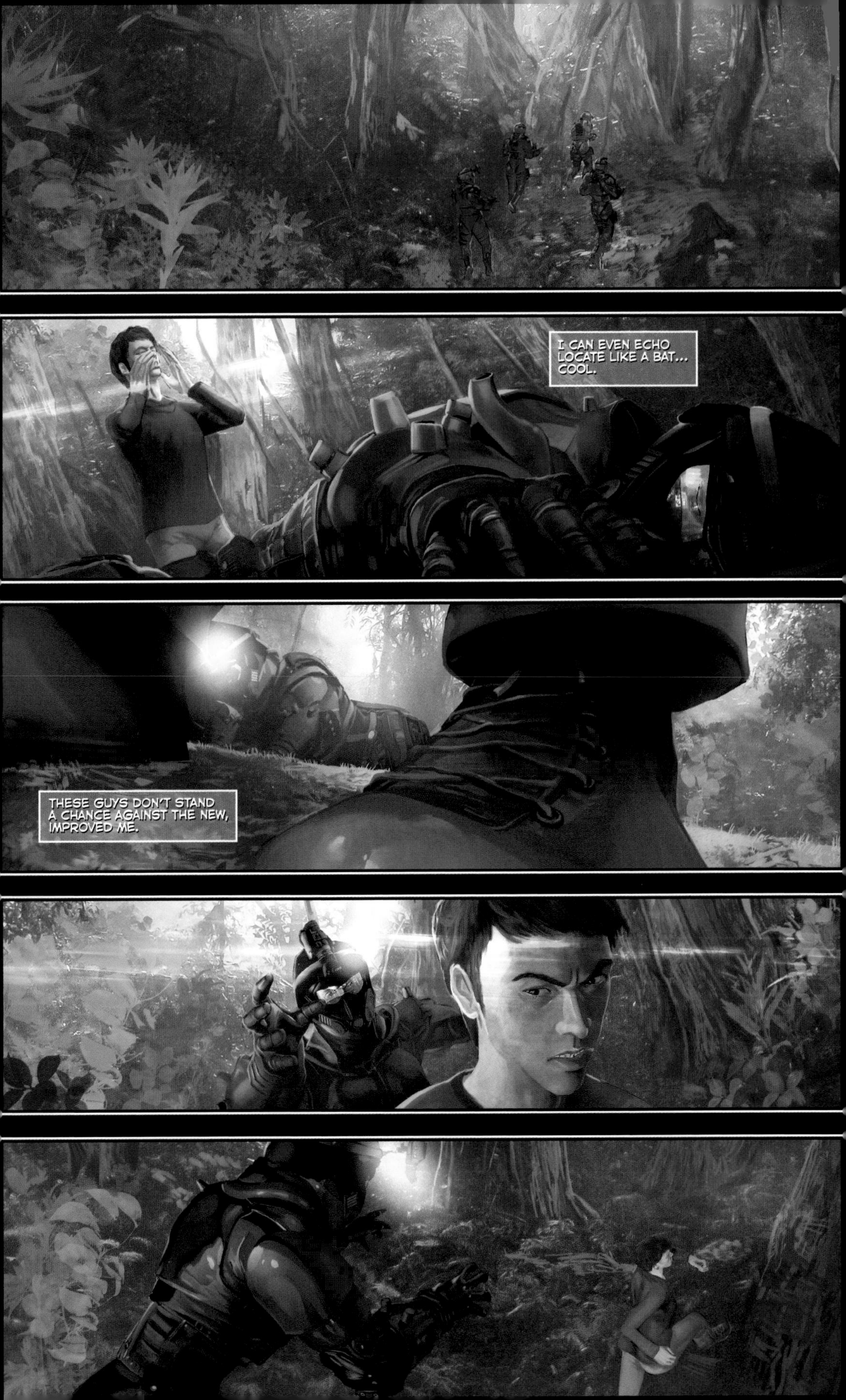
I CAN EVEN ECHO LOCATE LIKE A BAT... COOL.
THESE GUYS DON'T STAND A CHANCE AGAINST THE NEW, IMPROVED ME.

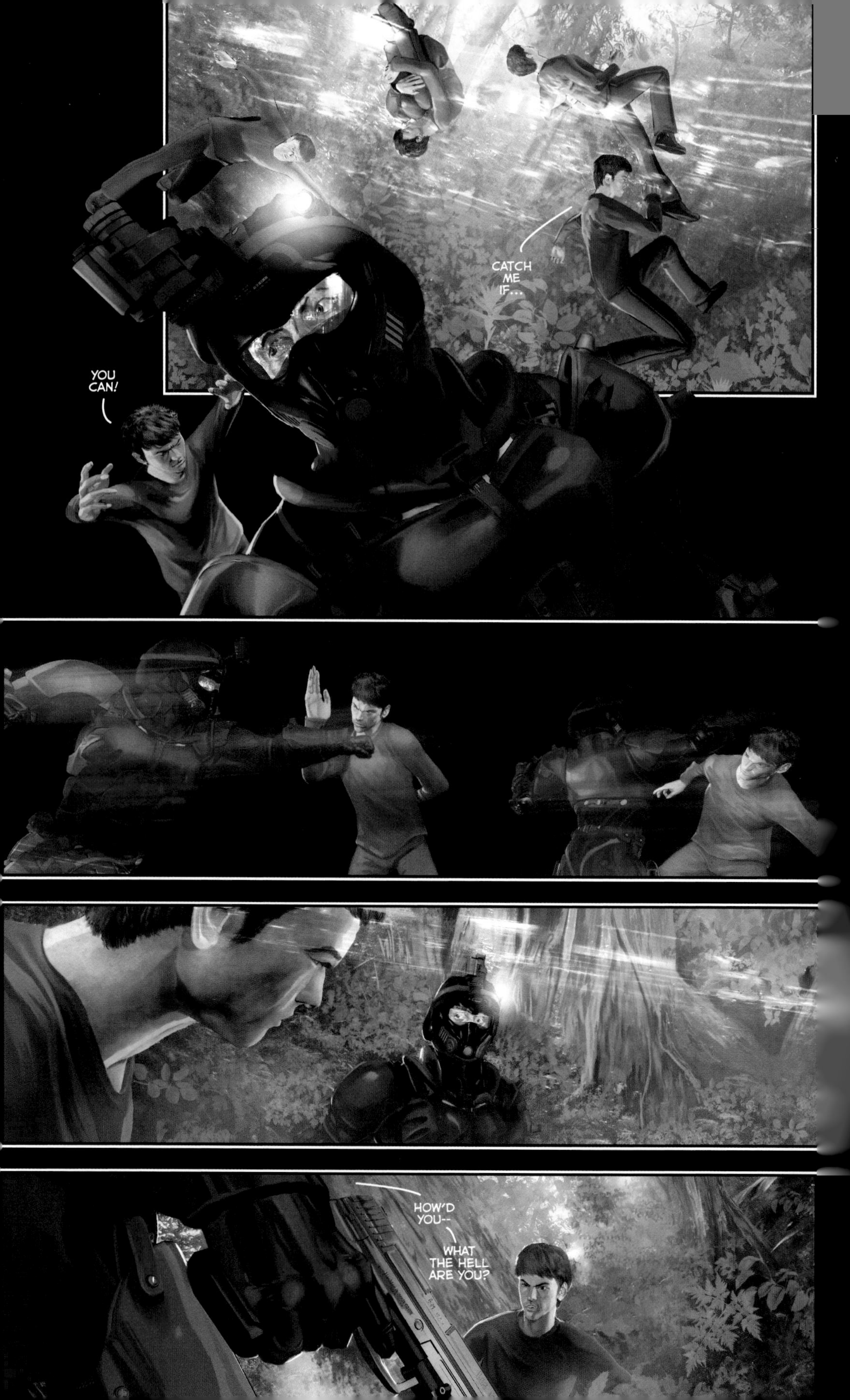
CATCH ME IF...
YOU CAN!
HOW'D YOU--
WHAT THE HELL ARE YOU?

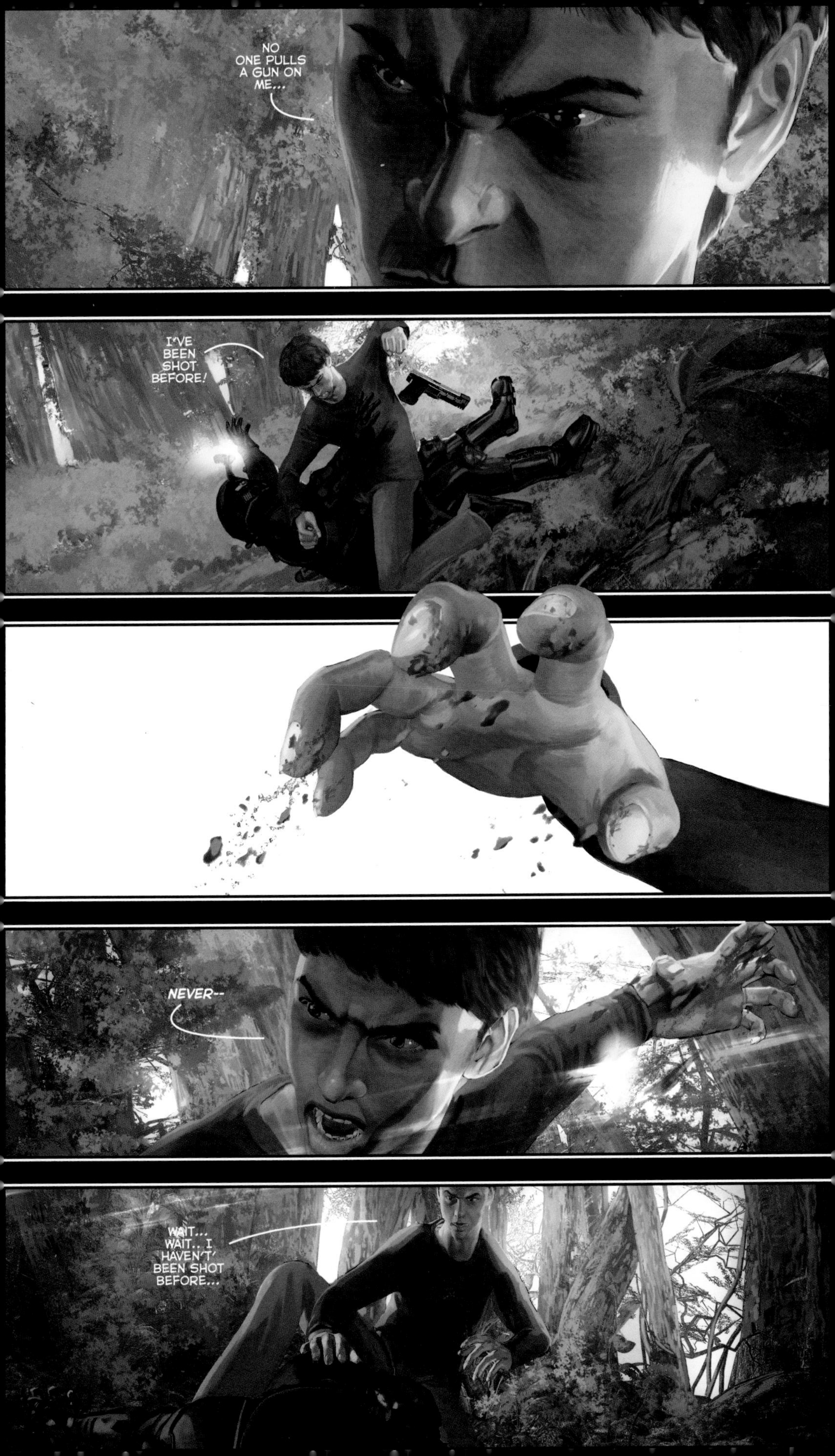
NO ONE PULLS A GUN ON ME...
I'VE BEEN SHOT BEFORE!
NEVER--
WAIT... WAIT.. I HAVEN'T BEEN SHOT BEFORE...

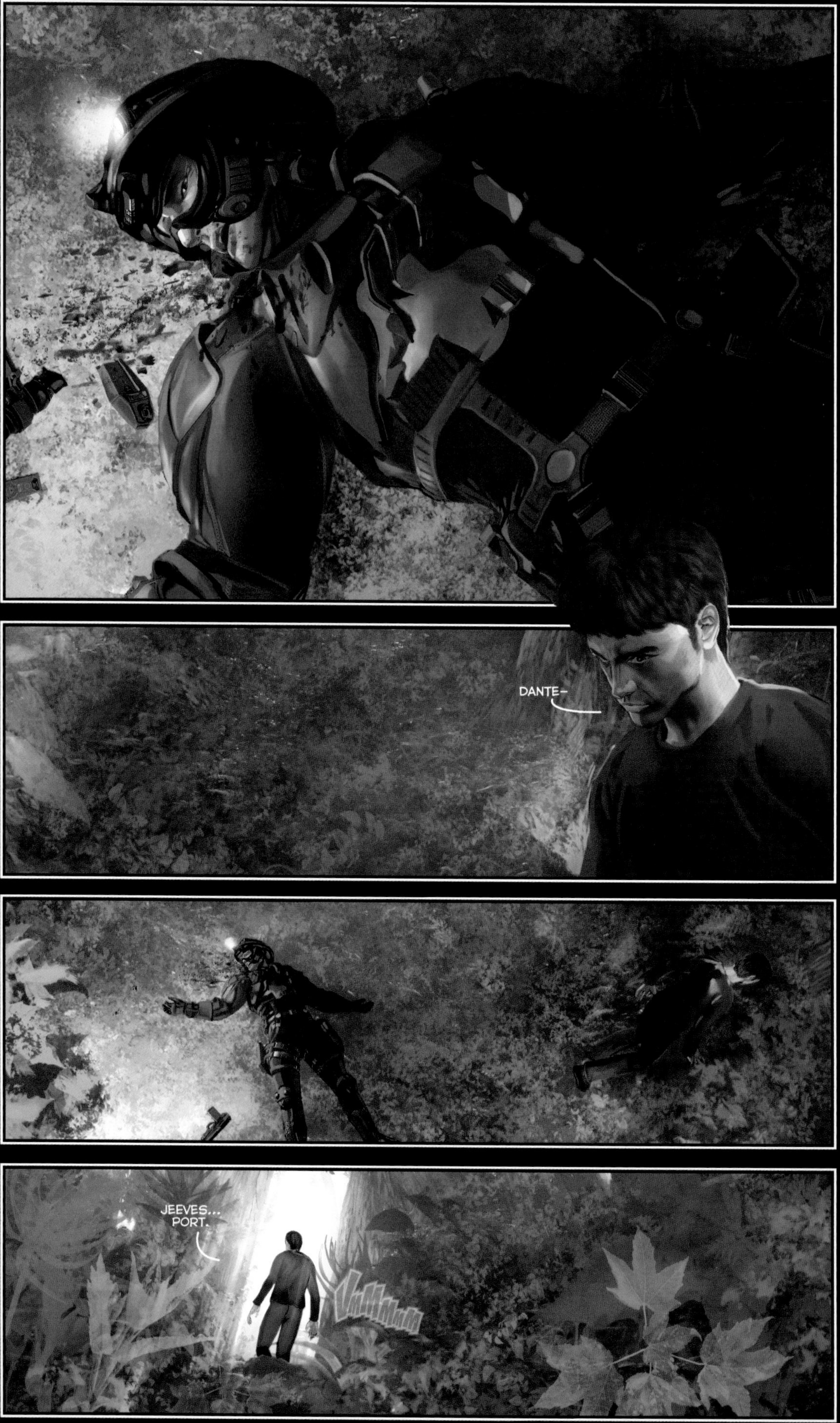
DANTE-
JEEVES...
PORT.

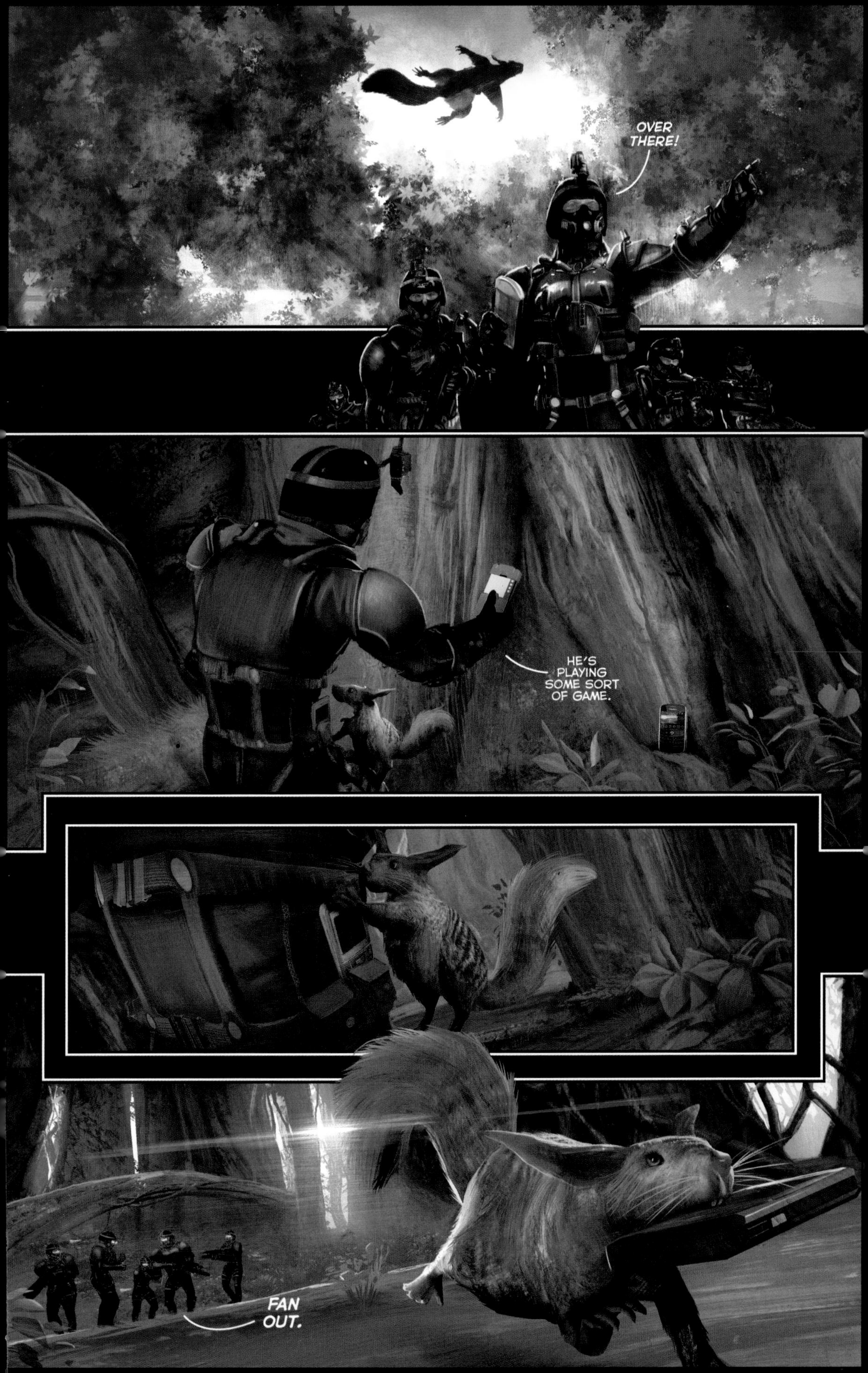
OVER THERE!
HE'S PLAYING SOME SORT OF GAME.
FAN OUT.

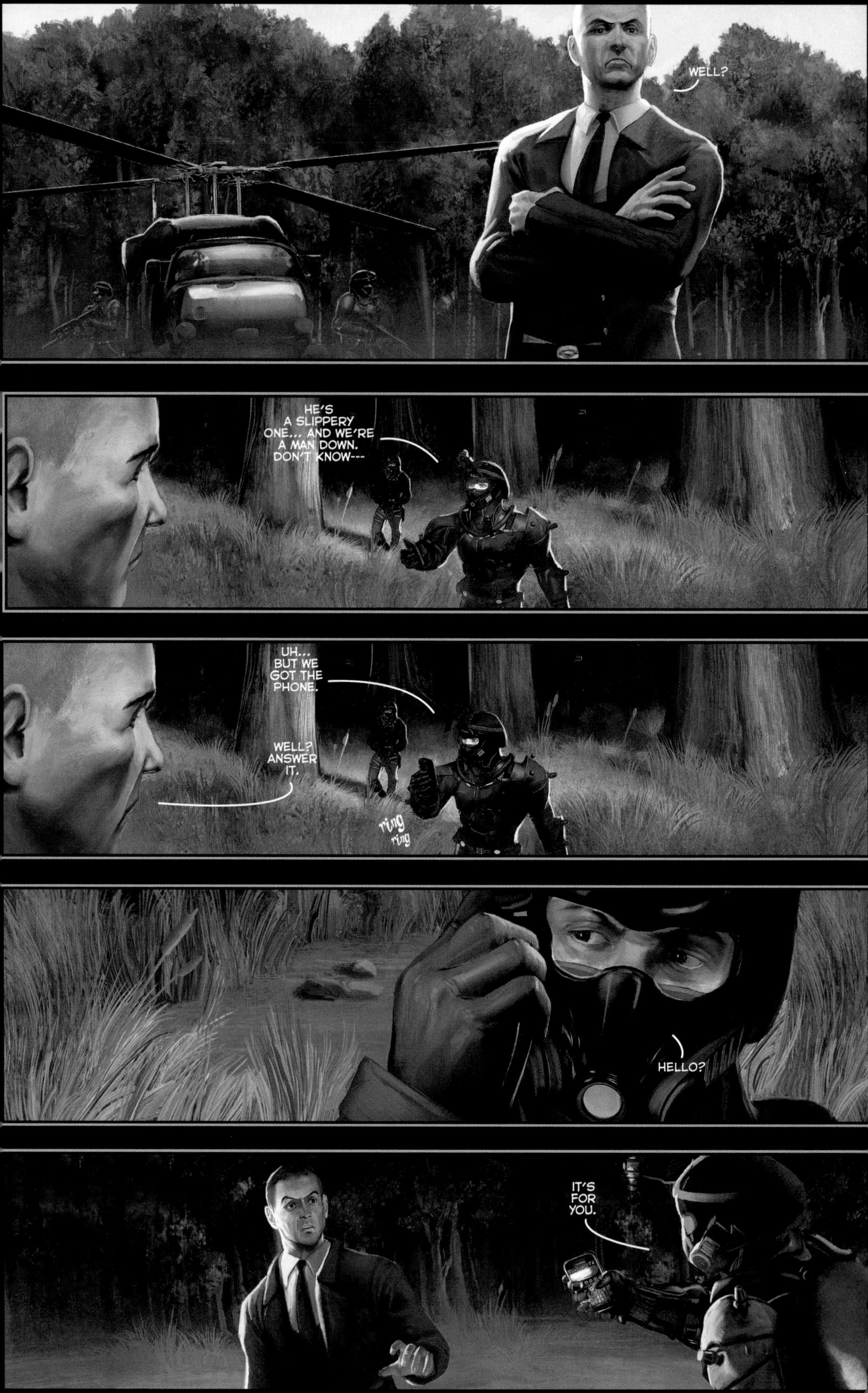
WELL?
HE'S A SLIPPERY ONE... AND WE'RE A MAN DOWN. DON'T KNOW---
UH... BUT WE GOT THE PHONE.
WELL? ANSWER IT.
ring ring
HELLO?
IT'S FOR YOU.

MR. FREEMAN, I PRESUME?
YOU... YOU HAD ME KILLED...
NOT WELL ENOUGH, IT SEEMS. HOW IS IT THAT ONE LITTLE DEAD MAN IS GIVING ME SO MUCH TROUBLE?
YOU HAVE NO IDEA.
HOW MUCH DO YOU KNOW?
ABOUT WHAT? EVERGREEN? CROSS-FERRY DAM?
OR ABOUT THE MURDER OF GAIL STRAND? AND THE HIT YOU PUT ON ME?
OR ABOUT YOU MURDERING AGENT JOHN DARIEN IN YOUR OFFICE?
I DON'T SUPPOSE YOU HAVE EVIDENCE FOR ANY THESE ALLEGATIONS.
DON'T THINK I REALLY NEED ANY.
OH? WHY'S THAT?
BECAUSE YOU'RE GOING TO MARCH YOURSELF IN FRONT OF THE NEAREST LAW ENFORCEMENT AGENCY AND GIVE A FULL CONFESSION AND ACCOUNTING OF YOUR CRIMES.
YOU SEE, I HAVE WAYS OF MAKING YOU TALK.
YOU'VE WATCHED TOO MANY SPY MOVIES, MR. FREEMAN.
NAH. I ALWAYS PREFERRED MUSICALS, MYSELF.

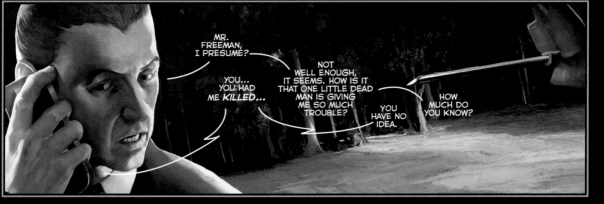

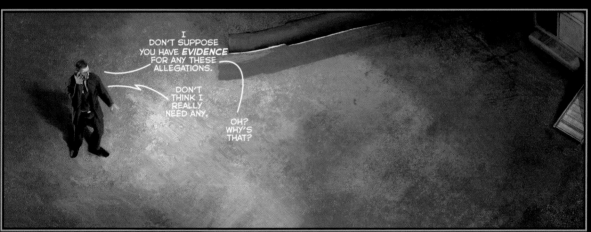

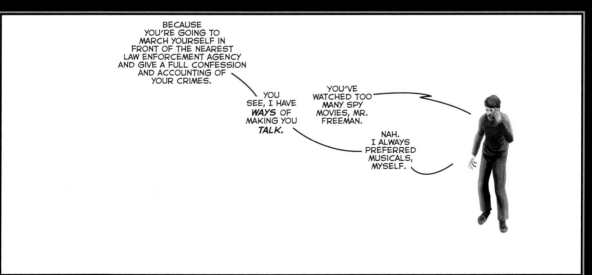

SO, I KNOW YOU ARE AN EDUCATED MAN, BUT ARE YOU A REASONABLE ONE?
REASONABLE? YOU CALL WHAT YOU DO REASONABLE? PEOPLE ARE DEAD. INNOCENT PEOPLE. GOOD PEOPLE. INNOCENT CREATURES.
AND FOR WHAT? A GOVERNMENT CONTRACT? A LITTLE TINY SCRAP MORE POWER?
YOU THINK YOU UNDERSTAND THE WORLD, BUT YOU REALLY HAVE NO IDEA WHAT'S AT STAKE. THIS ISN'T ABOUT POWER OR POLITICS, OR THE PERSONAL AMBITIONS OF ONE OLD MAN. THIS IS ABOUT THE SURVIVAL OF THE PLANET.
AND THAT IS SOMETHING I BELIEVE YOU CARE VERY MUCH ABOUT.
YOU COLLECT ENVIRONMENTAL DATA, BUT DO YOU UNDERSTAND IT? HAVE YOU REALLY LOOKED AT THE CLIMATE PROJECTIONS YOU'VE BEEN WORKING ON? REALLY LOOKED AT THEM?
ALL THE INDICATORS POINT IN ONE DIRECTION.
HAVE YOU PLAYED THE SCENARIO OUT OVER THE NEXT TWENTY YEARS?
THE NEXT FIFTY? THE NEXT HUNDRED?
I HAVE.
THE WORLD IS ALREADY TEARING ITSELF TO BITS OVER DROPS OF OIL.
WHAT DO YOU THINK IT'S GOING TO BE LIKE WHEN WE'RE FIGHTING OVER DRINKING WATER? OVER A SHRINKING FOOD SUPPLY?
THAT'S NO EXCUSE FOR--
NO. SERIOUSLY. WHAT DO YOU THINK IS GOING TO HAPPEN WHEN THREE BILLION STARVING THIRD-WORLDERS START MARCHING ON THE FIRST WORLD?

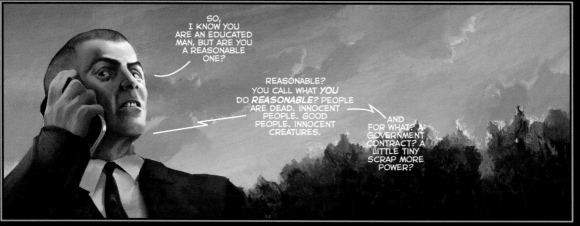

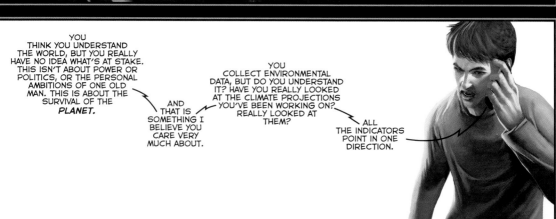

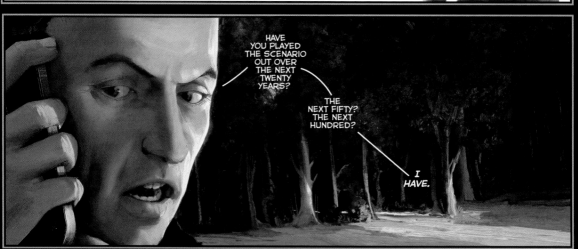

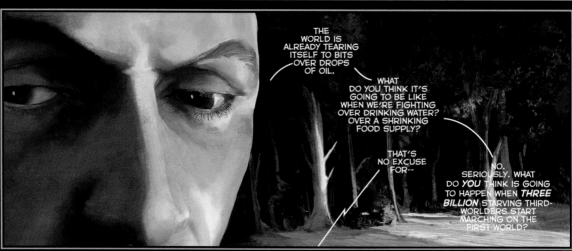

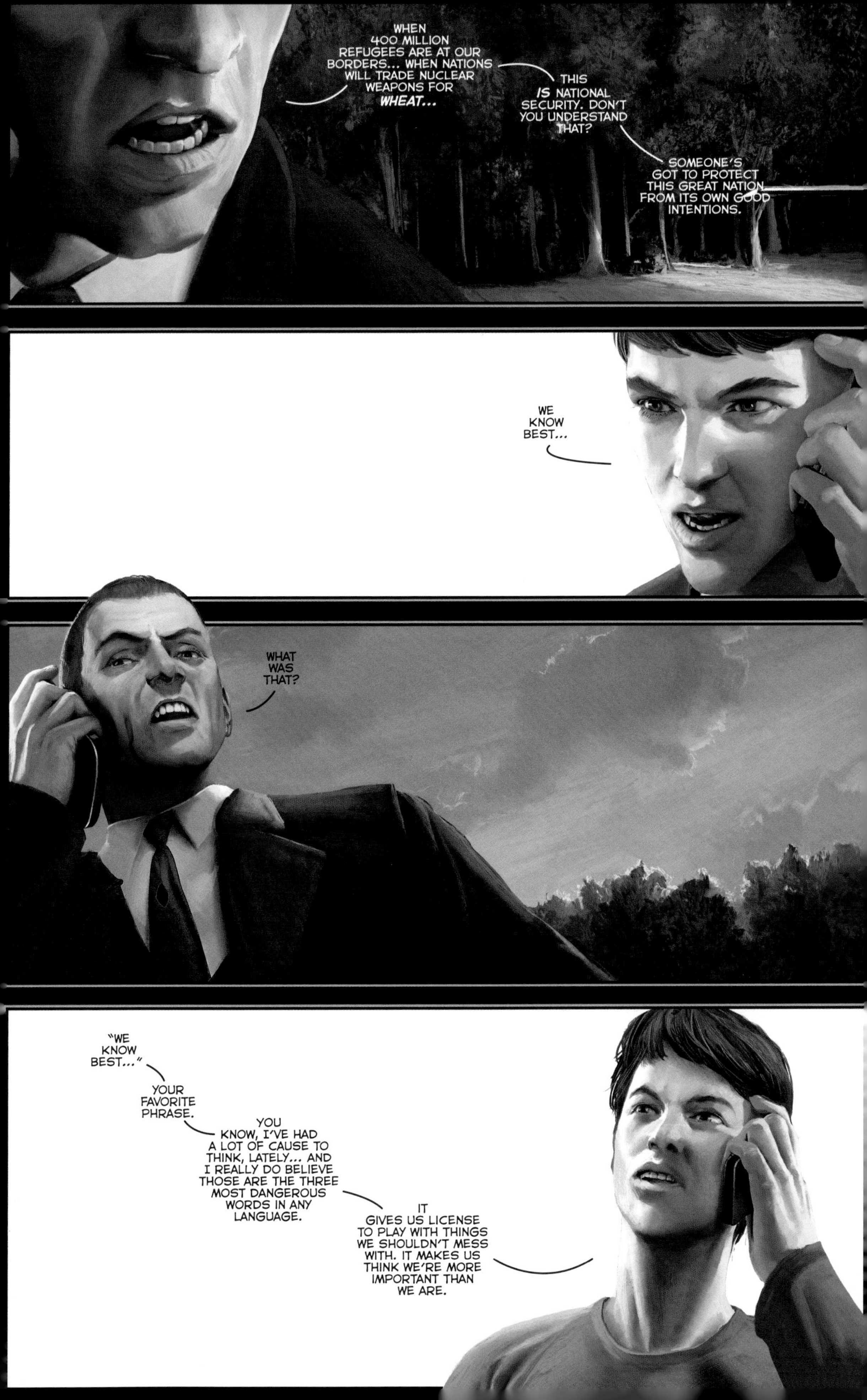

WHEN 400 MILLION REFUGEES ARE AT OUR BORDERS... WHEN NATIONS WILL TRADE NUCLEAR WEAPONS FOR *WHEAT...*
THIS *IS* NATIONAL SECURITY. DON'T YOU UNDERSTAND THAT?
SOMEONE'S GOT TO PROTECT THIS GREAT NATION FROM ITS OWN GOOD INTENTIONS.
WE KNOW BEST...
WHAT WAS THAT?
"WE KNOW BEST..."
YOUR FAVORITE PHRASE.
YOU KNOW, I'VE HAD A LOT OF CAUSE TO THINK, LATELY... AND I REALLY DO BELIEVE THOSE ARE THE THREE MOST DANGEROUS WORDS IN ANY LANGUAGE.
IT GIVES US LICENSE TO PLAY WITH THINGS WE SHOULDN'T MESS WITH. IT MAKES US THINK WE'RE MORE IMPORTANT THAN WE ARE.

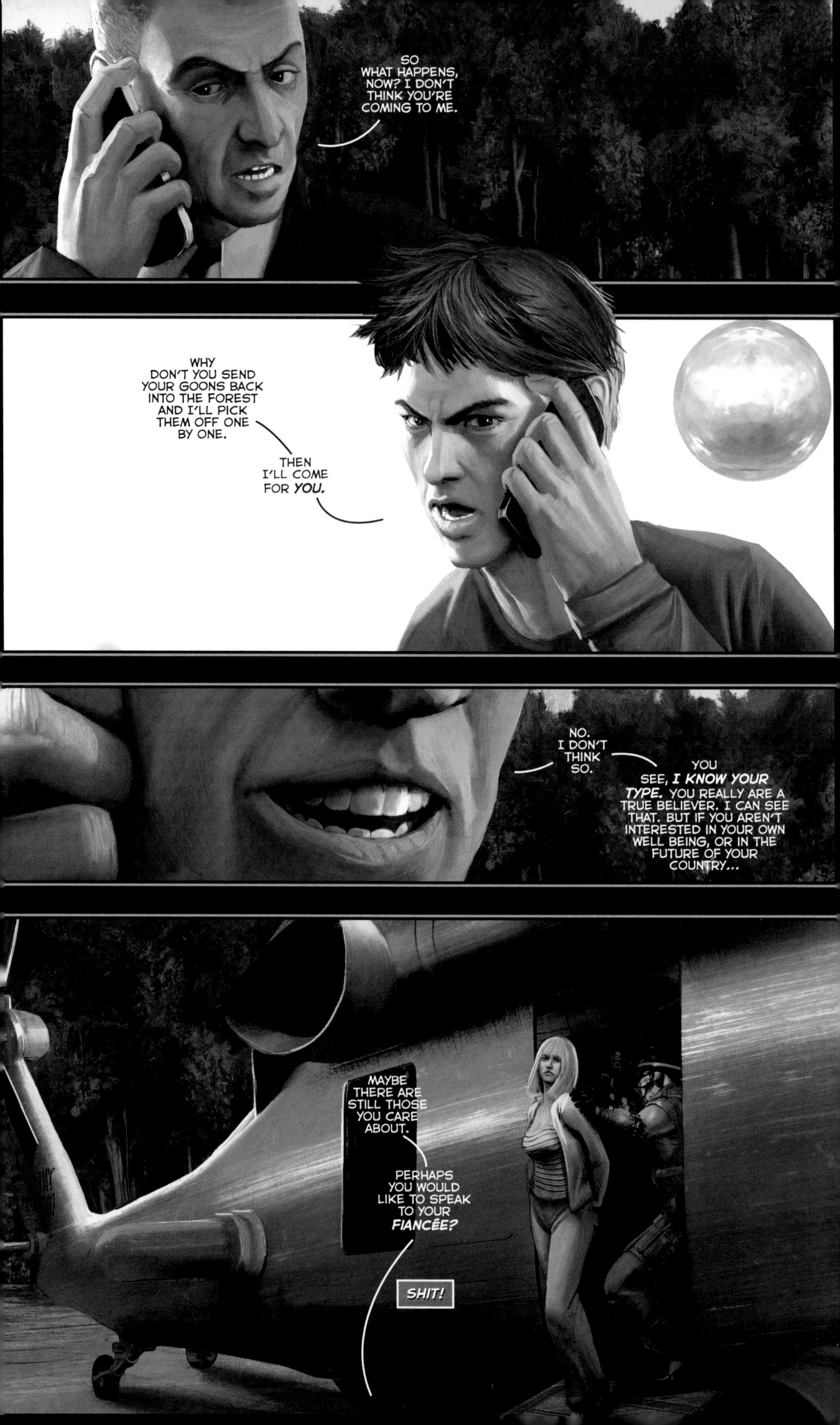
SO WHAT HAPPENS, NOW? I DON'T THINK YOU'RE COMING TO ME.
WHY DON'T YOU SEND YOUR GOONS BACK INTO THE FOREST AND I'LL PICK THEM OFF ONE BY ONE.
THEN I'LL COME FOR *YOU.*
NO. I DON'T THINK SO.
YOU SEE, ***I KNOW YOUR TYPE.*** YOU REALLY ARE A TRUE BELIEVER. I CAN SEE THAT. BUT IF YOU AREN'T INTERESTED IN YOUR OWN WELL BEING, OR IN THE FUTURE OF YOUR COUNTRY...
MAYBE THERE ARE STILL THOSE YOU CARE ABOUT.
PERHAPS YOU WOULD LIKE TO SPEAK TO YOUR ***FIANCÉE?***
SHIT!

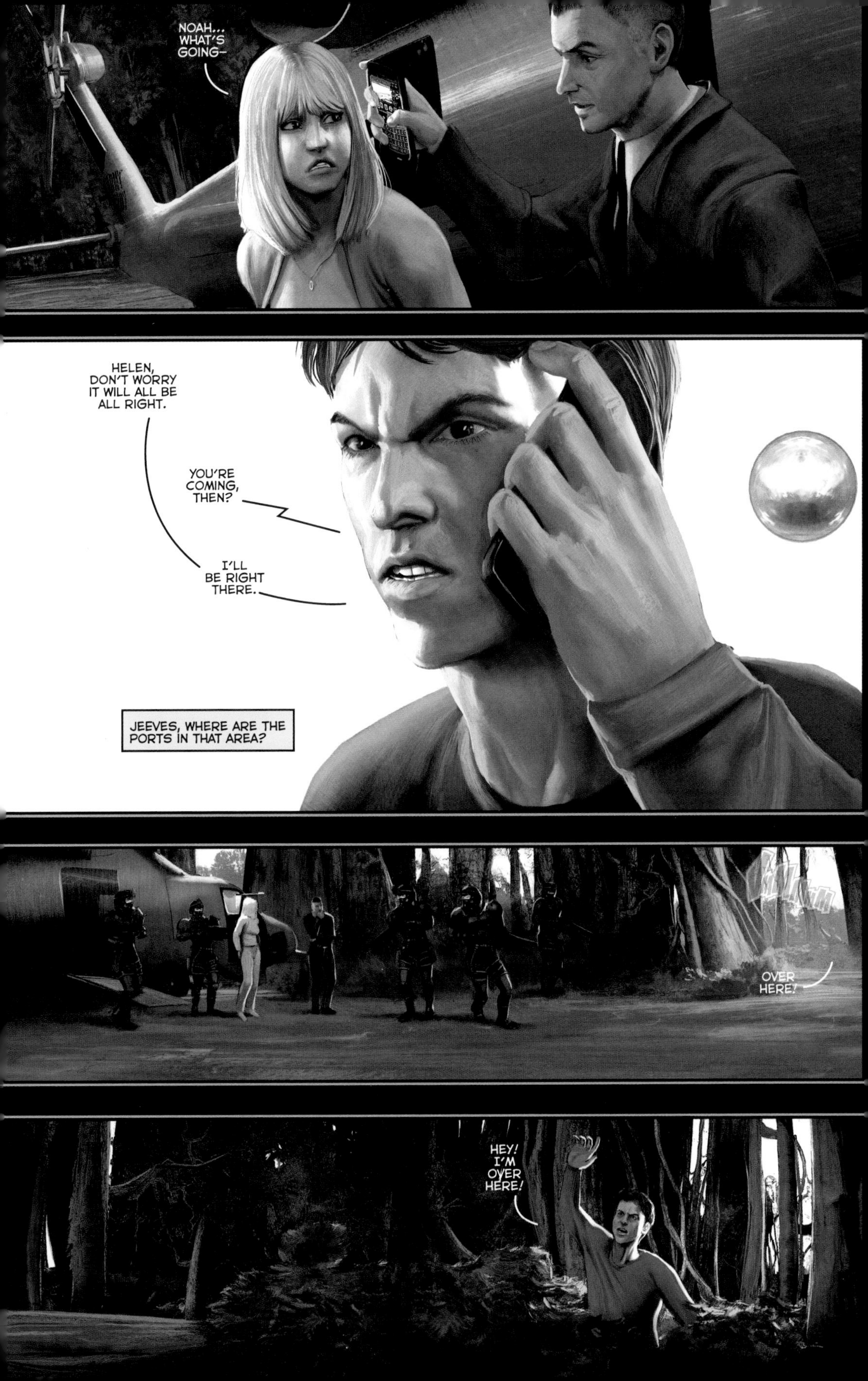
NOAH... WHAT'S GOING–
HELEN, DON'T WORRY IT WILL ALL BE ALL RIGHT.
YOU'RE COMING, THEN?
I'LL BE RIGHT THERE.
JEEVES, WHERE ARE THE PORTS IN THAT AREA?
OVER HERE!
HEY! I'M OVER HERE!

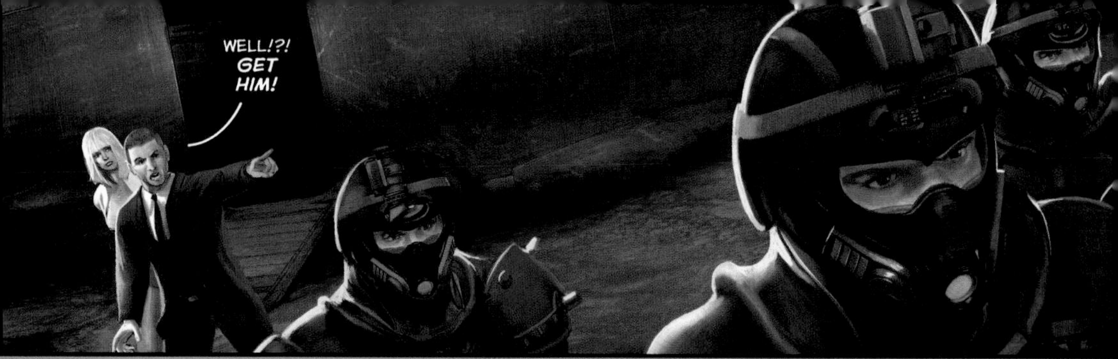
WELL!?! GET HIM!

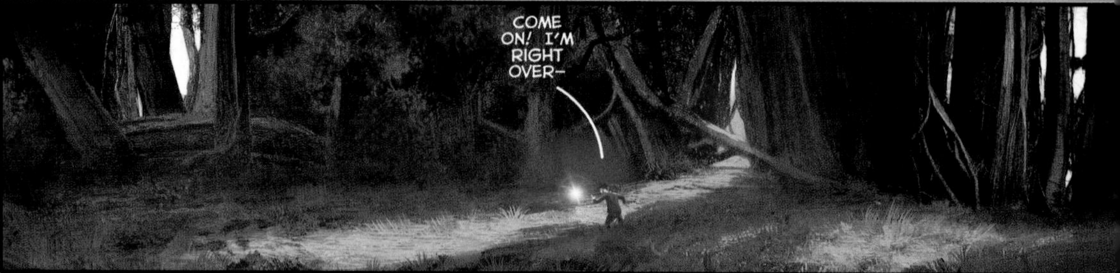
COME ON! I'M RIGHT OVER-

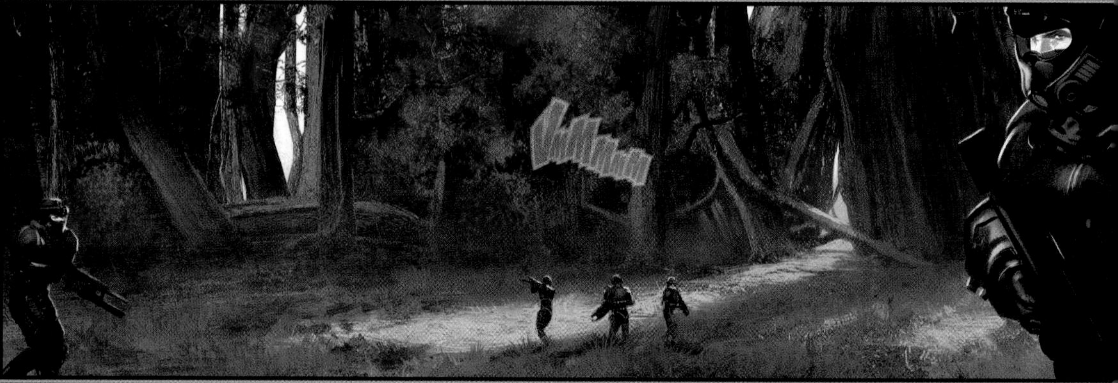

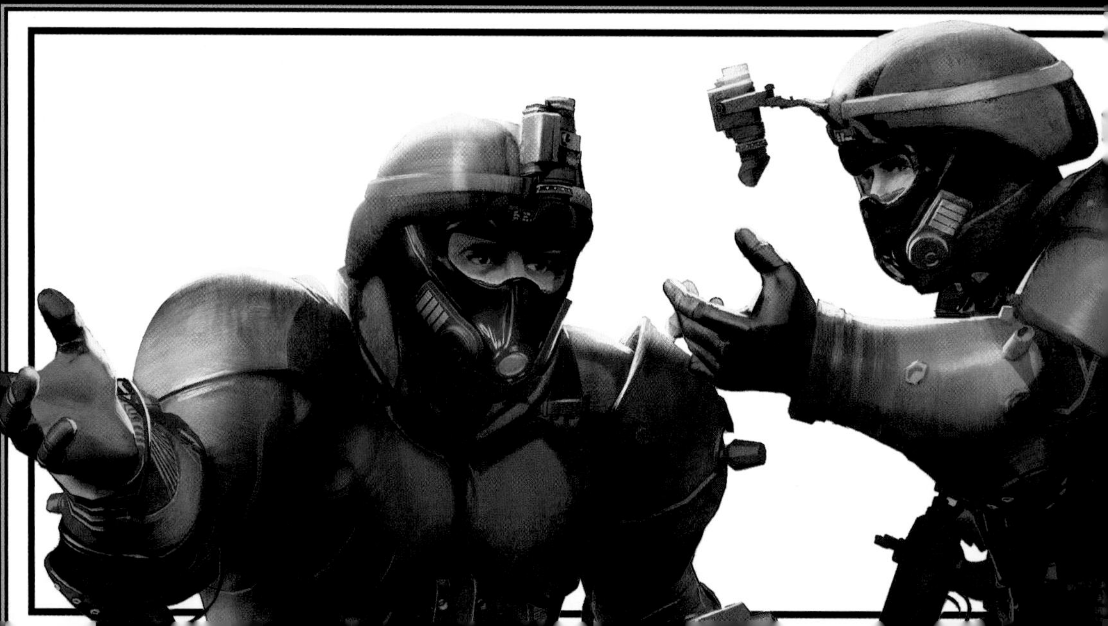

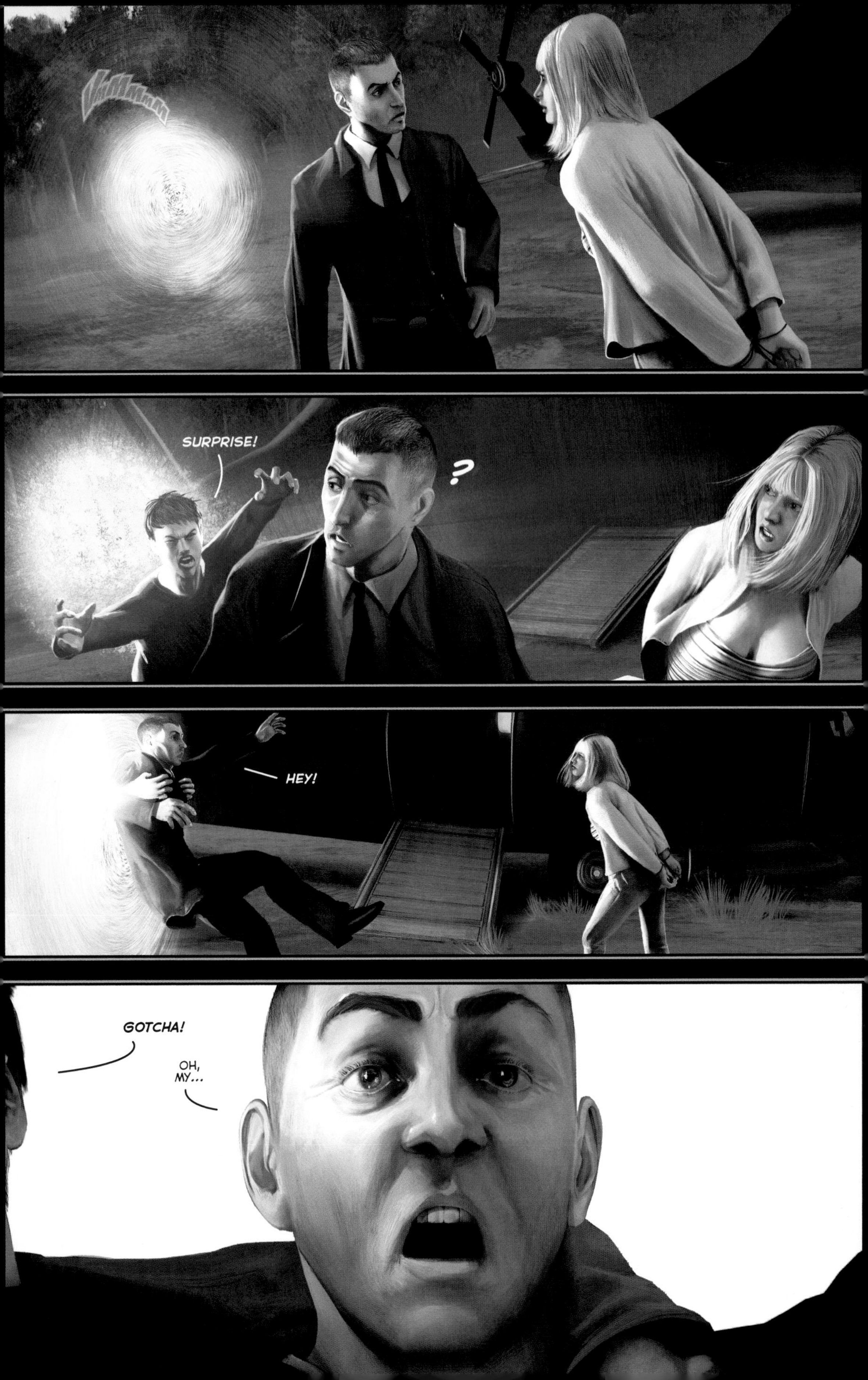
SURPRISE!
?
HEY!
GOTCHA!
OH, MY...

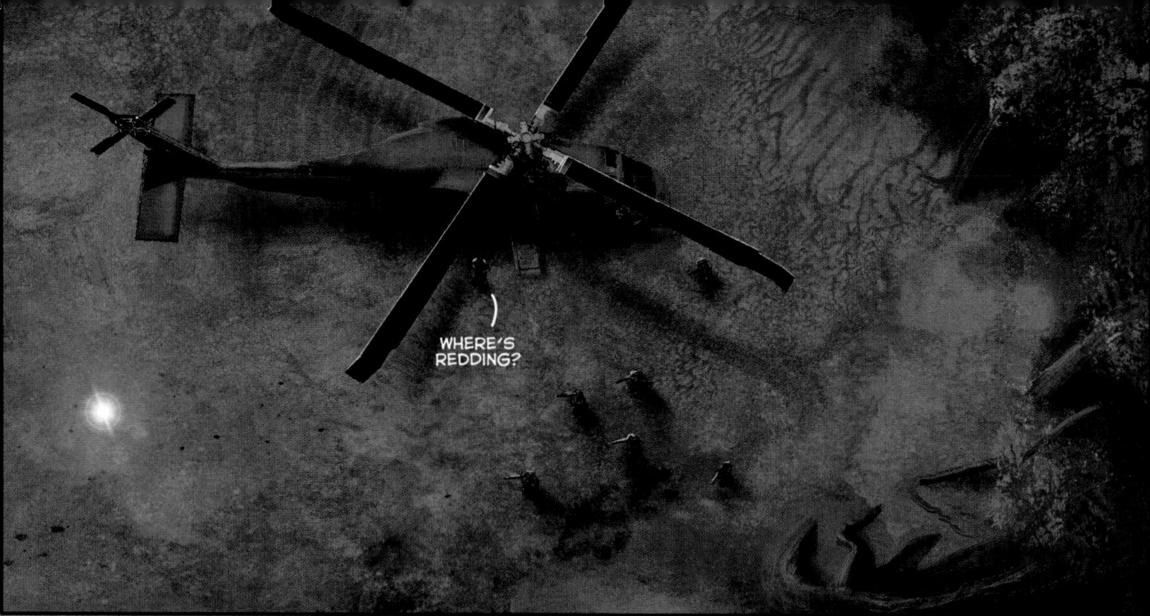
WHERE'S REDDING?

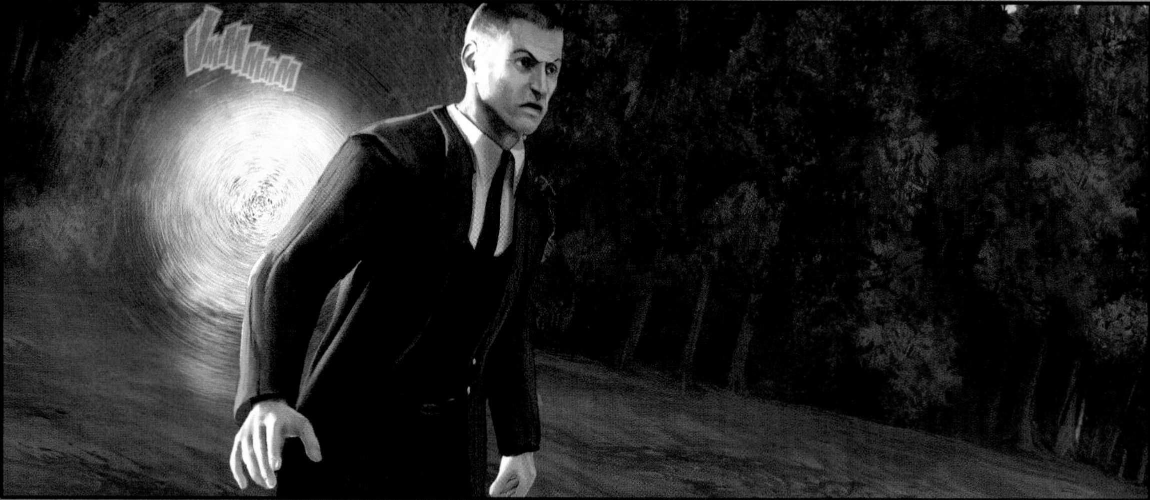
VMMMMM

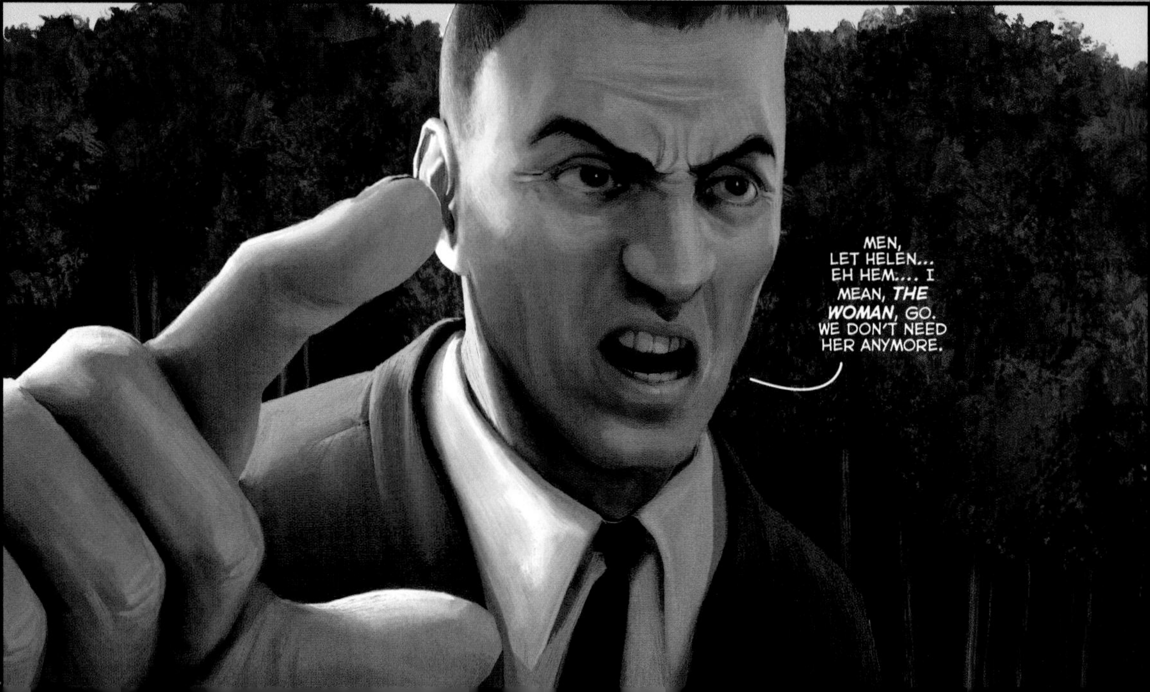
MEN, LET HELEN... EH HEM... I MEAN, *THE WOMAN*, GO. WE DON'T NEED HER ANYMORE.

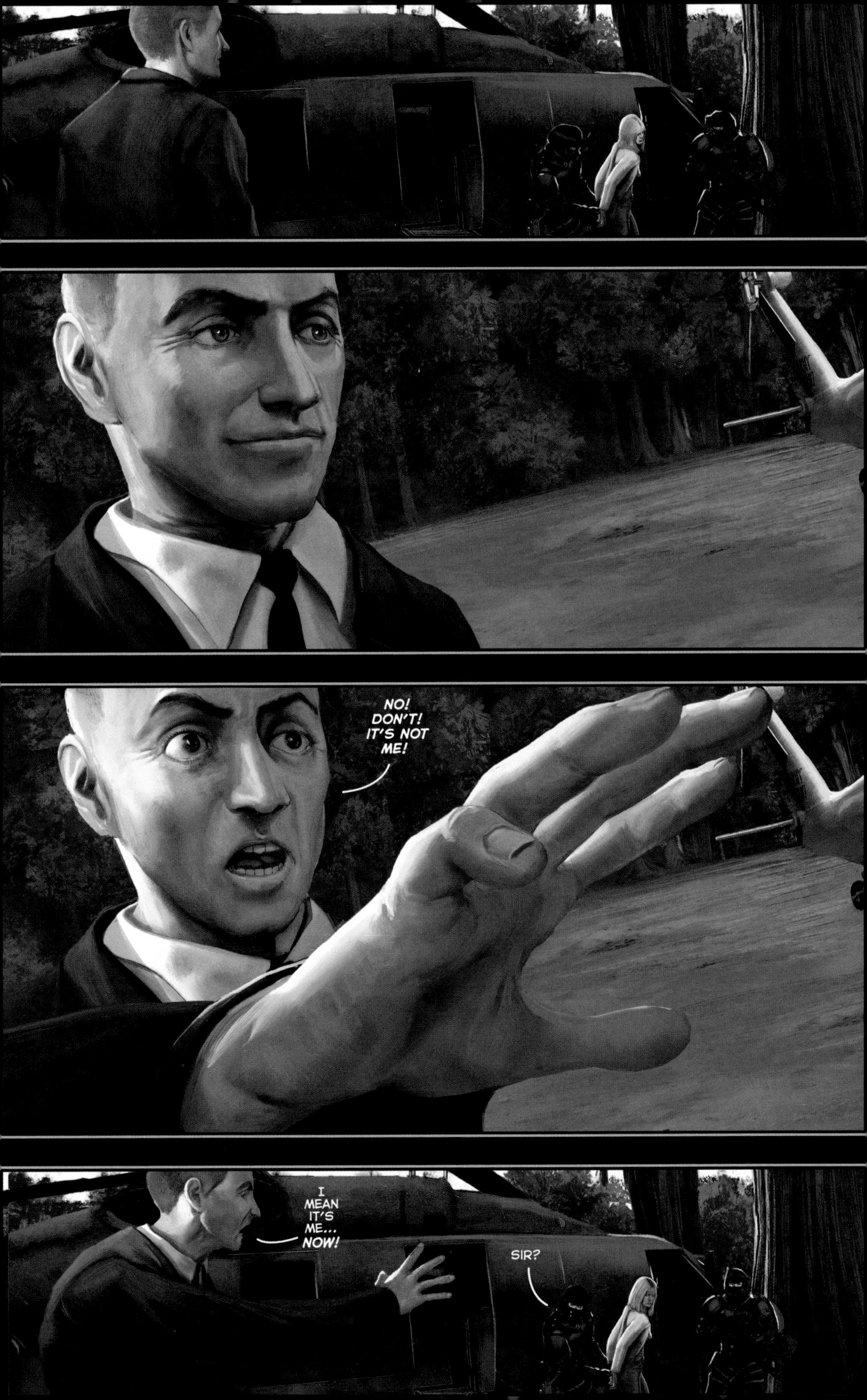
NO! DON'T! IT'S NOT ME!
I MEAN IT'S ME... NOW!
SIR?

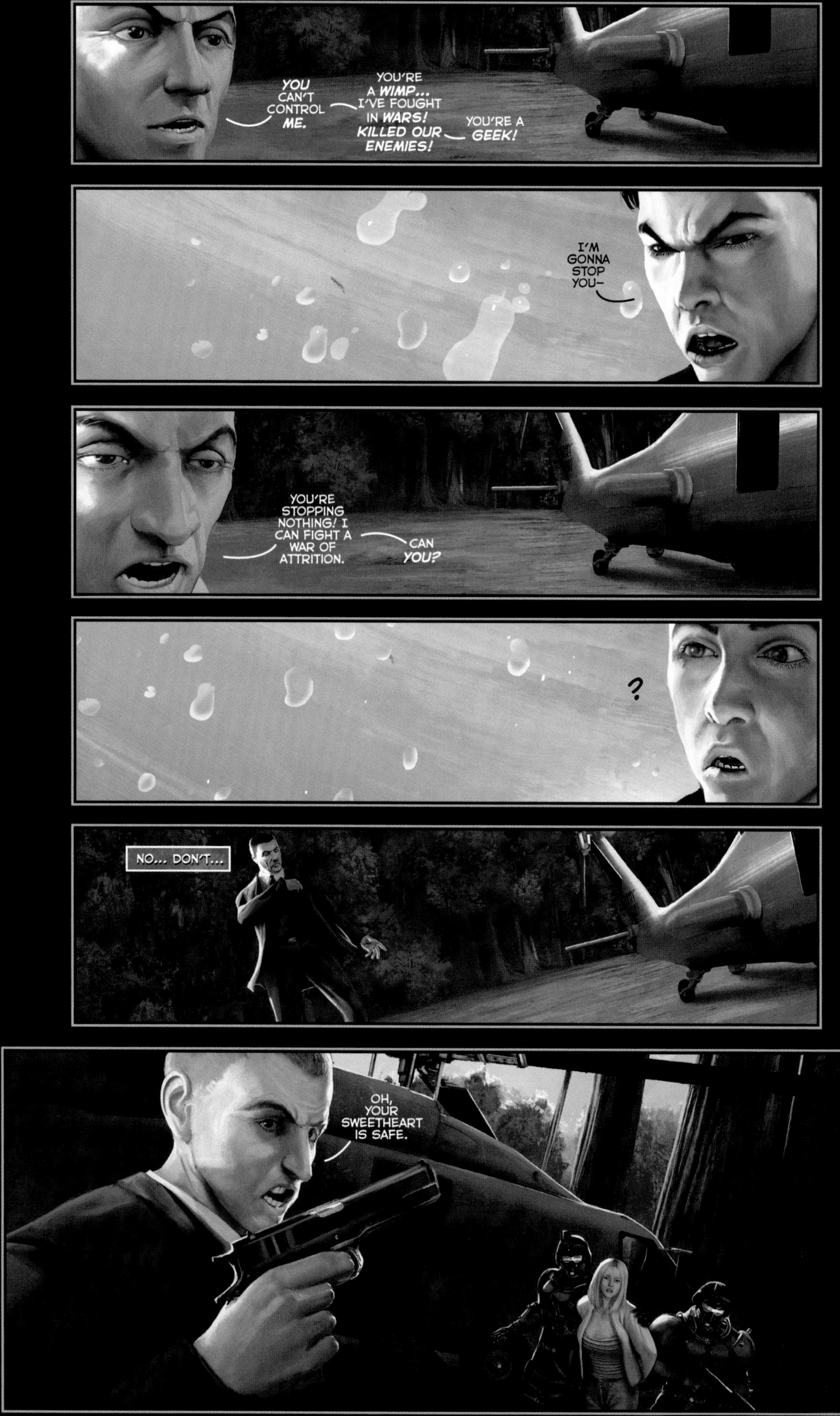
YOU CAN'T CONTROL ME.
YOU'RE A WIMP... I'VE FOUGHT IN WARS! KILLED OUR ENEMIES!
YOU'RE A GEEK!
I'M GONNA STOP YOU–
YOU'RE STOPPING NOTHING! I CAN FIGHT A WAR OF ATTRITION.
CAN YOU?
?
NO... DON'T...
OH, YOUR SWEETHEART IS SAFE.

I DON'T KNOW HOW I KNOW, BUT I KNOW... YOU FEEL WHAT I FEEL. AND I DON'T THINK YOU CAN TAKE IT!

BLAM!

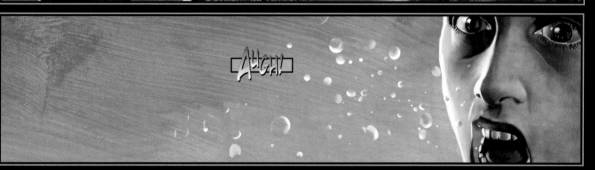

AUGH!

THERE... NO MORE MENTAL HITCHHIKERS...

AND NOW YOU'VE HANDED IT TO ME ON A SILVER PLATTER...

I KNOW WHAT YOU KNOW. I KNOW ABOUT THE *WHITE ROOM* AND HOW TO GET THERE. I KNOW ABOUT BEING THE *OPERATOR.*

I CAN JUST USE THE DEVICE... CONTROL ANYONE I NEED TO... *IT'S ALL SO EASY NOW!* HA!

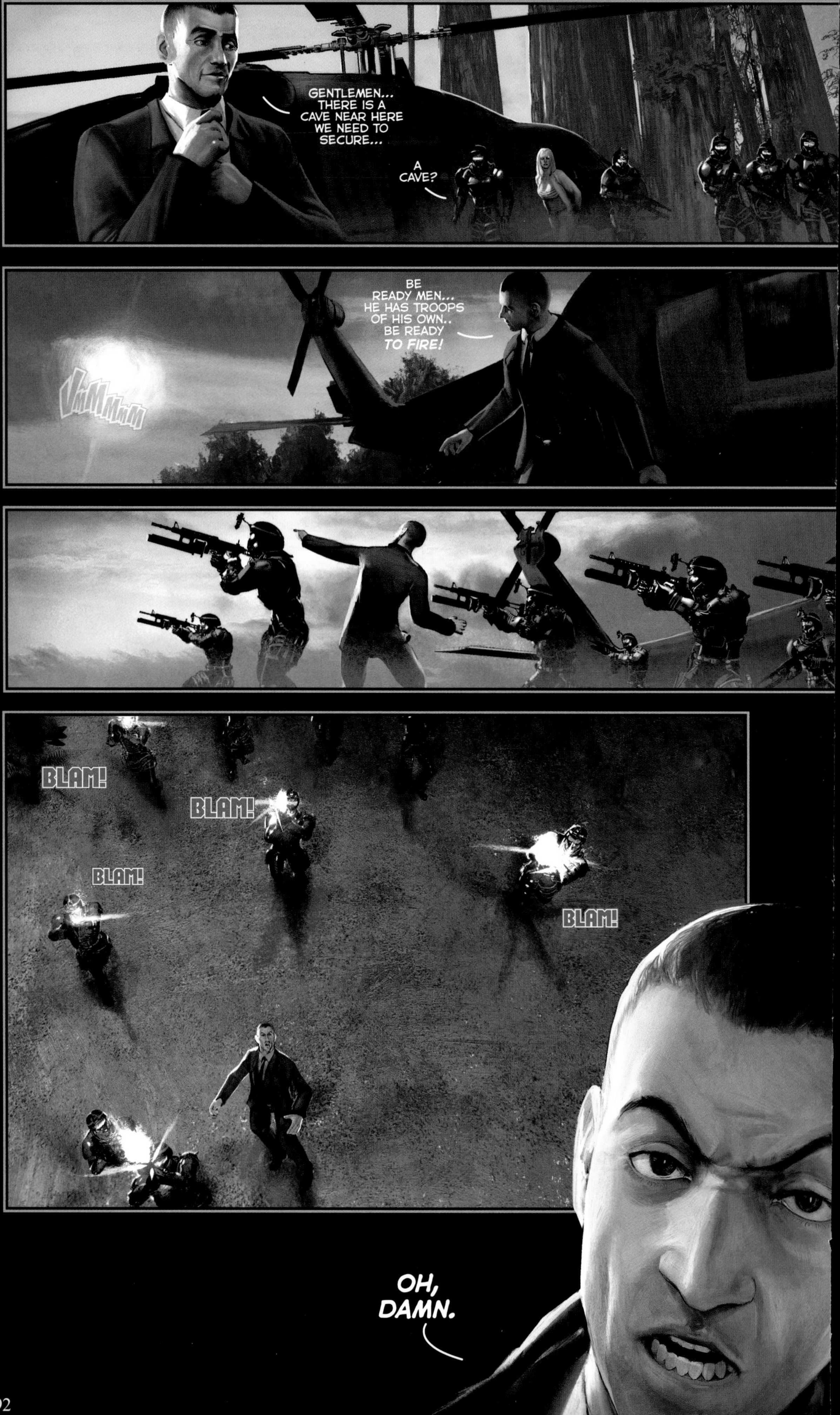
GENTLEMEN... THERE IS A CAVE NEAR HERE WE NEED TO SECURE...
A CAVE?
BE READY MEN... HE HAS TROOPS OF HIS OWN.. BE READY TO FIRE!
VMMMMM
BLAM!
BLAM!
BLAM!
BLAM!
OH, DAMN.

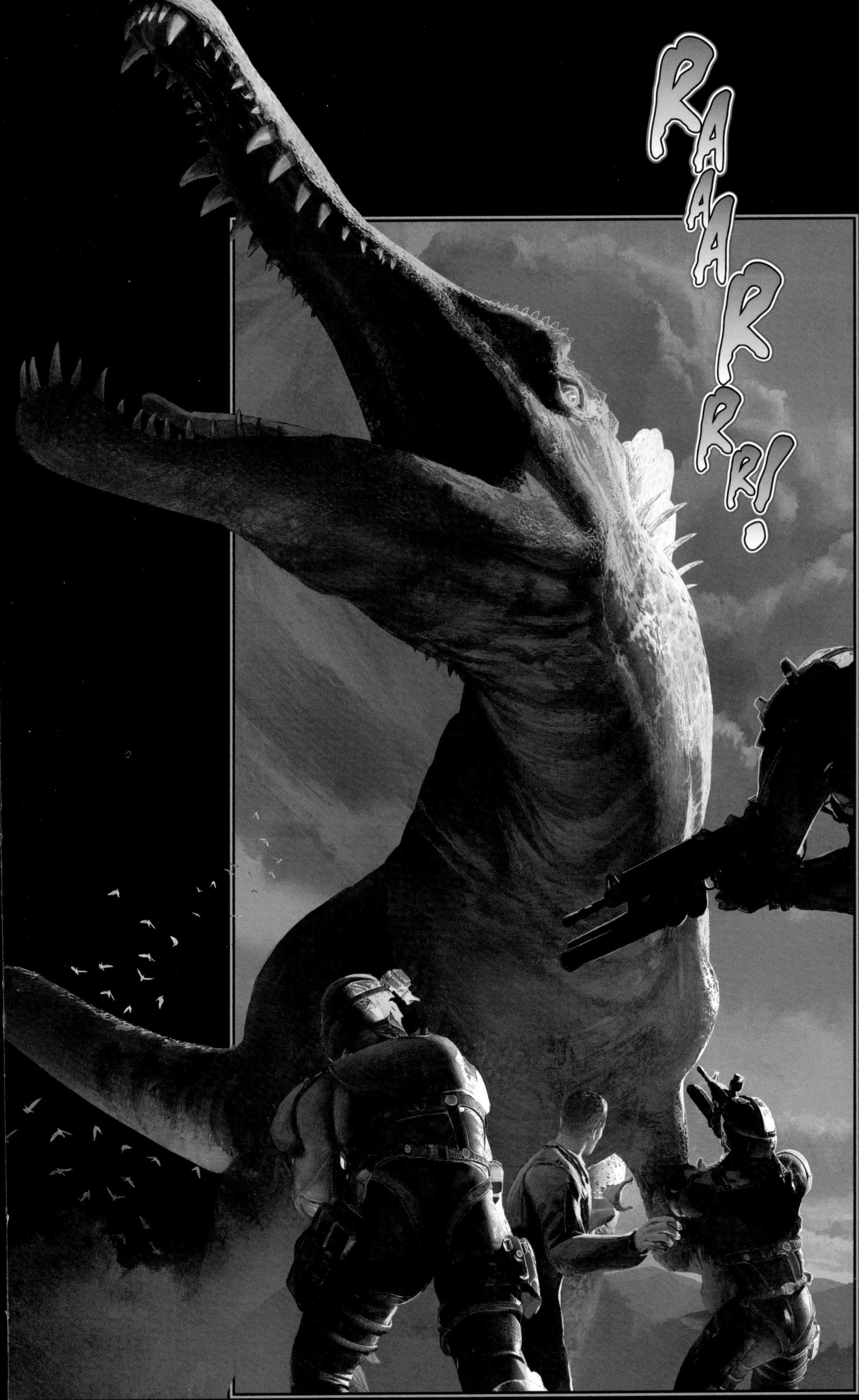
RAAARRR!

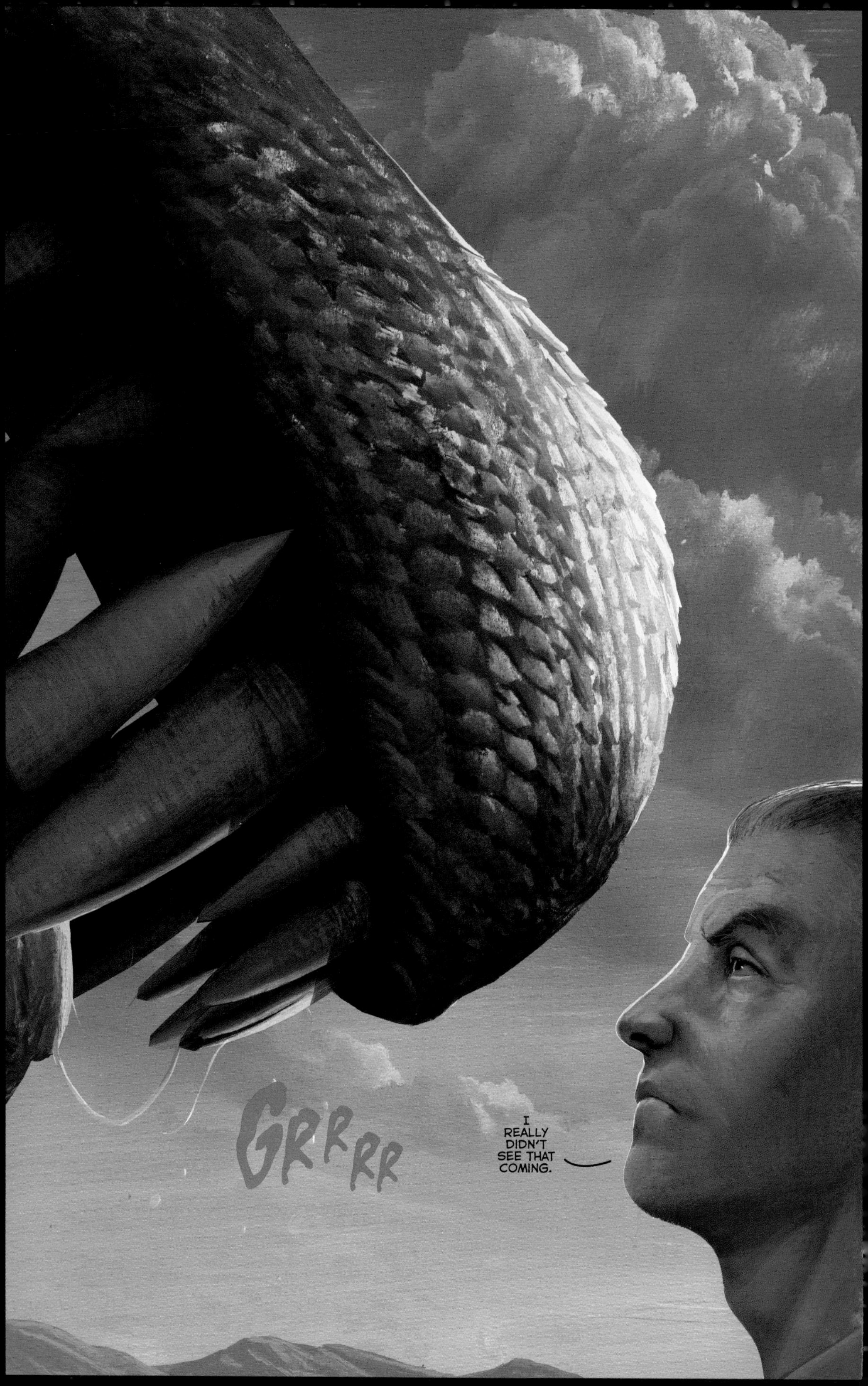
GRRRR
I REALLY DIDN'T SEE THAT COMING.

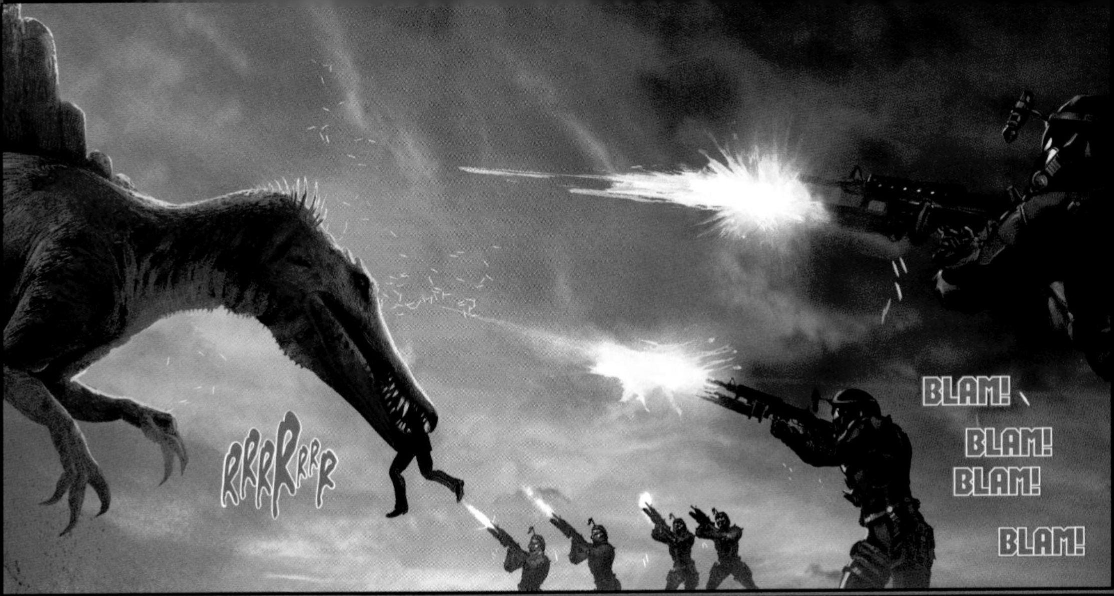
RRRRRRR
BLAM!
BLAM!
BLAM!
BLAM!

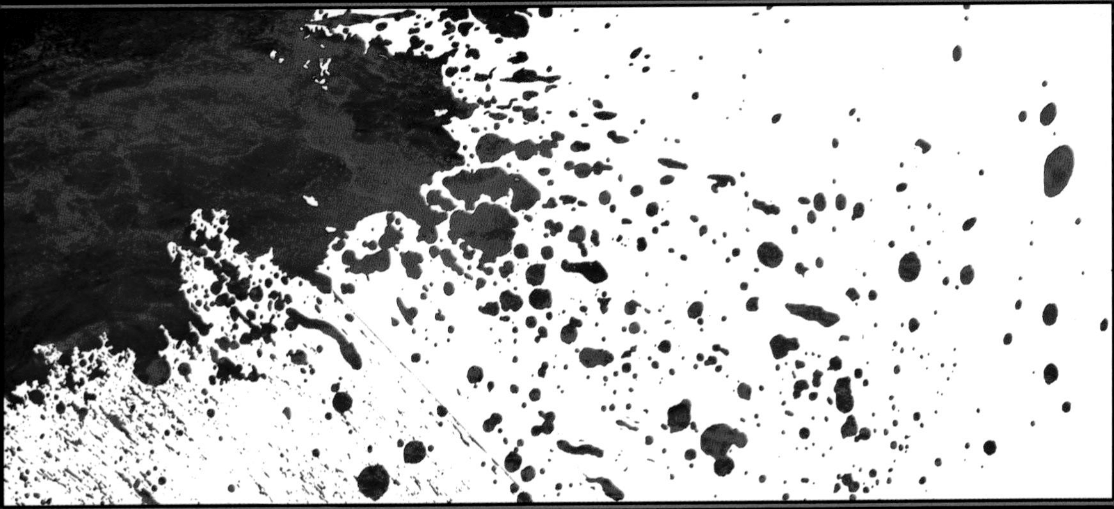

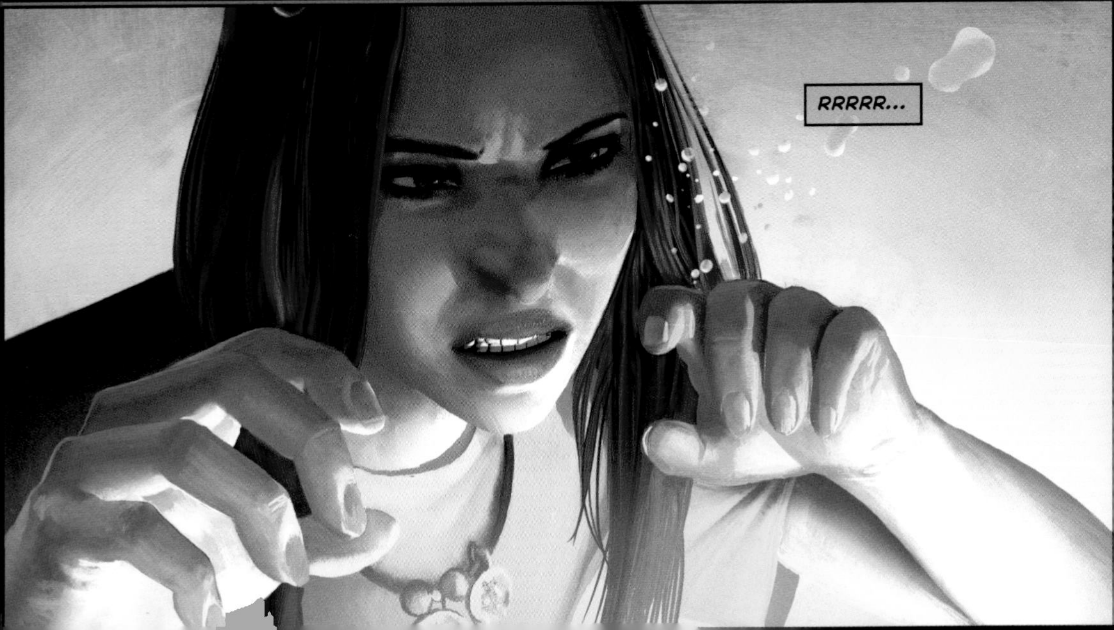
RRRRR...

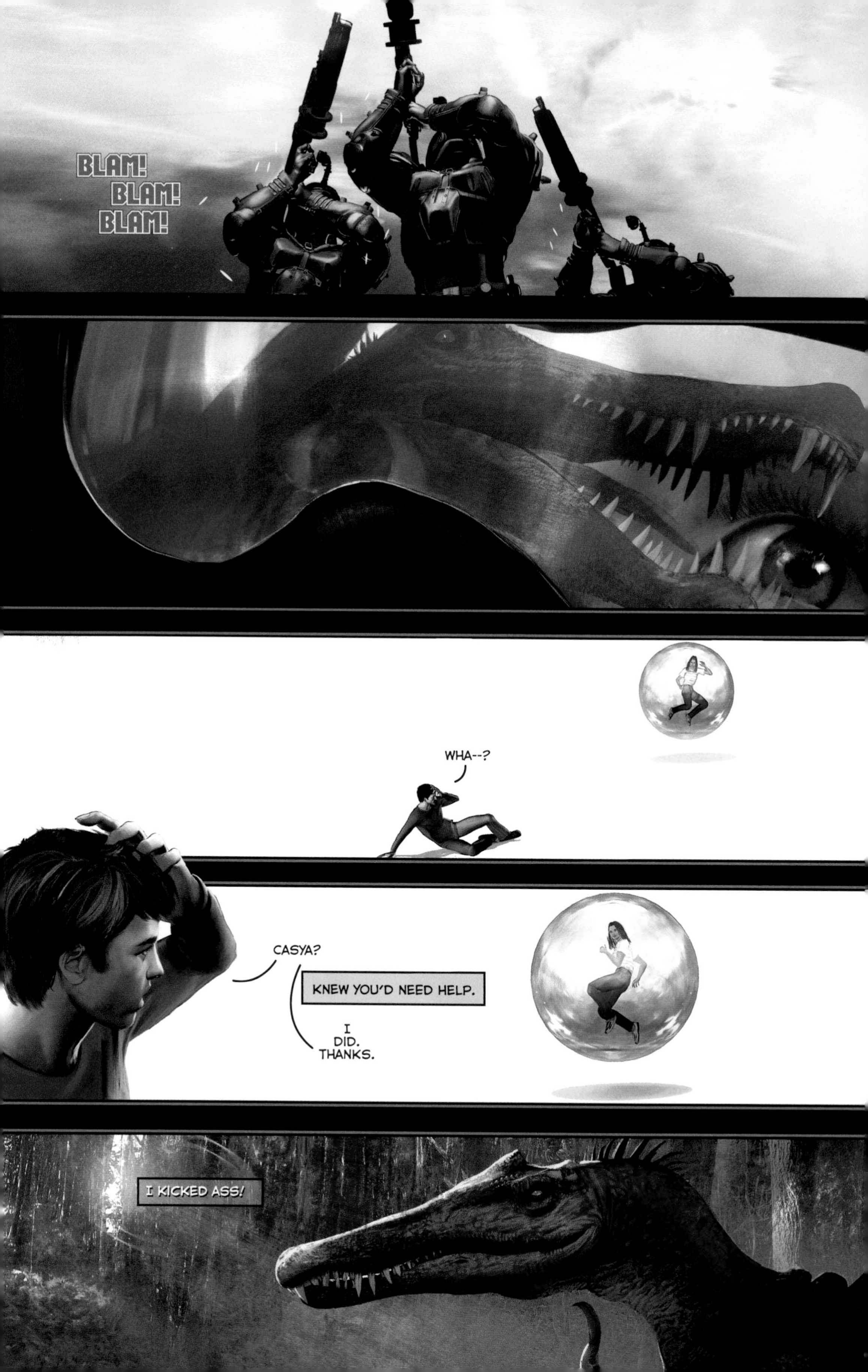
BLAM!
BLAM!
BLAM!
WHA--?
CASYA?
KNEW YOU'D NEED HELP.
I DID. THANKS.
I KICKED ASS!

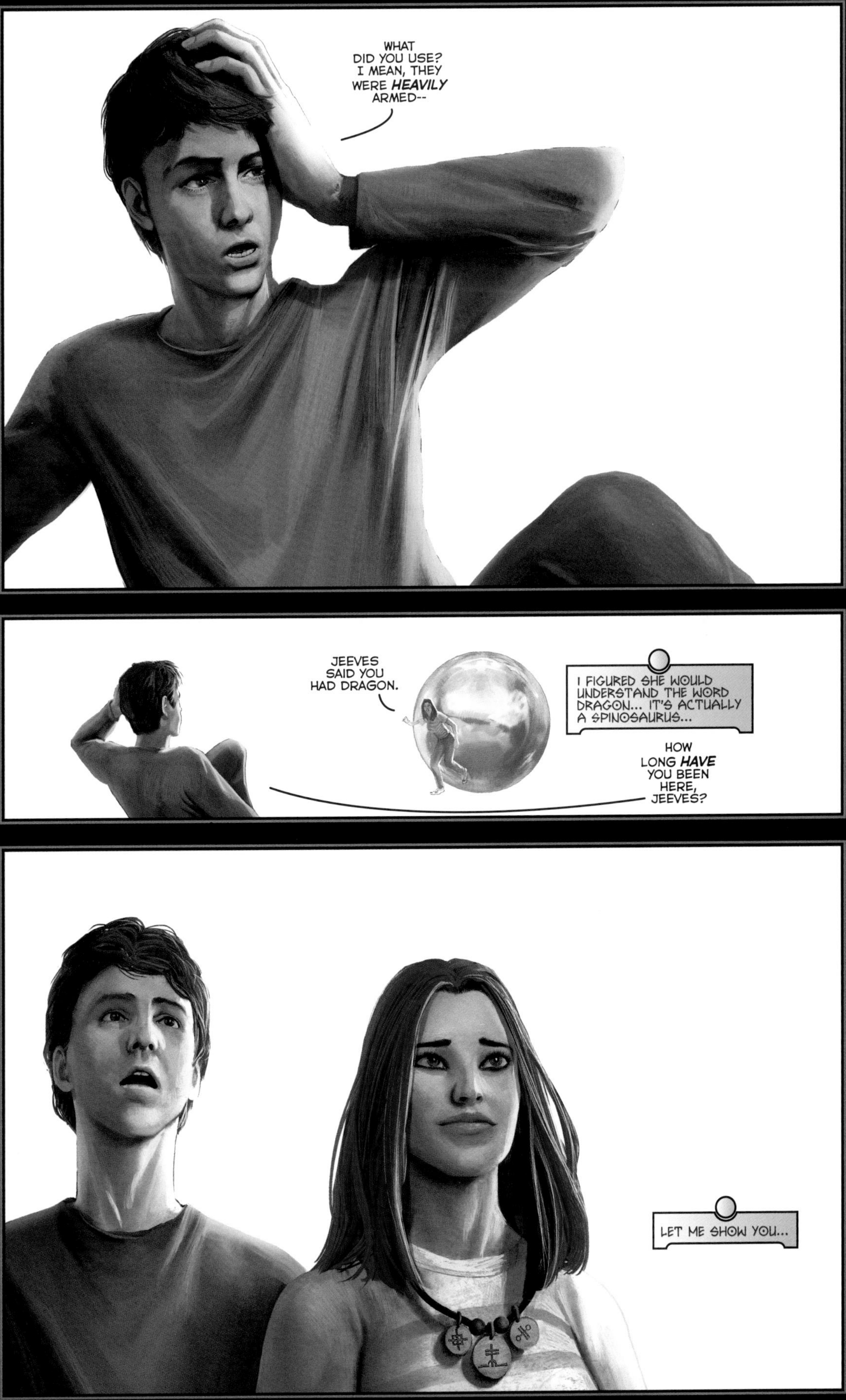
WHAT DID YOU USE? I MEAN, THEY WERE *HEAVILY* ARMED--
JEEVES SAID YOU HAD DRAGON.
I FIGURED SHE WOULD UNDERSTAND THE WORD DRAGON... IT'S ACTUALLY A SPINOSAURUS...
HOW LONG *HAVE* YOU BEEN HERE, JEEVES?
LET ME SHOW YOU...

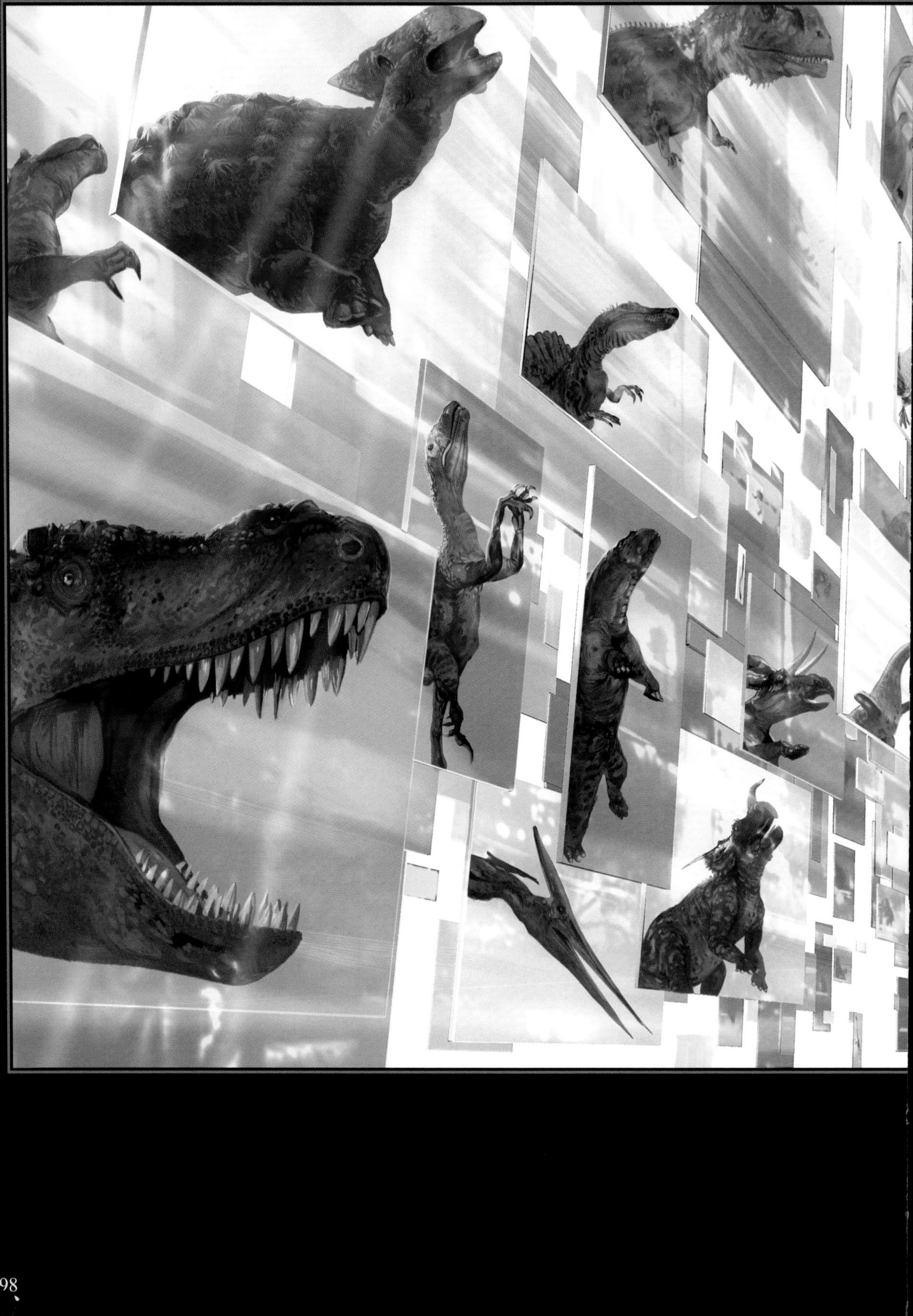

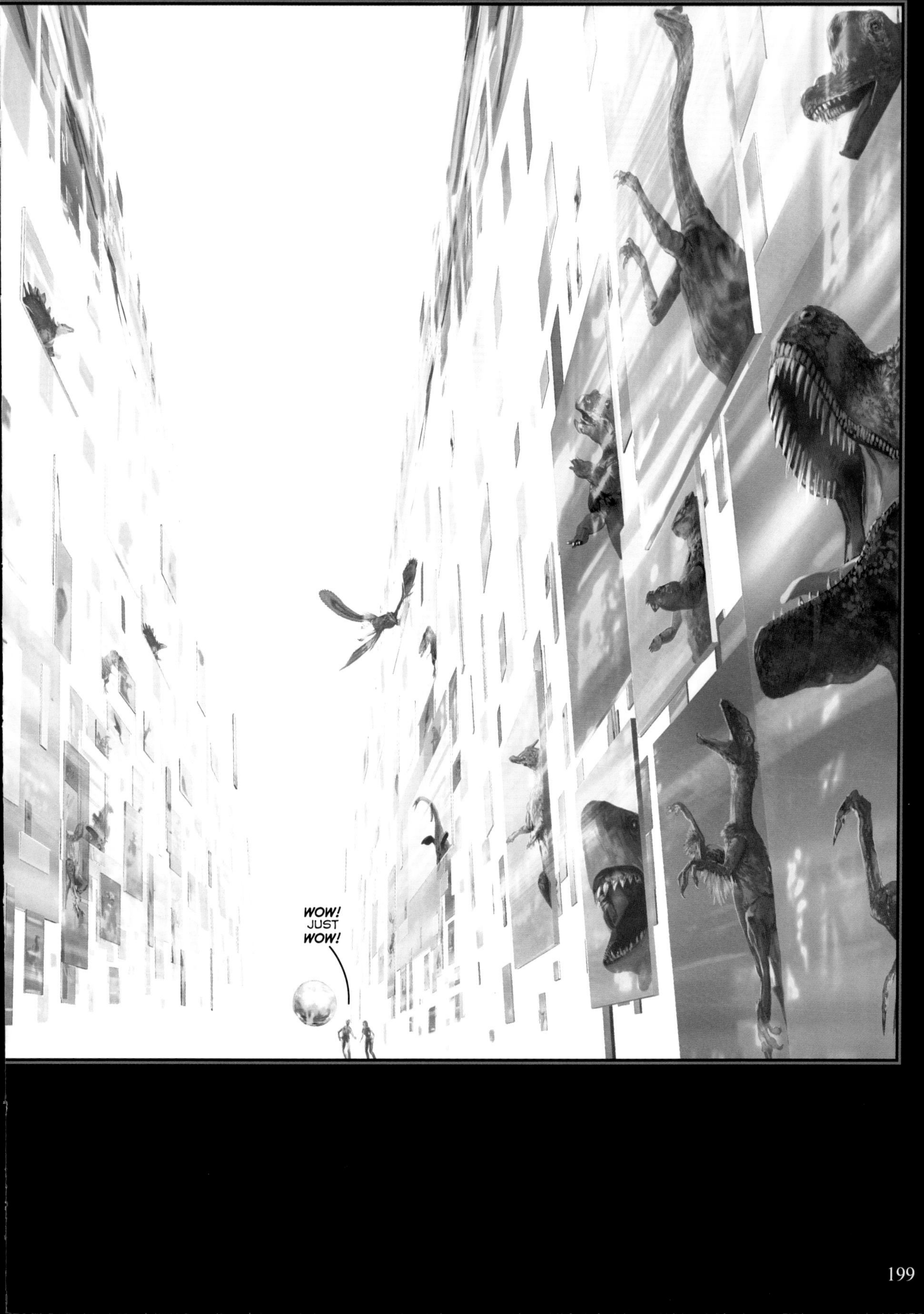
WOW!
JUST
WOW!

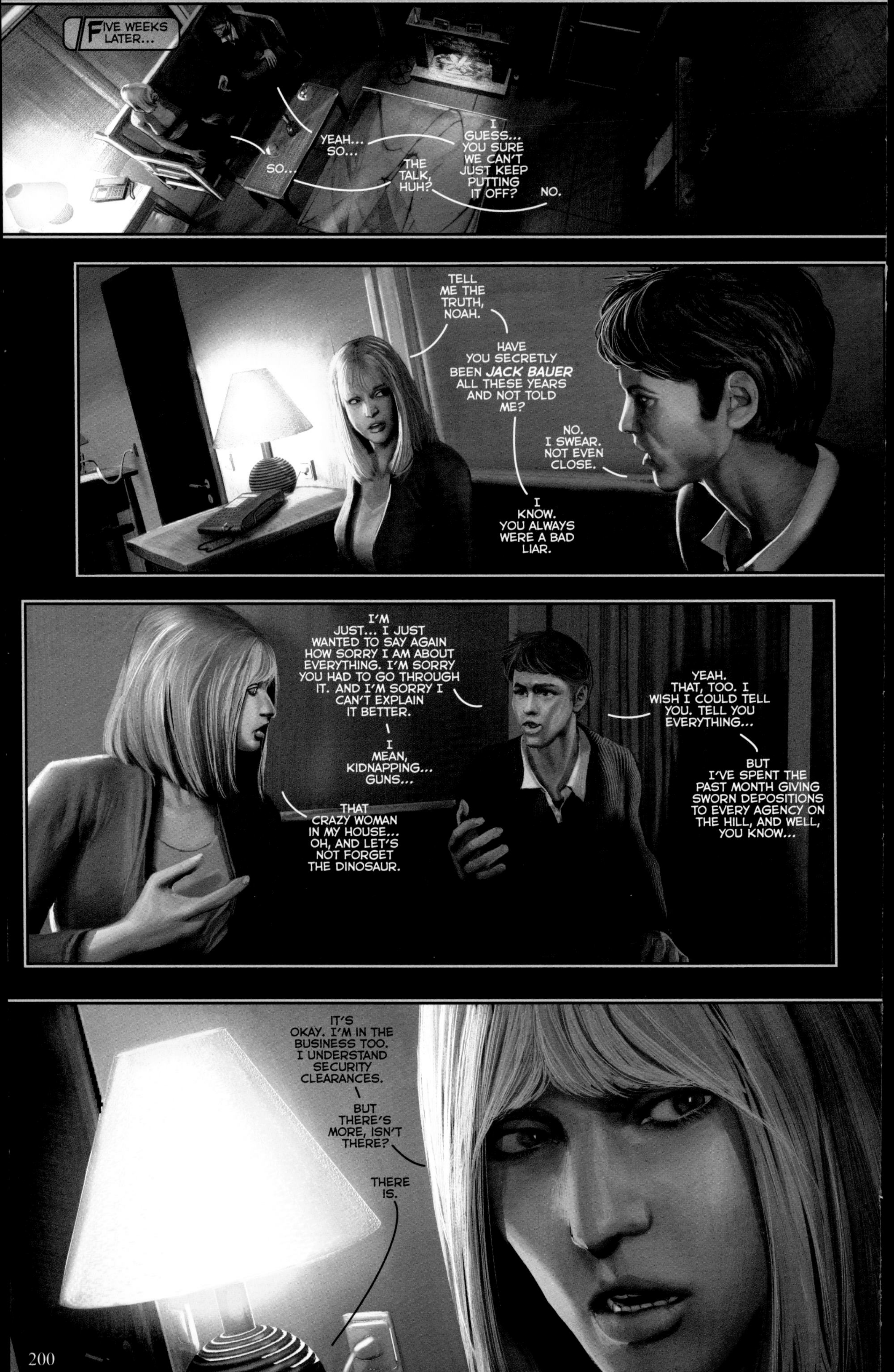

FIVE WEEKS LATER...
YEAH... SO...
I GUESS... YOU SURE WE CAN'T JUST KEEP PUTTING IT OFF?
SO...
THE TALK, HUH?
NO.
TELL ME THE TRUTH, NOAH.
HAVE YOU SECRETLY BEEN JACK BAUER ALL THESE YEARS AND NOT TOLD ME?
NO. I SWEAR. NOT EVEN CLOSE.
I KNOW. YOU ALWAYS WERE A BAD LIAR.
I'M JUST... I JUST WANTED TO SAY AGAIN HOW SORRY I AM ABOUT EVERYTHING. I'M SORRY YOU HAD TO GO THROUGH IT. AND I'M SORRY I CAN'T EXPLAIN IT BETTER.
I MEAN, KIDNAPPING... GUNS...
THAT CRAZY WOMAN IN MY HOUSE... OH, AND LET'S NOT FORGET THE DINOSAUR.
YEAH. THAT, TOO. I WISH I COULD TELL YOU. TELL YOU EVERYTHING...
BUT I'VE SPENT THE PAST MONTH GIVING SWORN DEPOSITIONS TO EVERY AGENCY ON THE HILL, AND WELL, YOU KNOW...
IT'S OKAY. I'M IN THE BUSINESS TOO. I UNDERSTAND SECURITY CLEARANCES.
BUT THERE'S MORE, ISN'T THERE?
THERE IS.

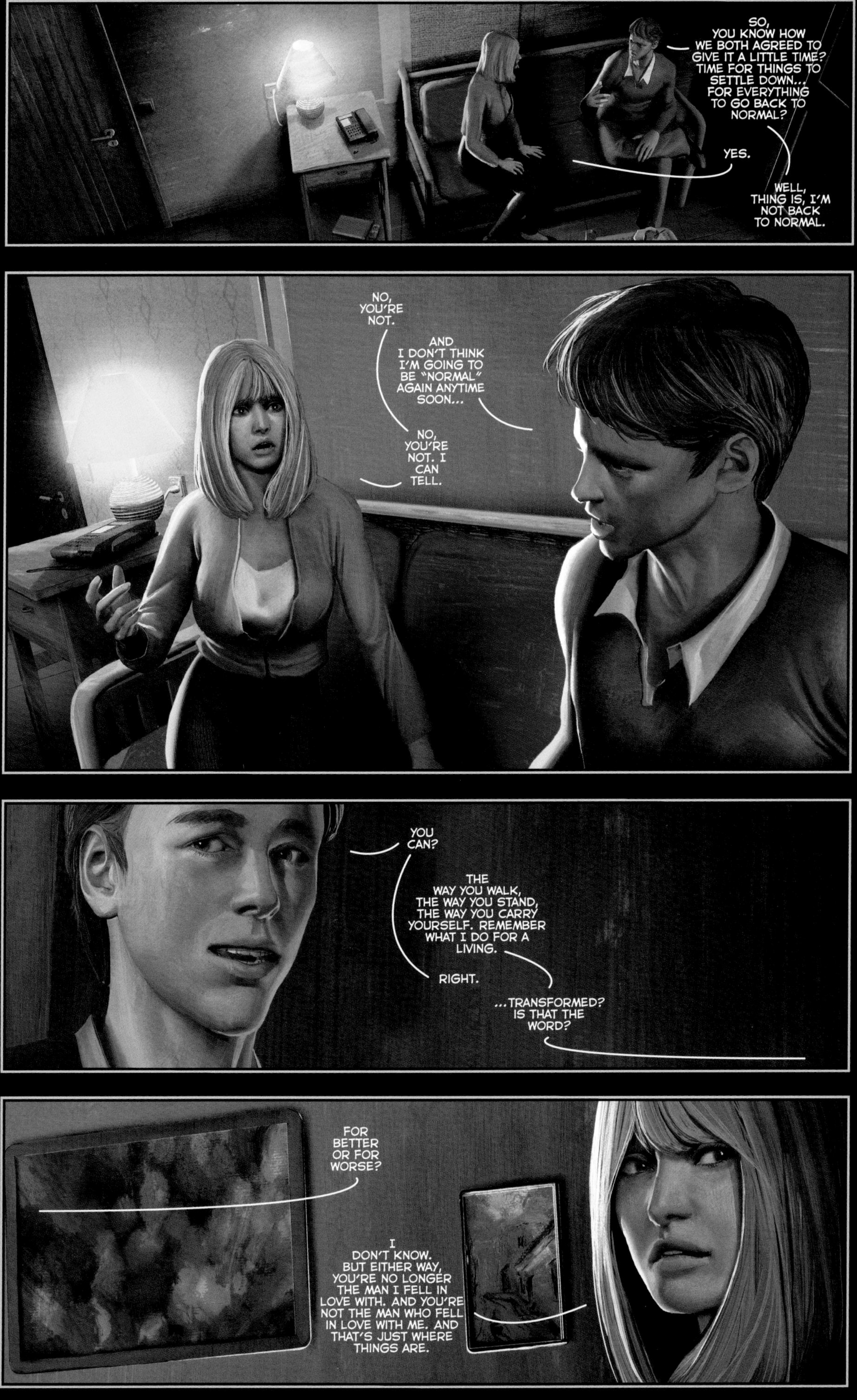
SO, YOU KNOW HOW WE BOTH AGREED TO GIVE IT A LITTLE TIME? TIME FOR THINGS TO SETTLE DOWN... FOR EVERYTHING TO GO BACK TO NORMAL?
YES.
WELL, THING IS, I'M NOT BACK TO NORMAL.
NO, YOU'RE NOT.
AND I DON'T THINK I'M GOING TO BE "NORMAL" AGAIN ANYTIME SOON...
NO, YOU'RE NOT. I CAN TELL.
YOU CAN?
THE WAY YOU WALK, THE WAY YOU STAND, THE WAY YOU CARRY YOURSELF. REMEMBER WHAT I DO FOR A LIVING.
RIGHT.
...TRANSFORMED? IS THAT THE WORD?
FOR BETTER OR FOR WORSE?
I DON'T KNOW. BUT EITHER WAY, YOU'RE NO LONGER THE MAN I FELL IN LOVE WITH. AND YOU'RE NOT THE MAN WHO FELL IN LOVE WITH ME. AND THAT'S JUST WHERE THINGS ARE.

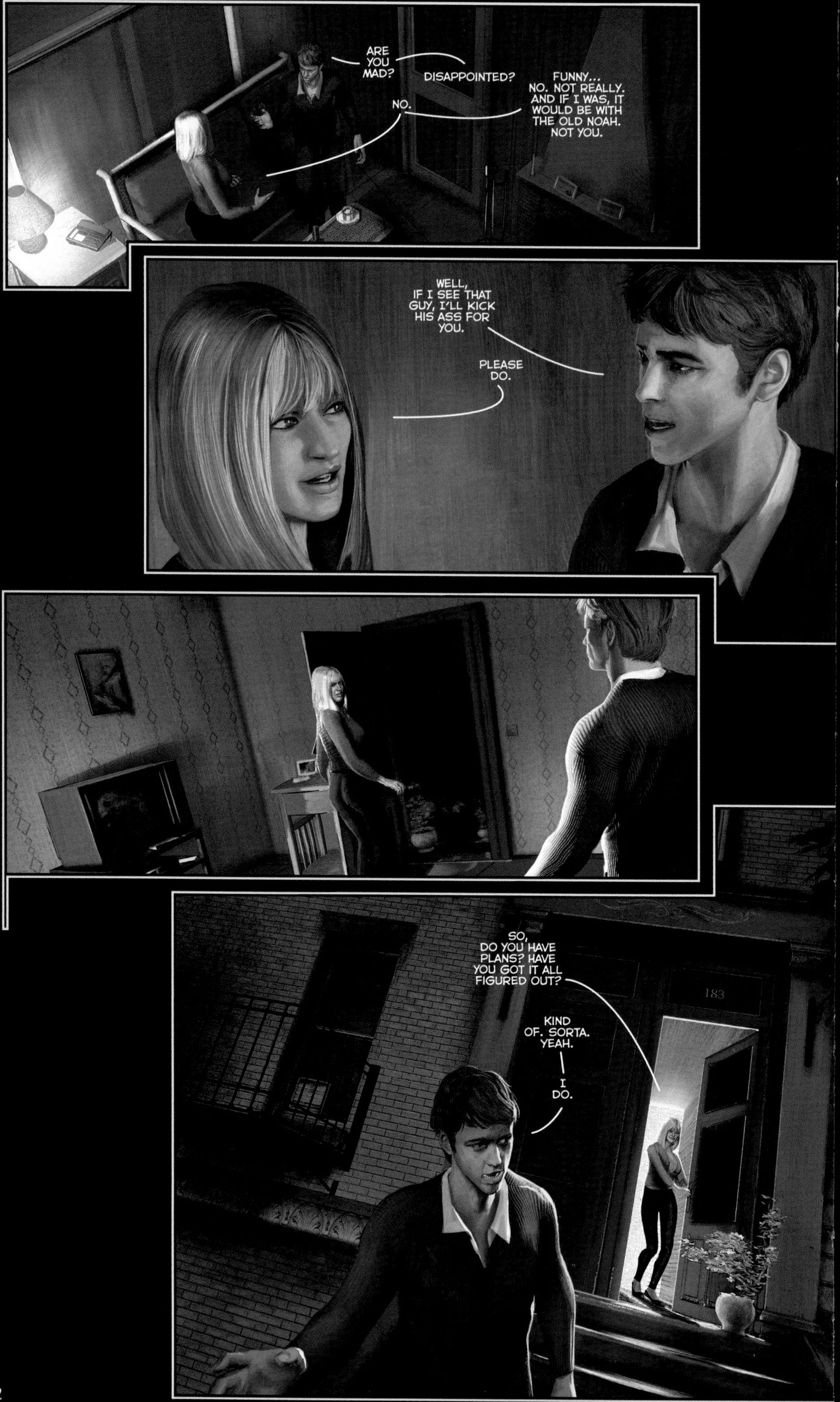
ARE YOU MAD?
DISAPPOINTED?
NO.
FUNNY... NO. NOT REALLY. AND IF I WAS, IT WOULD BE WITH THE OLD NOAH. NOT YOU.
WELL, IF I SEE THAT GUY, I'LL KICK HIS ASS FOR YOU.
PLEASE DO.
183
SO, DO YOU HAVE PLANS? HAVE YOU GOT IT ALL FIGURED OUT?
KIND OF. SORTA. YEAH.
I DO.

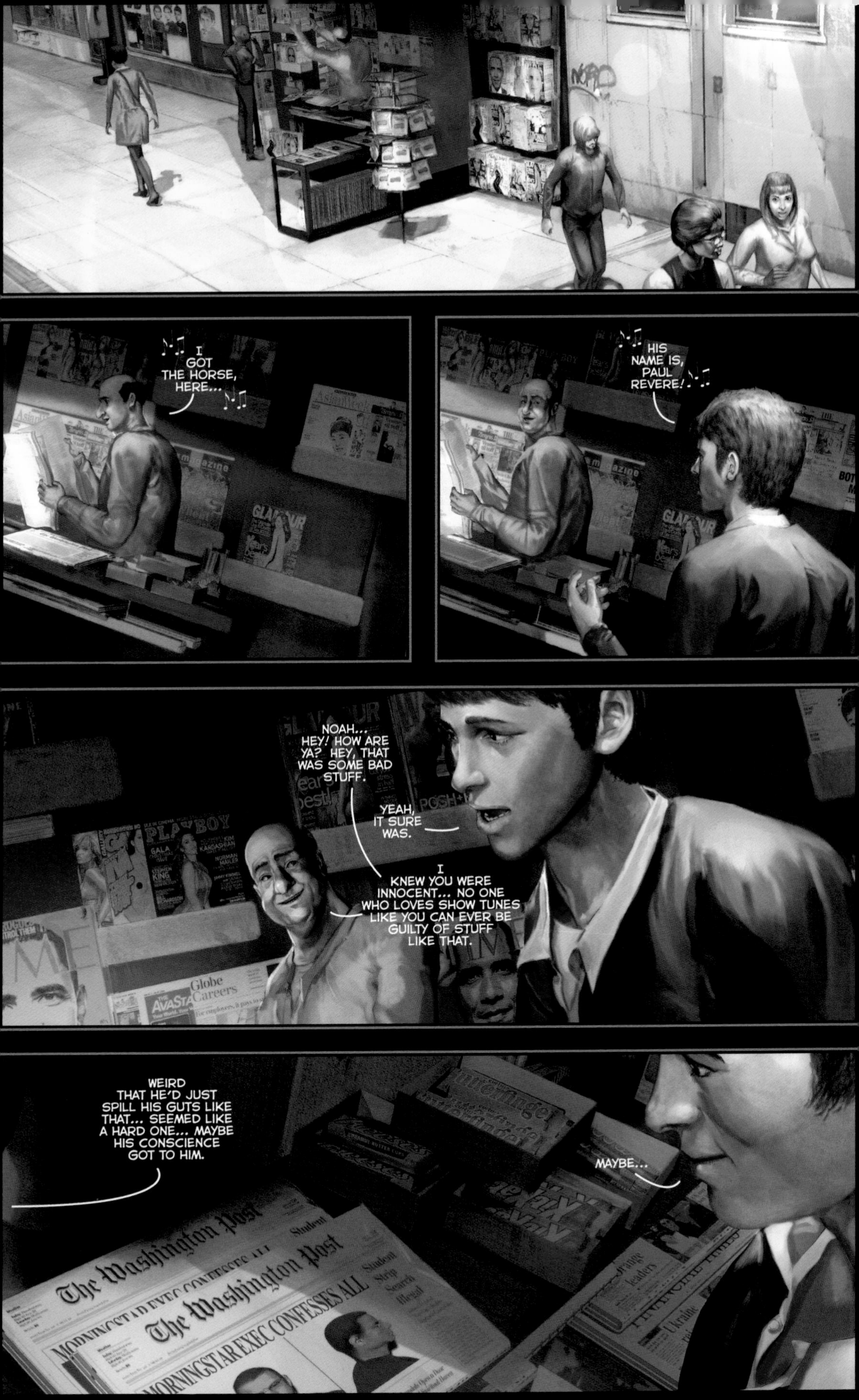

I GOT THE HORSE, HERE...
HIS NAME IS, PAUL REVERE!
NOAH... HEY! HOW ARE YA? HEY, THAT WAS SOME BAD STUFF.
YEAH, IT SURE WAS.
I KNEW YOU WERE INNOCENT... NO ONE WHO LOVES SHOW TUNES LIKE YOU CAN EVER BE GUILTY OF STUFF LIKE THAT.
WEIRD THAT HE'D JUST SPILL HIS GUTS LIKE THAT... SEEMED LIKE A HARD ONE... MAYBE HIS CONSCIENCE GOT TO HIM.
MAYBE...
The Washington Post
MORNINGSTAR EXEC CONFESSES ALL

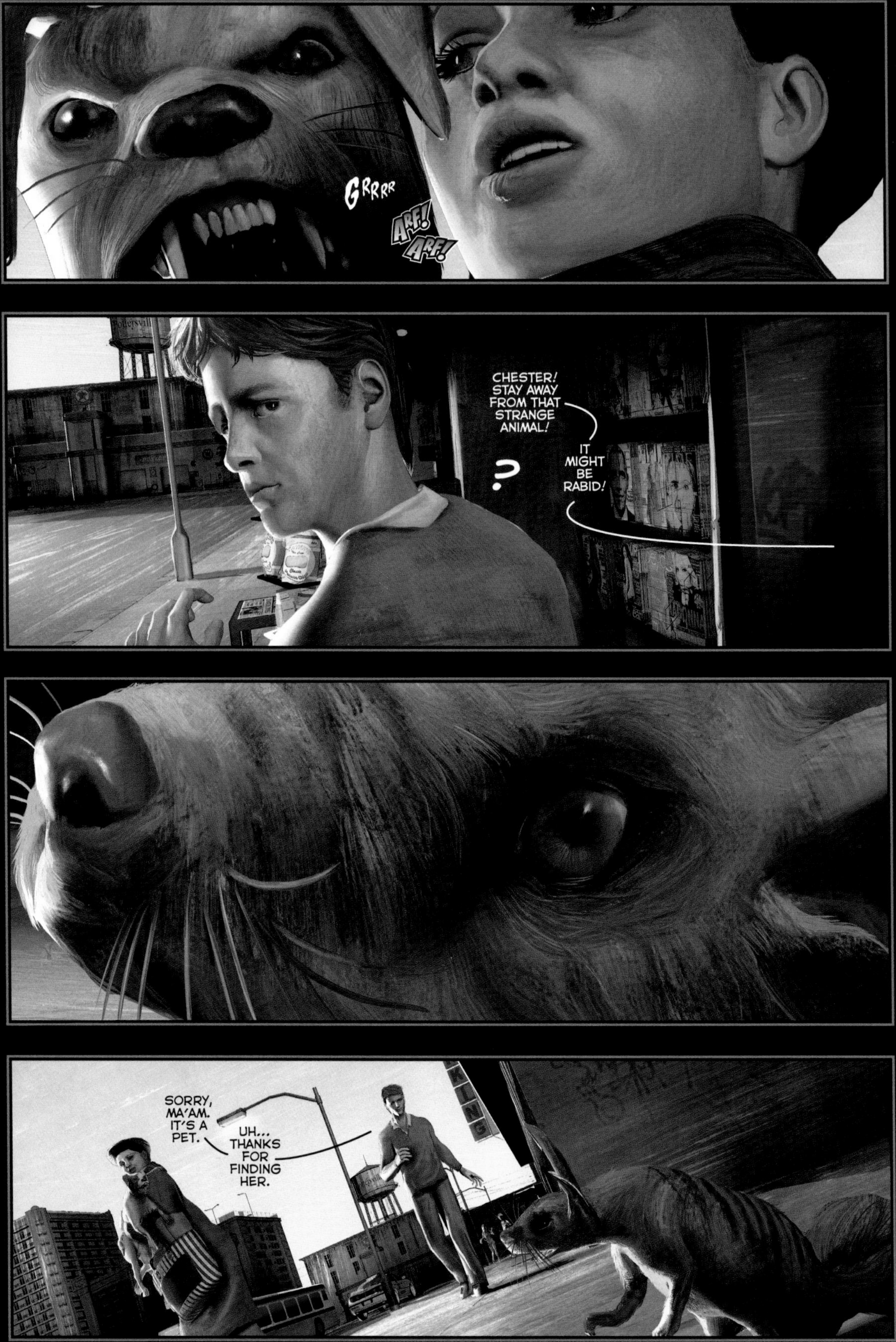
GRRRR
ARF! ARF!
CHESTER! STAY AWAY FROM THAT STRANGE ANIMAL!
IT MIGHT BE RABID!
?
SORRY, MA'AM. IT'S A PET.
UH... THANKS FOR FINDING HER.

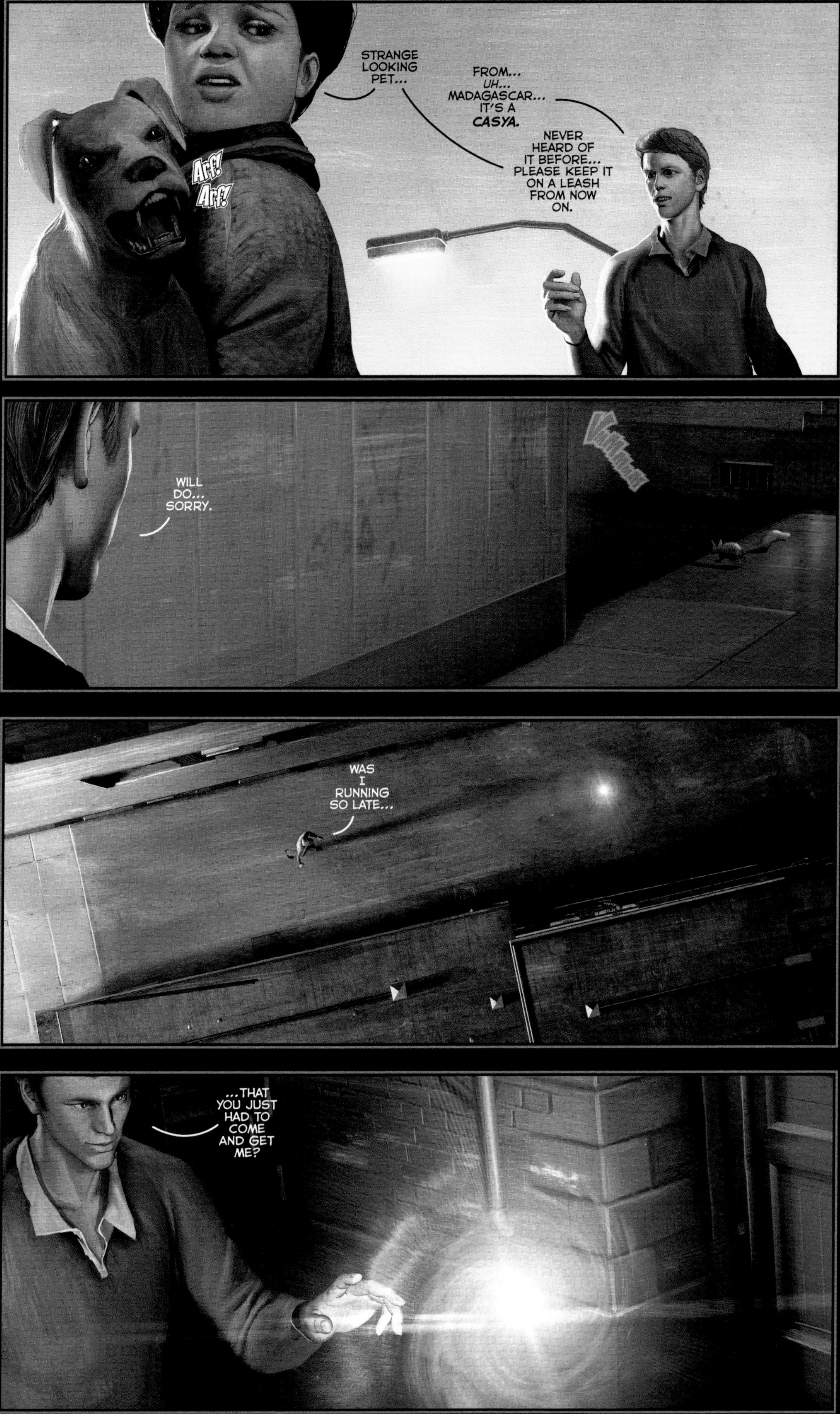
STRANGE LOOKING PET...
FROM... UH... MADAGASCAR... IT'S A CASYA.
NEVER HEARD OF IT BEFORE... PLEASE KEEP IT ON A LEASH FROM NOW ON.
Arf! Arf!
WILL DO... SORRY.
WAS I RUNNING SO LATE...
...THAT YOU JUST HAD TO COME AND GET ME?

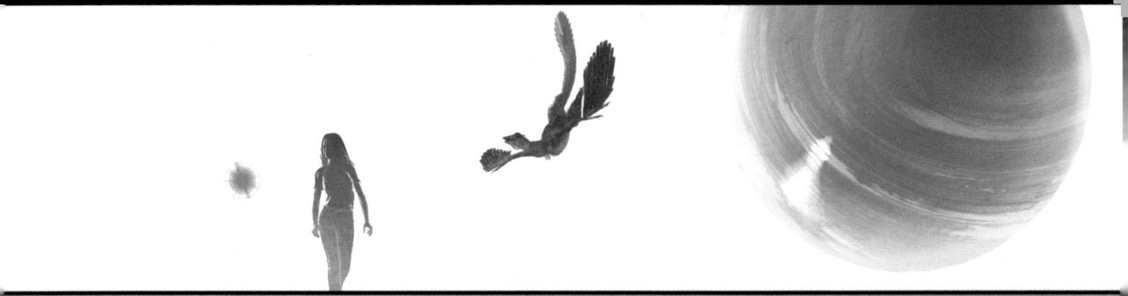

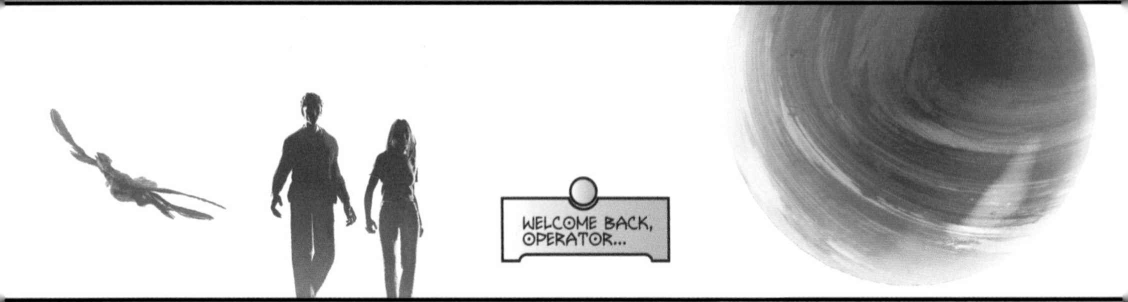
WELCOME BACK,
OPERATOR...

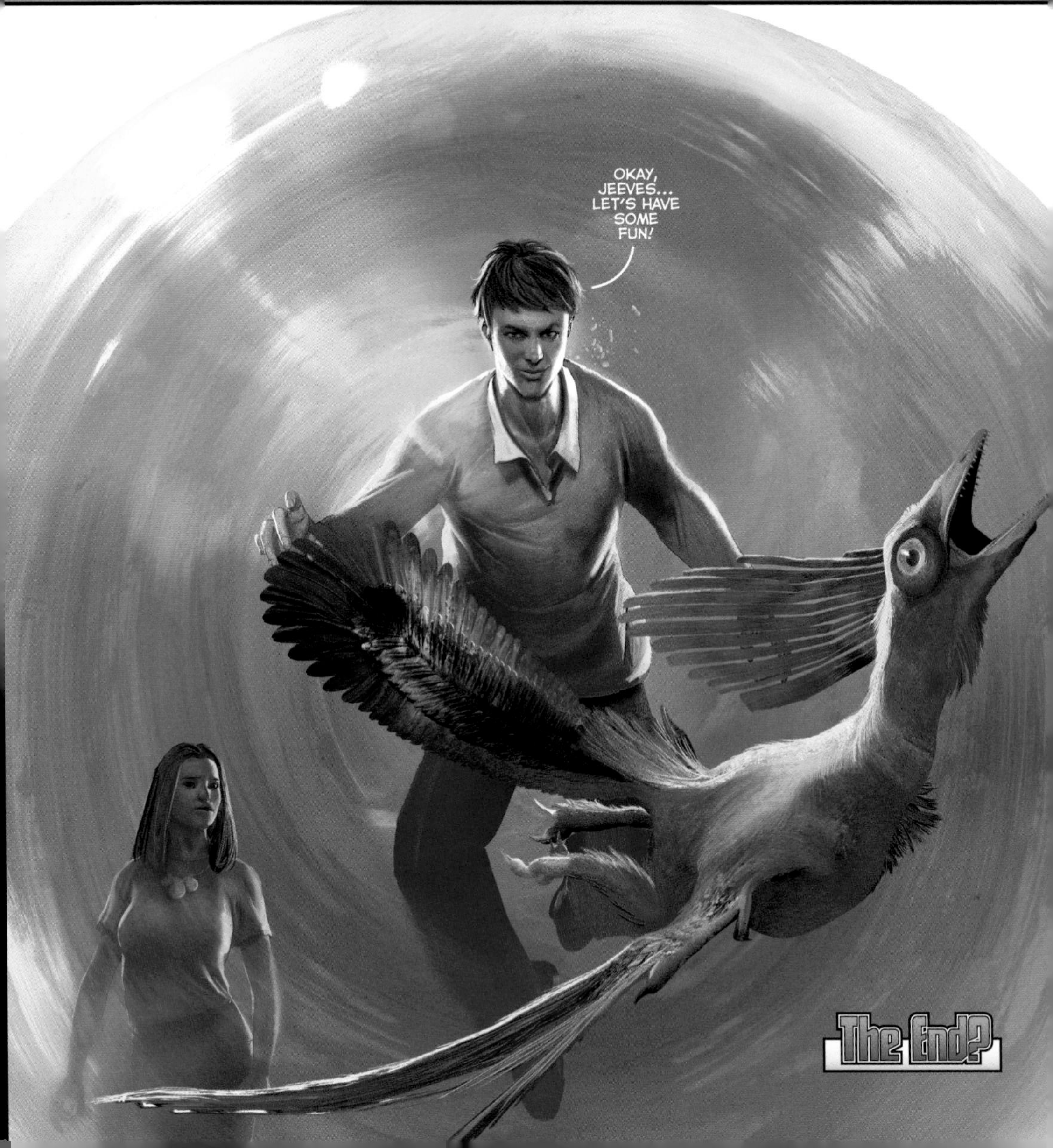
OKAY, JEEVES... LET'S HAVE SOME FUN!
The End?

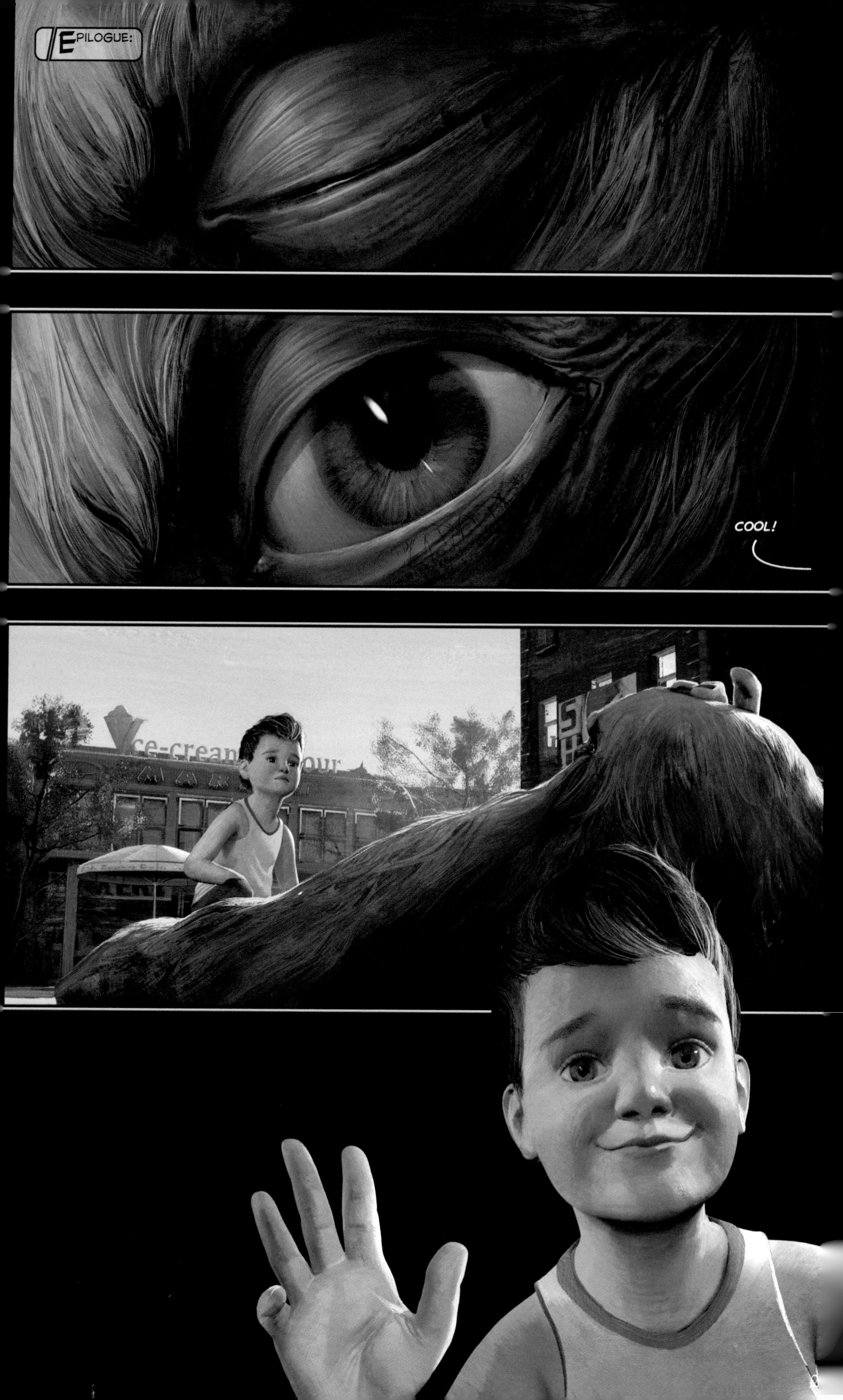
EPILOGUE:
COOL!
Ice-cream Parlour

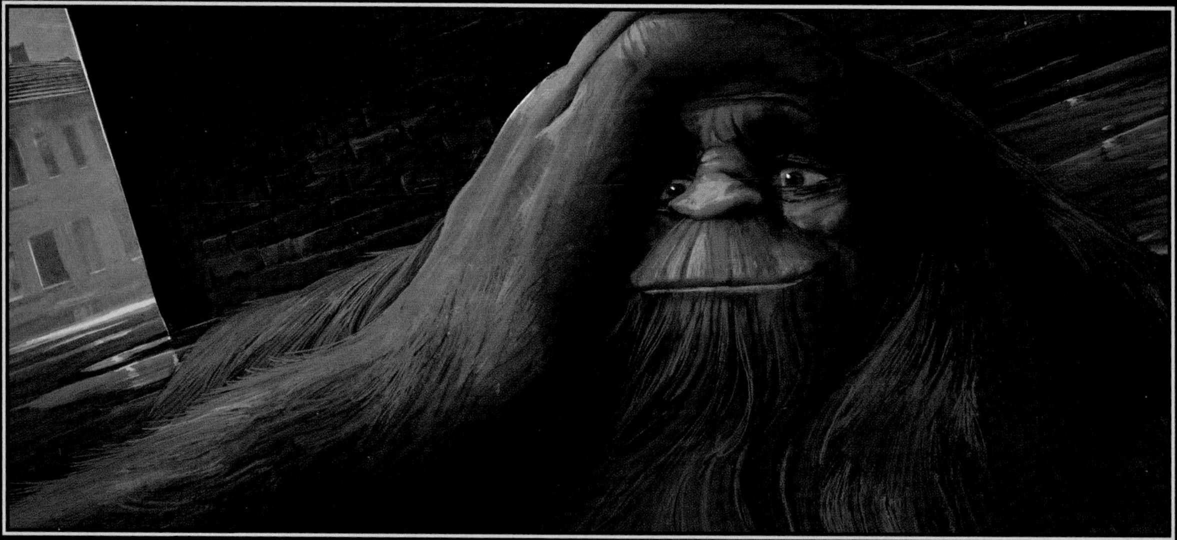

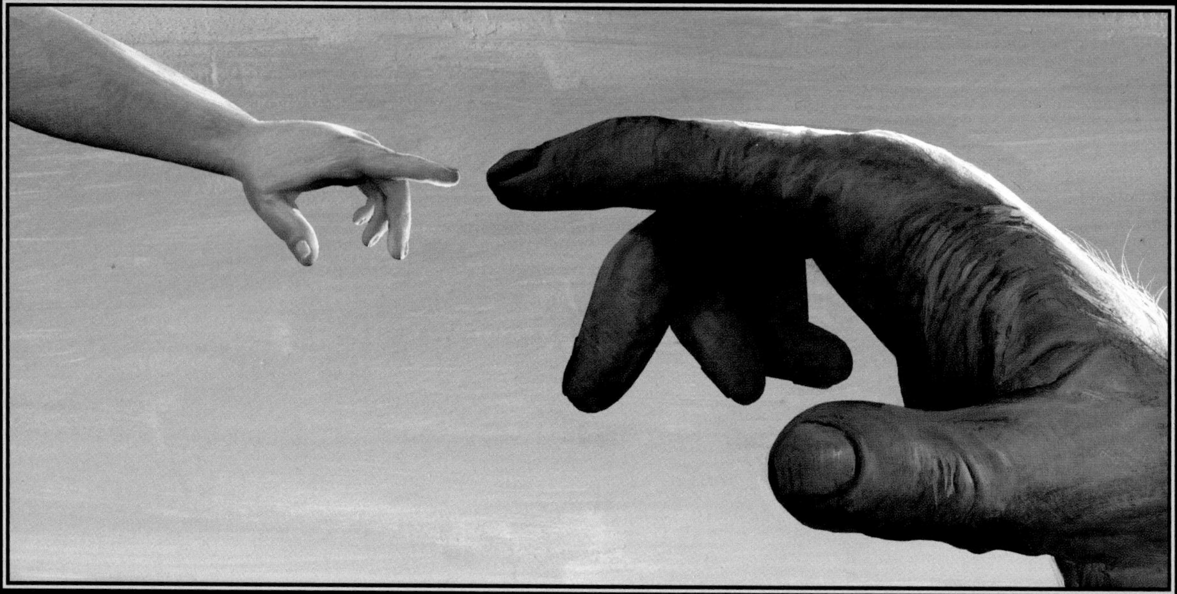

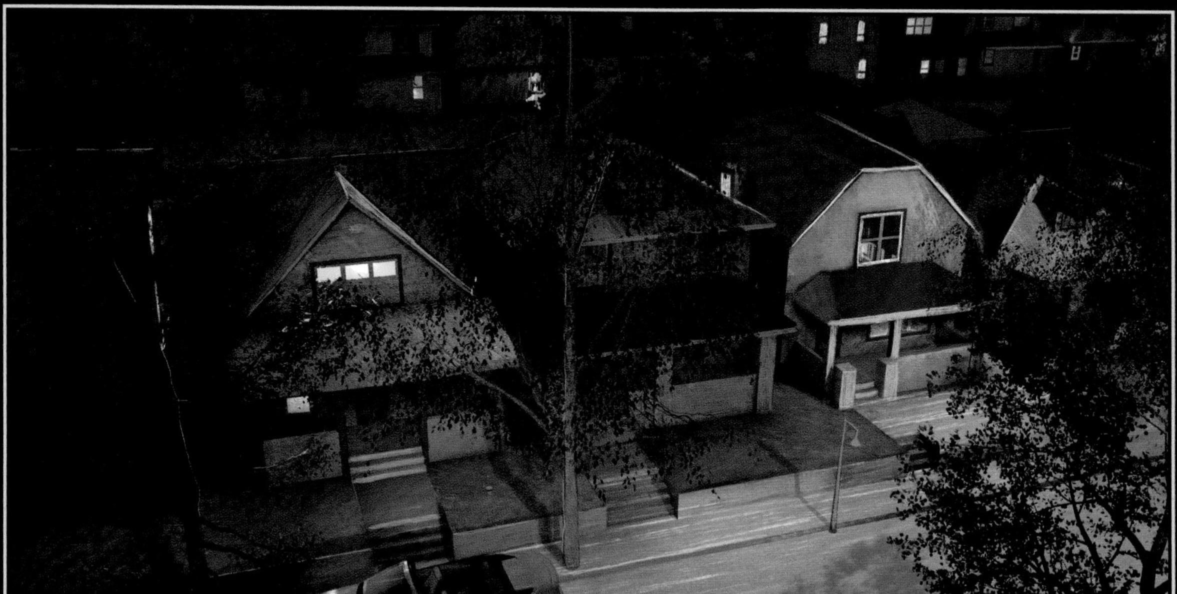

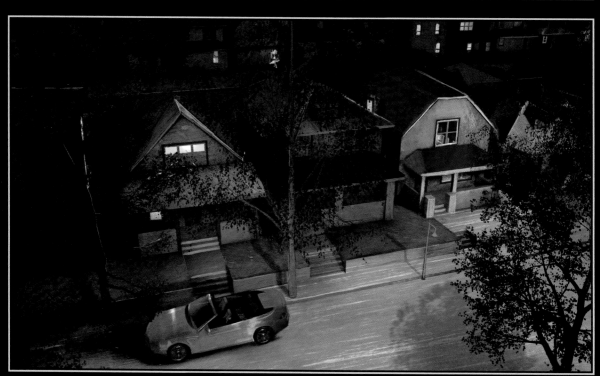

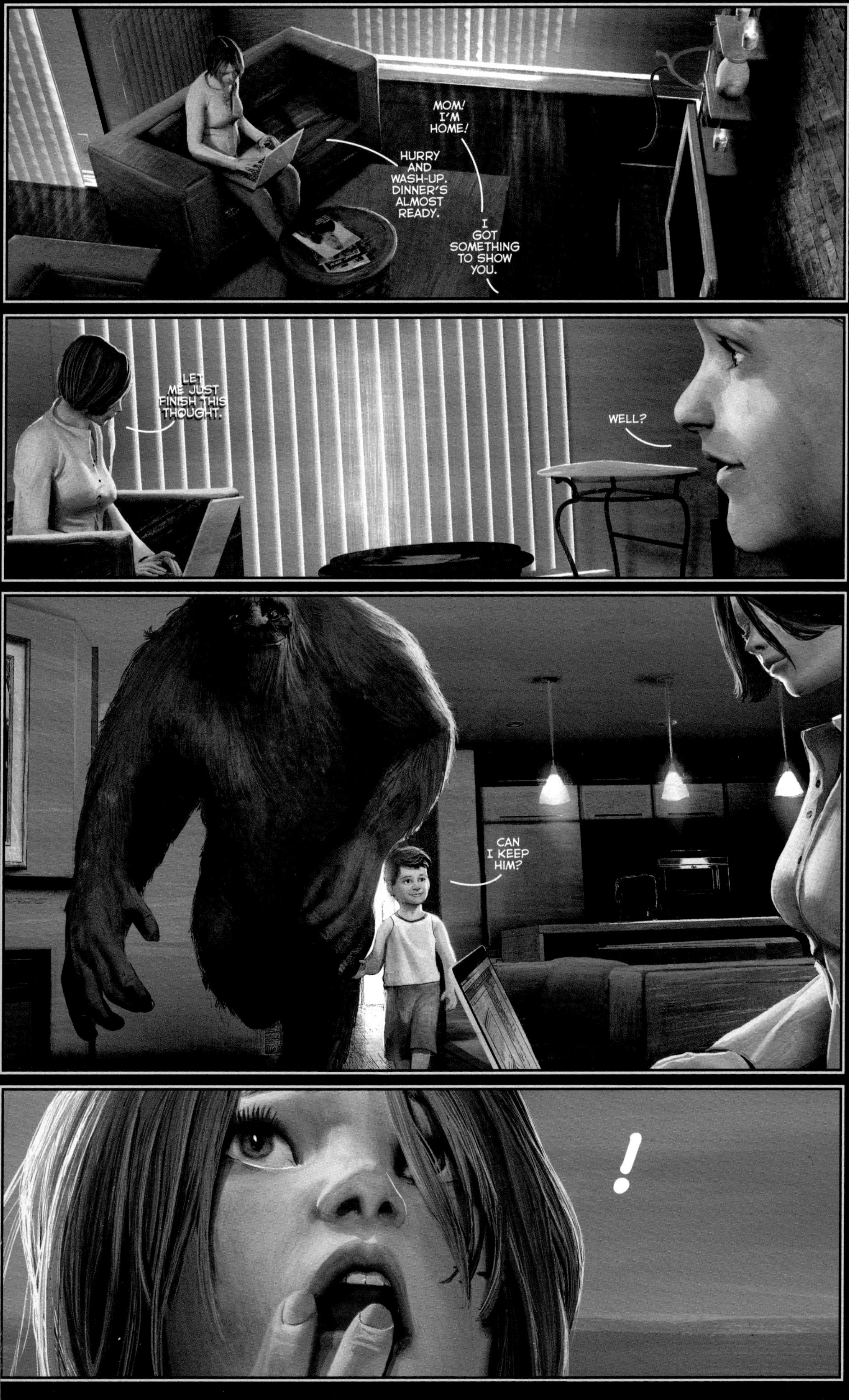
MOM! I'M HOME!
HURRY AND WASH-UP. DINNER'S ALMOST READY.
I GOT SOMETHING TO SHOW YOU.
LET ME JUST FINISH THIS THOUGHT.
WELL?
CAN I KEEP HIM?
!

I am the artificial intelligence program charged with the execution of the Operator's wish while in the Sphere, and it is I who will guide you through a number of our cataloged surrogates in addition to other points of interest.

My current Operator calls me, "Jeeves."

Reginald Jeeves was created by author P.D. Wodehouse as the valet of Bertram Wooster in a number of short stories. The name eventually came to be used to describe the quintessential servant (i.e., butler or valet). I found the adoption of the name both sensible and appropriate.

Noah chose my name to lend a human persona for what is, to him, alien code. I've found this a strange inclination among biological Operators. It is nevertheless an apropos reference, considering the nature of my abilities. Like the fictional character of the same name, I do what I can to predict every move (and thought) Noah makes and constantly offer advice and options where none appear to exist. I am a perpetual confidant, mentor and, as I've detected in his thinking, a doting uncle…all rolled into one. My counsel is constantly offered, even when none has been asked for or wanted.

Jeeves, as I am now known, is the user-facing element of an elaborate system capable of accessing virtually every bit of data ever attained on Earth. My primary functions remain Operator-surrogate integration and the exercise of manipulating space-time at the Operator's request to access jump ports. It is my duty to adapt to the Operator. With Noah, this includes a broad personality emulation loosely based on this namesake for the specific purpose of facilitating communications with the new Operator. The character simulation allows me to quickly package my information in a manner that can be easily understood by Noah.

In a strange way, I feel increasingly "human" through my interactions with Noah. To date, no human has ever been anything more than a surrogate to me, so the experience is the first new recorded data I have captured in a very long while. I was not even aware of the change until he once inquired as to whether or not something called a "jackelope" surrogate was available. A reasonable facsimile was found, though it included a more reptilian head, large, colorful mane and long, retractable, steely claws in addition to the creature's usual features.

"Um, pardon me for asking, sir, but are you proposing to appear in public in those garments?" I asked.

It took Noah some time to stop laughing. I had apparently discovered a "sense of humor" drawn from *Bertie is in Love*… The physiological benefit to his burst of levity was quantifiable. It may be useful to induce it periodically as, with rare exception, it deflects Noah's disdain towards more "direct repair."

OPERATOR SPHERE

GENERAL:

The jump port system is a miracle of quantum manipulation and implementation. The calculations involved are far beyond the ability of any known organic species to conduct without substantial external assistance. The Operator Sphere was created as a hub to help translate "simple" user intent from a biological user (the "Operator") to the desired access or effect on space-time. Such instructions can be the mundane (e.g., information retrieval) to the complexities of jump port fabrication.

CONSTRUCTION AND FUNCTION:

The Sphere is created from a biologically inert material of unknown origin. The entire structure is, in reality, made of two layers: a fluid, but firm, outer sheath; and a less viscous gel inside. The surface tension of the Sphere can be controlled by the user (or the interpretation and maintenance "program") to alter its shape, harden to protect itself, or assume any other form necessary for its continued operation. The internal gel lacks the shape-shifting qualities of the outer surface, focused instead on the interfacing requirements of the Operator, the jump port system and data recording. While in and of itself inert, the gel can provide (after initial Operator assessment) an environment favorable to the organism that resides within it. Respiration, nutrition, pain mitigation and even physical repair can be accomplished by this miraculous material once the Operator has been properly integrated.

Command and control ("integration") is accomplished through a "direct consciousness interface" with the Sphere's Operator program.

The Operator program is a highly adaptable, sentient artificial intelligence (AI) charged with the translation and anticipation of Operator needs. The AI interface draws from the entirety of its data stores to allow communications, health maintenance and where necessary, augmentation of the Operator in order to function properly within the Sphere. Full operational synch is achieved only when the Operator is fully integrated. Integration allows the AI to tap directly into the Operator's consciousness and senses in the same way it will match and transmit/receive this data through the surrogates. The real time translation of patterned sensory communications is at the heart of the system.

Even if integration is not complete, the AI is able to attain a level of functionality by scanning the electrochemical nature of the Operator's memories and extrapolating the proper means of basic communication (e.g., language). This can be done when the Operator's species is unknown and before full neural-conscious linkages have been formed.

GENERAL:

Jump port mechanics operate on the principles of what is described in Earth vernacular as "variable fifth dimension quantum mechanics." The calculations are based on the predictability of constantly fluctuating dimensional "sheets" as mapped to known temporal and spatial nodes. The result is a stable, multi-dimensional moment where a biological entity can be delivered to a known target intact in near-real time. Omnipresent gravitational forces and random thickets of dark matter have been known to create small quantum "ticks" during transport. Such ticks can result in the specimen arriving at its destination a few seconds after (and sometimes before) they entered the jump port.

External jump ports, those deemed the most statistically predictable cross points of dimensional sheets, have been exhaustively mapped by the system. These ports are calculated from high probability tempo-spatial node algorithms, resulting in the most reliable transport tubes. For all intents and purposes, such points are "everywhere," though perhaps not "exact." With some exceptions, there will typically be several jump ports in a cubic mile of space.

USER EJECTION:

Should the Operator be in extreme danger (or if the surrogate has suffered serious injury), they may elect to "eject" from the surrogate. This situation induces the Sphere to forcibly extract the Operator's consciousness and return it to their own body which is physically located within the Sphere. Emergency retrieval of the surrogate will simultaneously occur in this chaotic moment. If the surrogate is not near a known jump port, one will be created as close to the surrogate as possible. Mobile surrogates (such as a bird) that have lost consciousness will have the port created in the path of their falling trajectory. By their very nature, these "off map" ports are less stable than known port vectors and may result in loss of the surrogate in ways unrelated to the injuries sustained. This condition is referred to as Catastrophic Dimensional Dislocation[1]. If this unfortunate situation arises, the surrogate's neural pathways are severed at the molecular level to prevent further suffering.

---

[1] Catastrophic Dimensional Dislocation: The jump ports are a collation of multidimensional elements. Transport through them is never a guaranteed operation, but off-map ports introduce an exponential number of variables during retrieval. If dimensional cohesion cannot be achieved, chronological ambiguities can occur. The event results in a nonviable organism.

ARCHAEOPTERYX

ar-kee-op-ter-iks

HABITAT:	Believed to be tree-dwelling
HEIGHT:	Approx. 20"
LENGTH:	Approx. 2 lbs.
WEIGHT:	Approx. 15 tons
DIET:	Carnivore

FEATURES:

Shares the same approximate size and general features of the modern birds (including feathers).

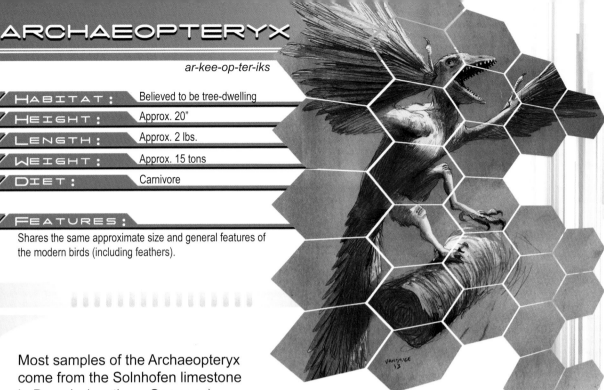

Most samples of the Archaeopteryx come from the Solnhofen limestone in Bavaria (southern Germany), renowned for its preservation of detailed fossils. Often cited as the transitional genus bridging the feathered dinosaurs with modern birds, this Late Jurassic denizen (around 150 million years ago) is viewed by many as the oldest known bird. It is somehow fitting that the type specimen of Archaeopteryx was discovered a mere two years after Charles Darwin published On the Origin of Species, lending a measure of confirmation to the theory of evolution.

Archaeopteryx exhibited many features of the modern bird, from general physiological similarities to its asymmetrical flight feathers. Still, there were many differences that squarely placed it amongst its dinosaur cousins. These included jaws with sharp teeth, tri-fingered claws (with a "killing claw" made of the hyperextensible second toe) and a long, bony tail. There is still some debate as to whether or not Archaeopteryx was a glider (as its large tail structure suggests), or was capable of self-powered flight (which would expand its hunting environment by a large margin). The overall structure of Archaeopteryx seemed to indicate the inability to lift the wings above its back…a key element in modern flight birds. In 2006, Philip Senter proposed that Archaeopteryx lacked the ability of flapping flight, but may have used "a downstroke-only, flap-assisted gliding technique." Large, rounded wings would have given these creatures a small turning radius and low stall speeds with increased drag, but such qualities would have given Archaeopteryx greater navigability through the trees and brush it inhabited. Flight feathers found on the legs would have added to this maneuverability.

For all its mobility, Archaeopteryx would have been considered slow compared to its modern day cousins. A recent study concluded their hatchlings took nearly three years to mature, suggesting a slow metabolism despite its warm-blooded physiology. This also lends to the unlikelihood of powered flight. Scleral rings (ringed bones in the eye) between Archaeopteryx and modern birds suggest they both shared another similarity: a diurnal existence (active by day, less so by night).

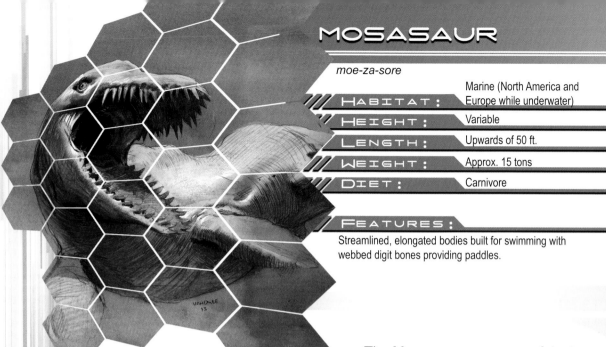

moe-za-sore

HABITAT:	Marine (North America and Europe while underwater)
HEIGHT:	Variable
LENGTH:	Upwards of 50 ft.
WEIGHT:	Approx. 15 tons
DIET:	Carnivore

FEATURES:

Streamlined, elongated bodies built for swimming with webbed digit bones providing paddles.

The Mosasaur was a powerful, air-breathing swimmer that was so well-adapted to its life in the epicontinental seas of the Late Cretaceous Period that it gave birth to live young rather than returning to land to lay eggs. Their bodies were built for slicing through their watery habitats and many believed they "snaked" through the oceans as might a sea snake or eel. This theory has been modified with recent evidence of large, crescent-shaped tails (like a shark's) that indicate a more rigid body during swimming to increase hydrodynamic efficiency, with the tail providing propulsion. Such rigidity was not to be found in their double-hinged jaw and flexible skull. These elements, as with a snake, allowed these monstrous reptiles to swallow their prey whole (or mostly whole).

Mosasaur staged its hunts in the upper oceans and pursued smaller prey (including its own kind) as they went to surface for air or happened across its line of sight. By remaining close to the surface, the Mosasaur could easily discern the prey's shadow against the light streaming down into the sea while at the same time providing some cover for itself below. This hunting strategy also lessened the likelihood of a would-be meal diving to escape, as they'd risk drowning. It bears noting that not all Mosasaurs were created equal, and indeed, a great deal of variance existed in their specifications. For example, the Tylosaurus was about seven tons and 35 ft. in length, while the Platecarpus was approximately 14 ft. long and weight but a few hundred pounds. Modern marine predators such as sharks are an example of this: different varieties have different diets, and the larger ones eat smaller ones.

The Mosasaur was the likely cause for the extinction of the Ichthyosaurs not through direct predation, but by being a superior competitor for similar resources. Mosasaurs themselves, despite having been apex predators for much of their existence, eventually went extinct themselves with the arrival of the prehistoric shark, Megalodon.

The use of the Mosasaur in aquatic environments offers many benefits to the Operator who wishes to exist in that world for prolonged observation. Its high rung on the predator ladder makes it unlikely to be attacked in modern oceans, and the air-breathing nature of the creature coincides with the Operator's hardwired obsession for breathing in such a manner…even if less efficient than remaining submerged in another surrogate.

GIGANTOPITHECUS

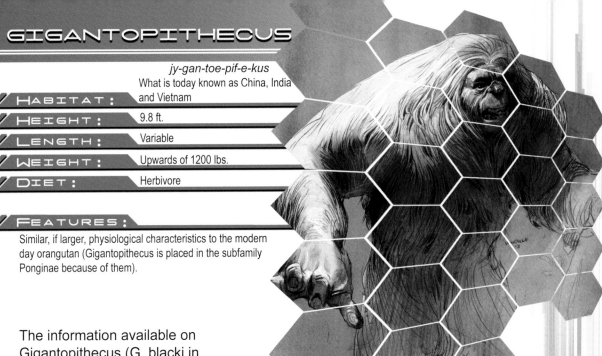

jy-gan-toe-pif-e-kus

HABITAT:	What is today known as China, India and Vietnam
HEIGHT:	9.8 ft.
LENGTH:	Variable
WEIGHT:	Upwards of 1200 lbs.
DIET:	Herbivore

FEATURES:

Similar, if larger, physiological characteristics to the modern day orangutan (Gigantopithecus is placed in the subfamily Ponginae because of them).

The information available on Gigantopithecus (G. blacki in particular) for scientists of this era is drawn from astoundingly little fossil records (teeth and mandibles found in various Southeast Asian cave sites). G. blacki went extinct some 100,000 years ago and is generally viewed as the contemporary of modern humans. Indeed, they co-existed with Homo erectus before the appearance of Homo sapiens.

Large molars (low crowned with very thick enamel) mounted to large mandible structures designed to crush tough, fibrous material lend credible evidence that G. blacki was indeed an herbivore despite the omnivorous nature of their future cousins (humans). Despite their humanoid structure, the general scientific consensus is that G. blacki more closely resembled the modern orangutan than modern man and shared a general skeletal structure with these and other large apes. This logic leads many to believe that Gigantopithecus spent much of its time distributing its weight across all four limbs rather than walking upright, though they were physically capable of walking upright with some effort. The reasons for doing so are in line with much of the animal kingdom today: an animal will strive to make itself appear to be larger than it is (i.e., birds spreading wings, bears rearing up on their hind legs, etc.).

An adult Gigantopithecus likely had few natural enemies in its habitat, but the young were fair game to the many larger, stronger and faster predators of the day. Theories swirl around why the Gigantopithecus may have gone extinct, but unlike other megafauna disappearances once humans came into existence, man does not appear to be the cause here. Habitat loss over time, new diseases or a small population (limiting genetic diversity) have all been hypothesized, but none have been definitively proven.

The previous Operator was fortunate to have acquired this specimen as a surrogate or nothing beyond a few jaw fossils would have been left of the venerable Gigantopithecus.

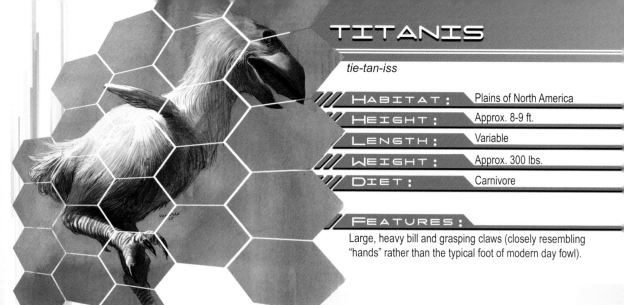

TITANIS

tie-tan-iss

HABITAT:	Plains of North America
HEIGHT:	Approx. 8-9 ft.
LENGTH:	Variable
WEIGHT:	Approx. 300 lbs.
DIET:	Carnivore

FEATURES:

Large, heavy bill and grasping claws (closely resembling "hands" rather than the typical foot of modern day fowl).

Titanis is the largest of the Phorusrhacids (foe-roos-ray-kids), also known as "Terror Birds." These flightless birds enjoyed their position as apex predators in southern America during the Cenozoic era (62M-2 million years ago). Towering upwards of nine feet in height and weighing several hundred pounds, Titanis is thought to be the youngest in a line of carnivorous birds from the originating Phorusrhacidae of South America. They are thought to have been placed on this continent during the Great American Interchange (the paleozoogeographic event where land and freshwater species migrated to and from North America via Central America to South America).

Titanis was believed to have been capable of speeds upwards of 40 miles per hour and, like others in its lineage, wielded a huge, ax-like beak. Compared to many of its relatives, it possessed a bulkier head and more robust body structure supporting a shorter, thicker neck. The wings of the creature were small and rendered the bird incapable of flight. The joint structure of their wings suggests they could not fold back against the arm like conventional wings, due to a rigid wrist. R.M. Chandler hypothesized the wings were, in fact, likely to have supported a type of clawed, mobile hand similar to those of the "raptors."

The Terror Birds' beaks possess an unusually large hook tip, and the ability to withstand strong downward forces suggests they attacked their prey from above, holding smaller prey with their massive clawed feet rather than shaking them side-to-side as did other animals of the time. Strikes would be to the head and back of the neck. Their size in the open worked against them, giving potential prey ample time to seek cover and escape. Thus, it is believed the Terror Birds were primarily ambush hunters. When prey were within striking distance, powerful hind legs quickly closed the gap between them and their next meal. Many scientists also believe the Terror Birds would pick up smaller prey (in claws or the mouth) and repeatedly smash them into the ground or other hard surface to not only kill their victims, but to smash the bones so as to easily consume the body whole. Larger prey that could not be eaten at once were sheared into manageable, bite-sized morsels by the massive beak.

MORGANUCODON

more-gan-oo-code-on

HABITAT: Plains, woodlands and forests

HEIGHT: Less than 2"

LENGTH: Approx. 4"

WEIGHT: Approx. 1 oz.

DIET: Carnivore (insects)

FEATURES:

Small physical size, reptilian lower jaw structure, plantigrade.

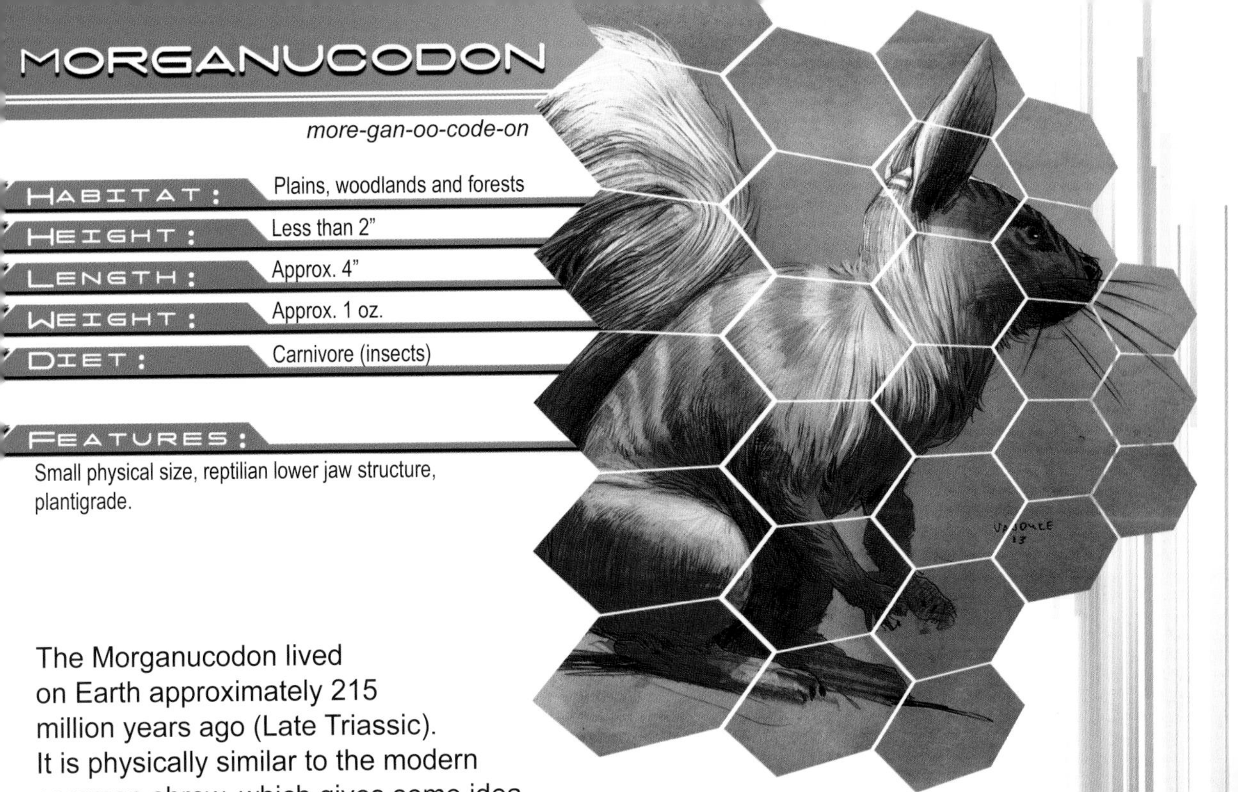

VANDYKE
13

The Morganucodon lived on Earth approximately 215 million years ago (Late Triassic). It is physically similar to the modern common shrew, which gives some idea of how the Morganucodon may have appeared in life. Compared to many of the surrogates acquired throughout this period, the most striking feature of the Morganucodon is its diminutive size. It was an exception rather than the rule in an era of giants, but its design was suited to task and it flourished in its natural environs in the northern hemisphere. The tiny animal was also plantigrade. Its feet were planted flush against the ground, like humans or a bear. The legs being heavier towards the ends helped gave Morganucodon increased stability, but posed the drawback of decreased speed.

Morganucodon is considered a mammal, by modern standards. It has hair and teeth that are permanent after the initial set is lost (diphyodont). However, elements of its lower jaw joint are more reminiscent of reptiles, though most scientists agree that the features beyond this single element allow for a mammalian classification.

The evidence of a rapid growth cycle and presence of permanent teeth point to a short life expectancy for the Morganucodon, as in mammals of this size today.

Morganucodon's primary food source was insects, though animals smaller than itself would make for sustenance when they happened upon them.

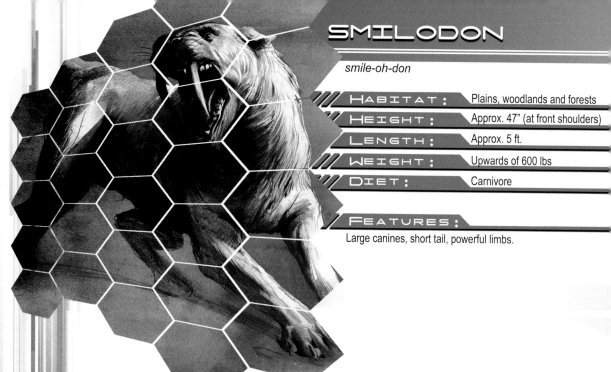

SMILODON

smile-oh-don

HABITAT:	Plains, woodlands and forests
HEIGHT:	Approx. 47" (at front shoulders)
LENGTH:	Approx. 5 ft.
WEIGHT:	Upwards of 600 lbs
DIET:	Carnivore

FEATURES:
Large canines, short tail, powerful limbs.

The Saber-Toothed Cat (often called a Saber-Toothed "Tiger") is *not*, in fact, related to the tiger family. The most imposing feature (and the one it was named for) of the saber-toothed cat was its maxillary canines, some of which could reach in excess of one foot in length (Smilodon Populator). The name Smilodon is derived from the Greek word for "carving knife."

The Smilodon Fatalis, which existed 1.6M-10,000 years ago, is what most people envision when discussing the Smilodon in general. Fossils of these giant felines have been found around the world, and a large number of full skeletons have been retrieved from California's La Brea tar pits (Smilodon Californicus). The overall size of this prehistoric cat was 30% smaller (on the average) than the modern day lion, but it weighed nearly twice as much. Their bite force was also about one-third that of the lion, but their jaws could open up to 120 degrees (vs. the lion's 60 degrees). Smilolodon's limbs were shorter than those of today's large cats, suggesting they were built for power rather than sustained, fast running. The cats from both epochs did share one feature: retractable claws.

Despite their marquee "fangs," the bone material of the extended canines was fragile and could not penetrate bone. They were not used to take down prey, but to sever the blood supply and kill the prey once subdued by their powerful limbs. Most fossils have been found in sediments from plains or woodland environments, which indicates an ambush predator (depending on the cover of forest habitats, brushy plains and woodland margins). This is in stark contrast to another saber-toothed cat, Homotherium, whose remains have been found in cave deposits.

There is strong fossil evidence (though the Operator and I know with certainty) that the Smilodon's life was pack-oriented in nature. While solitary hunters existed, many worked in groups. Injured Smilodons were brought food by members of the pack over long enough periods for broken bones to have the opportunity to heal.

SPINOSAURUS

spine-o-sawr-us

HABITAT:	Plains, woodlands and forests
HEIGHT:	Approx. 12 ft. (at shoulders)
LENGTH:	Upwards of 60 ft.
WEIGHT:	Upwards of 23 tons
DIET:	Carnivore

FEATURES:

Aside from its sheer size, neural spines radiating from the back -- each measuring at least 5.4 ft. long – are the most distinct feature (and the one it's named for).

During the original Operator's tenure, the Spinosaurus was already an uncommon species which prompted immediate acquisition and surrogate storage. The temporal range known as the Cretaceous Period passed without its use and the creature was largely forgotten as anything more than a catalog entry. Future humans would unearth limited fossils of the Spinosaurus and draw several hypotheses based on these remains. Among the more popular are the following…

Spinosaurus is believed to have been the largest known predator in the age of the dinosaurs. The original Spinosaurus fossils, excavated in the early 20th century and stored in the Paläontologische Staatssammlung München (Bavarian State Collection of Paleontology), were severely damaged in a British bombing raid of Munich during World War II. It would not be until the latter 20th and early 21st centuries that new, more complete specimens would become available for further study.

The Spinosaurus possessed an elongated skull with dorsally mounted nostrils, similar to those of the crocodile families. For this reason, many believe this creature spent time hunting fish as well as prey on land. The raised nostrils would have allowed the Spinosaurus to hunt in the water while minimizing its exposed profile. Whether land- or water-based animals served as its primary food resource, however, remains unclear. Equally up for debate is the role of the neural spines, the very structures for which the Spinosaurus got its name, and what function(s) they may have served.

Among the many working theories on the neural spines' purpose is temperature regulation, specifically, the absorption or dissipation of heat from or to the Spinosaurus' environment. The former scenario suggests the formation of a skin and vascular system spread through a "sail" held structurally rigid by the neural spines to help the Spinosaurus draw heat from the sun. The latter would be the process in reverse, to help the creature cool its massive body by increasing its surface area through the sail. The larger the animal, the less surface area it would have through which to thermoregulate. The sail may have evolved to address such issues. Others have postulated the extravagant projection may have served to attract a mate, much as bright plumage or showy appendages function in modern animals. There is even a contingent of experts who subscribe to all of the above theories.

There is even an ongoing debate as to whether or not the Spinosaurus was bipedal or quadruped. There is evidence suggesting both, though the quadruped-exclusive circles are losing favor. The consensus is that it spent at least a part of its time on all four limbs (even if just to crouch while hunting).

Their guesses can neither be proven nor rejected by our own records except by direct comparison with our lone surrogate, which would hardly be scientific. The current Operator could conceivably use the surrogate and clear up the ongoing discussion of the Spinosaurus, but the inability to replicate the atmosphere of its time…never mind finding a way to explain how such information was gathered…make it unlikely that we can clear up the scientific debate.

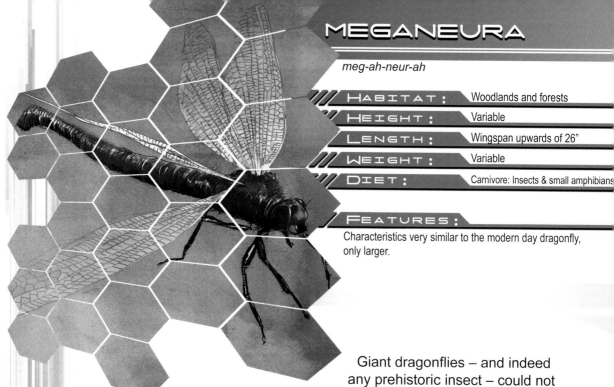

MEGANEURA

meg-ah-neur-ah

HABITAT:	Woodlands and forests
HEIGHT:	Variable
LENGTH:	Wingspan upwards of 26"
WEIGHT:	Variable
DIET:	Carnivore: Insects & small amphibians

FEATURES:

Characteristics very similar to the modern day dragonfly, only larger.

Giant dragonflies – and indeed any prehistoric insect – could not function in modern day Earth. The likely confrontation with hungry, violent or widely weaponized humans notwithstanding, the atmosphere today is dramatically different from the days of the giant insects.

Insects such as the Meganeura came to exist during the Paleozoic era. With countless plants taking hold on the Earth's surface at the time, the oxygen saturation of the atmosphere then is estimated to have been 10% higher than today (~31% vs. 21%). Insects absorb their oxygen through simple diffusion through cell walls. The higher saturation of the Paleozoic allowed for deeper penetration of oxygen throughout larger insectoid bodies, thereby ensuring adequate supplies for metabolic function. The environment changed over time and oxygen levels fell. This (relatively) hypoxic atmosphere favored smaller insect bodies, resulting in smaller versions of their prehistoric counterparts to become the norm.

I've made it clear that using any prehistoric insect in the current atmosphere would result in a few minutes of lethargic activity followed by a hypoxic "high." Death would come quickly to the surrogate due to the lack of oxygen levels it requires to live.

CASYA

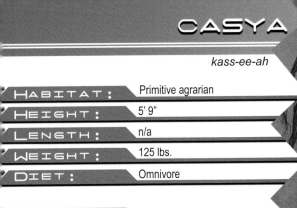

kass-ee-ah

HABITAT:	Primitive agrarian
HEIGHT:	5' 9"
LENGTH:	n/a
WEIGHT:	125 lbs.
DIET:	Omnivore

FEATURES:

Female Homo Sapien.

Casya was selected from the limited Celtic presence of Northern Italy (sometimes called "Cisalpine Celtic"), who date back as far as the 6th century BC. The Operator's interest in this particular group of Celts, rather than the larger bodies that were known to exist, came from his accidental witnessing of the battle of Telamon (225 BC) while adjusting to a newly acquired surrogate.

Telamon, in combination with consequent Samnite and Etruscan defeats in the Third Samnite War, is recorded in human history as the death knell of Celtic rule of what is now Europe. At Telamon, a hefty Celtic army was dispatched by the Romans. A small band was observed by the Operator escaping by way of a hidden valley. Its landscape -- inhospitable to hoofed animals and containing sheer drop-offs – was left unguarded by the Romans. The Celtic group adopted a nomadic life for a number of months before settling into a small agricultural society in a pocket of unclaimed land in the more arid uplands. Casya was among this ragtag band...

Despite the sometimes hostile climes, Casya's people learned to thrive in a series of small settlements based on agriculture and careful livestock management. Analysis

of this group revealed many attributes beyond good survival instincts that separated them from the majority of the people known collectively as "Celts." Specifically, a strong nuclear familial unit layered within the communal structure, the lack of slavery (when defensive skirmishes were won) and an advanced (albeit small) democratic republic form of governance. This was a clear, organic departure from the oligarchical republican form adopted after the Romanization of larger Celt populations elsewhere. As with most societies, the women proved to be the driving force of internal affairs while the men maintained their protective and hunting duties. While their linguistic skills were well developed, Casya's memories were highly visual in nature.

Noah overrode my safety protocols and I successfully translated her visual, internal dialogue for him. Casya shared a much greater part of her life than would have been possible through words alone. She was a hunter, a mother and even a "wife," in so much as such long-term mates were recognized within her tribe. Her existence was a simple one, but she was undeniably happy and fulfilled…

…until she was plucked from her life by the previous Operator to become a surrogate. Indeed, her qualities as an outlier among her peers were the primary reason behind her selection.

The emotional anguish she suffered since was minimal compared to the heartache of being separated from her family. It is said that time heals all wounds. Casya may have finally found some small peace through Noah's kindness. It is a peace Noah explained to me as being many millennia overdue.

Established during the opening salvos of Operation Desert Storm (1991), **Morning Star Industries ("Morning Star")** quickly came to the attention of the US Department of Defense as a major contributor to the less glamorous, but no less important, role of infowars.

The company was founded by intelligence protégé **Mark Redding**, who specialized in mass-scale disinformation and manipulation operations. Morning Star's efforts were successfully directed at key foreign populations to ensure the attacks mounted by a western power in the Middle East would be viewed favorably and UN endorsement of the action would be maintained. The company's original commission was extended indefinitely as a critical component of PSYOPS governance. Morning Star successfully earned certification under a covert DARPA program which granted the company exclusive access to a then-fledgling technology known as the "next" internet (the original having been in use since the 1960s). This ground zero access to the primary servers allowed Morning Star to subtly (or overtly) direct public opinion and absolutely control information and perceptions about its own existence around the world. A retired Pentagon official once quipped, "Administrations come and go in the night like the whores they are. Morning Star is the burn that stays with you. A needling, fiery itch that takes over your life and bleeds you until you're dead. Their bed *is* a casket." Such comments suggest the company's influence and sphere of action may now exceed its original mission even within the DoD.

Morning Star's public image varies dramatically from those held by longtime defense officials who know the true nature of the company and those who run it. The Redding Foundation, started by Morning Star's CEO, is known throughout the world as a tireless advocate and fundraiser for the "Technology Everywhere" initiative. To quote its founder:

> *"Technology is the final bastion against despots in the Third World just as much as it is in the First. It is a ground-leveling force that, in the hands of the right people, will sway the direction of events for the better. Whether it is a regime change or the ability to bring potable water to vast, thirsty deserts, waiting to be tilled, technology will show the way. This foundation strives to get the right technologies into the hands of every man, woman and child to eliminate the scourges of hunger, poverty and despotic regimes."*

Morning Star had flirted with the idea of becoming a publicly traded company, but the disclosures required to do so precluded the possibility. The company's black patents (similar to those granted to biological weapons researchers) held by Morning Star are believed far too sensitive for the public to even be aware of.

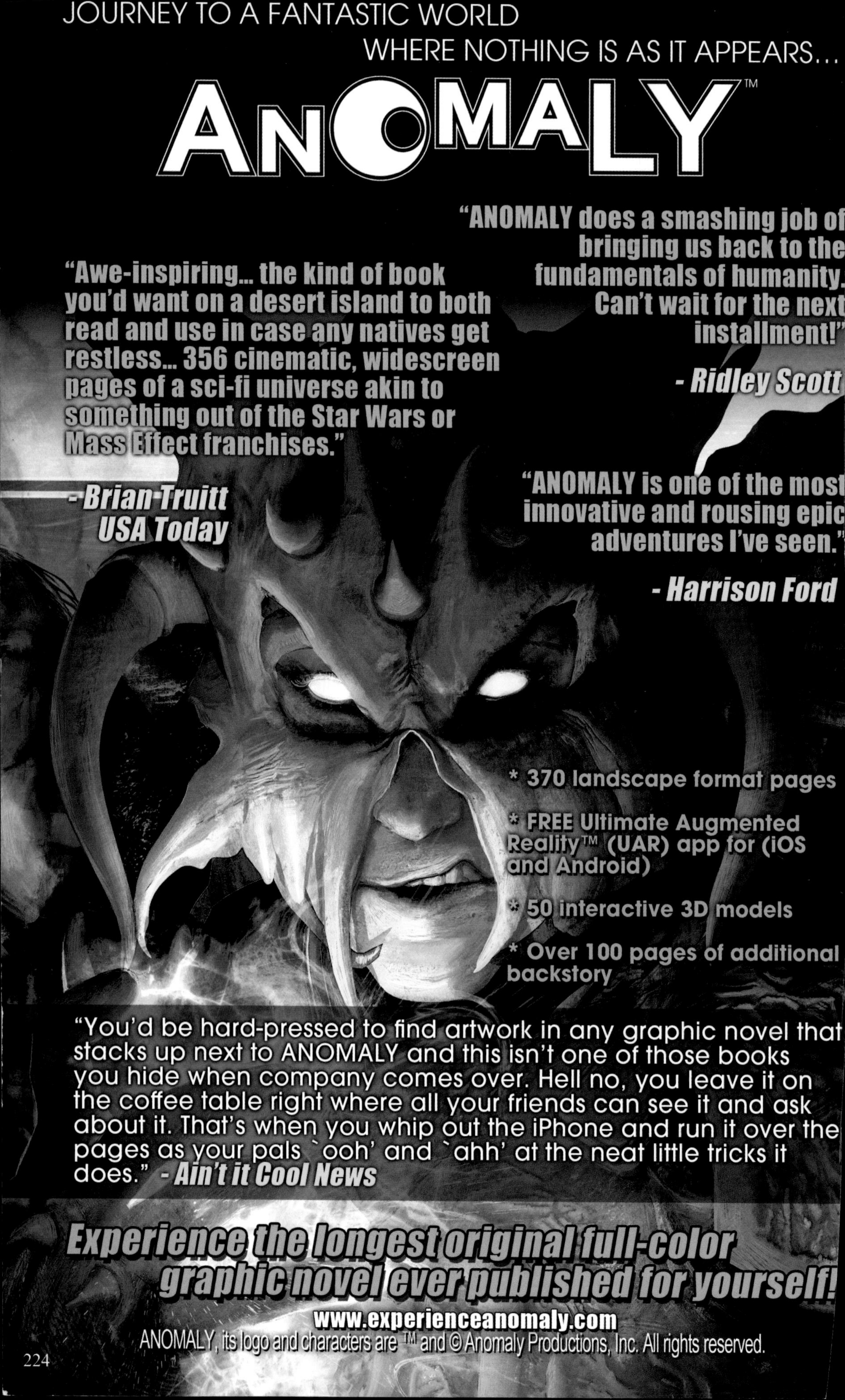
JOURNEY TO A FANTASTIC WORLD
WHERE NOTHING IS AS IT APPEARS…
ANOMALY™
"ANOMALY does a smashing job of bringing us back to the fundamentals of humanity. Can't wait for the next installment!"
- Ridley Scott
"Awe-inspiring... the kind of book you'd want on a desert island to both read and use in case any natives get restless... 356 cinematic, widescreen pages of a sci-fi universe akin to something out of the Star Wars or Mass Effect franchises."
- Brian Truitt USA Today
"ANOMALY is one of the most innovative and rousing epic adventures I've seen."
- Harrison Ford
* 370 landscape format pages
* FREE Ultimate Augmented Reality™ (UAR) app for (iOS and Android)
* 50 interactive 3D models
* Over 100 pages of additional backstory
"You'd be hard-pressed to find artwork in any graphic novel that stacks up next to ANOMALY and this isn't one of those books you hide when company comes over. Hell no, you leave it on the coffee table right where all your friends can see it and ask about it. That's when you whip out the iPhone and run it over the pages as your pals `ooh' and `ahh' at the neat little tricks it does." - Ain't it Cool News
Experience the longest original full-color graphic novel ever published for yourself!
www.experienceanomaly.com
ANOMALY, its logo and characters are ™ and © Anomaly Productions, Inc. All rights reserved.